In Search of Perfect Harmony: Tartini's Music and Music Theory in Local and European Contexts

Nejc Sukljan (ed.)

In Search of Perfect Harmony: Tartini's Music and Music Theory in Local and European Contexts

Bibliographic Information published by the Deutsche Nationalbibliothek
The Deutsche Nationalbibliothek lists this publication in the Deutsche Nationalbibliografie; detailed bibliographic data is available online at http://dnb.d-nb.de.

Library of Congress Cataloging-in-Publication Data
A CIP catalog record for this book has been applied for at the Library of Congress.

International review committee
Margherita Canale Degrassi, Paolo Da Col, Sergio Durante, Gabriele Taschetti, Neal Zaslaw

Cover illustration:
Tartini's concertos; score copied by Tartini's student Giulio Meneghini (IMSLP: Petrucci Music Library).
Tartini's circle (appendix to Tartini, Trattato di musica).
Tartini's third tone (Tartini, Trattato di musica).

This volume is one of the results of the research programme *Researches into the History of Music in Slovenia* (P6-0004), founded by the Slovenian Research Agency (ARRS), and the bilateral project *A Common Cultural Heritage: Life, Music, and Music Theories of Giuseppe Tartini in the European Context* between the Department of Musicology of the Faculty of Arts, University of Ljubljana and the Department of Linguistic and Literary Studies, University of Padua.

This volume was published with the support of the Community of Italians "Giuseppe Tartini" Piran, the Faculty of Arts, University of Ljubljana, and the Slovenian Musicological Society.

ISBN 978-3-631-86907-9 (Print)
E-ISBN 978-3-631-88783-7 (E-PDF)
E-ISBN 978-3-631-88784-4 (E-PUB)
10.3726/b20325
© Peter Lang GmbH
Internationaler Verlag der Wissenschaften
Berlin 2022
All rights reserved.
Peter Lang – Berlin · Bruxelles · Lausanne · New York · Oxford
All parts of this publication are protected by copyright. Any utilisation outside the strict limits of the copyright law, without the permission of the publisher, is forbidden and liable to prosecution. This applies in particular to reproductions, translations, microfilming, and storage and processing in electronic retrieval systems.
This volume has been copyedited by Peter Lang GmbH.
This publication has been peer reviewed.
www.peterlang.com

Table of Contents

List of Authors 7

Preface 9

Sergio Durante
Introduction: The Tartini Moment 13

In Search of Perfect Harmony in Music: Tartini's Musical Language

Baiba Jaunslaviete
Violin Sonatas by Giuseppe Tartini from the Perspective of Musical-Rhetorical Figures 27

Margherita Canale Degrassi
The Orchestral Accompaniments of Giuseppe Tartini's Concertos for Violin and Orchestra and the Third-Tone Theory: Hypotheses for an Analysis 55

Piotr Wilk
Tartini's Concertos Op. 1 and 2 against the Backdrop of the Venetian Concerto Tradition 77

Chiara Casarin
A Contribution to the Devotional Music of the Eighteenth Century: Giuseppe Tartini's Spiritual *laude* 101

Alan Maddox
"A great commotion of spirit": Tartini's "Ancona experience" and the Power of Affective Performance 123

In Search of Perfect Harmony in Musical Thought: Tartini's Theory and Beyond

Nejc Sukljan
Tartini and the Ancients: Traces of Ancient Music Theory in Tartini–Martini Correspondence 141

Walter Kurt Kreyszig
Giuseppe Tartini, the *philosophia naturae* and the *natura-ars* Dichotomy: In Defence of *natura* as the Key to His *Traité des agréments de la musique* 169

Bella Brover Lubovsky
"No Other Art than the Imitation of Nature": Tartini, Algarotti, and the Hermeneutics of Modal Dualism 203

Roberta Vidic
Tartini's "Musical Inference" between Epistemology and History of Harmony 223

Jerneja Umer Kljun
Understanding Tartini and His Thought: Overcoming Translation Difficulties in the Correspondence between Tartini and Martini 245

Maestro delle Nazioni: Tartini's Influence and Reception and Dispersion of His Work

Lucija Konfic
Giuseppe Michele Stratico's Theoretical Thinking: Transgressing the Boundaries of Tartini's School 263

Ana Lombardía
The Reception of Tartini's Violin Sonatas in Madrid (*ca.* 1750–*ca.* 1800) 279

Daniel E. Freeman
The Stylistic Legacy of Giuseppe Tartini's Violin Concertos as Revealed in the Violin Concertos of Josef Mysliveček and Wolfgang Mozart 309

Index 331

List of Authors

Bella Brover Lubovsky
Jerusalem Academy of Music and Dance
bella.brover@jamd.ac.il

Margherita Canale Degrassi
Conservatory of Music "Giuseppe Tartini", Trieste, Italy
margherita.canale@tiscali.it

Chiara Casarin
University of Padua
chiara.casarin.1991@gmail.com

Sergio Durante
University of Padua
sergio.durante@unipd.it

Daniel E. Freeman
University of Minnesota
freem593@umn.edu

Baiba Jaunslaviete
Jāzeps Vītols Latvian Academy of Music
baiba.jaunslaviete@jvlma.lv

Lucija Konfic
Department for History of Croatian Music of the Croatian Academy of Sciences and Arts
lucijam@hazu.hr

Walter Kurt Kreyszig
University of Saskatchewan, Saskatoon, Canada
Conservatory of Music Niccolò Paganini, Genoa, Italy
walter.kreyszig@usask.ca

Ana Lombardía
Universidad de Salamanca, Spain
ana.lombardia@usal.es

Alan Maddox
University of Sydney
alan.maddox@sydney.edu.au

Nejc Sukljan
University of Ljubljana
nejc.sukljan@ff.uni-lj.si

Jerneja Umer Kljun
University of Ljubljana
jerneja.umerkljun@ff.uni-lj.si

Roberta Vidic
University of Music and Theater Hamburg (HfMT)
roberta.vidic@hfmt-hamburg.de

Piotr Wilk
Jagiellonian University in Kraków
piotr.wilk@uj.edu.pl

Preface

The last few years have seen important occasions to revisit the life and work of the famous violinist, composer, music teacher and music theorist Giuseppe Tartini (1692–1770): 2020 was the 250th anniversary of his death and 2022 was the 330th anniversary of his birth. To mark the occasion, the Department of Linguistic and Literary Studies of the University of Padua, the Department of Musicology of the Faculty of Arts, University of Ljubljana and the "Giuseppe Tartini" Conservatory in Trieste joined forces and organized three international musicological conferences between 2019 and 2020, exploring topics related to Tartini's life, work and legacy. The present three-volume series, *Giuseppe Tartini and the Musical Culture of the Enlightenment*, edited by Margherita Canale Degrassi, Paolo Da Col, Nejc Sukljan, and Gabriele Taschetti, presents a thematically organized selection of the expanded and revised conference papers.

When in 1896 Tartini's monument was erected in Piran, one of the commemorative records named him as "*an artist and scientist of European reputation without an equal*" (*Amico*, 2 August, 1896). Indeed, not many musicians made history both as an outstanding composer (the renowned mathematician, physicist and Tartini's contemporary Leonhard Euler even called him the greatest composer of the time) and as an exceptional music theorist (beginning from traditional musical-theoretical ideas, Tartini laid the foundation for many later music-acoustical considerations). Especially after he began to devote himself to speculative reflections on music, Tartini seems to have been searching for *harmony* between music theory (which he studied in depth, even reaching back to ancient concepts of music) and musical practice (his daily routine as composer and violinist at St Anthony's Basilica in Padua and as violin teacher). The 2nd volume of the series *In Search of Perfect Harmony: Tartini's Music and Music Theory in Local and European Contexts* focuses on both Tartini's musical language and his theoretical deliberations.

After the introductory essay by Sergio Durante, the volume is divided into three parts. The first part, *In Search of Perfect Harmony in Music*, brings chapters dedicated to Tartini's musical language. In the first chapter, Baiba Jaunslaviete discusses the use of rhetorical figures in Tartini's violin sonatas and attempts to determine their influence on his musical style. In the second chapter, Margherita Canale Degrassi looks at possible links between Tartini's theoretical concepts and compositional practice, in particular the relationship between the third tone and orchestral accompaniment in violin concertos. In the next chapter, Piotr Wilk attempts to position Tartini's concertos within the tradition of the Venetian concerto of the first half of the eighteenth century by examining and comparing various compositional aspects, while Chiara Casarin's essay provides a detailed overview of Giuseppe Tartini's *laude*. The first part then concludes with Alan Maddox's discussion of Tartini's conception of musical effect, based on the famous account of the event in the opera house of Ancona where Tartini heard a recitative that profoundly influenced him.

The second part, *In Search of Perfect Harmony in Musical Thought*, includes four chapters dealing with various aspects of Tartini's theory. Nejc Sukljan's discussion of Tartini's knowledge and use of ancient theorems in his correspondence with Giovanni Battista Martini is followed by three chapters dealing with possible connections between Tartini's theoretical thought and practical music: Walter Kurt Kreyszig looks for connections between Tartini's preoccupation with *philosophia naturae* and musical practice in *Traité des agréments*; Bella Brover Lubovsky discusses the use of the parallel minor key in the context of Tartini's correspondence with Francesco Algarotti; and Roberta Vidic discusses the principles of harmony in the context of Tartini's correspondence with Francesco Antonio Calegari. The final chapter of this part by Jerneja Umer Kljun highlights another interesting approach to Tartini's theory, namely the translation difficulties in the theoretical letters to Martini.

The third part, *Maestro delle Nazioni*, concludes the volume with three chapters on Tartini's influence and the reception and dissemination of his work. Lucija Konfic writes about the theories of Michele Stratico, one of Tartini's many students; Ana Lombardía sheds light on the hitherto little-known reception of Tartini's music in Spain; and Daniel E. Freeman clearly shows how important and influential Tartini's legacy was for subsequent generations of composers, namely Josef Mysliveček and even Wolfgang Mozart.

We hope that this volume will be of interest and use to all who are drawn in one way or another to Tartini's fascinating personality and diverse musical legacy, whether scholars, performers or simply interested readers.

Nejc Sukljan,
editor

Introduction

Sergio Durante

University of Padua

The Tartini Moment

It is in the mindset of musicologists to consider performance the conclusion of a process that originates from a careful consideration of the sources, be they historical documents or properly musical texts. In the case of Tartini, however, the contrary might be honestly said: performers arrived before scholars and offered to their audiences, both in concert and in recordings, direct and effective musical experiences, notwithstanding that the scores in use were not necessarily up to the scholarly standard. We must then recognize that it is mainly the merit of practical musicians if Tartini is better known today than it was 30 years ago. A number of new recordings appeared before and/or in connection with the Tartini year 2020, marking a resurgence that is particularly noteworthy insofar as it does not depend on joint planning, on a major festival or institution but on the individual initiatives of performers. It is not only the quality of first-class performers in play but also the diverse concepts enlivening the projects. This is not the occasion for a complete discography, but at least a selection of cases must be mentioned: in the first place the complete recording of the violin concertos published by Dynamic, a huge enterprise planned and achieved over the years with unmeasurable determination, energy and competence by the late Giovanni Guglielmo, his son Federico and Carlo Lazari with period instruments ensemble *L'arte dell'arco*.[1] The fact of making available to the public 125 concertos in 29 CDs represents a turn in Tartini's reception. After the edition was completed, new concertos by (or attributed to) Tartini surfaced, thanks to researchers, but I suspect that a part of the newly found 30 works will need a prudent assessment of authenticity since the "Tartini" label encouraged forgery as was the case with other eighteenth-century-celebrated masters.[2] Another interesting collection of 13 CDs encloses all of Enrico Gatti's sonata recordings and nests the reprint of sonatas Op. I (Le Cène, 1734, the most circulated collection throughout Europe) and Op. II (Clèton, 1745, the only Italian print); this collection represents not only a homage to one brilliant violinist in historically informed performance but, more importantly, places Tartini within a frame of contemporary composers that stresses his peculiarity. Projects of lesser magnitude are equally important in that they offer original approaches to a music style that is appreciated more and more as its profundity is understood: David Plantier has published (with Annabelle

---

1 Giuseppe Tartini, *The Violin concertos (Complete) (box set)*, L'arte dell'arco, Dynamic CDS7713, 2015, CD.
2 On the sources for the solo concertos see Margherita Canale Degrassi, "The Solo Concertos by Giuseppe Tartini: Sources, Tradition and Thematic Catalogue," *Ad Parnassum* 11, no. 22 (2013): 11–49.

Luis, cello) various recordings in what is probably the phonic arrangement closest to the Paduan practice of the time, that is, with cello solo rather than cello and harpsichord.[3] The result is fully convincing for the emerging clarity of the contrapuntal texture no less than for the instrumental quality and interpretive sensibility. This apparently radical, certainly untraditional choice, anticipates and matches recent investigations of the sources (without, of course, excluding the possibility of a more traditional performance *à tre*). One of Plantier's CDs is based on the careful use of the ms. FR-Pc 9796, and is devoted to Tartini's last violin sonatas: the source itself directs the artist towards the choice of demonstrably late works of top quality, side by side with the early sonata D19. Yet another original approach is represented by Mathieu Camilleri CD titled *Senti lo mare* (Listen to the Sea), one of the literary incipits chosen by Tartini as "creative prompter":[4] besides offering a stylistically convincing performance, the artist aims at reviving the improvisational *manière* by Tartini offering, besides diminutions and embellishments, a *Prélude/Capriccio* entirely original, and yet shaped according to the long-internalized style of Tartini. Among the artists who are presently demonstrating a special interest for the piranese virtuoso, one should not forget Marie Rouquié, Leila Schayegh and Chouchane Siranossian,[5] protagonists of diverse but equally convincing renderings of Tartini's music. Of course, one should not neglect the gratitude due to violinists of the old school, among whom Piero Toso, Uto Ughi, Salvatore Accardo and others, but I feel that only in the vast and yet diverse region of historically informed practices, the peculiar greatness of Tartini will become fully transparent. This does not represent advocacy of a movement that does not need any but, more simply, the consequence of considering the foundations of Tartini's fortune in his time, no less than his substantial oblivion during the nineteenth and most of the twentieth centuries. First and more obviously he was a performer of exceptional skill who invented devices for the use of his instrument, sound combinations and effects that appeared new and surprising. His mastery of the bow, on one hand, and his expressive sound production, on the other, appeared unprecedented to contemporary listeners. We can only imagine the quality of that impression 250 years after the facts, but Tartini himself provides a clue about the indispensable relation between *his* compositions and a specific style of performance. In 1749 he was commissioned a number of compositions by Frederick the Great through Francesco Algarotti, and on the occasion, he cautioned his intermediary about the risks (in a letter of 20 November 1749):

---

3   Giuseppe Tartini, *Cantabile e suonabile*, Duo Tartini: David Plantier, Annabelle Luis, AgOgique AGO020, 2015, CD; Giuseppe Tartini, *Continuo addio!*, Duo Tartini: David Plantier, Annabelle Luis, Muso MU-031, 2019, CD; Giuseppe Tartini, *Vertigo (The Last Violin Sonatas)*, Duo Tartini: David Plantier, Annabelle Luis, Muso MU-040, 2020, CD.
4   Giuseppe Tartini, *Senti lo mare. Sonates pour violon seul*, Matthieu Camilleri, En Phases, ENP002, 2018, CD.
5   See her recordings of five concertos, including a first performance, in Giuseppe Tartini, *Tartini: Violin Concertos*, Chouchane Siranossian, Venice Baroque Orchestra, Andrea Marcon, Alpha ALPHA596, 2020, CD.

[...] I must inform you (as a good servant) to limit my praises with this marvelous monarch. As on the one hand he is too wise in every matter, and on the other your love for me exceeds any merit and any talent of mine. And although this love is very dear and most precious to me, I could never allow it to be harmful to such a patron of mine, as could easily happen in the present case, in which I am obliged by your command to send my compositions there to be examined and judged by this monarch. I blindly obey you, as I shall always do, but may God assist you. The gamble in the performance adds to this, since it is equally as impossible that another man (whoever he may be) might match my character and my expression with precision, as it is impossible for another man to look exactly like me.[6]

We have no way to know whether Frederick liked the pieces or not, but he was kind enough to Tartini with an original melody that was then used as a theme for a new concerto.[7] The text stresses the crucial importance of adequate performance and conversely that, in absence of such, the composer himself could raise doubts about the outcome. After Tartini died and his compositional style became old-fashioned, most of his music fell in oblivion for a long time. This does not diminish the value of Tartini's compositions but calls for a suitable approach: this music needs an eloquent, superior performance or, in other words, as Giulio Caccini wrote "non patisce mediocrità" (does not suffer mediocrity). One should add that it does not suffer equal temperament, poor intonation, constant vibrato and lack of

---

6   "[...] devo avvertirla (come buon servitore) a misurar le mie lodi con cotesto maraviglioso monarca. Perché da una parte egli è troppo veggente in ogni genere, e dall'altra il di lei amore verso di me eccede qualunque merito, e qualunque mia dote. E sebbene questo amore mi è carissimo, e pretiosis*si*mo non potrò mai permettere che ad un tale e tanto mio padrone, riesca dannoso, come può facilmente succedere nel caso presente in cui dal di lei comando sono obbligato mandar costà le mie compositioni all'esame e giudicio di cotesto monarca. Io la obedisco ciecamente, come la obedirò sempre, ma Dio gliela mandi buona. Vi si aggiunge l'azzardo della essecutione: essendo egualme*nte* impossibile che un altro uomo (qualunque sia) incontri di punto il mio carattere, e la mia espressione, com'è impossibile, che un altro uomo perfettamente mi rassomigli." Giorgia Malagò, ed., *Giuseppe Tartini: Lettere e documenti/Pisma in dokumenti/Letters and Documents*, trans. Jerneja Umer Kljun and Roberto Baldo, vol. 1 (Trieste: Edizioni Università di Trieste, 2020): 179. English translation in Malagò, *Tartini: Lettere*, 2:318. For a bibliographical survey on Tartini up to 2013 see Sergio Durante, "Tartini Studies: The State of the Art," *Ad Parnassum* 11, no. 22 (2013): 1–10.
7   This is reported in Francesco Fanzago, *Orazione del signor abate Francesco Fanzago padovano delle lodi di Giuseppe Tartini [...] con un breve compendio della vita del medesimo* (Padova: Stamperia Conzatti, 1770), 19; and in Sergio Durante, *Tartini, Padova, l'Europa* (Livorno: Le Sillabe 2017), 85; and represents a parallel to the *soggetto reale* presented to J.S. Bach. Both composers built on the king's gift a full-size work (or set of works), but unfortunately we have presently no clues leading to the identification of Tartini's one.

clarity. If it is true that (some) performers understood this first, the time has come for musicologists to provide musicians with critical editions of Tartini's oeuvre, amounting to approximately 420 catalogue numbers according to the most recent count.[8]

However, in order to provide an orientation within this massive musical and theoretical output, we also need a more detailed, and perhaps less eulogistic, narration about Tartini's life and ideas. Pierluigi Petrobelli, the most important Tartini scholar of the twentieth century, believed in the image of Giuseppe as a "totally honest" man,[9] but I would suggest that we inherited rather uncritically Tartini's self-representation while a reliable portrait of any personality must be more complicated and contradictory. Tartini's reputation was in reality not only the result of a candid devotion to music but also of a forward-looking career planning. He was hired at St Anthony's basilica in 1721, and with the exception of the three Prague years (1723–1726), he played there until his retirement in 1765 (30–35 performances each year). Not enough attention has been paid so far to the uniqueness of that position: how many violinists became the main musical attraction of a major sanctuary for the fascination of instrumental performance (and not of their liturgical compositions)? None to my knowledge. By staying in Padua, rather than accepting the more prestigious positions that he was repeatedly offered, Tartini was assuring to himself a composite audience not only of local population but also, much more importantly, of wealthy travellers on their *Grand tour* who became as many advertisers of their privileged musical experience at St Anthony's. When Burney reported in his *Musical travel through Italy* that he visited Padua with the attitude of "a pilgrim to Mecca" (months after Tartini's death), he was characterizing the city as a music-shrine and Tartini (rather than St Anthony) as the object of veneration: the overlapping of sanctuary and music venue was perfect in his imagination as it had been successfully functional to Tartini's international image.[10]

It is not far-fetched to say that, consciously or not (I believe consciously), Tartini devised a lucid planning: not by chance his first book of concertos was published in Amsterdam in 1726 or 1727, immediately after the opening in Padua of the school of violin and composition that was to become his main source of income. According to the report of Achilles Rhyner-Delon (and implicitly by the over 100 students who attended his lessons), he was a careful, charismatic and

---

8   The new thematic catalogue of Tartini has been realized with the support of the EU Interreg ITA-SLO. See Guido Viverit, Alba Luksich, and Simone Olivari, eds., "Catalogo tematico delle composizioni di Giuseppe Tartini," *Discover Tartini, tARTini-Turismo culturale all'insegna di Giuseppe Tartini Interreg ITA–SLO*, 2019–2020, http://catalog.discovertartini.eu/dcm/gt/navigation.xq.
9   This is a literal quote from personal discussions I had in the autumn of 2011 with Petrobelli; he probably derived this persuasion both from the eulogistic text of Fanzago and from his readings of the letters.
10 Read in the edition, Charles Burney, *Viaggio musicale in Italia*, trans. Enrico Fubini (Torino: EDT, 1979), 123.

effective teacher;[11] however, his special teaching talent is not a sufficient explanation: opening a private school that attracted students from all over the continent (and beyond) was also a form of self-promotion. Some of them were exceptionally good, like Bini, Pagin or Nardini; many more were wealthy amateurs of diverse proficiency, all equally eager to boast of their studies with Tartini, all trumpeting his virtuosity and his techniques, as witnessed in E.T.A. Hoffmann's tale recently reprinted as *L'allievo di Tartini* (Tartini's student).[12]

Even the too often repeated story of the devil's dream, reappraised from the psychoanalytical perspective by Roberta Guarnieri,[13] can be seen with new eyes: what was for Tartini the use of insisting in the narration of that story? If we believe de Lalande's report, the dream was the stimulus for the composition of a piece that he reputed "his best and yet inferior to the one heard in the dream";[14] we must also recall that, according to the visitor Christoph Gottlieb von Murr, a score of the *Devil's Trill* sonata was hanging at the wall of the room where Tartini taught,[15] like an emblem of his inspiration. The story of the dream must have been told time and again (as proved by its synthetic and variant version in Cartier's l'*Art du violon*).[16] We might then argue, with a degree of cynicism, that Tartini was using his dream as yet another element of self-mythography, possibly delineating a marketing strategy *avant-lettre*.[17] Therefore, he might have been an honest man, in his own way, but he was neither a saint nor indifferent to finances or to artistic and intellectual glory.

---

11 Martin Staehelin, "Giuseppe Tartini über seine künstlerische Entwicklung," *Archiv für Musikwissenschaft*, no. 35 (1978): 251–274.
12 The original title was *Der Baron von B.* (1818–1819). See Ernst Theodor Amadeus Hoffman, *L'allievo di Tartini ed altri racconti musicali* (Firenze: Passigli 1984), 103–119.
13 See Roberta Guarnieri, "Tartini and the Psychoanalyst: dream and musical creation," in *Giuseppe Tartini: Fundamental Questions*, ed. Gabriele Taschetti (Berlin: Peter Lang, 2022), 143–148.
14 Joseph Jérôme de Lalande, *Voyage d'un françois en Italie dans les années 1765 et 1766*, vol. 8 (Paris, 1769), 292–294.
15 Pierluigi Petrobelli, *Giuseppe Tartini: Le fonti biografiche* (Venice: Universal, 1968), 78–79; the visit must have taken place around 1760.
16 The caption of the devil "a pié del letto" (at the bed's foot) is a representation that differs from de Lalande's narration and introduces a third implicit protagonist, the reader who imagines Tartini dreaming in his sleep: the tale leaps from the subjective (Tartinian) perspective and is objectified. See Jean-Baptiste Cartier, *L'art du violon* (Paris: Decombe, 1803).
17 It is significant that Michele Stratico, one of Tartini's best students, left a manuscript dissertation titled *Lo spirito tartiniano* ("Lo spirito Tartiniano," by Michele Stratico, fols. 171–191, I-Vnm, Ms. It. Cl. IV, 343e [= 5348], National Library "Marciana", Venice), in which he imagines a fictitious dream and a discussion on music theory with his late master: the oniric dimension left evidently a mark in the *School of the nations*.

The historical investigation on Tartini leads us into regions that are unusual for a standard violinist of the mid-eighteenth century or, as he belittlingly liked to define himself, a "segatore di violino".[18] This "violin sawyer" was in reality a man of the highest ambitions that originated both from his natural talents and from his upbringing. Being the son of an important civil servant and member of a prominent family in Piran, he was expected from childhood to aim at a social status that could not be attained through the profession of music. Also, his achievements in music theory, mistakenly considered in the literature as a replacement for performance and composition in his late years, might be seen more convincingly as a psychological compensation of his social downgrading from the élite – where his family needed him to be – to the lower guild of practical musicians. While this interpretation is logical, it is also incomplete and in part unfair: the study of his epistolary shows that the passion for intellectual exercises of different sorts was alive since childhood and surfaced in diverse fields and different moments of his life: the early letters of 1731 to Giovanni Battista Martini, a younger and not yet famous colleague at the time, demonstrate interest for the art of enigmatic canons (the traditionally "higher craft" of composition). In 1741 he tried to convince Martini and through him Paolo Battista Balbi of having solved important mathematical problems. At a later stage, around 1751, his focus became the prestigious riddle of squaring the circle: he tried through Francesco Algarotti and the Venetian *doge* Pietro Grimani to obtain recognition (and possibly a dedication) from Frederick of Prussia. Then came his treatise of 1754 *Trattato di musica secondo la vera scienza dell'armonia* (Treatise on Music according to the True Science of Harmony) that can be seen from two different perspectives: it is in part a treatise on music through which Tartini assesses the physical and mathematical foundations of his art (conceived essentially as the combination of melody and harmony in relation to a diatonic scale defined by nature); it is also an attempt to provide and demonstrate a link between physics and metaphysics. In the second chapter, he explains to his noble student, Decio Agostino Trento:

> [...] I can praise myself of being perhaps the first (at least in present times) to discover the metaphysics of quantitative sciences, deducted from physical facts in such a way that it is impossible to separate them. I follow the truth which is found within the things, as far as it leads me; I am sure to have proceeded rigorously up to the present day. And so will I do until the end.[19]

---

18 Letter to P. B. Balbi of April 14, 1741. See Malagò, *Tartini: Lettere* 1:150.
19 "[...] posso tenermi in pregio di esser forse il primo (almeno in questi tempi) che scuopra la metafisica delle scienze di quantità, dedotta dalle cose fisiche in tal modo, che sia impossibile il separarla. Seguo il vero, ch'è nelle cose, fin dove mi conduce; e son certo di averlo fin'ora seguito a tutto rigore. Così farò fino alla fine." Giuseppe Tartini, *Trattato di musica secondo la vera scienza dell'armonia* (Padova: Stamperia del Seminario, 1754), 32. English translation by the author.

This quite-unheard-of goal is very telling of Tartini's excessive intellectual ambition.[20] Was it the disproportionate consequence of a mentally unbalanced personality, of senility perhaps? The answer is more complex. We must recall that in his cultural context the connection between the science of sound and that of number descended from a long tradition reflected, with different outcomes, in Jean Philippe Rameau's theoretical works. In other words, if a musician tried to elevate his craft to the level of science, the effort had to focus on the so-called *historia naturalis* (science of nature) rather than on the crono-historical, anthropological or linguistic plan.

One of the troubles in the approach to Tartini's theoretical writings comes from the impression of obscurity – in reality dissolved by Patrizio Barbieri in his numerous writings[21] – and of their idleness with respect to its applicability to practice. But the application to music practice was not at all the main preoccupation of the author: we must realize that the notion of "music theory" as it came to be elaborated in the nineteenth and twentieth centuries has little to do with Tartini's (or Rameau's) purposes. The cultural limits of the time provided as many straitjackets to their investigations. Two in particular need mention: eurocentrism and the related idea that the music of their time had achieved a degree of perfection as never before. As a consequence the investigation of music as language did not question the inherited principle of the *numero senario* (representing the natural legitimation of the intervals in current use) nor took into deep consideration the theoretical consequences of the upper harmonic pitches so that their sight was self-limited to the "nature" of lower harmonics (the theoretically more convenient 5th and 3rd).[22] In the end the theoretical process aimed almost by necessity to the discovery of the originating principle of harmony, be it the fundamental bass (for Rameau) or the third tone (for Tartini). This so-called "theory" did not extend to, nor explain, the existing musical objects but rather collapsed on itself. The extreme consequence of this conceptual loop is the treatise *Scienza platonica fondata nel cerchio* (Platonic Science Founded in the Circle) where Tartini tried to reconnect all the steps of his intellectual development: the empirical investigation

---

20 See also Sergio Durante, "Giuseppe Tartini nella rete dei *savants*," in *Padua als Europäisches Wissenschaftszentrum von der Renaissance bis zur Aufklärung*, ed. Dietrich von Engelhardt, Gian Franco Frigo (Aachen: Shaker, 2017), 195–204; Sergio Durante, "Lungo il solco tracciato: esperienza acustiche e riflessioni estetiche da Galileo a Tartini," *Atti e memorie dell'Accademia galileiana di scienze, lettere ed arti* (2016–2017): 33–42.
21 See, in particular, Patrizio Barbieri, *Acustica, accordatura e temperamento nell'Illuminismo Veneto* (Rome: Torre d'Orfeo, 1987); and the fundamental Patrizio Barbieri, *Quarrels on harmonic theories in the Venetian Enlightenment* (Lucca: LIM, 2020).
22 For the meaning of *senario* and the relevance of the lower harmonics in eighteenth-century music theories, see Barbieri, *Quarrels*, and Sergio Durante, "Giuseppe Tartini nella rete dei savants".

of combination tones, their arithmetical consequences on pitch relations, and their supposed ties to Plato's writings (at the origin of Western culture) and far back to Hermes Trismegistos,[23] whose "fragments" were discredited for many by the mid-eighteenth century but still valuable for Tartini.

The scholar is tempted to dismiss this whole field as irrelevant for the purpose of music history: after all our focus and interest is Tartini's compositional output while speculations bordering with hermetic philosophy will lead us nowhere, as much as they led the aging Tartini to frustration and conflict. However, this is only half true because, from a different vantage point, those ideas represent the intimate persuasion of a creative artist and, within such limits, they are precious evidence of an aesthetical and ethical outlook that supported the art works we investigate today. In sum, assuming that Tartini's speculations are irrelevant to his music is even less convincing than his metaphysical intuitions, not intended after all to development but to coincide with his intense and somewhat anguished catholic faith. On the larger canvas Tartini's theories can be seen as a significant if underrated episode in the intellectual history of the mid-eighteenth century, illustrating a possibly darker side of the Enlightenment and at the same time representing evidence of the inherent contradictions of that time and culture. Tartini's speculations, in sum, add to our understanding of the broader European culture while providing material for a truthful investigation of the artist's mindset.

The collective effort that characterizes the current scholarly interest in Tartini faces tasks that concern not only the assessment of one composer's output but also shed light on the age. In the first place we should get rid of what I might call the "baroque" misunderstanding: since this term came to be applied with substantial superficiality to music, composers, musical instruments of the period until 1760 or even later, it finally came to mean nothing. We should refrain from applying it to Tartini or to any of the styles and/or personalities that consciously adhered to the anti-baroque ideals of the Enlightenment (to what degree the Enlightenment realized its ideals is of course another question). Once we take this step, it will be easy to see the diverse and non-directional multiplicity of styles and individual aesthetic attitudes coexisting at the time. In the past, the value of Tartini's music has been supported by considering him a link towards Classicism, or a Pre-romantic personality: none of the above is necessary nor true, but reflects the attitude to represent history as an orderly, teleological, linear process: it is more complicated than that. We might ask, conversely, how we should represent Tartini's "case" within the tangle of European music, the intricate overlapping of social and institutional macro-structures: that of the temples, courts and scriptoria, characterized by higher stability and that of the commercial theatres, concert venues, music prints characterized by circulation of artists and repertories. In that intricate old-régime reality Tartini realized an intermediate and original professional pattern, his own personal style and his own repertory.

***

---

23 Malagò, *Tartini: Lettere*, 1:186.

If it is true, as stated in the beginning, that performers arrived first, it is now time to provide them with reliable editions of the approximately 420 opus numbers. If we look at Tartini's oeuvre at a distance, we realize the complexity of the enterprise because, in a sense, he composed too much music in too few genres and without caring to date them, generating one of the most intricate chronology riddles. At least some of his most important prints were authorized and provide a chronological frame for the early- to mid-life production. These are all the works published by Michel Charles Le Cène: the 17 concertos of Op. I, books 1–3, to be considered significant early works; his 19 sonatas of Op. I (1734) and Op. II (the penultimate print by Le Cène, completed after his death in 1743), the 12 *Sonatas* (also as Op. II) printed in Rome by Cléton (1745). This accounts for 17 concertos (24 if we tentatively add the Witvogel editions) and 31 sonatas over a total of 161 and 204, respectively (one set of Trio sonatas printed in London "at the author expense" in 1750 is in doubt of authenticity). Tartini considered at least two more publication projects for concertos (12 and 6, respectively) and one set of sonatas, but they never materialized. It is impossible to say why but I surmise that there were sufficient works by Tartini on the market by the mid-eighteenth century (both authorized and not), at a point in his career when he was famous and his teaching earned him more money than any new print would. It is noteworthy that he kept composing until his last years, contrary to the traditional notion that he abandoned composition in favour of music theory. Of this huge heritage only a fraction is available today in reliable editions: we must be grateful to Edoardo Farina and Claudio Scimone for their editorial work in the 1970s, without which almost no Tartini music would be circulating,[24] but it must be stressed that the only truly critical edition available today is Agnese Pavanello's *Devil's Trill* sonata (Brainard g5) published by Bärenreiter. The next step will be Tartini's *Opera omnia*, a difficult yet overdue enterprise that confronts one of the most intricate transmissions.[25] Despite the current expansion of research we are not yet in the position to have a complete grasp of his stylistic development, except for the valuable but too general characterizations by Dounias and Brainard. We will certainly know more as the patient work of text criticism for the new edition is carried forward, but this will take time. In the while, a few impressions on characteristic aspects are in order. The form of Tartini's compositions is stable to the point of letting us suspect his indifference to formal invention as such. In concertos the *ritornello form* remains basically unvaried through his career with few exceptions (e.g. the concerto for Lunardo Venier); in sonatas he adopts almost exclusively the binary form or rarely

---

24 A reconsideration is found in Sergio Durante, "Il contributo di Claudio Scimone alla conoscenza di Giuseppe Tartini," in *Claudio Scimone (1934–2018). Contributi per una storicizzazione*, ed. Sergio Durante and Claudio Griggio (Firenze: Olschki, 2021), 27–35.
25 The first volume of the series is due in 2022 and represents a completely new edition of *L'arte dell'arco*, ed. Matteo Cossu and published by Bärenreiter.

the variation (possibly a relic of the final *ciaccona*). In mainstream musicological tradition this leads to a negative aesthetical evaluation, but it may suggest instead that the value of this music must be searched elsewhere. It would be misleading to expect a renovation or complication of forms: if anything, the contrary is true and can be seen in his relatively late "little sonatas", traditionally identified with the pieces (or part of them) transmitted in the important autograph I-Pca, 1888. Here not only the standard movement is short but also the performing medium tends to a minimum, renouncing the accompaniment of the bass while entrusting its function to the double stops of the cello or to the underlying (and more "theoretical" than actually audible) third tone. In this we might read a trend towards simplification or even aphoristic form, coherent on one hand with the idea that the kernel of compositional application is the primary melodic invention and its aural (i.e. timbral) articulation, and on the other with the practical use of such pieces, probably intended by Tartini for private use in solo performances (and in fact never published in his lifetime). Tartini's concept of form as a simple functional frame rather than object of invention is also clear in the concertos. The potential monotony of this approach is balanced in the fast movements by the unending inventiveness of thematic gestures and by the progressive technical complication of the solo sections delineating a climactic, elementary, additive structure. The essentially virtuosic poetics of the fast movements is not denied but balanced by the intense expressivity of the slow ones where Tartini's originality of ethos and *Stimmung* comes to the fore. If this reading is correct, I find all the more dubious to recognize Tartini's concerto style as a step towards Classicism, and even less towards Romanticism on account of his demonstrably "sentimental" aesthetics,[26] unless this reference is meant in its most generic terms.

A lot has been done in the past 40 years and more is happening today in Tartini's research, but the vast continent of Tartini's music remains superficially explored or, more optimistically, is in the process of laborious analysis, a collective task entrusted to a new generation of scholars and to their willingness to explain and narrate the connections between the many facets of an intriguing personality: the man, the violinist, the composer, the scientist, the enlightened prophet of music science.

Bibliography

Barbieri, Patrizio. *Acustica, accordatura e temperamento nell'illuminismo veneto. Con scritti inediti di Alessandro Barca, Giordano Riccati e altri autori*. Roma: Torre d'Orfeo, 1987.

Barbieri, Patrizio. *Quarrels on harmonic theories in the Venetian Enlightenment*. Lucca: LIM, 2020.

---

26 On this see Pierpaolo Polzonetti, *Tartini e la musica secondo natura* (Lucca: LIM, 2001).

Burney, Charles. *Viaggio musicale in Italia*. Translated by Enrico Fubini. Torino: EDT, 1979.

Canale, Margherita. "The Solo Concertos by Giuseppe Tartini: Sources, Tradition and Thematic Catalogue." *Ad Parnassum* 11, no. 22 (2013): 11–49.

Cartier, Jean-Baptiste. *L'art du violon*. Paris: Decombe, 1803.

Durante, Sergio. "Giuseppe Tartini nella rete dei *savants*." In *Padua als Europäisches Wissenschaftszentrum von der Renaissance bis zur Aufklärung*, edited by Dietrich von Engelhardt and Gian Franco Frigo, 195–204. Aachen: Shaker, 2017.

Durante, Sergio. "Tartini Studies: The State of the Art." *Ad Parnassum* 11, no. 22 (2013): 1–10.

Durante, Sergio. "Lungo il solco tracciato: esperienza acustiche e riflessioni estetiche da Galileo a Tartini." *Atti e memorie dell'Accademia galileiana di scienze, lettere ed arti* (2016–2017): 33–42.

Durante, Sergio. *Tartini, Padova, L'Europa*. Livorno: Le Sillabe, 2017.

Durante, Sergio. "Il contributo di Claudio Scimone alla conoscenza di Giuseppe Tartini." In *Claudio Scimone (1934–2018). Contributi per una storicizzazione*, edited by Sergio Durante and Claudio Griggio, 27–35. Firenze: Olschki, 2021.

Fanzago, Francesco. *Orazione del signor abate Francesco Fanzago padovano delle lodi di Giuseppe Tartini recitata nella chiesa de' rr. pp. Serviti in Padova li 31. marzo l'anno 1770. Con varie note illustrata, e con un breve compendio della vita del medesimo*. Padova: Stamperia Conzatti, 1770.

Guarnieri, Roberta. "Tartini and the Psychoanalyst: dream and musical creation." In *Giuseppe Tartini: Fundamental Questions*, edited by Gabriele Taschetti, 143–148. Berlin: Peter Lang, 2022.

Hoffmann, Ernst Theodor Amadeus. *L'allievo di Tartini ed altri racconti musicali*. Firenze: Passigli 1984.

Lalande, Joseph Jérôme. *Voyage d'un françois en Italie dans les années 1765 et 1766*, vol. 8. Paris: n.p., 1769.

Malagò, Giorgia, ed. *Giuseppe Tartini: Lettere e documenti/Pisma in dokumenti/ Letters and Documents*. 2 vols. Translated by Jerneja Umer Kljun and Roberto Baldo. Trieste: Edizioni Università di Trieste, 2020.

Petrobelli, Pierluigi. *Giuseppe Tartini: Le fonti biografiche*. Venice-Vienna: Universal, 1968.

Polzonetti, Pierpaolo. *Tartini e la musica secondo natura*. Lucca: LIM, 2001.

Staehelin, Martin. "Giuseppe Tartini über seine künstlerische Entwicklung." *Archiv für Musikwissenschaft* 35 (1978): 251–274.

Stratico, Michele. "Lo spirito Tartiniano." Fols. 171–191, I-Vnm, Ms. It. Cl. IV, 343e [= 5348], National Library "Marciana", Venice.

Tartini, Giuseppe. *Trattato di musica secondo la vera scienza dell'armonia.* Padova: Stamperia del Seminario, 1754.

Viverit, Guido, Alba Luksich, Simone Olivari, eds. "Catalogo tematico delle composizioni di Giuseppe Tartini." *Discover Tartini, tARTini-Turismo culturale all'insegna di Giuseppe Tartini (Interreg ITA–SLO),* 2019–2020. http://catalog.discovertartini.eu/dcm/gt/navigation.xq

Discography

Tartini, Giuseppe. *Cantabile e suonabile.* Duo Tartini: David Plantier, Annabelle Luis. AgOgique, CD AGO020. 2015.

Tartini, Giuseppe. *Continuo addio!* Duo Tartini: David Plantier, Annabelle Luis. Muso CD MU- 031. 2019.

Tartini, Giuseppe. *Senti lo mare. Sonates pour violon seul.* Matthieu Camilleri. En Phases, CD ENP002. 2018.

Tartini, Giuseppe. *Tartini: Violin Concertos.* Chouchane Siranossian, Venice Baroque Orchestra, Andrea Marcon. Alpha CD ALPHA596. 2020.

Tartini, Giuseppe. *The Violin concertos (Complete) (box set).* L'arte dell'arco. Dynamic CDS7713. 2015.

Tartini, Giuseppe. *Vertigo (The Last Violin Sonatas).* Duo Tartini: David Plantier, Annabelle Luis. Muso CD MU- 040. 2020.

In Search of Perfect Harmony
in Music: Tartini's Musical Language

Baiba Jaunslaviete

Jāzeps Vītols Latvian Academy of Music

Violin Sonatas by Giuseppe Tartini from the Perspective of Musical-Rhetorical Figures

Abstract: During the seventeenth and eighteenth centuries, concepts of musical-rhetorical figures were intensively developed, for the most part, by German theorists. However, in this time period, we can find similar musical formulas also in the works created by composers from other European regions, among them, Tartini. Many scholars have already noted his innovative approach to the expressive possibilities of the violin, bringing it close to human speech or singing. This feature suggested the aim of this chapter – to find out how rhetorical figures used in Tartini's violin sonatas reflect his musical style.

The theory of musical-rhetorical figures has never been developed to a homogeneous system. However, with all its variability, it provides a valuable basis for comparing how composers interpret typical musical formulas of their time and how they reveal their own stylistic uniqueness through it. Therefore, the research on Tartini's violin sonatas from this viewpoint could be a significant contribution to the understanding of his musical style.

Keywords: Baroque, Classicism, opera, Metastasio, program music

1 Introduction

Over time, many scholars have provided various explanations of the individual features of Giuseppe Tartini's musical style. However, one of the aspects where opinions often coincide is regarding the composer's innovative approach to the expressive possibilities of the violin, bringing it as close as possible to human speech or singing. The first evidence of this is found already in the eighteenth century. In 1789, the well-known English music historian, organist and composer Charles Burney noted: "Many of his adagios want nothing but words to be excellent pathetic opera songs."[1]

In the twentieth and twenty-first centuries, Tartini's music researchers also drew attention primarily to its vocal analogies and the literary sources of inspiration. Several studies were dedicated to more than 70 of his works (concertos

---

1 Charles Burney, *A General History of Music, from the Earliest Age to the Present Period*, vol. 3 (London: Printed for the author, 1789), 566.

and sonatas) that are supplemented with poetic mottos,[2] borrowed from opera librettos by Metastasio and the poem *La Gerusalemme liberata* (Jerusalem Delivered) by Tasso. Piotr Wilk concludes that this thematic had already been discussed in the first monographs on Tartini's concertos and sonatas, as well as in the newest research papers by Maddalena Pietribiasi and Alessio Ruffatti, Sergio Durante and Alessandro Zattarin.[3] These mottos have been studied both in an attempt to decipher their sources, which are still not entirely clear today, and striving to reveal the reflection of the literary source in the music. Pierpaolo Polzonetti references Tartini's biography that allows to explain the parallels with opera in his music: the composer began his career as a violinist in an opera orchestra in Marche.[4]

Meanwhile, Pierluigi Petrobelli highlights the influence of speech and singing in Tartini's works, revealing its relation to the aesthetic views of the composer presented in his *Trattato di musica secondo la vera scienza dell' armonia* (Treatise on Music according to the True Science of Harmony, 1754). He notes that nature and a manifestation of the naturalness, the human voice, were essential ideals for Tartini. Explaining this idea, Petrobelli cites the *Trattato di musica*: "If the intention of the Greeks was to move, not indiscriminately but rather by exciting a specific passion, it is surely a certitude of nature that each passion has its own peculiar movements and its particular tone of voice."[5]

---

2 Paul Brainard differentiates two kinds of mottos given by Tartini to his works: "[...] either as motto-like quotations of one or two central words, generally noted down in cipher, or as a fully written-out incipit of one or more lines, usually in normal script. The motto form is the earlier of the two." Paul Brainard, "Tartini and the Sonata for Unaccompanied Violin," *Journal of the American Musicological Society* 14, no. 3 (Autumn, 1961): 391.

3 Alessio Ruffatti and Maddalena Pietribiasi, "Motti Tartiniani: nuove concordanze, nuovi problemi," in *Tartini. Il tempo e le opere*, ed. Andrea Bombi, Maria Nevilla Massaro (Bologna: Il Mulino, 1994), 389–394; Sergio Durante, "Tartini and his texts," in *The Century of Bach and Mozart. Perspectives on Historiography, Composition, Theory and Performance*, ed. Sean Gallagher, Thomas Forest Kelly (Cambridge, MA: Harvard University Press, 2008), 145–186; Alessandro Zattarin, "Vidi in sogno un guerrier: Tasso, Metastasio e altri fantasmi nelle sonate a violino solo di Giuseppe Tartini," *Ad Parnassum* 11, no. 22 (October 2013): 151–159. See: Piotr Wilk, "Poetical Mottos in Tartini's Concertos – the Latest Concordances and Questions," *Musica Iagellonica* 9 (2018): 81.

4 Pierpaolo Polzonetti, "Tartini and the Tongue of Saint Anthony," *Journal of the American Musicological Society* 67, no. 2 (2014): 440, https://doi.org/10.1525/jams.2014.67.2.429.

5 "Se l'intento de' Greci era di eccitare non qualunque commozione in genere, ma la tal passione in ispecie, è certo di certezza di natura, che ciascuna passione ha li suoi moti particolari, e il suo tuono particolare di voce." Giuseppe Tartini, *Trattato di musica secondo la vera scienza dell' armonia* (Padova: Stamperia del Seminario, 1754), 141. English translation in Pierluigi Petrobelli, "Tartini, Giuseppe," in *Grove Music Online*, Oxford Music Online, accessed January 1, 2022, https://doi.org/10.1093/gmo/9781561592630.article.27529.

As Petrobelli concludes, such an interest in the naturalness and the human voice was strongly expressed in the music by Tartini starting with the 1740s (in the earlier works, the virtuosity was more in the forefront), and this was also characteristic of his latest period: "[...] the musical language of these sonatas is very different from that of the earlier ones; it is a language reduced to its basic elements, and its 'speaking' character is emphasized by rests and by the melodic contour."[6]

Another author, Martin Staehelin, describes such essential terms as *cantabile* and *sonabile* formulated by Tartini himself – it is felt that his sympathy belonged to the first.[7]

The significant influence of speech, singing and extramusical sources on Tartini's works inspired the main goal of this chapter – to look at one of his favourite genres, violin sonatas, from the viewpoint of musical-rhetorical figures. Their role will be discussed in the following contexts:

- the unity of sonata cycle,
- the thematic material of individual movements,
- the development of this material.

It is well known that interest in rhetorics among musicians and music theorists increased significantly already on the eve of the Baroque era, the sixteenth century. As noted by Blake Wilson, "musical-rhetorical relations developed along more radical lines in Italy, where they unfolded in the more rarefied air of the humanist courts and academies, which sustained [...] [an] interaction between music and emerging theories of vernacular poetry".[8] Meanwhile, the teaching of musical-rhetorical figures (*Figurenlehre*) originated at the turn of the seventeenth century in Germany where Joachim Burmeister published several treatises on this theme, starting with *Hypomnematum musicae poeticae* (Notes on Musical Poetics, 1599). However, most intensely, the concepts of figures were developed in the eighteenth century, just during Tartini's lifetime, for example, by Johann Gottfried Walther in *Praecepta der musicalischen Composition* (Precepts of Musical Composition, 1708) and *Musicalisches Lexicon* (Musical Lexicon, 1732), Johann Mattheson in *Der Vollkommene Capellmeister* (The Perfect Chapelmaster, 1739). In this period, the lists or figures were compiled more with the idea of helping composers to create music by convincingly highlighting specific text details or affects. At the same time, they could be considered an essential tool for analysing the music language. Therefore, such lists are also used enthusiastically by many contemporary scholars in their research of Baroque music.

---

6 Petrobelli, "Tartini, Giuseppe."
7 Martin Staehelin, "Giuseppe Tartini über seine künstlerische Entwicklung. Ein unbekanntes Selbstzeugnis," *Archiv für Musikwissenschaft* 35, no. 4 (1978): 263.
8 Blake Wilson, George J. Buelow, and Peter A. Hoyt, "Rhetoric and music," in *Grove Music Online*, Oxford Music Online, accessed January 1, 2022, https://doi.org/10.1093/gmo/9781561592630.article.43166.

As it has been repeatedly noted in musicological literature, German composers of the Baroque age were strongly influenced by Italian music.[9] Therefore, it is not surprising that in works by Italian composers, we find analogues for practically all of the figures that got their names from the German *Figurenlehre*. It also applies to the works by Giuseppe Tartini, who tried to bring his instrumental music as close as possible to vocal music and speech. The closeness of these two areas with rhetoric is especially highlighted in the literature. "Almost always, rhetorical figures have clear declamatory implications," notes Tom Beghin in *The Oxford Handbook of Topic Theory*.[10] Meanwhile, Dietrich Bartel, in his *Musica Poetica* (Musical Poetics, 1997), summarizes the views by music rhetoric theorist Johann Gottfried Walther: "[...] musica poetica is essentially vocal music in which the 'music-poet' was to present the text in a Klang-rede or musical oration."[11]

In the treatises created during the seventeenth–eighteenth century, we see a lot of similar features in the explanations of the figures; however, contradictions can also be found. It is one of the reasons why musical rhetoric has not become a terminologically unified theoretical system. Nevertheless, the aim of this chapter is not to go into the contradictions and different understandings but to take, from the offerings of various authors, the terms that seem most suitable for the characterisation of Tartini's **music semantics** and his **stylistic individuality**. The chosen figure definitions will mainly be borrowed from *Musica Poetica* (1997) by Dietrich Bartel – the monograph that is based on a detailed comparative analysis of their descriptions in various sources.

2 Sonata Cycle by Tartini: Rhetorical Figures as Tools for Uniting the Movements

The period when Tartini created his sonatas is described by Paul Brainard as a time of a historical transition when the cycles of da chiesa and da camera no longer existed in their previous form; however, the Classical cycle had not yet developed. Most of the sonatas by Tartini are three-movement cycles (slow–fast–fast), where the first movement with its solemn seriousness continues the tradition of the introduction movement of sonata da chiesa.[12] The second movement, Allegro, is named by Pierluigi Petrobelli "the centrepiece of the composition, in which

---

9   See, for example, Owen Rees, "Hamburg to Vienna: German and Austrian Baroque," *Early Music* 49, no. 1 (February, 2021): 158, https://doi.org/10.1093/em/caab019.
10 Tom Beghin, "Recognizing Musical Topics versus Executing Rhetorical Figures," in *The Oxford Handbook of Topic Theory*, ed. Danuta Mirka (Oxford, etc.: Oxford University Press, 2014), 552.
11 Dietrich Bartel, *Musica Poetica. Musical-Rhetorical Figures in German Baroque Music* (Lincoln and London: University of Nebraska Press, 1997), 22.
12 Paul Brainard, "Die Violinsonaten Giuseppe Tartinis," (Doctoral dissertation, University of Göttingen, 1959), 102–103.

[...] the contrapuntal display of the three voices [...] is given ample room".[13] The third movement is also Allegro, frequently lighter and dancing.[14] Less common are four-movement cycles; they are characterized by two alternating slow and fast movements (da chiesa tradition), a higher proportion of polyphony in the second movement and a dance in the finale (in later sonatas, it is represented mainly by minuet). Regarding the structure of individual movements, Brainard especially highlights *"forma bipartite"*,[15] and this same feature is mentioned by Pierluigi Petrobelli: "[...] all three movements are in the same key and, with rare exceptions,[16] use the same binary structure, moving to the dominant in the first section and returning to the tonic in the second, with each section repeated."[17]

Meanwhile, the mentioned binary structures are mostly quite complicated and can, in fact, be seen as manifestations of early sonata form, similarly used, for example, in the sonatas by Domenico Scarlatti: there are demarcated first and second subjects in the exposition, and the second subject appears in the main key in the recapitulation. Therefore, in further analysis, the sonata form's terminology will sometimes be used. This will be applied to both the full sonata form and the movements, in which the characteristic features of this form are found at least in the exposition (the first subject, transition and second subject with typical tonal relations).

Paul Brainard has already mentioned intervallic and other arches that frequently unite individual movements of the cycle – mainly both Allegros or, less often, movements in a different tempo.[18] It could be concluded that such uniting elements could also be considered musical-rhetorical figures. Just a few examples:

- In the Sonata B.g.10,[19] *Didone abbandonata* (Dido Abandoned), the composer uses the same thematic material in the codetta of the second and the third movement (see Figure 1, mm. 1–8, and Figure 2, mm. 3–5). Thus, the principle of *epiphora* is realized. It is defined by Johann Gottfried Walther in his *Musicalisches Lexicon* as follows: "The *epiphora* or *epistrophe* is a rhetorical figure in which one or more words are repeated at the end of numerous phrases, elaborations, or similar passages."[20] Both codettas are based on a rapid *catabasis* – a melodic fall that, according to the theory of music rhetoric, "expresses descending, lowly,

---

13 Petrobelli, "Tartini, Giuseppe."
14 Petrobelli, "Tartini, Giuseppe."
15 Brainard, "Die Violinsonaten Giuseppe Tartinis," 122.
16 Several fugues and variations could be mentioned among these exceptions.
17 Petrobelli, "Tartini, Giuseppe."
18 Brainard, "Die Violinsonaten Giuseppe Tartinis," 117–119.
19 Here and further, references are given according to Paul Brainard's cataloguing.
20 "Epiphora, ἐπιφορά oder Epistrophe, ἐπιστροφή, ist eine Rhetorische Figur, da ein oder mehr Worte zu Ende der Commatum, Colorum, u.s.f. wiederholt werden." Johann Gottfried Walther, *Musicalisches Lexicon* (Leipzig: Wolfgang Deer, 1732), 227–228. English translation in Bartel, *Musica Poetica*, 261.

or negative images or affections".[21] It confirms the dramatic, impetuous mood of the music. In the fourth movement, this musical material is given in a rhythmical diminution (the *diminutio* figure).

Figure 1: Tartini, *Sonata* B.g10 (Didone abbandonata), mvm. 2: the ending. (Giuseppe Tartini, *XII Sonate a Violino e Violoncello o Cimbalo*, Op. 1 ([Rome:] Undefined publisher, 1745), 45, https://s9.imslp.org/files/imglnks/usimg/e/e7/IMSLP387572-PMLP90962--AC_E2-886-_12_Sonate_Op.1_07-12.pdf.)

Figure 2: Tartini, *Sonata* B.g10 (Didone abbandonata), mvm. 3: the ending. (Tartini, *XII Sonate*, Op. 1, 45, https://s9.imslp.org/files/imglnks/usimg/e/e7/IMSLP387572-PMLP90962--AC_E2-886-_12_Sonate_Op.1_07-12.pdf.)

- The subject of the second (fugal) movement from *Sonata* in E minor B.e6 is based on the tones of the minor triad, which are also repeated at the beginning of the final movement, however, with an additional melodic figuration. Here we see the *variatio* figure, which is defined by Wolfgang Caspar Printz in his *Phrynis Mytilenaeus oder Satyrischer Componist* (Phrynis Mytilenaeus, or the Satirical Composer, 1676–1696) as follows: "In a strict sense, *Variatio* refers to an artful alteration (figuration) of a given melodic passage, yet in which the original melody is always noticed and recognised."[22]

---

21 Bartel, *Musica Poetica*, 214.
22 "In stricta Significatione ist Variatio eine künstliche Veränderung eines vorgegebenen Moduli, da man dieses allezeit in jener mercken und abnehmen kan." Wolfgang

Violin Sonatas by Giuseppe Tartini: Musical-Rhetorical Figures 33

The same figure is found in the *Sonata* in G major B.G17: the subjects of its second (fugal) movement and finale have similar melodic contours (compare Figure 3, mm. 1–2, and Figure 4, mm. 1–4); however, the role of figuration in the finale even increases.

Figure 3: Tartini, *Sonata* B.G17, mvm. 2: the beginning. (Tartini, *XII Sonate*, Op. 1, 18, IMSLP387573-PMLP90962--AC_E2-886-_12_Sonate_Op.1_01-06.pdf.)

Figure 4: Tartini, *Sonata* B.G17, mvm. 3: the beginning. (Tartini, *XII Sonate*, Op. 1, 20, IMSLP387573-PMLP90962--AC_E2-886-_12_Sonate_Op.1_01-06.pdf.)

- In the first movement of the *Sonata* in B minor (B.h6), a *saltus durisculus* figure, or dissonant leap, is used. It is noteworthy that the developer of the latter term, Christoph Bernhard, has described it in his treatises *Tractatus compositionis augmentatus* (An Augmented Treatise on Composition, ca. 1657) and *Ausführlicher Bericht vom Gebrauche der Con- und Dissonantien* (Detailed Report on the Use of Consonances and Dissonances, after 1663) with a slightly negative connotation as forbidden, unnatural leaps or *verbothene* and *unnatürliche Sprünge* which could be used only in recitatives or *stylus luxurians communis* where they accommodate certain affections.[23] However, the praxis of Baroque music significantly contrasted to this theoretical position, and *saltus duriusculus* was broadly used in many genres. In the discussed example, it is represented by a leap of a ninth that is not frequently found in other slow movements by Tartini and leaves a very expressive, pathetic impression. A descending sequence (*gradatio* figure) of this motif follows. We see the same combination of two

---

Caspar Printz, *Phrynis Mytilenaeus oder Satyrischer Componist*, vol. 2 (Quedlinburg: In Verlegung Christian Okels, 1677), 46. English translation in Bartel, *Musica Poetica*, 435.
23 Bartel, *Musica Poetica*, 381.

figures in the second movement (compare mvm. 1, mm. 5-6, and mvm. 2, mm. 9-12).

Also, there are many other examples among Tartini's sonatas with arches created between different movements.

The tendency to unite the cycle in such a way was strongly expressed in music only starting with Beethoven (*Symphonies* No. 5, 9, and others). However, in the age of Tartini, such arches, though sometimes found as barely perceptible allusions, cannot be considered characteristic in general. In this case, they reflect more the composer's individual style, his striving for diverse manifestations of unity in the cyclical works.

3 Thematic Material and Rhetorical Figures: The Case of Didona

Sonatas inspired by poetic mottos represent only a part of the works by Tartini. However, it is useful to start researching his thematic material with the question: whether and how the chosen literary texts influenced the use of figures? An important insight that could help the search for the answer is expressed by Pyotr Wilk. He notes that the influence of additional literary texts on the instrumental works by Tartini was mostly limited with the general idea without going into details:

> [...] the poetic mottos often served him as an aid in reflecting the mood to be created. Unlike Vivaldi in *Le quattro stagioni*, and not following the madrigal convention, Tartini was not literally trying to illustrate the meaning of the words, but was, rather, conveying the atmosphere and the emotions which the given text evoked in him. While Vivaldi gave more of an epic character to his illustrative and programmatic concertos, Tartini's works with poetic mottos aim to be more lyrical.[24]

In the continuation, an example of the realization of such a general idea will be observed, discussing several excerpts from the famous *Sonata* in G minor B.g10 (*Didone abbandonata*). The composition was published under this naming and with mottos from the opera libretto *Didone abbandonata* by Metastasio, not in the first edition (1734) but only in the nineteenth century. However, the expressive title and a certain program are indirectly evidenced by the testimony of a contemporary of Tartini – the French mathematician, philosopher and music theorist of the eighteenth century Jean le Rond d'Alembert. He was sceptical about the instrumental music of his time, including sonatas. Nevertheless, d'Alembert admitted that there are also several pleasant exceptions in this genre:

> Composers of instrumental music will make just a vain noise unless they have in mind (like the celebrated Tartini) an action or expression to paint. Only a very few

---

24 Wilk, "Poetical Mottos," 91.

sonatas reflect this focus, which is so necessary for pleasing people of taste. The one entitled *Didone abbandonata* [by Giuseppe Tartini] is a very beautiful monologue in which we see sadness, hope, and despair depicted successively. A very vivid and pathetique scene could easily be made of this sonata.[25]

Didone abbandonata consists of three movements and includes the already mentioned order of tempos (slow–fast–fast). Poetic mottos are attached to all movements. The first could be classified as a lyrical reflection, the second – as a drama and the third – as an epilogue that preserves the restless mood of the second movement; however, the development is less intensive, and a song-like flow is hidden in the rapid passages.

In this case, my goal is not to review the whole musical material of the Sonata: only three of its themes will be further described in detail. They stand out representing many of the features that are characteristic of Tartini's sonatas and, at the same time, reflecting the affects mentioned in the previous citation by d'Alembert: "[...] sadness, hope, and despair depicted successive".

A manifestation of **sadness** is already the first subject of the first movement (sonata form). It is inspired by the following motto from the *Didone abbandonata* libretto by Metastasio: *Eccomi sola, tradita, abbandonata senza Enea, senza amici e senza regno* (Here I am, betrayed, abandoned without Aeneas, without friends and without kingdom).[26]

Comparing this theme with the beginnings of other sonatas by Tartini, we see that many of his first movements created in minor keys tend to a similar, elegiac, simple and song-like way of expression. In all these cases, we also find a similar use of several rhetoric figures:

- *catabasis* – a melodic fall that, according to the theory of music rhetoric, "expresses descending, lowly, or negative images or affections"[27] and corresponds

---

25 "Les auteurs qui composent de la musique instrumentale ne feront qu'un vain bruit, tant qu'ils n'auront pas dans la (à l'exemple, dit-on, du célebre Tartini), une action ou une expression à peindre. Quelques sonates, mais en assez petit nombre, ont cet avantage si désirable, et si nécessaire pour les rendre agréables aux gens de goût. Nous en citerons une qui a pour titre Didone abbandonata. C'est une très-beau monologue; on y voit se succéder rapidement et d'une manière très-marquée, la douleur, l'espérance, le désespoir, avec des degrés et suivant des nuances différentes; et on pourrait de cette sonate faire aisément une scène très-animée et très-pathétique." Jean Le Rond D'Alembert, "De la liberté de la musique," *Mélanges de littérature, d'histoire et de philosophie*, vol. 4 (Amsterdam: Zacharie Chatelain, 1759), 455–456. English translation in Beverly Jerold, "Fontenelle's Famous Question and Performance Standards of the Day," *College Music Symposium* 43 (2003): 152.
26 English translation in Mary P. Ogletree, "Giuseppe Tartini: His Influence on Violin Technique and Literature," (Doctoral dissertation, University of Kentucky, The Graduate School, 1979), 56, https://www.proquest.com/docview/302931832?pq-origsite=gscholar&fromopenview=true.
27 Bartel, *Musica Poetica*, 214.

to the elegiac mood. Tartini has sometimes individualized it with his favourite melodic formula combining the 6th, 5th, and 1st degrees of the minor scale;
- *catabasis* is complemented with specific figures of repetitions (*palilogia*, sometimes expressed as a sequence – *gradatio*).

Besides *Didone abbandonata* (see Figure 5), several examples are the first movements from the *Sonatas* in G minor B.g4, G minor B.g5, *Il trillo del diavolo* (The Devil's Trill, see Figure 6), and in D minor B.d4.

Figure 5: Tartini, *Sonata* B.g10 (Didone abbandonata), mvm. 1: the beginning. (Tartini, *XII Sonate*, Op. 1, 42. https://s9.imslp.org/files/imglnks/usimg/e/e7/IMSLP387572-PMLP90962--AC_E2-886-_12_Sonate_Op.1_07-12.pdf.)

Figure 6: Tartini, *Sonata* B.g5 (Il trillo del diavolo), mvm. 1: the beginning. (Giuseppe Tartini, *Sonate de Tartini que son ecole avoit nommèe Le Trille du Diable* (Paris: Decombe, [1799]), 307, https://s9.imslp.org/files/imglnks/usimg/e/e0/IMSLP361282-PMLP346890-Tartini_vn_son_g_Devis_Trill.pdf.)

A very similar combination of figures (also *catabasis*, repetitions, a painful and longing expression of the minor second between the 6th and 5th degree) can be found in well-known works of a later epoch, such as the 40th symphony by Mozart (the main theme of the first movement). Meanwhile, the figure of silence *suspiratio* – a rest that imitates a sigh,[28] – in the context of the above-mentioned figures appears less often and reflects an exceptionally personal, intimate and lyrical expression. Besides *Didone abbandonata*, the first movements of *Sonatas* in D minor B.d4 and E minor B.e6 (see Figure 7, mm. 1–3) can be mentioned here.

Figure 7: Tartini, *Sonata* B.e6, mvm. 1: the beginning. (Tartini, *XII Sonate*, Op. 1, 21, IMSLP387573-PMLP90962--AC_E2-886-_12_Sonate_Op.1_01-06.pdf.)

Returning to the *Didone abbandonata*, it can be concluded that the second subject of the first movement with its major key (B flat major) obtains a lighter and more optimistic mood. Continuing the analogy expressed by d'Alembert, it is associated with **hope**. The second subject consists of two themes. The first of them is highlighted through a rapid pulse of semiquavers, clear and transparent texture (figure *fuga*: violin performs imitations in two parts almost unaccompanied, leaps of ascending fourths are dominant); thus, a playful, flirty character is achieved. However, the second theme of the second subject should be especially highlighted because it represents another characteristic of Tartini's thematic material. This theme includes a combination of the following figures:

- *exclamatio*: the latter is described in the theory of music rhetoric as an exclamation that expresses "all kinds of desire and fervent longing, all pleading, beseeching, complaining, as well as frightening, fearing, dreading, etc." (from *Der Vollkommene Capellmeister* by Johann Matheson).[29] This figure is mainly manifested through intervallic laps; so, in the melancholic themes by Tartini, the fifths and sixths, sometimes also broader or narrower intervals, are especially characteristic;
- *catabasis* is used before or, more often, after *exclamatio*;
- the musical phrase is usually concluded with a syncope (*syncopatio*);

---

28 Bartel, *Musica Poetica*, 392.
29 "Die zweite Art der Ausbrüche oder Exclamationen hält alles Wünschen und hertzliches Sehnen in sich; alle Bitten, Anrufungen, Klagen; auch Schrecken β, Grauen, Entsetzen, etc." Johann Matheson, *Der vollkommene Capellmeister* (Hamburg: Christian Herold, 1739), 193–194. English translation in Bartel, *Musica Poetica*, 268.

- a following descending or, less frequently, ascending sequence (*gradatio*) of all previously mentioned musical material is highly characteristic.

Besides *Didone abbandonata* (see Figure 8, from m. 3), several examples are the first movements of the *Sonatas* in G major – B.G17 (see Figure 9) and B.G19 (see Figure 10, mm. 1–4).

Figure 8: Tartini, *Sonata* B.g10 (Didone abbandonata), mvm. 1: a fragment from the second subject. (Giuseppe Tartini, *XII Solos for a Violin with a Thorough Bass for the Harpsichord or Violoncello* (London: John Walsh, n.d. [1734]), 42, https://s9.imslp.org/files/imglnks/usimg/4/4c/IMSLP362105-PMLP90962-Tartini_12_Sonatas_%26_Pastorale_Op_1.pdf.)

Figure 9: Tartini, *Sonata* B.G17, mvm. 1: the beginning. (Tartini, *XII Sonate*, Op. 1, 17, IMSLP387573-PMLP90962--AC_E2-886-_12_Sonate_Op.1_01-06.pdf.)

Figure 10: Tartini, *Sonata* B.G19, mvm. 1: the beginning. (Giuseppe Tartini, *XII Sonate a Violino e Basso*, Op. 2 (Rome: Antonius Cleton, 1745), 60, https://s9.imslp.org/files/imglnks/usimg/9/94/IMSLP387564-PMLP411073--AC_E2-885-_12_Sonate_Op.2_07-12.pdf.)

Also, this type of thematic material is used for expressing melancholic modes. However, the broad and rising *exclamatio* does not sound as painful as the previously described sigh motifs that include the 6th and the 5th degree of the minor scale. Rather, the nostalgia of memories and dreams stands out here. The discussed combinations of figures are frequently found in the sonatas, both in major and minor keys.

The third keyword in the citation by d'Alembert, **despair**, can undoubtedly be associated with the second movement inspired by the motto – words of Metastasio *Precipiti Cartago, / Arda la reggia, e sia / Il cenere di lei la tomba mia* (Let Carthage fall, the palace burn, and its ashes will be my grave).[30] The music very well reflects the drama of the demise of Carthago. The thematic material is based on a rapid movement up/down (*anabasis/catabasis*) the tonic degrees, the so-called fanfare motif (see Figure 11).

Also, in the fast movements of other Tartini's sonatas, we frequently find a similar harsh fanfare in a minor key. Some examples are *Allegro assai* from *Il trillo del diavolo* (mvm. 3, *catabasis*; see Figure 12, mm. 3–8), as well as *Sonata* in G minor B.g4 (the initial theme of the mvm. 2, *catabasis*) and *Sonata* in D minor B.d3 (the beginning of the mvm. 4, *anabasis*).

Figure 11: Tartini, *Sonata* B.g10 (Didone abbandonata), mvm. 2: the beginning. (Tartini, *XII Sonate*, Op. 1, 44, https://s9.imslp.org/files/imglnks/usimg/e/e7/IMSLP387572-PMLP90962--AC_E2-886-_12_Sonate_Op.1_07-12.pdf.)

Figure 12: Tartini, *Sonata* B.g5 (Il trillo del diavolo), mvm. 3 (an excerpt). (Tartini, *Sonate de Tartini*, 312.)

---

30 Translation in Ogletree, "Giuseppe Tartini," 56.

Some of the mentioned examples – excerpts from *Didone abbadonata* and *Il trillo del diavolo* – also include a *subsumptio*, i.e., second figurations whose more personal mood contrasts to the tonic triads. Generally, this kind of thematic material is a predecessor for the first subjects of several Classical works, such as the *Farewell Symphony* by Haydn (mvm. 1 and partially mvm. 4) or the *Piano Sonata* no. 1 by Beethoven (mvm. 1).

Of course, the previous review describes only a few of the many themes found in the violin sonatas by Tartini. In any case, the chosen examples allow us to see how the composer's individual style is represented through the use of specific figures. Its manifestations have many similar features both in sonatas inspired by poetic mottos and without them.

***

Tartini's melodies, which include rapidly changing, "capricious" rhythmic figures, should be highlighted when regarding other kinds of thematic material. They are found both in slow and fast movements and reflect an essential feature of Italian music in this time, the Lombard style. David Fuller notes in *The Harvard Dictionary of Music*, that this term was occasionally mentioned with disfavour by several eighteenth-century writers from other European regions. For example, Johann Joachim Quantz, in his *Versuch einer Anweisung die Flöte traversiere zu spielen* (On Playing the Transverse Flute, 1752), criticizes two Lombardic violinists, "unnamed but identifiable as Vivaldi and Tartini".[31] Meanwhile, Tartini, in his *Regole per arrivare a saper ben suonar il Violino* (Rules for Learning to Play the Violin Well), describes with sympathy, a "gay and lively composition" created "according to the current style, which is called Lombardo".[32] Fuller concludes that the Lombard style, characterized by "much fussy rhythmic detail such as triplets, syncopations, gruppetti, ornaments of all kinds, and the Lombard rhythm", was also important for other Italian composers, among them Antonio Locatelli and Pietro Nardini. However, Tartini should be especially highlighted: his contemporary Johann Adolph Scheibe in the work *Compendium musices* (Musical Compendium, 1736) expresses the opinion that the "currently fashionable *galanterie*", such as the Lombard rhythm (reversed dotting, an essential component of the Lombard style), "stemmed from

---

31 D[avid] F[uller], "Lombard Rhythm," in *The New Harvard Dictionary of Music*, ed. Don Michael Randel, 456 (Cambridge, Mass.: Belknap Press of Harvard University Press, 1986).

32 "[...] *composizione gaja, vivace, e secondo lo stile corrente (che si chiama Lombardo).*" Giuseppe Tartini, *Regole per arrivare a saper ben suonar il Violino*, manuscript, 6, Conservatorio di Musica "Benedetto Marcello", Venice, accessed May 9, 2022, http://vmirror.imslp.org/files/imglnks/usimg/c/c9/IMSLP597862-PMLP667235-TARTINI-Regole-Nicolai_MS.pdf. English translation in D[avid] F[uller], "Lombard Style," *The New Harvard Dictionary of Music*, ed. Don Michael Randel, 456 (Cambridge, Mass.: Belknap Press of Harvard University Press, 1986).

Tartini".[33] Consequently, this feature reflects not only the general tendencies of the Italian Baroque music but also the individuality of Tartini. The Lombard style is found, for example, in the second movement of the *Sonata* in A minor B.a10 and in the first movement of the *Sonata* in D major B.D11 (see Figure 13, Lombard rhythm in mm. 1, 3, 5, 6; see also Figure 14 in chapter 4.1, mm. 10–11).

Figure 13: Tartini, *Sonata* B.a10, mvm. 2: the beginning. (Tartini, *XII Sonate*, Op. 2, 26. https://s9.imslp.org/files/imglnks/usimg/0/09/IMSLP387565-PMLP411073--AC_E2-885-_12_Sonate_Op.2_01-06.pdf.)

From a rhetorical viewpoint, the Lombard style includes many figures of melodic ornamentation such as *trillo, accentus, subsumptio* and others – they are used in Tartini's music also in other contexts, but in less dense concentrations. Meanwhile, the Lombard rhythm could be described as a specific manifestation of a *syncopatio*. In the theory of rhetoric, this term is defined as removing a letter or a syllable "from the middle of a word".[34] Tartini frequently used its musical analogues of all kinds because they stress the dynamic, precipitate character of his music.

4 Development of the Thematic Material

Not only the thematic cores but their development can also be explained in terms of rhetorical figures. A comprehensive listing of them would be very broad, especially in the field of various figures of repetitions that were meticulously classified by eighteenth-century music theorists and widely used by Baroque composers – various sequences (also the already-mentioned *gradatio*), imitations (*fuga*) or formal arches (*anaphora, epiphora*, etc.) can be found in the works of every composer from this epoch, and Tartini is no exception. Therefore, in the continuation, I will focus only on some of the "rhetorical" types of development that seem to be especially characteristic for the composer's style.

---

33 Fuller, "Lombard Rhythm," 456.
34 "[…] dictionis medio". Joannes Susenbrotus, *Epitome troporum ac schematum et grammaticorum et rhetoricum* (Tiguri: Apud Christophorum Froschouerem, 1540?), 22. English translation in Bartel, *Musica Poetica*, 399.

4.1 Antithesis as a Driving Force of Development

Among the rhetorical figures which manifest themselves most diversely, the *antitheton* (*antithesis*) should be highlighted. It is described in *Der Vollkommene Capellmeister* by Matheson as follows: "When explicit opposites occur in the text, the matter is quite different. For opposition in the text demands a comparable expression in the music. [...] Opposites can be expressed in various ways in music, be it through certain notes which invert their progression, through intervals which oppose each other, through sudden changes of the key or the rhythm, etc."[35]

The music by Tartini (and Baroque music in general) is rich in examples of *antithetons* of all kinds. However, only two of them will be further described in this chapter because they best reflect the composer's individual style.

In the sonata movements by Tartini, the relationship between the first and second subject often differs from the main dramaturgical tendency of the later eighteen-century sonata form. Respectively, in his sonatas, we rarely find the contrast between a more dynamic, active first subject and a more lyrical, calmer second subject. Both subjects are either at approximately the same level of tension or – and this second possibility is also related to antithesis as a rhetorical figure – frequently just the second subject stands out with a more intense, dramatic expression than the first one. Therefore, it includes means that could be described in terms of rhetorical figures aimed at **affected** expression. Among them, the rising or falling chromatic lines, or the so-called *passus duriusculus* could be mentioned – this naming was introduced approximately in 1657 by Christoph Bernhard, the student and assistant of Heinrich Schütz, in his *Tractatus compositionis augmentatus*.[36] One of the examples from Tartini's sonatas, where it initially appears in the section of the second subject, is the first movement from his *Sonata* in A minor B.a10. Although a sad mood is common here both for the first and second subject, the antithesis is expressed in an opposition between two ways of expression: simple, song-like diatonic melodic flow of the first subject (mostly seconds, enriched by *exclamatio* of a minor sixth, mm. 1–2); and *passus duriusculus* (continuo part) as well as *salto semplice* (intervallic leaps) of the second subject (see mm. 8–10).

Another possibility of dramatizing the second subject is the use of the figure *pathopoeia* – "a musical passage which seeks to arouse a passionate affection through chromaticism or some other means".[37] An example is the *Sonata* in

---

35 "Wenn ausdrückliche Gegensätze vorkommen, so verhält sich die Sache gantz anders. Denn der Worte Wiederstand erfordert daselbst auch ein gleiches in den Klängen. [...] Gegensätze können auf verschiedene Weise im Gesange ausgedruckt werden, es sey durch gewisse Klänge, die ihren Gang umkehren; durch Intervalle, die einander zuwieder lauffen; durch plötzliche Veränderung der Ton-Art, des Tacts etc." Mattheson, *Der vollkommene Capellmeister*, 188. English translation in Bartel, *Musica Poetica*, 199.
36 Bartel, *Musica Poetica*, 357.
37 Bartel, *Musica Poetica*, 359.

D major B.D11 (see Figure 14). Its second movement includes a strongly expressed *antitheton* (*antithesis*) between two ways of expression:

- diatonic melodic flow with several consonant leaps, or *salto semplice* (the first subject, mm. 1–4, and the first theme of the second subject, mm. 10–13),
- harmonic instability and *saltus duriusculus* (the second theme of the second subject which begins on m. 14; the mentioned figures from m. 15).

Figure 14: Tartini, *Sonata* B.D11, mvm. 2: the exposition. (Giuseppe Tartini, *Sonate a Violino Solo col Basso*, Op. 7 (Paris: Boivin, n.d.), 2, https://s9.imslp.org/files/imglnks/usimg/f/f3/IMSLP571788-PMLP411075-Tart_Sonate_Op.7.pdf.)

A similar opposition of two subjects presents the second movement of the *Sonata* in A major B.A6 where the beginning of the second subject, with its minor key, brings a sudden turn in the composition (E minor; see Figure 15, from m. 9).

Figure 15: Tartini, *Sonata* B.A6, mvm. 2: the exposition (an excerpt). (Giuseppe Tartini, *Sei Sonate a Violino e Violoncello o Cimbalo*, Op. 6 (Paris: Le Clerc, Mme. Boivin, n.d.[ca.1748]), 14, https://s9.imslp.org/files/imglnks/usimg/d/dd/IMSLP417081-PMLP411072-Tartini_Opera_VI.pdf.)

Meanwhile, in the fourth, final movement from the *Sonata* in D major B.D13, *antitheton* of the first and second subject is manifested in harmony. The first subject leaves an impression of stability due to consonant chords on strong beats. The second subject (from m. 41) is based on the transposition of the first subject in the dominant key; however, in its continuation, Tartini prefers dissonant double notes on the strong beats (mm. 50, 52) that could be perceived as a special kind of accentuation (*emphasis*[38]): a major seventh is intertwined, and it is a feature that gives the music an exacerbated expression, different from the first subject. Frequent use

---

38 It is described by Johann Mattheson as follows: "Emphasis occurs when certain expressions are given singular power and efficacy." ("Emphasis est, cum vocabulum adhibitum singularem habet vim & efficaciam." Mattheson, *Der vollkommene Capellmeister*, 174). English translation in Bartel, *Musica Poetica*, 254.

of various accents is characteristic of Tartini's music in general, and it confirms the extraverted nature of the composer.

At least several fragments of the development section in the sonatas by Tartini include a rapid alternating of oppositions or even their "fighting". In this respect, too, he is ahead of his time because in general, such intensity and confrontations are characteristics of the development in the Classical rather than in Baroque sonata. An alternating of deeply contrasting motifs from exposition, each in the length of a measure, is found, for example, in the development of the first movement of *Didone abbandonata* (see Figure 16, after the repeat sign).

Figure 16: Tartini, *Sonata* B.g10 (Didone abbandonata), mvm. 1: the development (an excerpt). (Tartini, *XII Sonate*, Op. 1, 42, https://s9.imslp.org/files/imglnks/usimg/e/e7/IMSLP387572-PMLP90962--AC_E2-886-_12_Sonate_Op.1_07-12.pdf.)

In the second movement of the same sonata, we see similar confrontations between the above-mentioned harsh fanfare based on changes of *anabasis* and *catabasis*, and lyrical song-like motifs. It is interesting to note that the lyrical material, due to its melodic and rhythmic construction, evokes clear associations with *Sento nel core* (I feel in my heart a certain sorrow) by Alessandro Scarlatti (see Figure 17, mm. 9–14).

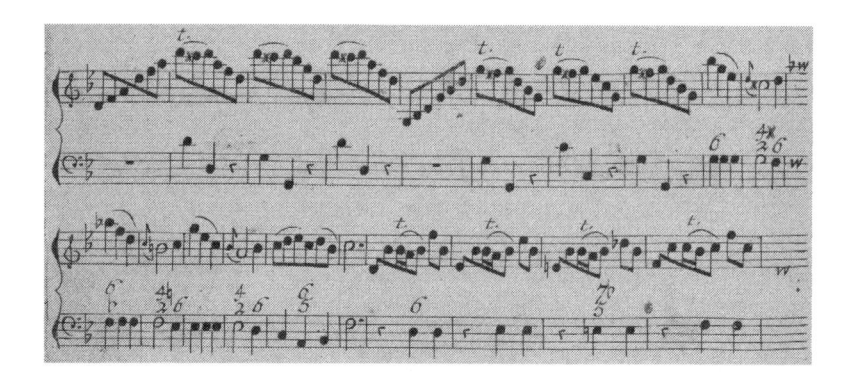

Figure 17: Tartini, *Sonata* B.g10 (Didone abbandonata), mvm. 2: the development (an excerpt). (Tartini, *XII Sonate*, Op. 1, 44, https://s9.imslp.org/files/imglnks/usimg/e/e7/ IMSLP387572-PMLP90962--AC_E2-886-_12_Sonate_Op.1_07-12.pdf.)

In the context of the possible program of this sonata, such confrontation can be perceived as an opposition between the dramatic fate of Carthago and nostalgic memories about Dido and her unfulfilled dreams. The sad mood of these lyrical motifs is highlighted by the figurations based on unstable harmonies (seventh chords of D minor and C minor). It is a *pathopoiea* figure – one of the many manifestations of the expressive use of dissonances and alterations in harmony by Tartini.

A unique antitheton that possibly was inspired by the autobiographic program[39] is found in the *Sonata* B.g5 in G minor (*Il trillo del diavolo*). Its final movement includes repeated confrontations of two tempos and corresponding ways of expression (a lyrical Andante and a harsh Allegro assai). For Tartini, this kind of juxtaposition is unusual. However, in this case, it can be explained with the opposition of two storylines: on one hand, the composer's dreams reflected in his autobiographic message and, on the other, the devil's figure.

4.2 Rhetoric Means of Repetitions as a Basis for a Dramatic Rise

The repetitions of some remarkable rhetorical figures are focused on acquiring a higher and higher grade of dramatic tension. The **trill (*trillo*)** has an important place among them. Tartini himself has characterized his attitude towards trill as follows: "[...] a perfect ornament of music; but it should be used in the same way

---

39 As is well known, this program is included not in the score but in the memories of Tartini's contemporary Jérôme Lalande. See more about it in Polzonetti, "Tartini and the Tongue of Saint Anthony," 440.

as one uses salt in eating. Too much or too little salt spoils the taste, and it should not be put on everything one eats."[40]

In the typology of musical-rhetorical figures, the trill is included in the section of ornamentation.[41] Many trills in Tartini's works meet this standard. However, there are also other cases, and they will be discussed in this chapter: namely, the trill extends beyond the borders of ornamentation and acquires an **affected** emotional expression. The best known but not the only example of this kind is the sonata *Il trillo del diavolo*.

The dramatization is often manifested only in the second subjects of the sonata form. There are two main ways how this effect is achieved. First, an ascending sequence (*gradatio*) is frequently used, resulting in intense modulations and chromatic alterations. Several examples are the second subjects of the third movement from *Il trillo del diavolo* (see Figure 18, from m. 6) and the second movement from the *Sonata* in B minor B.h6 (see Figure 19).

Figure 18: Tartini, *Sonata* B.g5 (Il trillo del diavolo), mvm. 3, Allegro assai: the exposition (an excerpt). (Tartini, *Sonate de Tartini*, 312.)

Figure 19: Tartini, *Sonata* B.h6, mvm. 2: the exposition (an excerpt). (Giuseppe Tartini, XII Sonate a Violino e Basso, Op. 3 (Paris: Le Clerc, 1747), 17, https://s9.imslp.org/files/imglnks/usimg/0/06/IMSLP331600-PMLP411073-xiisonateviolino00tart_op3.pdf.)

---

40 "[...] Il Trillo è ottima cosa, ed è un perfetto ornamento nella Musica; ma con la stessa riserva che si ha per il Sale nelle vivande, il troppo, il poco le guasta, e non si deve usare in tutti li Cibi." Tartini, *Regole,* 10. English translation by Sol Babitz in: Giuseppe Tartini, *Treatise on the Ornaments of Music* (Los Angeles: Early Music Laboratory, 1970), 7.
41 Bartel, *Musica Poetica*, 447–448.

In the latter case, although not so prolonged as in *Il trillo del diavolo*, the trills are used soon after *saltus duriusculus* – a dissonant intervallic leap (a ninth in m. 25), thus enhancing its effect. A combination of four rhetorical figures could be mentioned in both examples: a trill (*trillo*) itself, *gradatio*, *pathopoeia* and *parrhesia*. The latter is described as the introduction of dissonance on a weak beat. Meanwhile, in the theory of rhetoric itself, *parrhesia* is defined as a free, frank and fearless speech; already in ancient Greece, this term has meant striving to speak candidly. Renaissance literature and culture researcher David Colclough notes that the Greek uses of *parrhesia* highly influenced the sixteenth- and seventeenth-century works on rhetoric and political advice;[42] this analogy allows for a better understanding of the vital role of the corresponding figure in the Baroque music.

Alongside trills, *saltus duriusculus* is another affected figure whose potential is often fully revealed in the second subjects. In many cases, it could be perceived as a further development of an intervallic leap from the first subject. An example is the second movement from the *Sonata* in C major B.C12: *saltus duriusculus* as a seventh appears already in the first subject (m. 2); however, right at the end of the second subject (mm. 13–14), it is used especially intensely. This figure reflects both Tartini's temperament and the virtuosic possibilities of his violin music that were unprecedented for his era.

Thus, the emotionally affected figures in the exposition frequently culminate in the second subject. Meanwhile, in the context of the entire movement, we often see a dramaturgical crescendo with its peak towards the recapitulation or coda, and it is also reflected using rhetorical means. Several examples of using *pathopoiea* in theses sections could be found in the second movements of the *Sonatas* in D major B.D11 (the end of the recapitulation: see Figure 20, especially mm. 3–7) and in A major B.a6 (coda; see Figure 21, especially mm. 5–6).

Figure 20: Tartini, *Sonata* B.D11, mvm. 2: the ending. (Tartini, *Sonate*, Op. 7, 3.)

---

42 David Colclough, "Parrhesia: The Rhetoric of Free Speech in Early Modern England," *Rhetorica: A Journal of the History of Rhetoric* 17, no. 2 (Spring, 1999): 178, https://doi.org/10.1525/rh.1999.17.2.177.

Violin Sonatas by Giuseppe Tartini: Musical-Rhetorical Figures   49

Figure 21: Tartini, *Sonata* B.a6, mvm. 2: the ending. (Tartini, *Sei Sonate*, Op. 6, 15.)

Sometimes, the increase in tension is based on a thorough development of a certain potentially dramatic figure during the whole movement. For example, in the finale of the sonata *Il trillo del diavolo*, the trill combined with *pathopoeia* can already be found in the second subject of the exposition; however, in the coda, it obtains an especially threatening character because here it is reduced on insistent repetitions of only one D pitch, which, as a dominant of G minor, is also harmonically tense[43] (see Figure 22). Thus, its, figuratively speaking, devilish mood is particularly clearly reflected.

---

43 In several cases, such interpretations of the trill – repetitions of the same pitch that are highlighted with different harmonies – reveal their dramatic potential already in previous sections of the form. For example, in the second movement of *Didone abbandonata*, the B flat pitch in the development sections gains rapidly changing harmonizations, including a diminished seventh chord.

Figure 22: Tartini, *Sonata* B.g5 (Il trillo del diavolo), mvm. 3: coda (an excerpt). (Tartini, *Sonate de Tartini*, 313.)

A similar, although not as intense, increase in the role of trill, culminating in the recapitulation, is also manifested in the third (final) movement from the *Sonata* in B minor B.h2 (mm. 84–88).

5 Conclusion

The sonatas by Tartini reveal a strongly expressed succession to Baroque traditions: it follows from the use of rhetorical figures as more or less typified elements of musical language, from the above-mentioned Lombard style as an essential characteristic of the Italian late Baroque, and other features. At the same time, the interpretation of rhetorical means confirms that Tartini's music had even more features in common with the emerging Classicism. The choice of many figures of vocal origin, such as *suspiratio*, or *exclamatio*, reflect the previously mentioned influence of opera – a genre of a predominantly homophone style even in the Baroque age.

As a forerunner of future eras, Tartini strives to intense use of various confrontations (*antitheton*) in the development sections of his sonatas and to strongly expressed arches between the movements of cycles, uniting them with specific rhetorical figures.

Besides the influences and parallels, the analysis of figures also reveals important individual stylistic qualities of Tartini's music. Here such means as the dramatization of the trill (*trillo*) and combining it with certain rhetorical figures like *parrhesia*, *pathopoeia* or *saltus duriusculus* should be highlighted. Also, the particular interpretation of the sonata form (or, at least, its exposition) with the second subject as one of the dramatic centres is determined by the use of the earlier-mentioned figures. The most expressive rhetorical figures also appear in the recapitulations and codas that are not simply supplementary but become culminations of the whole movement; they may include, for example, a sudden, unprepared *pathopoeia*, or *passus duriusculus*, or the broadest *saltus duriusculus*, etc.

This chapter provides only a partial insight into the diverse use of rhetorical figures in the music by Tartini. In the future, the approach presented in this study could also be helpful for a more detailed discussion of his works of different genres and from different creative periods, as well as comparison with his contemporaries. The study conducted also confirms that searching for rhetorical figures is a good, although, of course, not a universal tool for analysis of eighteenth-century music because the individual interpretations of certain figures are very different and cannot be placed in the frames of standardized techniques.

Bibliography

Literature

Bartel, Dietrich. *Musica Poetica. Musical-Rhetorical Figures in German Baroque Music*. Lincoln and London: University of Nebraska Press, 1997.

Beghin, Tom. "Recognizing Musical Topics versus Executing Rhetorical Figures." In *The Oxford Handbook of Topic Theory*, edited by Danuta Mirka, 551–576. Oxford: Oxford University Press, 2014.

Brainard, Paul. "Die Violinsonaten Giuseppe Tartinis." Doctoral dissertation, University of Göttingen, 1959.

Brainard, Paul. "Tartini and the Sonata for Unaccompanied Violin." *Journal of the American Musicological Society* 14, no. 3 (Autumn, 1961): 383–393.

Burney, Charles. *A General History of Music, from the Earliest Age to the Present Period*, vol. 3. London: Printed for the author, 1789.

Colclough, David. "Parrhesia: The Rhetoric of Free Speech in Early Modern England." *Rhetorica: A Journal of the History of Rhetoric* 17, no. 2 (Spring, 1999): 177–212, https://doi.org/10.1525/rh.1999.17.2.177.

D'Alembert, Jean Le Rond. "De la liberté de la musique." In *Mélanges de littérature, d'histoire et de philosophie*, vol. 4, 383–462. Amsterdam: Zacharie Chatelain, 1759.

Durante, Sergio. "Tartini and His Texts." In *The Century of Bach and Mozart. Perspectives on Historiography, Composition, Theory and Performance*, edited by Sean Gallagher and Thomas Forrest Kelly, 145–186. Cambridge, Mass.: Harvard University Press, 2008.

Fuller, David. "Lombard Rhythm." In *The New Harvard Dictionary of Music*, edited by Don Michael Randel, 456. Cambridge, Mass.: Belknap Press of Harvard University Press, 1986.

Fuller, David. "Lombard Style." In *The New Harvard Dictionary of Music*, edited by Don Michael Randel, 456. Cambridge, Mass.: Belknap Press of Harvard University Press, 1986.

Jerold, Beverly. "Fontenelle's Famous Question and Performance Standards of the Day." *College Music Symposium* 43 (2003): 150–160.

Mattheson, Johann. *Der vollkommene Capellmeister*. Hamburg: Christian Herold, 1739.

Ogletree, Mary P. "Giuseppe Tartini: His Influence on Violin Technique and Literature." Doctoral dissertation, University of Kentucky, The Graduate School, 1979. https://www.proquest.com/docview/302931832?pq-origsite=gscholar&fromopenview=true.

Petrobelli, Pierluigi. "Tartini, Giuseppe." In *Grove Music Online*. Oxford Music Online. Accessed January 1, 2022. https://doi.org/10.1093/gmo/9781561592630.article.27529.

Polzonetti, Pierpaolo. "Tartini and the Tongue of Saint Anthony." *Journal of the American Musicological Society* 67, no. 2 (2014): 429–486. https://doi.org/10.1525/jams.2014.67.2.429.

Printz, Wolfgang Caspar. *Phrynis Mytilenaeus oder Satyrischer Componist*, vol. 2. Quedlinburg: In Verlegung Christian Okels, 1677.

Rees, Owen. "Hamburg to Vienna: German and Austrian Baroque." *Early Music* 49, no. 1 (February, 2021): 158–161. https://doi.org/10.1093/em/caab019

Ruffatti, Alessio, and Maddalena Pietribiasi. "Motti Tartiniani: nuove concordanze, nuovi problemi." In *Tartini. Il tempo e le opera*, edited by Andrea Bombi and Maria Nevilla Massaro, 389–394. Bologna: Il Mulino, 1994.

Staehelin, Martin. "Giuseppe Tartini über seine künstlerische Entwicklung. Ein unbekanntes Selbstzeugnis." *Archiv für Musikwissenschaft* 35, no. 4 (1978): 251–274.

Susenbrotus, Joannes. *Epitome troporum ac schematum et grammaticorum et rhetoricum*. Tiguri: Apud Christophorum Froschouerem, 1540 (?).

Tartini, Giuseppe. *Regole per arrivare a saper ben suonar il Violino*. Manuscript. Conservatorio di Musica "Benedetto Marcello", Venice. Accessed May 9, 2022. http://vmirror.imslp.org/files/imglnks/usimg/c/c9/IMSLP597862-PMLP667235-TARTINI-Regole-Nicolai_MS.pdf.

Tartini, Giuseppe. *Trattato di musica secondo la vera scienza dell'armonia*. Padova: Stamperia del Seminario, 1754.

Tartini, Giuseppe. *Treatise on the Ornaments of Music*. Translated and edited by Sol Babitz. Los Angeles: Early Music Laboratory, 1970.

Walther, Johann Gottfried. *Musicalisches Lexicon*. Leipzig: Wolfgang Deer, 1732.

Wilk, Piotr. "Poetical Mottos in Tartini's Concertos – the Latest Concordances and Questions." *Musica Iagellonica* 9 (2018): 81–99.

Wilson, Blake, George J. Buelow, and Peter A. Hoyt. "Rhetoric and music." In *Grove Music Online*. Oxford Music Online. Accessed January 1, 2022. https://doi.org/10.1093/gmo/9781561592630.article.43166.

Zattarin, Alessandro. "Vidi in sogno un guerrier: Tasso, Metastasio e altri fantasmi nelle sonate a violino solo di Giuseppe Tartini." *Ad Parnassum* 11, no. 22 (October 2013): 151–159.

Scores

Tartini, Giuseppe. *XII Solos for a Violin with a Thorough Bass for the Harpsichord or Violoncello.* London: John Walsh, n.d. [1734]. https://s9.imslp.org/files/imglnks/usimg/4/4c/IMSLP362105-PMLP90962-Tartini_12_Sonatas_%26_Pastorale_Op_1.pdf.

Tartini, Giuseppe. *XII Sonate a Violino e Basso*, Op. 2. Rome: Antonius Cleton, 1745. https://s9.imslp.org/files/imglnks/usimg/0/09/IMSLP387565-PMLP411073--AC_E2-885-_12_Sonate_Op.2_01-06.pdf; https://s9.imslp.org/files/imglnks/usimg/9/94/IMSLP387564-PMLP411073--AC_E2-885-_12_Sonate_Op.2_07-12.pdf.

Tartini, Giuseppe. *XII Sonate a Violino e Basso*, Op. 3. Paris: Le Clerc, 1747. https://s9.imslp.org/files/imglnks/usimg/0/06/IMSLP331600-PMLP411073-xiisonateviolino00tart_op3.pdf.

Tartini, Giuseppe. *XII Sonate a Violino e Violoncello o Cimbalo*, Op. 1. [Rome:] Undefined publisher, 1745. https://s9.imslp.org/files/imglnks/usimg/4/4d/IMSLP387573-PMLP90962--AC_E2-886-_12_Sonate_Op.1_01-06.pdf; https://s9.imslp.org/files/imglnks/usimg/e/e7/IMSLP387572-PMLP90962--AC_E2-886-_12_Sonate_Op.1_07-12.pdf.

Tartini, Giuseppe. *Sei Sonate a Violino e Violoncello o Cimbalo*, Op. 6. Paris: Le Clerc, Mme. Boivin, n.d. [ca.1748]. https://s9.imslp.org/files/imglnks/usimg/d/dd/IMSLP417081-PMLP411072-Tartini_Opera_VI.pdf.

Tartini, Giuseppe. *Sonate a Violino solo col Basso*, Op. 7. Paris: Boivin, n.d. https://s9.imslp.org/files/imglnks/usimg/f/f3/IMSLP571788-PMLP411075-Tart_Sonate_Op.7.pdf.

Tartini, Giuseppe. *Sonate de Tartini que son ecole avoit nommèe Le Trille du Diable.* Paris: Decombe, n.d. [1799]. https://s9.imslp.org/files/imglnks/usimg/e/e0/IMSLP361282-PMLP346890-Tartini_vn_son_g_Devis_Trill.pdf.

Margherita Canale Degrassi

Conservatory of Music "Giuseppe Tartini", Trieste, Italy

The Orchestral Accompaniments of Giuseppe Tartini's Concertos for Violin and Orchestra and the Third-Tone Theory: Hypotheses for an Analysis

Abstract: Giuseppe Tartini (1692–1770) is known for his compositions, in particular the over 160 violin concertos; at the same time, Tartini contributed to the science of acoustics with his discovery of the *third tone* or *difference tone*, also called the *Tartini tone*. His theoretical works contain a theory of harmony based on the third tone as well as on algebra and geometry. However, the connection between theory and his compositions comes second in Tartini's studies. This chapter examines in particular some aspects of orchestration and orchestral revisions in violin concertos, exploring the hypothesis of the use of the third tone.

Keywords: third tone, acoustic, orchestration, orchestral accompaniments, violin concertos

1 Introduction

Giuseppe Tartini (Piran 1692 - Padua 1770) was not only an important composer, violinist and violin teacher, but also a lucid music theorist who devoted himself extensively to the study of subjects related to harmony and the physical acoustic foundations of sound. In addition to his correspondence and manuscript documents, his research can also be found in two theoretical treatises published in Padua in 1754 and 1767, namely the *Trattato secondo la vera scienza dell'armonia* (Treatise on Music according to the True Science of Harmony) and the *De' Principj dell'armonia musicale contenuta nel diatonico genere* (On the Principles of Musical Harmony Contained in the Diatonic Genus).[1]

According to what he writes in *De' Principj*, Tartini discovered the *terzo suono* (third tone) in 1714[2] but in an autograph manuscript recently acquired by the Conservatory of Trieste, which appears to be a draft of the treatise, he seems to claim

---

1 Giuseppe Tartini, *Trattato di musica secondo la vera scienza dell'armonia* (Padova: Stamperia del Seminario, 1754); Giuseppe Tartini, *De' Principj dell'armonia musicale contenuta nel diatonico genere* (Padova: Stamperia del Seminario, 1767).
2 Tartini, *De' Principj*, 36.

that the discovery was made in 1713.³ A comparison between the published treatise and the autograph is shown in Figure 1.

> 36 CAPO SECONDO
>
> ne, e reazione da due suoni simultanei, siano in qualsivoglia ragione, o musicale di razional quantità, o geometrica d'irrazional quantità, si ha, e deve averfi fenfibile quefto terzo fuono, il quale intanto non è fenfibile nelle ragioni fummultiplici 1, 2; 1, 3; 1, 4 ec., inquanto per la formola 1×2=2, 1×3=3, 1×4=4 ec. rifultando fempre unifono al termine maggiore, che nelle multiplici 1, 2; 1, 3 ec. è fempre il tutto dato nella fifico-armonica unità, il di cui fuono è molto più forte del rifultato terzo fuono, fi fente quello, e non quefto. Ma più. Nell'acuftica fi fa ftato di fcienza fulle vibrazioni, e coincidenze delle tefe corde fonore, e non dovrà farfi ful terzo fuono, la di cui formola è la fteffa delle vibrazioni, e coincidenze? Troppo di più vi farebbe d'aggiungere alla prova della univerfalità di quefto fenomeno, e della foftanzial diverfità del medefimo da qualunque altro. Ma bafta, e avanza il fin qui efpofto per far tacere per fempre chi lo accomuna con gli altri, e chi lo tiene in niun conto. Il di più che potrebbe dirfi, arrivarebbe all'infulto, e però fi rifparmia ben volentieri.
>
> §. 3. Non così l'autore può rifparmiar il di più ch'è coftretto a pubblicare fulla fcoperta di quefto fenomeno. Nell'anno 1714. giovine di anni 22. incirca fcopre fortunatamente ful Violino quefto fenomeno in Ancona, dove non pochi ricordevoli teftimonj fopravvivono ancora. Lo comunica fin da quel tempo fenza riferva, e miftero ai Profeffori di Violino. Lo fa regola fondamentale di perfetto accordo per i Giovani della fua fcuola nell'anno 1728 incominciata in Padova, dove ancora fuffifte; e con ciò fi diffonde la notizia del fenomeno per tutta Europa. Pubblica nel 1754 il fuo trattato di mufica, in cui enuncia quefto fenomeno nel Capitolo primo, lo coftituifce fifico principal fondamento del fuo fiftema, e per modeftia non fi vanta autore della fcoperta. Che ne fegue? Efteri accreditati Autori volendo dar l'onore della fcoperta alla propria Nazione, la pretendono feguita tra loro, perchè fu pubblicamente enunciata con la ftampa nell'anno antecedente 1753, e profeguono a pubblicamente confermare in più modi la loro pretenfione. Almeno aveffero avuto la cautela di enunciar la fcoperta come poffibile a farfi da molti fenza faputa, e commercio dell'uno con l'altro, in tempi diverfi, ed anche nello fteffo tempo, ma in luoghi diverfi ec. Nò: fi vuole attribuire fenza riferva alla propria Nazione. Convien dire, che qualche loro dominante paffione non gli abbia permeffo di confiderare la inevitabile confeguenza di effere fmentiti da più migliaja di teftimonj di fatto, tra i quali ve n'è buon numero della fteffa loro Nazione, e di coftringer l'autore a por da parte la modeftia per rivelar pubblicamente il fatto. E pur quefto è il meno, fe fi rifguarda il fatto in altro afpetto. Il cafo è curiofo, e merita rifleffione particolare. Da quefti tali fi vuol attribuire la fcoperta alla propria Nazione, e fi vuole afficurare il Pubblico,

---

3 Draft of the treatise "De' Principj dell'armonia musicale", by Giuseppe Tartini, n. d., p. 4, I–TSc, GT/FA/23 ms2, *Tartiniana Collection*, Library of the Conservatory of Music "Giuseppe Tartini", Trieste, Italy. http://www.internetculturale.it/it/16/search/detail?id=oai%3Awww.internetculturale.sbn.it%2FTeca%3A20%3ANT0000%3AN%3ATSA2769169

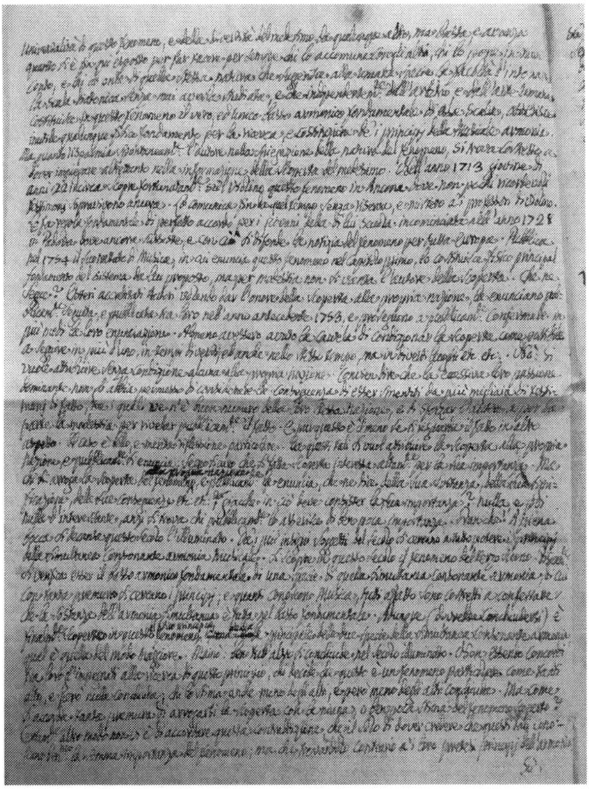

Accompaniments of Tartini's Concertos and the Third-Tone 57

Figure 1: A comparison between the published treatise *De' principj* and the autograph kept at the Conservatory of Trieste.

The *third tone* is of crucial importance to Tartini, and he discusses it in all his theoretical treatises. In addition, there is a large number of autograph documents that have not yet been analysed in detail. Of these, the documents kept in the Piran unit of the Regional Archives of Koper are of particular importance[4] (the first page of one of these documents is shown in Figure 2[5]). Here he developed his ideas

---

4 *Collection Giuseppe Tartini*, SI PAK PI 334, Regional archives Koper, Piran Unit, Slovenia. http://www.internetculturale.it/it/16/search?q=&searchType=avanzato&channel_ _subject=%22Tartini%2C+Giuseppe+-+Documenti%22&opCha__subject=AND&_ _meta_locationStringOnlyBib=archivio+regionale+di+capodistria+-+sezione+pir ano+%28pokrajinski+arhiva+koper+upravnih+enota+piran%29+-+slovenia
5 Notebook with musical-theoretical writings intitled "Terzo", by Giuseppe Tartini, Si-Pit, SI PAK KP 334, box 3, ms.140, *Collection Giuseppe Tartini*, Regional archives Koper, Piran Unit, Slovenia. http://www.internetculturale.it/it/16/search/detail?id=oai%3Awww. internetculturale.sbn.it%2FTeca%3A20%3ANT0000%3AN%3ASI-PIt-003140

about his theories that led him to consider the third tone as the basis for the rules of musical harmony.

Figure 2: The first page of one of the Tartini's manuscripts kept in the Piran unit of the Regional Archives of Koper.

The questions of harmony, mathematics and physical acoustics, which lasted throughout the eighteenth century and were present in most of Tartini's scientific reflections and led to debates, correspondence and contacts with theorists, scientists and renowned mathematicians of his time, have already been examined in detail elsewhere.[6] The aim of this paper is therefore to present some ideas for an alternative "reading" of the third tone, in particular about the way it is used in Tartini's compositions and about its function in orchestral accompaniments for concertos for violin and orchestra.

2 What Is the Third Tone?

In musical acoustics, the term *harmonic* is used to define complementary tones to a fundamental frequency at which they are produced, and with which they determine the timbre of an instrument or voice.

Tartini also began to study the vibrations of the strings and their frequencies: he examined the sound of an instrument called *tromba marina* (also called *trumpet marine* or *nun's fiddle*, see Figure 3), which was still in use in his time and for which Vivaldi wrote a concerto. Tartini's discussions on this topic can be found both in surviving autograph manuscripts[7] and in his treatises[8] (see Figure 4).

---

[6] See Patrizio Barbieri, "Il sistema armonico di Tartini nelle 'censure' di due celebri fisicomatematici: Eulero e Riccati," in *Tartini: il tempo e le opere*, ed. Andrea Bombi and Maria Nevilla Massaro (Bologna: Il Mulino, 1994): 321–344; Patrizio Barbieri, *Quarrels on Harmonic Theories in the Venetian Enlightenment* (Lucca: LIM, 2020); Angela Lohri, "The Tartini Tones and their relevance in Music Theory and Performance," in *CroArtScia 2011*, ed. Sonja Nikolić, Vesna Meštrić, Igor Peteh and Vesna Rastija (Zagreb: Croatian Academy of Sciences and Arts, 2014), 96–98; Angela Lohri, Sandra Carral, and Vasileios Chatziioannou, "Combination Tones in Violins," *Archives of Acoustics* 36, no.4 (2011): 727–740; Angela Lohri, *Kombinationstöne und Tartinis "terzo suono"* (Mainz: Schott Music GmbH & Co.KG, 2016); Marta Mion, "Between music and molecular studies: the third tone according to Hermann von Helmholtz," *Audiologia&Foniatria: Italian Journal of Audiology and Phoniatrics*, no. 6 (2021): 1–3. https://doi.org/10.14658/pupj-ijap-2021-1-2. See also Sukljan's chapter in this volume: Nejc Sukljan, "Tartini and the Ancients: Traces of Ancient Music Theory in Tartini-Martin Correspondence," in *In Search of Perfect Harmony: Tartini's Music and Music Theory in Local and European Contexts*, ed. Nejc Sukljan (Berlin: Peter Lang, 2022), 141–167.
[7] Short study of the string on tromba marina, by Giuseppe Tartini, SI-Pit, SI PAK PI 334, box 3, ms.147, *Collection Giuseppe Tartini*, Regional archives Koper, Piran Unit, Slovenia.
[8] Tartini, *Trattato di musica*, 11.

1. 2. Kleine Poschen / Geigen ein Octav höher. 3. Discant-Geig ein Quart höher. 4. Rechte Discant-Geig. 5. Tenor-Geig. 6 Bas-Geig de bracio. 7. Trumscheit. 8. Scheidtholtt.

Figure 3: Two examples of *tromba marina*: the first (instrument no. 7) is from the *Syntagma Musicum* by Michael Praetorius (1619) and the other from the *Gabinetto Armonico* by Filippo Buonanni (1722). (Michael Praetorius, *Syntagma musicum II: De Organographia* (Kassel: Bärenreiter, 2001), plate XXI; Filippo Bonanni, *Gabinetto armonico* (Roma: nella stamperia di Giorgio Placho, 1722), plate LXII.)

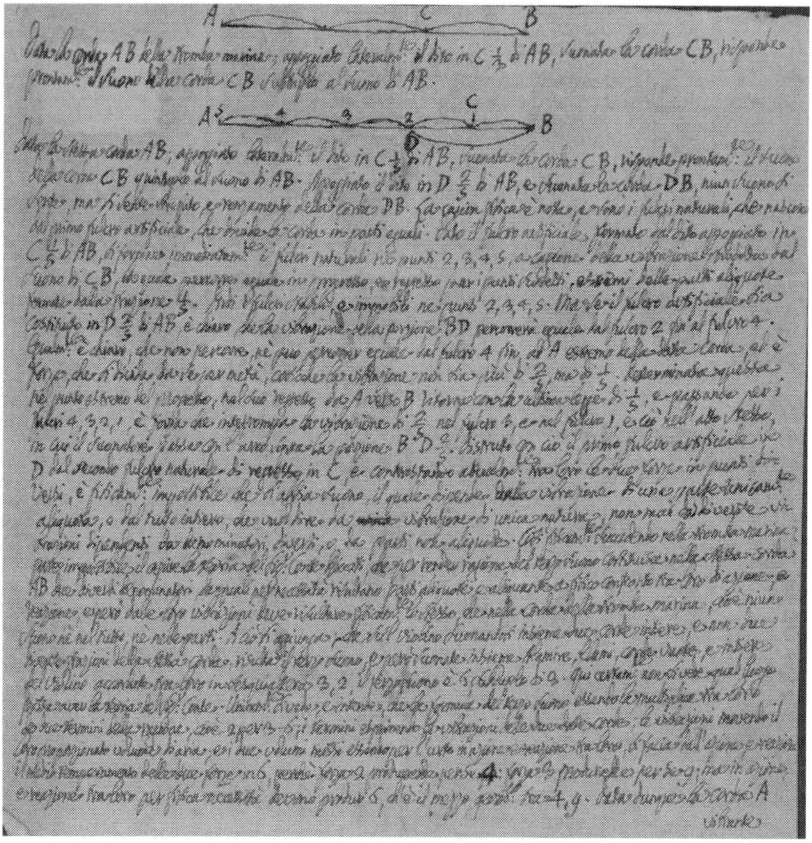

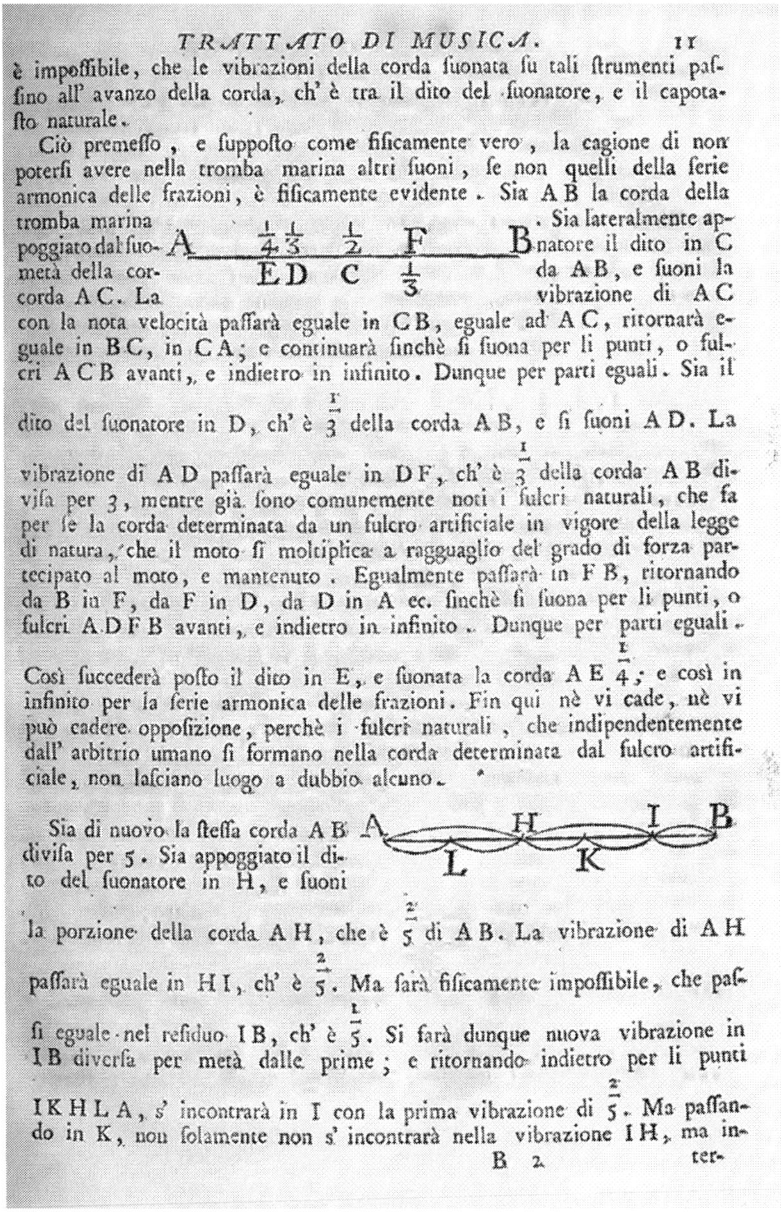

> *TRATTATO DI MUSICA.* 11
> è impoffibile, che le vibrazioni della corda fuonata fu tali ftrumenti paffino all' avanzo della corda, ch' è tra il dito del fuonatore, e il capotafto naturale.
> Ciò premeffo, e fuppofto come fificamente vero, la cagione di non poterfi avere nella tromba marina altri fuoni, fe non quelli della ferie armonica delle frazioni, è fificamente evidente. Sia AB la corda della tromba marina . Sia lateralmente appoggiato dal fuo- A $\frac{1}{4}\frac{1}{3}$ $\frac{1}{2}$ F B natore il dito in C metà della cor- ED C $\frac{1}{3}$ da AB, e fuoni la corda AC. La vibrazione di AC con la nota velocità paffarà eguale in CB, eguale ad AC, ritornarà eguale in BC, in CA; e continuarà finchè fi fuona per li punti, o fulcri ACB avanti, e indietro in infinito. Dunque per parti eguali. Sia il dito del fuonatore in D, ch' è $\frac{1}{3}$ della corda AB, e fi fuoni AD. La vibrazione di AD paffarà eguale in DF, ch' è $\frac{1}{3}$ della corda AB divifa per 3, mentre già fono comunemente noti i fulcri naturali, che fa per fe la corda determinata da un fulcro artificiale in vigore della legge di natura, che il moto fi moltiplica a ragguaglio del grado di forza partecipato al moto, e mantenuto. Egualmente paffarà in FB, ritornando da B in F, da F in D, da D in A ec. finchè fi fuona per li punti, o fulcri ADFB avanti, e indietro in infinito. Dunque per parti eguali.
> Così succederà pofto il dito in E, e fuonata la corda AE $\frac{1}{4}$; e così in infinito per la ferie armonica delle frazioni. Fin qui nè vi cade, nè vi può cadere oppofizione, perchè i fulcri naturali, che indipendentemente dall' arbitrio umano fi formano nella corda determinata dal fulcro artificiale, non lafciano luogo a dubbio alcuno.
> Sia di nuovo la fteffa corda AB divifa per 5. Sia appoggiato il dito del fuonatore in H, e fuoni
> la porzione della corda AH, che è $\frac{2}{5}$ di AB. La vibrazione di AH paffarà eguale in HI, ch' è $\frac{2}{5}$. Ma farà fificamente impoffibile, che paffi eguale nel refiduo IB, ch' è $\frac{1}{5}$. Si farà dunque nuova vibrazione in IB diverfa per metà dalle prime; e ritornando indietro per li punti IKHLA, s' incontrarà in I con la prima vibrazione di $\frac{2}{5}$. Ma paffando in K, non folamente non s' incontrarà nella vibrazione IH, ma in-
> B 2 ter-

Figure 4: A page of Tartini's autograph manuscript and page 11 of the *Trattato di musica*, in which Tartini discusses the vibration of the strings in the trumpet marine.

Harmonic tones follow the laws of natural frequencies and do not fit into the system of equal temperament. However, their frequencies, can be combined, creating new frequencies called *combination tones*. The frequencies of the harmonic tones are always integer multiples of the fundamental frequency of the basic tone. This does not explain or justify the creation of combination tones, since their frequencies are lower than those of the basictone. This is why the more recent studies on the so-called third tone go in two directions: that of physical analysis and that of psychological or psychoacoustic analysis, which looks for answers in psychology and neurology.[9] In this context, the question arises whether these combination tones are to be regarded as subjective or objective. According to Tartini, they are of objective nature and have a real existence: "It is physically certain that, when two simultaneous sounds are played loudly and in a prolonged way, [...] a third simultaneous [lower] tone can be heard, different from the two given sounds."[10] This is commonly referred to as the *Tartini tone* or *combination tone*.

In *De' Principj*, Tartini even presents a formula for calculating the third tone. He explains: "The formula of the third tone is the multiplication of the two [co]-prime numbers."[11] This calculation is equal to the least common multiple of the two numbers.[12]

An important question before Tartini's orchestral accompaniments can be discussed is how the third tone relates to the rules of harmony. Figure 2 shows an example from Tartini's notebook with a C major scale (black notes) and the chords added to each of the degrees. The third tones in the lower staff result from bichords of the upper staff (white notes) and correspond to the harmonic bass, as Tartini explains under the example: "The harmonic ground bass that results from all the harmonic parts that resonate in the third tone."[13] In Figure 5 the degrees that result from the chords are added.

---

9 According to recent studies published by two researchers from the University of Pisa, we can represent the spectrum of a bichord produced by a violin in which we can perceive the third tone, which is the difference between the fundamental frequencies. See Claudio Bini and Guglielmo Lami, *I suoni di combinazione ed il terzo suono di Tartini: fisica, storia e musica* (Pisa: il Campano, 2019).
10 "[...] è fisicamente certo, che dati due suoni simultanei forti, e prolungati [...] si sente un terzo suono simultaneo, diverso dai due dati suoni [...]" (Tartini, *De' Principj*, 5), quoted and english translation in Lohri, »The Tartini tones«, 88.
11 "[...] di questo terzo suono vi è la formula, che lo assicura, ed è la moltiplica tra loro de' due numeri sempre primi, disegnanti la forma, in cui sono i due dati suoni." (Tartini, *De' Principj*, 5), quoted and English translation in Lohri, "The Tartini tones," 89.
12 Patrizio Barbieri, "Tartinis Dritter Ton Eulers Harmonische Exponenten. Mit einem unveröffentlichten Manuskript Tartinis," *Musiktheorie* 7, no. 3 (1992): 220 and 227.
13 "Basso arm.[oni]co fondamentale, che nel terzo suono risulta da tutte insieme le parti dell'armonia." Tartini, Notebook "Terzo". English translation by the author. Tartini also discusses this precise example of the harmonized scale in his last published theoretical treatise (*De' Principj*), which testifies to the great importance he believed the third tone had in establishing the fundamental rules of tonal harmony. See Tartini, *De' Principj*, 80.

80   *C A P O   T E R Z O*

Si cerca il vero dove non è: non fi troverà mai. Per natura convengono al grave le cadenze, all' acuto la fcala; e per arte fi trasforma l' acuto in grave, le cadenze nella fcala con l' ufo della feconda, e terza formola, o fia bafe a comodo, e arbitrio de' compofitori, ch'è appunto la cagione per cui non vi è, nè può effervi certa legge di baffo, che proceda per fcala. La certiffima legge originale delle formole organiche della fcala, determinate non dall' arte, o dall' arbitrio, ma dalla fifico-armonica natura, fi trova unicamente in quefto efemplare, che appunto per tal cagione non può non effer il primo. A quefto punto di vifta l' autore invita Mufici, Dotti, chiunque, per efiger pubblica precifa rifpofta ful fatto, che qui efpone fotto gli occhi loro, e che minutamente anderà fvogliendo. Ecco qui efpofte le fifiche leggi di natura nel terzo fuono baffo armonico fondamentale della fcala dimoftrativamente dedotta dalla congiunzione delle due confonanti armonie, fimultanea, e fucceffiva, e qui fpiegata nelle quattro parti reali della fimultanea confonante armonia, dedotte dalla formola di ciafcuna nota fucceffiva di effa fcala.

Scala diatonica nelle fue forme

Baffo fondamentale terzo fuono cadenze ordinate

I   V   I   IV   I   IV   V   I

La fcala fi è fegnata con note chiufe per diftinguerla dalle altre aperte, che non formano fcala; e nel fettimo, e ottavo grado fi trovano le due note della fcala con due note aperte fottopofte per evitar a norma della legge muficale due ottave, e due quinte fucceffive, che fi formarebbero col baffo, fe le due della fcala foffero le fottopofte. Ora fi paffi all' efame.

§. 11. Ciò che cade in principal oggetto di efame, fi è il fatto della fcala fopra efpofta. Qui fi trova, che data la fcala a tre parti reali dedotte dalla formola di ciafcuna nota, la fifico-armonica natura forma da fe il baffo fondamentale di effa fcala. Quefto baffo fondamentale fi trova effer lo fteffo, che fi ha dalle tre cadenze ordinate. Le cadenze fi hanno dalla dupla geometrica difcreta. Quefta fi ha dagli avanzi delle frazioni di AB relativo al terzo fuono. Dagli avanzi fteffi fi ha egualmente la fefquialtera geometrica difcreta, da cui fi ha la formola organica fondamentale 1, 3, 5, e da quefta formola applicata alle tre lettere C, F,

Figure 5: Tartin's harmonization of the C major scale with the third tones in the lower staff and added degrees resulting from the chords.

Tartini also addresses the subject in the first pages of *Trattato di musica*.[14] In his opinion, the third tones can function as a harmonic bass in musical compositions or performances. He applied this view in some of his solo violin works, especially in the so-called *Piccole Sonate* (Little sonatas).[15] In a letter to Count Algarotti (dated 24 February 1750), he wrote that these kinds of compositions do not require accompaniment: "My little violin sonatas sent there have the bass as a formality [...] I play them without the *bassetto*, and this is my true intention."[16] In the *Trattato di musica*, Tartini explains that "the third tone [...] will demonstratively be the harmonic bass of the given intervals and the introduction of any other bass would be a paralogism."[17] His exploration of the third tone was not only aimed at ensuring the advantage of favourable acoustic effect in compositions. He proved that the use of the third tone would lead to a better understanding of music theory, as well as better violin playing: "When I play my violin on two strings, I can physically meet the form of the interval: the third tone which must result is its physical sign and proof. I thus have for myself and for my students the benefit of reliable intonation."[18]

3 The Orchestral Accompaniments

Let us now turn to some musical examples to further illustrate the application of Tartini's third tone theory in his compositions. Among the musical autographs preserved in the Musical Archives of the *Cappella Antoniana* of Padua is the score of a concerto for violin and orchestra in A major.[19] After the first movement

---

14 Tartini, *Trattato di musica*, 10–19.
15 Pierluigi Petrobelli, *Tartini, le sue idee e il suo tempo* (Lucca: LIM, 1992): 81–82.
16 "[...] Le piccole sonate mie a violino solo mandate costà hanno il basso per cerimonia [...]. Io le suono senza bassetto, e questa è la mia vera intentione." Giorgia Malagò, ed., *Giuseppe Tartini: Lettere e documenti/Pisma in dokumenti/Letters and Documents*, trans. Jerneja Umer Kljun and Roberto Baldo, vol. 1 (Trieste 2020): 180. English translation in Malagò, *Tartini: Lettere*, 2:319. Also see Črtomir Šiškovič, "Giuseppe Tartini: le 'Piccole sonate'," *A tutto arco* 10, no.13 (2017): 16–40.
17 "[...] dati i seguenti intervalli, de' quali è rispettivo terzo suono il sottoposto, questo sarà dimostrativamente il Basso armonico de' dati intervalli, e sarà paralogismo qualunque altro Basso vi si sottoponga." Tartini, *Trattato di musica*, 17. English translation by the author.
18 "Io nel mio Violino, dove suonando a doppia corda posso incontrar fisicamente la forma dell'intervallo, di cui è segno fisico dimostrativo il tal terzo suono, che deve risultare, ho il vantaggio per me, e per i miei scolari della sicura intonazione." Tartini, *Trattato di musica*, 100, quoted and english translation in Lohri, "The Tartini tones", 92.
19 Giuseppe Tartini, "Concerto per violino e orchestra in A major, D 110 (GT 1. A23)," autograph score. I-Pca, Ms. D VII 1902/51. Archivio musicale della Pontificia Biblioteca Antoniana, Padova, Italia. See: http://catalog.discovertartini.eu/dcm/gt/document.xq?doc=Concerto_per_violino_D110.xml

(*Allegro assai*) we find the second movement (*Larghetto* in 3/4, with the motto "Se mai saprai") on page 4. The piece is written for four parts: violino concertante, first violin, second violin and viola, but as Figure 6a shows, the sheet has been crossed out and at the top left Tartini wrote: "The *Grave* is at the end" ("in fine è il Grave"). One would expect a completely different movement, a new piece with a different melody. Instead, a simple comparison with the final *Grave*, which begins on page 8 of the manuscript after the third movement (Figure 6b), proves that the melody of the leading violin and the number of bars of the entire piece are the same. Why did Tartini write a movement that is almost the same as before? We immediately notice that it was written for three parts instead of four: violino concertante, first violin and second violin. The part for the viola is missing, and a closer analysis shows that the texture of the accompaniment is lighter and more essential: it is structured with many open chords and the harmony is expressed mainly in the higher register. Moreover, the first violin plays the part of the second, often in the upper octave and with some changes at the end of the phrase, while the second violin plays the part of the viola. In the final chords, the fifths are not present and sometimes there is only the unison with the root. Why was this movement crossed out and then rewritten in almost the same way?

We can assume that the only reason the first version was omitted is that Tartini wanted to emphasize the third tone as the fundamental bass of the chords. He wanted it to be heard, not written. The change of tempo marking from *Larghetto* to *Grave* also seems to have the purpose of slowing down the music, with the precise intention of allowing the perception of the third tone.

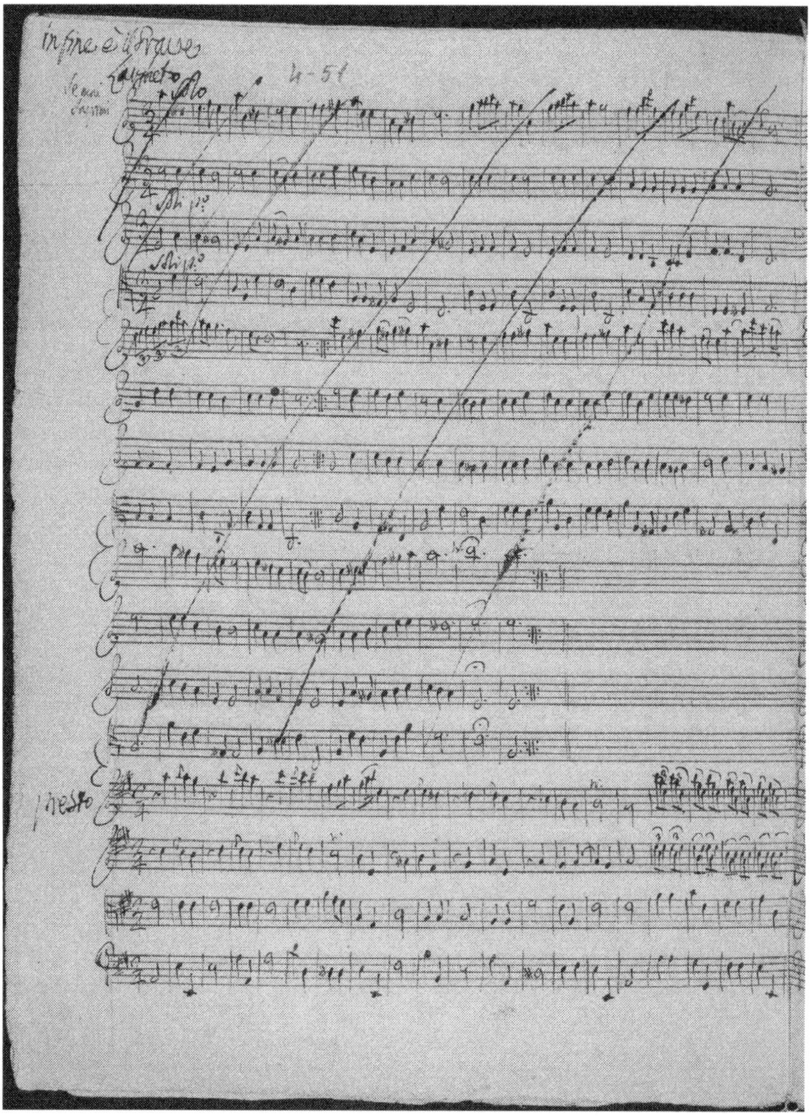

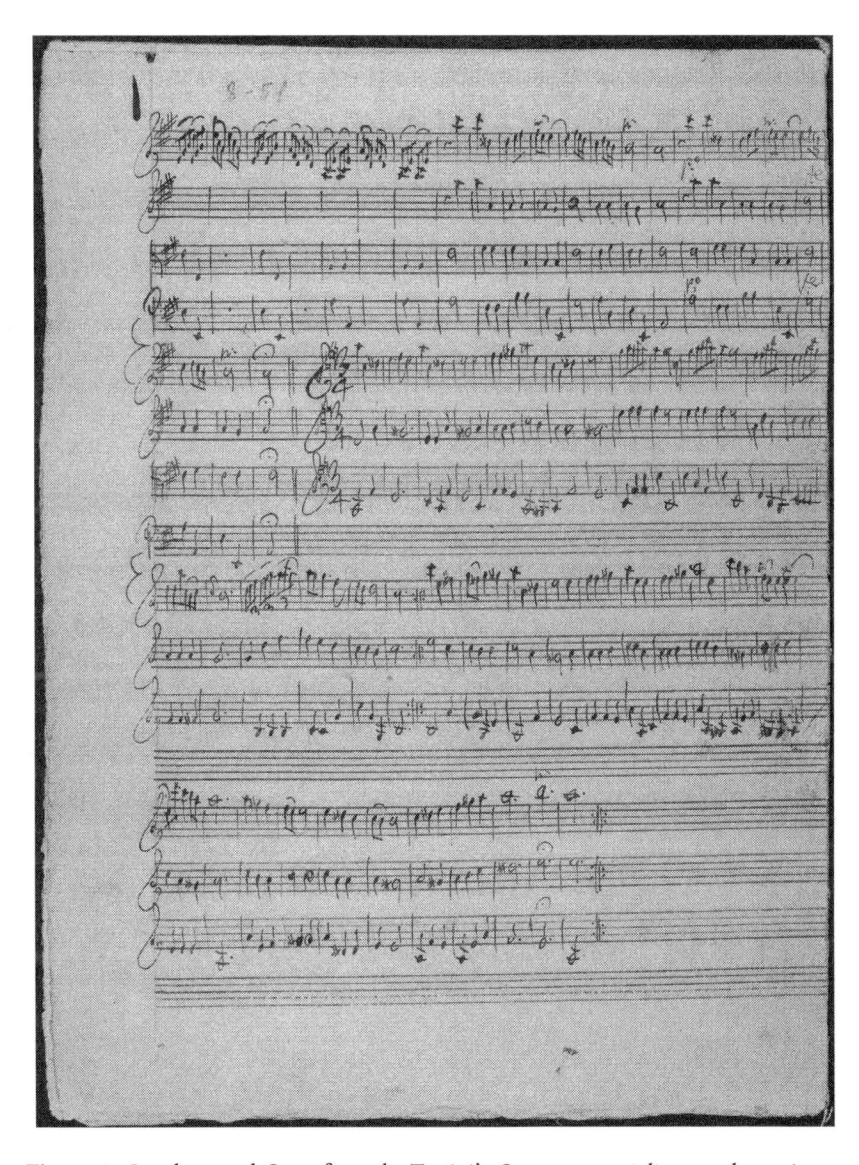

Figure 6: *Larghetto* and *Grave* from the Tartini's *Concerto per violino e orchestra* in A major, D 110 (GT 1. A23).

The type of accompaniment just analysed consists of only a few notes in the higher register of the first and second violins without bass accompaniment. Such a musical texture is found in numerous solo parts of Tartini's concertos for violin and orchestra. Figure 7, for example, shows a score of Tartini's *Concerto* in D major D 41 (GT 1.D27)[20] copied by Giulio Meneghini (1741–1824), a student of Tartini and his successor in the orchestra of the *Cappella Antoniana* in 1765. In the score, one can clearly see the accompaniment of the solo parts played only by the first and second violins.

Figure 7: Manuscript score by Giulio Meneghini of the Tartini's *Concerto per violino e orchestra* in D major, D 41 (GT 1. A09).

---

20 Tartini, "Concerto per violino e orchestra in D Major," D 41 (GT 1.D27). http://cata log.discovertartini.eu/dcm/gt/document.xq?doc=Concerto_per_violino_D41.xml. Today the score is kept in the library of the Conservatory of Paris: Giuseppe Tartini, "Concerto per violino e orchestra in D Major, D 41 (GT 1D27)," manuscript score by Giulio Meneghini. F-Pn MS-9795/21. Bibliotèque nationale de France, Département de la Musique, Paris, France.
  The score is archived in one of the three folders containing 84 Tartini concertos copied in Padua in the late eighteenth century and captured by the French occupying

Furthermore, we can see in Figure 8 that when in the *Concerto* D 96 (GT 1.A09)[21] the accompaniment of the solo part requires a bass, Meneghini makes this clear by adding "with the obligatory cello" ("Con violoncello obbligato") to the title.

Figure 8: Score by Giulio Meneghini of the Tartini's *Concerto per violino e orchestra* in D major, D 96 (GT 1.A09), "*Con violoncello obbligato*".

Similar inscriptions are found in other manuscripts located in the same folder, such as "with obligatory cello and violetta" ("Con Violoncello e violetta obbligati"). This suggests the theory that in his last years as a composer Tartini regularly opted for a lighter accompaniment, i.e. played only by the first and second violins, and that this type of accompaniment then became common for performances of Tartini's repertoire in late eighteenth-century Padua.

---

forces during the Napoleonic Wars. These manuscripts were amongst the very first documents in the library of the Conservatory of Paris, which was founded in 1801. See Pierluigi Petrobelli, *Giuseppe Tartini. Le fonti biografiche* (Venezia: Universal Edition, 1968), 76.

21 Giuseppe Tartini, "Concerto per violino e orchestra in D Major, D 96 (GT 1.A09), Con violoncello obbligato," manuscript score by Giulio Meneghini. F-Pn MS-9795/15. Bibliotèque nationale de France, Département de la Musique, Paris, France. Accessed http://catalog.discovertartini.eu/dcm/gt/document.xq?doc=Concerto_per_violino_D96.xml

This theory could be confirmed by a further analysis of other manuscripts by Tartini, especially of the so-called "draft scores" of his compositions. Tartini frequently revised his autograph scores, and during our work on Tartini's concertos we assumed that these revision sheets could be considered prior to the final drafts because of the particular writing and ink.[22] Now the presence of the bass in the soloist's accompaniment in these revision sheets seems to confirm this hypothesis. Figure 9 shows an autograph manuscript of the solo part after some erasures with an accompaniment of two violins and a bass.[23]

Figure 9: Autograph score of the Tartini's *Concerto per violino e orchestra* in D major, D 17 (GT 1. D03).

---

22 Margherita Canale, "I concerti solistici di Giuseppe Tartini. Testimoni, tradizione e catalogo tematico," (Doctoral dissertation, Padua University, 2010), vol. I, 48–53, http://paduaresearch.cab.unipd.it/3658/; Margherita Canale, "The Solo Concertos by Giuseppe Tartini: Sources, Tradition and Thematic Catalogue," *Ad Parnassum* 11, no. 22 (2013): 11–49.
23 Giuseppe Tartini, "Concerto per violino e orchestra in D Major, D 17 (GT 1.D03)," autograph score. I-Pca, Ms. D VII 1902/101. Archivio musicale della Pontificia Biblioteca Antoniana, Padova, Italia. http://catalog.discovertartini.eu/dcm/gt/document.xq?doc=Concerto_per_violino_D17.xml

Would it therefore be possible to consider the discussed connections between the theory of thirds and the use of lighter accompaniments with only first and second violins as a means of dating Tartini's manuscript scores?

4 Conclusions

The open harmonies used in these accompaniments of violin solos, with many empty fifth chords and a transparent texture, aimed to emphasize the third tone in the form of a harmonic bass and required an extremely precise natural intonation that could only be achieved by string instruments and was impossible to achieve with instruments such as the organ or the harpsichord. This fact speaks for the decision not to play the fundamental bass in Tartini's violin concertos witht the harpsichord. In this context, it is also significant that there was no harpsichord player among the musicians of the *Cappella* orchestra.[24] The bass should only be played by the organ in the *tutti* sections and, of course, never in the solo sections when the manuscript only calls for the use of the first and second violins.

Bibliography

Barbieri, Patrizio. "Il sistema armonico di Tartini nelle 'censure' di due celebri fisico-matematici: Eulero e Riccati." In *Tartini: il tempo e le opere*, edited by Andrea Bombi and Maria Nevilla Massaro, 321–344. Bologna: Il Mulino, 1994.

Barbieri, Patrizio. *Quarrels on Harmonic Theories in the Venetian Enlightenment*. Lucca: LIM, 2020.

Barbieri, Patrizio. "Tartinis Dritter Ton Eulers Harmonische Exponenten. Mit einem unveröffentlichten Manuskript Tartinis." *Musiktheorie* 7, no. 3 (1992): 219–234.

Bini, Claudio, and Guglielmo Lami. *I suoni di combinazione ed il terzo suono di Tartini: fisica, storia e musica*. Pisa: Il Campano, 2019.

Bonanni, Filippo. *Gabinetto armonico*. Roma: nella stamperia di Giorgio Placho, 1722.

Canale, Margherita. "I concerti solistici di Giuseppe Tartini. Testimoni, tradizione e catalogo tematico, vol. 1." Doctoral dissertation, Padua University, 2010. Accessed August 22, 2022. http://paduaresearch.cab.unipd.it/3658/

Canale, Margherita. "The Solo Concertos by Giuseppe Tartini: Sources, Tradition and Thematic Catalogue." *Ad Parnassum* 11, no. 22 (2013): 11–49.

Dalla Vecchia, Jolanda. *L'organizzazione della Cappella musicale antoniana di Padova nel Settecento*. Padova: Centro studi antoniani, 1995.

---

24 Jolanda Dalla Vecchia, *L'organizzazione della Cappella musicale antoniana di Padova nel Settecento* (Padova: Centro studi antoniani, 1995), 59.

Lohri, Angela, Sandra Carral, and Vasileios Chatziioannou. "Combination Tones in Violins." *Archives of Acoustics* 36, no.4 (2011): 727–740.

Lohri, Angela. *Kombinationstöne und Tartinis "terzo suono"*. Mainz: Schott Music GmbH & Co.KG, 2016.

Lohri, Angela. "The Tartini Tones and their relevance in Music Theory and Performance." In *CroArtScia 2011*, edited by Sonja Nikolić, Vesna Meštric, Igor Peteh, and Vesna Rastija, 87–98. Zagreb: Croatian Academy of Sciences and Arts, 2014.

Malagò, Giorgia, ed. *Giuseppe Tartini: Lettere e documenti/Pisma in dokumenti/ Letters and Documents*. 2 vols. Translated by Jerneja Umer Kljun and Roberto Baldo. Trieste: Edizioni Università di Trieste, 2020.

Mion, Marta. "Between music and molecular studies: the third tone according to Hermann von Helmholtz." *Audiologia&Foniatria: Italian Journal of Audiology and Phoniatrics*, no. 6 (2021): 1–3. https://doi.org/10.14658/pupj-ijap-2021-1-2.

Petrobelli, Pierluigi. *Giuseppe Tartini. Le fonti biografiche*. Venezia: Universal Edition, 1968.

Petrobelli, Pierluigi. *Tartini, le sue idee e il suo tempo*. Lucca: LIM, 1992.

Praetorius, Michael. *Syntagma musicum II: De organographia*. Facsimile of the Wittenberg edition, 1614–1615. Kassel: Bärenreiter, 2001.

Sukljan Nejc. "Tartini and the Ancients: Traces of Ancient Music Theory in Tartini-Martin Correspondence." In *In Search of Perfect Harmony: Tartini's Music and Music Theory in Local and European Contexts*, edited by Nejc Sukljan, 141–167. Berlin: Peter Lang, 2022.

Šiškovič, Črtomir. "Giuseppe Tartini: le 'Piccole sonate'." *A tutto arco* 10, no. 13 (2017): 16–40.

Tartini, Giuseppe. "Concerto per violino e orchestra in D major, D 17 (GT 1. D03)." Autograph score, I-Pca, Ms. D VII 1902/101. Archivio musicale della Pontificia Biblioteca Antoniana, Padova, Italia.

Tartini, Giuseppe. "Concerto per violino e orchestra in D major, D 41 (GT 1. A09)." Manuscript score by Giulio Meneghini, F-Pn MS-9795/21. Bibliotèque nationale de France, Département de la Musique, Paris, France.

Tartini, Giuseppe. "Concerto per violino e orchestra in D major, D 96 (GT 1.A09), Con violoncello obbligato." Manuscript score by Giulio Meneghini, F-Pn MS-9795/15. Bibliotèque nationale de France, Département de la Musique, Paris, France.

Tartini, Giuseppe. "Concerto per violino e orchestra in A major, D 110 (GT 1. A23)." Autograph score, I-Pca, Ms. D VII 1902/51. Archivio musicale della Pontificia Biblioteca Antoniana, Padova, Italia.

Tartini, Giuseppe. *De' Principj dell'armonia musicale contenuta nel diatonico genere*. Padova: Stamperia del Seminario, 1767.

Tartini, Giuseppe. Draft of the treatise "De' Principj dell'armonia musicale". I - TSc, GT/ FA/ 23 ms2, *Tartiniana Collection*, Library of the Conservatory of Music "Giuseppe Tartini", Trieste, Italy. http:// www.intern etcu ltur ale. it/ it/16/ sea rch/ det ail?id= oai%3Awww.intern etcu ltur ale.sbn.it%2FT eca%3A20%3ANT0000%3AN%3ATSA 2769 169.

Tartini, Giuseppe. Notebook "Terzo". SI- Pit, SI PAK PI 334, box 3, ms. 140, *Collection Giuseppe Tartini*, Regional archives Koper, Piran Unit, Slovenia.

Tartini, Giuseppe. Short study of the string on tromba marina. SI- Pit, SI PAK PI 334, box 3, ms. 147, *Collection Giuseppe Tartini*, Regional archives Koper, Piran Unit, Slovenia.

Tartini, Giuseppe. *Trattato di musica secondo la vera scienza dell'armonia*. Padova: Stamperia del Seminario, 1754.

Viverit, Guido, Alba Luksich, and Simone Olivari. *Catalogo tematico online delle composizioni di Giuseppe Tartini*. Accessed August 28, 2022. http://catalog.disc overtartini.eu/dcm/gt/navigation.xq.

Piotr Wilk

Jagiellonian University in Kraków

Tartini's Concertos Op. 1 and 2 against the Backdrop of the Venetian Concerto Tradition

Abstract: Giuseppe Tartini explored the secrets of the violin playing and the art of composition in Assisi and Ancona. It was not until the age of 30 that he settled permanently in Padua, and his first concertos, published as Op. 1 and 2 in the years 1727–1733, date roughly from that period. In this chapter, these works have been compared with the concertos composed in the Republic of Venice in the first four decades of the eighteenth century in order to answer the question of whether the composer worked according to the patterns prevailing in that music centre. The instrumental concerto was the leading music genre cultivated in the Republic of Venice at the time. About 1,000 compositions of this type have survived, establishing the Serenissima as the main centre of concerto production in Europe. Despite evident Venetian influences, Tartini's works are distinguished by an original melodic style, seemingly inspired by Dalmatian folklore. The composer also followed different aesthetic norms, already foreshadowing the era of Classicism.

Keywords: Tartini's Op. 1 and Op. 2, violin concerto, Venetian Baroque concerto, ritornello form, scoring

Of the genres of instrumental music practised in the Venetian Republic during Giuseppe Tartini's lifetime, the concerto was unquestionably the most important. The number of artists active in this field and the number of concertos preserved to our times are among the largest in Europe at that time. Only in the era of Vivaldi, which more or less coincides with the first period of Tartini's work according to Burney,[1] there were 15 composers in Veneto who wrote concertos (Table 1). In total, nearly 1,000 pieces of this type have been preserved from this musical centre![2] We are talking about the works of the citizens of the Serenissima who were active in Venice, Padua, Brescia and Bergamo.[3] We can also include in this

---

1 Cf. Charles Burney, *A General History of Music*, ed. Frank Mercer, vol. 2 (New York: Harcourt, Brece and Company, 1935), 446.
2 These concertos are the subject of my monograph. Cf. Piotr Wilk, *The Venetian Instrumental Concerto During Vivaldi's Time*, trans. John Comber (Berlin: Peter Lang, 2020).
3 Although Pietro Locatelli, born in Bergamo, was a citizen of the Republic of Venice, he operated mainly away from his homeland. Only the concertos from Op. 3 are in the Venetian style, written during his several-year stay in Venice in 1723–1727.

group the concertos of the Florentine Francesco Maria Veracini, written during his stay in Venice and published in anthologies with concertos by Tomaso Albinoni, Antonio Vivaldi, Giuseppe Tartini and Alessandro Marcello.[4] As we know, Veracini's violin playing in July 1716 during an *accademia* at the Venetian palace of Alvise and Pisana Mocenigo had a great influence on the young Tartini.[5]

In terms of the number of concertos preserved, Padua was the second centre of concerto production in the Republic of Venice after Venice. The city owes this position, of course, to Tartini, who left about 160 concertos. It was only in 1721 that Tartini settled permanently in Padua and, apart from his three-year stay in Prague, he continued to work there until his death. Since he was rather self-taught and his violin and composition skills were shaped outside Veneto – in Umbria and Marche – it is worth asking oneself whether and to what extent his concertos belong stylistically to the model cultivated in the Venetian Republic.

---

4   Cf. Giuseppe Valentini, et. al., *Concerti a cinque, con violini, oboè, violetta, violoncello e basso continuo*, vol. 1 [2] (Amsterdam: Jeanne Roger [Michel Charles Le Cène], [1717, 1730]), 143; Francesco Maria Veracini, et. al., *VI Concerti a 5 stromenti, 3 violini, alto viola e basso continuo* (Amsterdam: Jeanne Roger [Michel Charles Le Cène], [1719, 1720]), 144; Angelo Maria Scaccia, et. al, *VI Concerti a cinque stromenti a violino principale, violino primo, violino secondo, alto viola, organo e violoncello*, vol. 2 (Amsterdam: Gerhard Fredrik Witvogel, [1736]), 144; George Friedrich Handel, Giuseppe Tartini, and Francesco Maria Veracini, *Select Harmony. Fourth collection. Six concertos in seven parts for violins and other instruments* (London: I. Walsh, [1740]), 145.
5   Cf. Pierluigi Petrobelli, *Giuseppe Tartini. Le fonti biografiche* (Wien: Universal Edition, 1967), 56–57; John Walter Hill, "Veracini in Italy," *Music & Letters* 56, no. 3/4 (1975): 260–261; Sergio Durante, *Tartini, Padova, L'Europa* (Livorno: Sillabe, 2017), 23.

Table 1: Concerto composers active in the Republic of Venice until 1741

Composer	Place of activity	Number of concertos	Dating
1. Giorgio Gentili (1669–1737)	Venice	25	1708–1725
2. Alessandro Marcello (1669–1747)	Venice	12	1712–1740
3. Tomaso Albinoni (1671–1751)	Venice	60	1700–1740
4. Giacomo Facco (1676–1753)	Venice	13	1713–1750
5. Antonio Vivaldi (1678–1741)	Venice	548	1700–1740
6. Benedetto Marcello (1686–1739)	Venice	19	1705–1739
7. Carlo Tessarini (1690–1766)	Venice	53	1716–1749
8. Francesco Maria Veracini (1690–1768)	Venice	5	1712–1736
9. Pietro Locatelli (1695–1764)	Venice	12	1733 (op. 3)
10. Giulio Taglietti (1660–ca 1724)	Brescia	30	1709–1716
11. Luigi Taglietti (1668–ca 1744)	Brescia	5	1708
12. Francisco José de Castro (fl. 1695–1708)	Brescia	8	1708
13. Pietro Gnocchi (1689–1775)	Brescia	12	1740
14. Carlo Antonio Marino (1670–1735)	Bergamo	13	1697–1720
15. Giuseppe Tartini (1692–1770)	Padua	159	1724–1770

The specificity of Tartini's composing work, consisting in the constant reworking of finished pieces and the lack of dating of his manuscripts, is difficult to make rational comparisons. However, by limiting our considerations only to the published concertos, and thus the easiest to date, such a task should be possible. We will limit ourselves here to the works published in the two books of Op. 1 and the concertos from Op. 2:

1. *Sei concerti a cinque e sei stromenti a violino principale, violino primo di ripieno, violino secondo, alto viola, organo e violoncello, opera prima, libro primo*, Amsterdam, Michel-Charles Le Cène, [1727]; the *Concertos*: Op. 1, No. 1 (D 85), No. 2 (D 55), No. 3 (D 60), No. 4 (D 15), No. 5 (D 58), No. 6 (D 89);[6]

---

6 Manuscript sources are kept in: Padua, Basilica del Santo, Biblioteca Antoniana (I-Pca), Berkeley, University of California at Berkeley, Music Library (US-BEm), Dresden, Sächsische Landesbibliothek – Staats- und Universitätsbibliothek (D-Dl), Schwerin, Landesbibliothek Mecklenburg-Vorpommern, Musiksammlung (D-SWl), Berlin, Staatsbibliothek zu Berlin Preussischer Kulutrbesitz (D-Bsb), Cambridge, Fitzwilliam Museum (GB-Cfm).

2. *Sei concerti a cinque stromenti a violino principale, violino primo e secondo, alto viola, organo e violoncello, opera prima, libro secondo*, Amsterdam, Michel-Charles Le Cène, [1729]; the *Concertos*: Op. 1, No. 7 (D 111), No. 8 (D 91), No. 9 (D 59), No. 10 (D 71), No. 11 (D 88), No. 12 (D 18);[7]

3. *VI Concerti a otto stromenti, a violino principale, violino primo, violino secondo, violino primo de ripieno, violino secondo de ripieno, alto viola, organo, e violoncello obligato, opera seconda*, Amsterdam, Gerhard Fredrik Witvogel [1733]; the *Concertos*: Op. 2, No. 1 (D 73), No. 2 (D 2), No. 3 (D 124), No. 4 (D 62), No. 5 (D 3), No. 6 (D 46).[8]

Dutch prints of these 18 works were published between 1727 and 1733.[9] At that time, Tartini opened his famous School of Nations, Vivaldi released in Amsterdam the last concerto collections – Opp. 9–12, and Pietro Locatelli *L'arte del violino* (The art of violin), Op. 3.[10] We have little evidence that some of the concertos from Tartini's Op. 1 and 2 of Tartini were written before their publication.

---

7 Manuscript sources are kept in: Padua, Basilica del Santo, Biblioteca Antoniana (I-Pca), Berkeley, University of California at Berkeley, Music Library (US-BEm), Naples, Biblioteca del Conservatorio di Musica San Pietro a Majella (I-Nc), Ancona, Biblioteca Comunale Luciano Benincasa (I-AN), Bergamo, Biblioteca Civica Angelo Mai (I-BGc), Verona, Archivio di Stato (I-VEas), Berlin, Staatsbibliothek zu Berlin Preussischer Kulutrbesitz (D-Bsb), Vienna, Gesellschaft der Musikfreunde (A-Wgm), Paris, Conservatoire (F-Pc).

8 Manuscript sources are kept in: Padua, Basilica del Santo, Biblioteca Antoniana (I-Pca), Berkeley, University of California at Berkeley, Musi (US-BEm), Paris, Bibliotèque nationale de France (F-Pn), Naples, Biblioteca del Conservatorio di Musica San Pietro a Majella (I-Nc), Udine, Bibioteca Comunale Vincenzo Joppi (I-UDc), Berlin, Staatsbibliothek zu Berlin Preussischer Kulutrbesitz (D-Bsb), Ancona, Biblioteca Comunale Luciano Benincasa (I-AN), Stockholm, Statens Musikbibliothek (S-Skma).

9 Regarding the dating of these collections cf. François Lèsure, *Bibliographie des editions musicales publiées par Estienne Roger et Michel-Charles Le Cène (Amsterdam, 1696–1743)* (Paris: Heugel, 1969); Sofia Teresa Bisi, "Contributo per un'edizione critica dei Sei concerti opera prima libro primo di Giuseppe Tartini," *Ad Parnassum: A Journal of Eighteenth- and Nineteenth-Century Instrumental Music* 11, No. 22, (2013): 65; Vanessa Elisabetta Ruggieri, "Per un'edizione critica dei Sei concerti opera seconda di Giuseppe Tartini: riflessioni sui problemi di edizione e di datazione," *Ad Parnassum: A Journal of Eighteenth- and Nineteenth-Century Instrumental Music* 11, no. 22 (2013): 56.

10 Cf. Antonio Vivaldi, *La Cetra*, Op. 9, vol. 1 [2] (Amsterdam: Michele Carlo Le Cène, [1727]); Antonio Vivaldi, *VI concerti a flauto traverso, violino primo e secondo, alto viola, organo e violoncello*, Op. 10 (Amsterdam: Michele Carlo Le Cène, [1728]); Antonio Vivaldi, *Sei concerti a violino principale, violino primo e secondo, alto viola, organo e violoncello*, Op. 11 (Amsterdam: Michele Carlo Le Cène, [1729]); Antonio Vivaldi, *Sei concerti a violino principale, violino primo e secondo, alto viola, organo e violoncello*, Op. 12 (Amsterdam: Michele Carlo Le Cène, [1729]); Pietro Locatelli, *L'Arte del violino. XII Concerti Cioè, Violino solo, con XXIV Capricci ad Libitum, che si potrà Finire al segno*, Op. 3 (Amsterdam: Michele Carlo Le Cène, [1733]).

Only in the manuscript of the *Concerto*, Op. 1, No. 6 (D 89) from the Sächsische Landesbibliothek – Staats- und Universitätsbibliothek (Mus. 2456-O-1, 4) is a date (1724) clearly visible (Illustration 1).

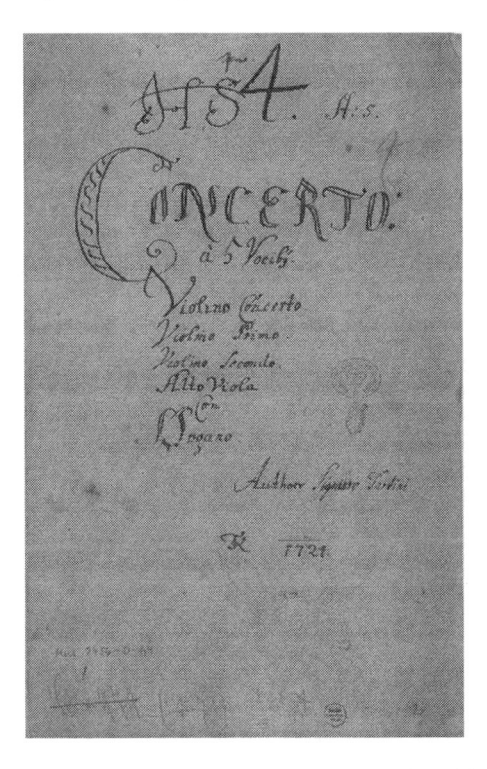

Illustration 1: Title page of Tartini's *Concerto* Op. 1, No. 6 (D 89) from the Sächsische *Landesbibliothek* – Staats- und Universitätsbibliothek in Dresden (Mus. 2456-O-1, 4).

Another Dresden copy of this concerto by Georg Pisendel (Mus. 2456-O-15, Mus. 2456-O-15a) has been dated quite hastily by RISM to the years 1715–1725.[11] It seems controversial to date Concerto Op. 2, No. 2 (D 2) to the year 1714 on the sole basis of the poetic motto *Il dì senza splendor* (The day without splendour) which accompanies its finale and comes from Vivaldi's opera *Orlando finto pazzo* (Orlando, the fake madman), staged in Venice in the same year.[12] If this method

---

11 Cf. RISM ID no.: 212001486.
12 Cf. Ruggieri, "Per un'edizione critica," 58–59; Sofia Teresa Bisi, Booklet to Giuseppe Tartini, *12 Violin Concertos op. 1*, L'arte dell'arco, Giovanni Guglielmo, Dynamic CDS 160/1–3, 1996, CD.

of dating Tartini's works were used, the concerto could have well been written as early as 1707. The motto *Se mai saprai* (If you ever know), from Giovanni Bononcini's opera *Etearco* (Etearcus), staged in the same year, appears with its second movement. The same motto also accompanies the middle movement of the *Concerto* Op. 2, No. 3 (D 124).[13]

1 Scoring

With regard to the scoring of Tartini's concertos, those in Op. 1 and Op. 2 as well as the others, the composer consistently cultivates the typical Venetian concerto *a cinque*, for three violins (violino principale, violino primo and violino secondo), viola, cello and basso continuo. The majority of concertos by Tomaso Albinoni (Opp. 7, 9, 10), the Marcello brothers, Antonio Vivaldi, Giacomo Facco and Carlo Tessarini, as well as concertos by Francesco Maria Veracini and Pietro Locatelli (Op. 3) written during their stay in Venice are also intended for such a scoring.[14] In addition, Tartini, alongside Vivaldi and Tessarini, contributes to the most widely represented repertory of the concerto for solo violin in the Republic of Venice (over 450 works).

Most Venetian concertos of the Vivaldi era have a fast harmonic rhythm with chord changes on every quarter note. Its slowing down can be seen most clearly in Tartini's concertos from Op. 1 and 2 (Example 1), which can be taken as an indication that they were probably conceived as works to be performed by an ensemble with more than one instrument to a part, despite their publication and preservation in manuscripts as single part books. A confirmation of this possibility can be found in the way in which Op. 2 was published with two ripieno violin parts. Before Tartini, however, single or double ripieno parts had already been introduced by Tomaso Albinoni, Giorgio Gentili and Giulio Taglietti.[15] Looking at Tartini's

---

13 Meanwhile, the motto *Bagna le piume in Lete placido sonno* (Wet the feathers in Lethe placid sleep) from Marc'Antonio Ziani's opera *Il duello d'Amore e di Vendetta* (The duel of Love and Revenge), staged at the Teatro di San Salvatore in 1700, appears in the second movement of the D 56 concerto. Tartini was 8 years old at the time. Cf. Piotr Wilk, "Poetical Mottos in Tartini's Concertos – the Latest Concordances and Questions," *Musica Iagellonica*, 9 (2018): 97.
14 Francesco Maria Veracini seems to have encountered the concerto genre only during his first stay in Venice (1711–1713). His earliest concerto is a youthful *Concerto* D 1, performed in person at the Venetian Basilica of Santa Maria Gloriosa dei Frari on 1 February 1712 in honour of the recently crowned Holy Roman Emperor Charles VI and his newly appointed ambassador to Venice. Pietro Locatelli came into contact with the Venetian concerto between 1723 and 1727 when he hosted and gave concerts at the palace of the Venetian patrician Girolamo Michiel Lini. In the preface to *L'arte del violino*, Op. 3, dedicated to Lini, the composer mentions that he performed the concertos there in his presence. Cf. Piotr Wilk, *Venetian Instrumental Concerto*, 13–14, 24, 339, 348.
15 Cf. Tomaso Albinoni, *Sinfonie e Concerti a cinque, due Violini, Alto, Tenore, Violoncello, e Basso*, Op. 2 (Venetia: Giuseppe Sala, 1700); Tomaso Albinoni, *Concerti a cinque, Due,*

concertos preserved in manuscripts, the two ripieno violins are found in only eight works (Table 2). The presence of ripienists in Op. 2 shows the growing European tendency since around 1740 to multiply ripieno parts, as a result of which 36 of Tartini's concertos have been preserved in the form of 9–24 part books (Table 2).[16] The practice of the orchestral performance of Tartini's concertos can also be confirmed by the size of the string orchestra at the Basilica of San Antonio in Padua. Between 1733 and 1773, i.e. after the publication of Opp. 1–2, it consisted of eight violins, four violas, two cellos and two violones or double basses.[17]

Example 1: G. Tartini, *Concerto* Op. 1 No. 2/i (D 55), bars 1–6. In this chapter, I have adopted a short notation referring precisely to specific movements of a work. In this notation, the exact number of a concerto (e.g. Op. 1, No. 1) is followed, after an oblique, by the specific movement of the work, given in small Roman numerals. Op. 1, No. 1/iii means the third movement of the *Concerto* Op. 1, No. 1.

Tre Violini, Alto, Tenore, Violoncello e Basso per il Cembalo, Op. 5 (Venetia: Giuseppe Sala, 1707); Giorgio Gentili, *Concerti a quattro, e cinque*, Op. 5 (Venezia: Appresso Antonio Bortoli, 1708); Giulio Taglietti, *Concerti a cinque, quattro Violini e Viola, Violone, Violoncello, e Basso Continuo*, Op. 8 (Venetia: Giuseppe Sala, 1710); Giulio Taglietti, *Concerti a quattro con suoi rinforzi*, Op. 11 (Bologna: Per li Fratelli Silvani, 1713).

16 Richard Maunder points to 1740 as the conventional date when the practice of performing concertos one-to-a-part was abandoned in Europe in favour of orchestral performance with more than one instrument to a part. Cf. Richard Maunder, *The Scoring of Baroque Concertos* (Woodbridge: The Boydell Press, 2004), 1.

17 Cf. Margherita Canale Degrassi, "Destinazioni e aspetti esecutivi dei concerti per violino di Giuseppe Tartini: contributi per un approfondimento," in *Intorno a Locatelli. Studi in occasione del tricentenario della nascita di Pietro Antonio Locatelli (1695–1764)*, ed. Albert Dunning (Lucca: LIM, 1995), 1:160.

Table 2: Multiple instruments per part in Tartini's concertos except for Op. 2

Number of ripieno parts	Concertos
Two ripieno violins	D 10, 21, 47, 50, 61, 86, 93, 118
More ripienists	D 6, 9, 11, 14, 22, 24, 26, 27, 30, 31, 38, 39, 42, 45, 48, 51, 66, 75, 76, 78–81, 83, 87, 97, 98, 100, 101, 103, 105, 106, 110, 119, 122, 125

2 Form

The three-movement form with ritornello structures in the outer movements was typical of concertos from the Republic of Venice. Its inventors were Albinoni and Vivaldi, and from them the model was taken over by composers of the younger generation: Tessarini, Veracini, Locatelli (in Op. 3) and Tartini. In the latter's oeuvre, the only example of a four-movement *Concerto*, Op. 1, No. 1, should rather be regarded as an interference by the publisher Le Cène with the original text of "Maestro delle Nazioni" (Master of Nations). Instead of the expected slow middle movement, a four-voice fugue in motet style appears here (Example 2). Manuscript versions of this concerto from Dresden, Venice and Naples do not include the fugue.[18] It appears only in the manuscript from the Fitzwilliam Museum, Cambridge, but this is an obvious *descriptus* from Le Cène's edition.[19] The 70-bar *Fuga alla breve* is in all likelihood a foreign element in the entire work, which is further evidenced by the fact that it is the only movement in the concerto without a solo part. Violino principale is consistently duplicated here by Violino I.

Tartini, like Locatelli in Op. 3, likes to introduce the ritornello form also in the concerto's middle movement. His concertos with three ritornello movements constitute one-third of his published works: in Op. 1, these are *Concertos* No. 3 (D 60), No. 7 (D 111), No. 10 (D 71) and No. 11 (D 88), and in Op. 2, No. 1 (D 73), No. 3 (D 124) and No. 5 (D 3). In other cases, as in Vivaldi's works, the middle movement in an example of a binary, arch or through-composed form. The ritornellos of Tartini's concertos are expansive, but not excessively so – usually spanning around 20 bars, with the longest one slightly exceeding 40 bars.[20] In this respect he was far surpassed by Locatelli in the latter's Op. 3. Even in the longest ritornellos, however, Tartini does not employ more than four themes; most often he limits himself to two, and in three works he uses only one theme.[21] In comparison with

---

18 Cf. Dresden, Sächsische Landesbibliothek – Staats- und Universitätsbibliothek, Mus.2456-O-1,6 and Mus.2456-O-1,6a; Venezia, Biblioteca del Conservatorio di Musica Benedetto Marcello, Correr, Busta 55.1; Napoli, Biblioteca del Conservatorio di Musica S. Pietro a Majella, M. S. 9948–9953.
19 Cf. Cambridge, Fitzwilliam Museum, Mus. Ms. 68.
20 E.g. Op. 1, No. 4/i; Op. 1, No. 8/iii.
21 E.g., Op. 1, No. 11/I; Op. 1, No. 12/i and Op. 2 No. 2/i.

the multi-thematic ritornellos of Vivaldi, Tessarini and Locatelli (Op. 3), Tartini's work is striking for its great thematic homogeneity of the ritornellos, and even of entire movements. The opening theme (motto) not only runs through all the ritornellos but is also repeated in all the solo episodes, which usually begin with the development of the motto. This treatment is not without its effects on the sense of compactness and monothematicity of the whole form. Against the background of the overall concerto output of the Venetian Republic, Tartini's monothematic ritornellos are an exception that may be regarded as a manifestation of the emerging classical aesthetic. In the first movement of the concerto Op. 2, No. 1 (D 73), these harbingers of early Classicism are even clearer when, in the opening ritornello (R1), the entrance of the new key coincides with the introduction of the second theme (Formal scheme 1).

Example 2: The beginning of the second movement of Tartini's *Concerto* Op. 1, No. 1 (D 85), bars 1–7.

Formal scheme 1: G. Tartini, *Concerto* Op. 2, No. 1/i (D 73).

Function	R1					S1	R2			S2	R3	S3		R4		S4	R5	
Themes	a	a1	a2 b	a3	c	a4 a5	b1 a6	d		a7 a8	e			a9 b2	f	a10	b2 a3	
Bars	5	4	4 2	2	12	5 4	2 2	17		4 2	15			3 3	14 4		2 2	
Key	I		i	I	→	V	v	V	→	vi			→iii	I				

In the Op. 2 concertos, the homogeneity of the individual movements is even greater than in Op 1. In the middle movements of the *Concertos* Op. 2, No. 1 (D 73) and Op. 2, No. 4 (D 62), despite the distribution of thematic material into, respectively, three and one solo episodes and four and two tutti segments, their almost complete monothematicity (in Op. 2, No. 1/ii, only the second episode introduces new thematic material), brings the form closer to variation rather than ritornello or arch. In general, the R1 material of Tartini's concertos recurs in all the ritornellos. In Op. 1, the composer repeated R1 literally as many as five times at the end of the movement: in Op. 1, No. 1/iii (D 85), Op. 1, No. 3/i (D 60), Op. 1, No. 6/iii (D 89), Op. 1, No. 7/iii (D 111) and Op. 1, No. 11/ii (D 88).

In the outer movements Tartini usually introduces three or four solo episodes, as did Antonio Vivaldi, Giacomo Facco, Pietro Locatelli and Carlo Tessarini. Exceptions include forms with five (Op. 1, No. 7/i D 111) or even six solos (Op. 1, No. 9/i D 59). There are only two solos in the middle ritornello movements of the concerto. Unlike the case in the concertos of most Venetian composers, Tartini blurs the thematic contrast between the ritornello material and the solo episodes, as the latter usually begin with the ritornello motto. The solos rarely operate with completely different thematic material. If the composer follows in the footsteps of Vivaldi here and introduces a thematic contrast between solo and tutti, it is only in forms with monothematic R1 (Op. 1, No. 11/i D 88). It is very characteristic of Tartini's concertos to weaken the correlation between structural divisions and contrasting textures.

The solo interpolations within the ritornello or tutti insertions in the solo episodes significantly blur the clarity of the ritornello form as well as its auditive perception, and they also destroy the logic of the division of roles played by the soloist and the orchestra, typical of Vivaldi's concertos. Both the frequent introduction of solo interventions within the ritornello and the important role given to the soloist in the recapitulation mean that it is the soloist who definitely dominates in Tartini's concertos. Solo sections take up proportionately more space than the tuttis on a scale not seen in other artists from the Republic of Venice. While in Vivaldi's early concertos the solo episodes constitute from a third to a half of the movement's duration, and in the late ones 56 %, in Tartini's published concertos, not including the capriccios, they already occupy 59 %, and in the late ones they reach 70 %.

Tartini's concerto forms exemplify the expansion of size characteristic of the third and fourth decades of the eighteenth century, also evident in concertos by Tessarini, Locatelli and in the late works of Vivaldi. Like them, the composer usually uses cells of 1–4 bars in the construction of a piece. In contrast to them, however, Tartini's phrasing much more often takes the form of periodicity, already foreshadowing the Classical style. It is full of repeats, continuous transformation and it sometimes even features an antecedent-consequent relationship (Example 3). Compared to the output of composers of the Venetian Republic, Tartini's concertos are among the most elaborate, averaging around 400 bars and often exceeding 500 bars (not including the solo capriccios).

Example 3: G. Tartini, *Concerto* Op. 1, No. 12/iii (D 18), bars 1–17.

3 Tonal Plans

The tonal plans of the ritornello movements of Tartini's early concertos are richer than those in his later works. In almost every concerto from Op 1 and 2, Tartini used a pendulum tonal scheme at least once, with a return to tonic within the course of the movement. In his later works, the pendulum model lost its primacy in favour of a circuit one, in which the main key returns in the final phase of the piece (Table 3).[22] In the course of the movement, Tartini, unlike Vivaldi, likes to return to keys previously reached by, even when it is not the main key:

I–V–vi–V–ii–iii–vi–iii–I–V–I (Op. 1, No. 4/i)
I–V–ii–vi–iv–I–vi–I–V–I (Op. 1, No. 8/iii)
I–V–ii–iv–vi–ii–I–III–I (Op. 1, No. 12/iii)
I–V–iii–V–iii–V–vi–I–vi–I (Op. 2, No. 1/iii)
i–III–i–iv–v–VII–iv–vi–v–i (Op. 2, No. 3/iii).

Table 3: Tonal plans in Tartini's *Concertos* from Opp. 1–2

Pendulum scheme	Circuit scheme
I–vi–I–vi–I (Op. 1, No. 6/iii)	i–V–v–III–i (Op. 1, No. 1/i)
I–V–ii–I–vi–iii–I (Op. 1, No. 9/iii)	i–V–III–V–i (Op. 2, No. 1/ii)
i–III–i–V–VII–iv–vi–V–i (Op. 2, No. 3/iii)	I–V–ii–I (Op. 1, No. 5/i, Op. 2, No. 6/iii)
I–V–vi–I–vi–iii–V–I (Op. 2, No. 2/i)	i–III–iv–v–iv–VII–i (Op. 1, No. 7/iii)
I–V–vi–I–iii–I (Op. 2, No. 6/i)	I–V–ii–V–I (Op. 1, No. 11/ii)

Unlike other Venetian composers, Tartini generally emphasizes the return to tonic at the end of a work with a tonal hiatus between the end of a solo episode and the beginning of a ritornello. The recapitulation of the tonic occurs abruptly after a cadence of the III[23] or VI degree.[24] Albinoni acted in a similar way in his concertos, when the recapitulation suddenly entered immediately after a presentation of the motto in a different key. Uniquely among the composers active in the Venetian Republic, Tartini's return to the tonic in the final phase of a concerto movement is shifted more and more towards the middle of the movement, with the result that the main key is often reasserted already in the penultimate ritornello.[25] As Johann Joachim Quantz recommended,[26] Tartini usually organizes all the ritornello

---

22 The concepts of pendulum and circuit plan were introduced into musicological discourse by Michael Talbot. Cf. Michael Talbot, *The Sacred Vocal Music of Antonio Vivaldi* (Firenze: Olschi,1995), 128–129.
23 Cf. Op. 1, No. 7/i; Op. 1, No. 9/iii; Op. 1, No. 12/iii; Op. 2, No. 1/i; Op. 2, No. 2/i; Op. 2, No. 4/i; Op. 2, No. 5/i; Op. 2, No. 6/i.
24 Cf. Op. 1, No. 8/i; Op. 1, No. 11/iii; Op. 2, No. 2/iii.
25 Cf. Op. 1, No. 2/i, iii; Op. 1, No. 3/iii; Op. 1, No. 4/iii; Op. 1, No. 6/i; Op. 1, No. 7/i; Op. 1, No. 8/i, iii; Op. 1, No. 11/i, iii; Op. 2, No. 1/i; Op. 2, Nos. 3–6/i.
26 See Chapter *Das XVIII Hauptstük: Wie ein Musikus und eine Musik zu beurtheilen sey*, in Johann Joachim Quantz, *Versuch einer Anweisung die Flöte traversiere zu spielen* (Berlin: Johann Friedrich Voß, 1752), § 38.

movements of a concerto on different tonal plans, with the exception being the *Concerto* Op. 1, No. 3 (D 60), where both outer movements are built on the same I–V–vi–I plane. Twice in Opp. 1–2, Tartini used the tonal plan I–V–ii–I with the characteristic sequence ii–I.[27] He often repeated this pattern in later concertos, and it became one of his trademarks.[28]

4 Solo Episodes, Cadenzas, Capriccios

The solo episodes in Tartini's violin concertos are among the most extensive. As with Vivaldi and Locatelli, not counting the capriccios, in extreme cases they range in length from 40 to 90 bars (e.g. the finale of Op. 1, No. 11 D 88). In their concertos these three violinists also attained the heights of violin technique, to be surpassed only by Paganini. The solo part of Tartini's concertos usually moves within the limits of the 7th position (up to a‴), rarely exceeding this limit, e.g. the 9th position (c⁗) in the finale's cadenza of the *Concerto* Op. 2, No. 6, while Vivaldi and Locatelli occasionally require the 14th (RV 212) and 17th (Op. 3, No. 11) positions. Tartini, like Veracini and Locatelli, makes extensive use of chordal playing, arpeggio and bariolage. In Op. 1, the solo part is saturated with virtuoso-shaped figurations which are etude-like in expression, but at the same time rather artificial sounding and drawn out. In Op. 2, the composer already presents virtuosity of a much better quality. In the melody of the soloist, there is less artificiality and more care for the deepening of expression. Tartini reduces harmonic figurations and multi-stops in favour of passages and melodies with an attractive line.

In the 10 concertos from Op. 1 and Op. 2 (List 1), the penultimate solo episode in its entirety or in its second phase takes the form of an improvised or notated cadenza or capriccio. The composer thus joins the likes of Vivaldi, Veracini, Tessarini and Locatelli. Since the composer very inconsistently uses the terms *cadenza, capriccio, ad libitum* both after a cadence to the tonic and a suspended cadence to the dominant, it is difficult today to say unequivocally when he intended to perform a short cadenza and when an extended, fanciful capriccio.[29] Such variously marked sections span from 4 to over 50 bars. A characteristic feature of Tartini's capriccios, distinguishing him from other Venetian composers, is their thematic link with the ritornello. At the end of some of them, the composer still implied the *ad libitum* performance of a short, improvised cadenza (Example 4).[30]

---

27 In Op. 1, No. 5/i and Op. 2, No. 6/iii.
28 Cf. Jehoash Hirshberg and Simon McVeigh, *The Italian Solo Concerto, 1700–1760. Rhetorical Strategies and Style History* (Woodbridge: The Boydell Press, 2004), 292–293.
29 The differences between cadenza and capriccio are explained by Philip Whitmore, cf. Philip Whitmore, "Towards an Understanding of the Capriccio," *Journal of the Royal Musical Association* 113, No. 1 (1988): 47–56.
30 Cf. Op. 1, No. 2/iii and Op. 2, No. 6/iii.

List 1: Cadenzas or capriccios (written or suggested) in Tartini's Op. 1 and Op. 2 concertos.

1. *Concerto* op. 1, no 1/i (D 85)
2. *Concerto* op. 1, no 2/i, iii (D 55)
3. *Concerto* op. 1, no 3/iii (D 60)
4. *Concerto* op. 1, no 4/i, iii (D 15)
5. *Concerto* op. 1, no 8/iii (D 91)
6. *Concerto* op. 1, no 10/iii (D 71)
7. *Concerto* op. 1, no 11/iii (D 88)
8. *Concerto* op. 1, no 12/iii (D 18)
9. *Concerto* op. 2, no 1/iii (D 73)
10. *Concerto* op. 2, no 6/iii (D 46)

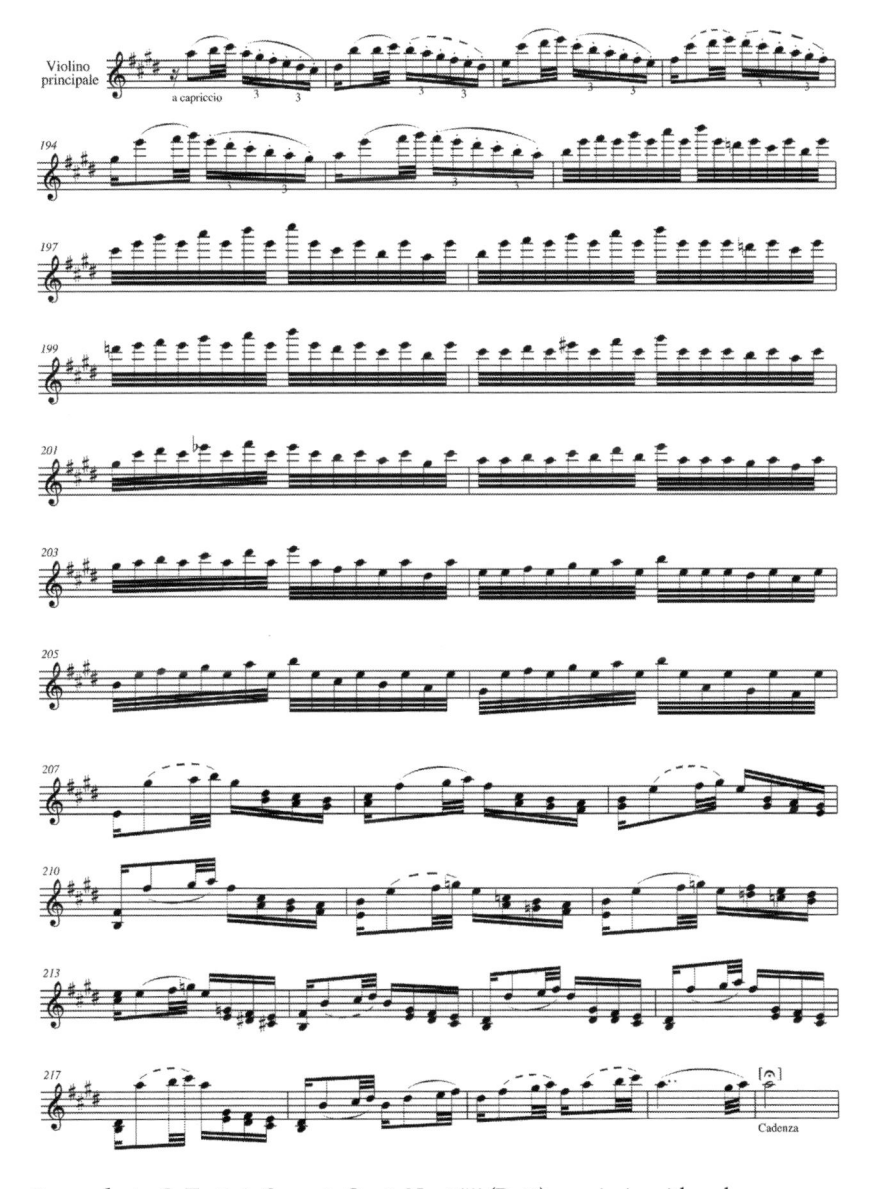

Example 4: G. Tartini, *Concerto* Op. 2, No. 6/iii (D 46), capriccio with cadenza.

5 Style

Tartini's published concertos belong to his early period, although it must be remembered that at the time of their publication the author had already reached his 35th year, and was therefore no youngster. In these concertos, there is already a clear melodic line of the *galant* style, full of ornaments, triplets, dotted and syncopated rhythms, and sudden contrasts of the modes (major versus minor). In terms of melodics, however, these concertos show a lot of shortcomings. They feature not very subtle and rather angular lines, where the composer wants at all costs to show off his great mastery of violin technique at the expense of the cantilena that was so characteristic of the Italian style (Example 5). Those qualities, sometimes found in genuine works of youth, are striking in a mature artist. Against the background of Venetian concerto works, Tartini's melodic style is admittedly original in its quasi-folk rapaciousness. However, Quantz judged him very harshly,[31] and Tartini himself seemed to have seen his very own limitations, working out just the right method of composing melodies by drawing inspiration from the texts of arias by such masters of the cantilena as Alessandro Scarlatti, Giovanni Bononcini, Benedetto Marcello and Antonio Vivaldi (Table 4).

Example 5: G. Tartini, *Concerto* Op. 2, No. 1/i (D 73), bars 95–101.

---

31 Cf. Quantz, *Versuch*, § 59.

Table 4: Poetical mottos in the concertos from Op. 1 and Op. 2 by Tartini

Concerto/ movement	Motto	Provenance (opera titles unless otherwise stated)
Op. 1, No. 9/ii (D 59)	*O pecorelle mie fuggite il rio perché col pianto mio s'avelenò* (O my sheep, flee the stream because with my tears it will be poisoned)	?
	Pecorelle che pascete, non bevete a questo rio perché col pianto mio s'intorbidò (Sheep that you feed, do not drink in this stream because with my tears it became silted)	Cantata A 248 by B. Marcello /?
Op. 2, No. 1/ii (D 73)	*Se regna in sù quest'alma il tuo sembiante vieni a regnar ancor sovra il mio trono* (If this soul reigns above your likeness, come and reign over my throne again)	*Costanza e fortezza*, I, 5 (1723) J. J. Fux / P. Pariati
Op. 2, No. 2/i (D 2)	*Torna ritorna o mia dolce speranza o dolce mio conforto sebben tu mi voi morto io t'amo ancora* (Come back, my sweet hope or my sweet comfort, although you wish me dead I still love you)	?
Op. 2, No. 2/ii (D 2)	*Se mai saprai [che il ciel crudele]* (If you ever know that heaven is cruel)	*Etearco*, II, 6 (1707) G. Bononcini / S. Stampiglia
Op. 2, No. 2/iii (D 2)	*Il dì senza splendor la notte senza orror prima vedrai* (You will see first the day without splendor and the night without horror)	*Orlando finto pazzo*, III, 3 (1714) A. Vivaldi / G. Braccioli
Op. 2, No. 3/ii (D 124)	*Se mai saprai che il ciel crudele* (If you ever know that heaven is cruel)	*Etearco*, II, 6 (1707) G. Bononcini / S. Stampiglia
Op. 2, No. 6/ii (D 46)	*Al mare al bosco al rio io cerco l'idol mio e non lo trovo* (At the sea, at the woods, at the river, I look for my idol and I can't find it)	Cantata by A. Scarlatti (ante 1714) /?

Taking into account Tartini's critical opinion on Vivaldi's way of mixing instrumental and vocal idioms,[32] paradoxically, among the most singing fragments of his Op. 1 and 2 are those in which he tries to imitate the Red Priest. The siciliana-like *Adagio* from the *Concerto* Op. 2, No. 6 (D 46) or the *Largo cantabile* from the *Concerto*

---

32 This was reported in Charles De Brosses, *Lettres historiques et critiques sur l'Italie* (Paris: Ponthieu, 1799), 243.

Op. 1, No. 1 (D 85) can even be seen as a paraphrase of the slow movements of Vivaldi's *Concertos Il gardellino* (The Goldfinch) RV 90 and *La pastorella* (The shepherdess) RV 95 (Example 6). There are more examples of clear imitation of Vivaldi's melodies in Tartini's concertos, not only in the cantilena.[33]

Example 6: Melodic similarities between Tartini's and Vivaldi's concertos.
a) G. Tartini, *Concerto* Op. 1, No. 1/iii (D 85), bars 1–9.
b) A. Vivaldi, *Concerto* "Il gardellino" RV 90/ii, bars 1–6.

---

33 There is a striking coincidence, for example, between the ritornello opening the finale of Vivaldi's *Concerto* RV 208, *Grosso Mogul* (Great Mogul) and its counterpart in the first movement of Tartini's *Concerto* Op 1, No 4 (D 15).

Whereas in concertos by Antonio Vivaldi, Giacomo Facco, Francesco Antonio Veracini, Carlo Tessarini and Pietro Locatelli (Op. 3), the middle movement takes on the character of a song or an aria, Tartini in Opp. 1 and 2 seems to be just experimenting and searching for his own way. Some of his most original arrangements are more reminiscent of a romantic *preghiera* than a Baroque aria (Example 7). In his later concertos, Tartini would develop this idea, as Charles Burney also seems to have noticed, stating that after 1744 the composer changed his style to a "more pleasing" and "more expressive".[34]

Example 7: G. Tartini, *Concerto* Op. 1, No. 6/ii, bars 1–4.

In Tartini's concertos, the so-called continuo homophony reigns supreme with the absolute melodic primacy of the soloist. The composer usually operates with four voices; ritornello themes are emphasized by the unison of only two violins,

---

34 Burney, *A General History of Music*, 446.

and in the solo episodes, the violinist may appear without any accompaniment, as in Veracini's concertos, or against a discreet accompaniment of one to four instruments. Given the liturgical purpose of many of Tartini's concertos,[35] one is surprised by his clear aversion to polyphony. Due to the absolute dominance of homophonic texture in those works, they can only be compared to Tessarini's concertos, as even in Vivaldi's violin concertos we find more fuging than in Tartini's. Tartini did not combine fugal technique with the ritornello form as did Vivaldi, Albinoni, Gentili and Facco. Apart from the aforementioned fugue from Op. 1, No. 1 (D 85), short fragments shaped by counterpoint are very rare in Tartini's published concertos: these are the fugal ritornello of the finale of the Op. 1, No. 4 *Concerto* (D 15), the imitative motto in the outer movements of the Op. 2, No. 2 *Concerto* (D 2), and the imitative beginning of the middle movement of the Op. 1, No. 12 *Concerto* (D 18). Instead of a linear counterpoint within a simple, few-voiced homophonic texture, Tartini exposes dance structures more often than his Venetian colleagues. In their rhythmic and harmonic simplicity, they seem to be taken directly from folk music (Example 8).

Example 8: G. Tartini, *Concerto* Op. 1, No. 7/iii, bars 183–189.

6 Conclusion

Judging by the example of *Concertos* Op. 1 and Op. 2, Tartini undoubtedly appears as a representative of the Baroque Venetian concerto, and one of the most eminent continuators of Vivaldi's model of the violin concerto. The influences of the Red Priest are manifold, and they manifest themselves most strongly in the work's form,

---

35 Cf. Pierpaolo Polzonetti, "Tartini and the Tongue of Saint Anthony," *Journal of the American Musicological Society* 67, no. 2 (2014): 464–465.

texture, its tonal organization and the soloist's relationship with the ensemble. In Tartini's approach, however, the ritornello form departs from Vivaldi's original, as the composer significantly redefined the role of its constituent parts, following different aesthetic premises. Restricting ourselves to the published works alone, we should state that his ritornello forms are the least Baroque. Tartini uses contrasts much less frequently than his Venetian colleagues. He limits the number of themes in ritornellos and relies more on reworking one or two ideas than on sequencing many contrasting sections. He also reduces the number of keys visited, aiming for the polarized, dominant-tonic tonal plans characteristic of early Classical concertos. As a result, his forms are quite uniform, clear and moderate in their expression. Tartini also works much more schematically and is more predictable than Vivaldi or other Venetian composers of the early eighteenth century.

The violin technique and the tendency to chordal playing as well as to frequent introduction of tutti insertions in solo episodes and to polarized tonal plans of movements, are common to concertos by Tartini and Veracini. In terms of the ornamentation used, the emphasis on violin virtuosity and the introduction of capriccios, Tartini's concertos resemble Locatelli's Op. 3. In spite of their evident links to the Venetian tradition, Tartini's concertos are distinguished by an original melodic style, which seems to have been widely inspired by folk music, as well as by the seeds of techniques which gradually led to the transformation of the Baroque model of the genre into the Classical violin concerto. The composer operates with a new melodic language based on short motifs developed into symmetrical two- and four-bar phrases; he makes extensive use not only of simple repetition of phrases and motifs but also of their constant transformation. The movements of his concertos are homogeneous and unified in expression, in which, by virtue of the reduction of the number of themes, the theatrically dramatic expression typical of Baroque concertos is softened.

Bibliography

Albinoni, Tomaso. *Concerti a cinque, Due, Tre Violini, Alto, Tenore, Violoncello e Basso per il Cembalo*, Op. 5. Venezia: Giuseppe Sala, 1707.

Albinoni, Tomaso. *Sinfonie e Concerti a cinque, due Violini, Alto, Tenore, Violoncello, e Basso*, Op. 2. Venezia: Giuseppe Sala, 1700.

Bisi, Sofia Teresa. Booklet, *Giuseppe Tartini, 12 Violin Concertos op. 1*, L'arte dell'arco, Giovanni Guglielmo. Dynamic CDS 160/1–3, 1996.

Bisi, Sofia Teresa. "Contributo per un'edizione critica dei Sei concerti opera prima libro primo di Giuseppe Tartini." *Ad Parnassum: A Journal of Eighteenth- and Nineteenth-Century Instrumental Music* 11, no. 22 (2013): 65–71.

Burney, Charles. *A General History of Music*. Edited by Frank Mercer. New York: Harcourt, Brece and Company, 1935.

Canale Degrassi, Margherita. "Destinazioni e aspetti esecutivi dei concerti per violino di Giuseppe Tartini: contributi per un approfondimento." In

Intorno a Locatelli. Studi in occasione del tricentenario della nascita di Pietro Antonio Locatelli (1695–1764), edited by Albert Dunning, vol. 1, 151–173. Lucca: LIM, 1995.

De Brosses, Charles. *Lettres historiques et critiques sur l'Italie*. Paris: Ponthieu, 1799.

Durante, Sergio. *Tartini, Padova, L'Europa*. Livorno: Sillabe, 2017.

Gentili, Giorgio. *Concerti a quattro, e cinque*, Op. 5. Venezia: Antonio Bortoli, 1708.

Handel, George Friderich, Giuseppe Tartini, and Francesco Maria Veracini. *Select Harmony. Fourth collection. Six concertos in seven parts for violins and other instruments*. London: John Walsh, [1740].

Hill, John Walter. "Veracini in Italy." *Music & Letters* 56, no. 3/4 (1975): 257–276.

Hirshberg, Jehoash, and Timothy McVeigh. *The Italian Solo Concerto, 1700–1760. Rhetorical Strategies and Style History*. Woodbridge: The Boydell Press, 2004.

Lèsure, François. *Bibliographie des editions musicales publiées par Estienne Roger et Michel-Charles Le Cène (Amsterdam, 1696–1743)*. Paris: Heugel, 1969.

Locatelli, Pietro. *L'Arte del violino. XII Concerti Cioè, Violino solo, con XXIV Capricci ad Libitum, che si potrà Finire al segno*, Op. 3. Amsterdam: Michele Carlo Le Cène, [1733].

Maunder, Richard. *The Scoring of Baroque Concertos*. Woodbridge: The Boydell Press, 2004.

Petrobelli, Pierluigi. *Giuseppe Tartini. Le fonti biografiche*. Wien: Universal Edition, 1967.

Polzonetti, Pierpaolo. "Tartini and the Tongue of Saint Anthony." *Journal of the American Musicological Society* 67, no. 2 (2014): 429–486.

Quantz, Johann Joachim. *Versuch einer Anweisung die Flöte traversiere zu spielen*. Berlin: Johann Friedrich Voß, 1752.

Ruggieri, Vanessa Elisabetta. "Per un'edizione critica dei Sei concerti opera seconda di Giuseppe Tartini: riflessioni sui problemi di edizione e di datazione." *Ad Parnassum: A Journal of Eighteenth- and Nineteenth-Century Instrumental Music* 11, no. 22 (2013): 51–63.

Scaccia, Angelo Maria, et al. *VI Concerti a cinque stromenti a violino principale, violino primo, violino secondo, alto viola, organo e violoncello*. Amsterdam: Gerhard Fredrik Witvogel, [1736].

Taglietti, Giulio. *Concerti a cinque, quattro Violini e Viola, Violone, Violoncello, e Basso Continuo*, Op. 8. Venezia: Giuseppe Sala, 1710.

Taglietti, Giulio. *Concerti a quattro con suoi rinforzi*, Op. 11. Bologna: Fratelli Silvani, 1713.

Talbot, Michael. *The Sacred Vocal Music of Antonio Vivaldi*. Firenze: Olschi, 1995.

Valentini, Giuseppe, et al. *Concerti a cinque, con violini, oboè, violetta, violoncello e basso continuo.* Amsterdam: Jeanne Roger, [1717].

Veracini, Francesco Maria, et al. *VI Concerti a 5 stromenti, 3 violini, alto viola e basso continuo.* Amsterdam: Jeanne Roger, [1719].

Vivaldi, Antonio *La Cetra*, Op. 9. Amsterdam: Michele Carlo Le Cène, [1727].

Vivaldi, Antonio. *VI concerti a flauto traverso, violino primo e secondo, alto viola, organo e violoncello*, Op. 10. Amsterdam: Michele Carlo Le Cène, [1728].

Vivaldi, Antonio. *Sei concerti a violino principale, violino primo e secondo, alto viola, organo e violoncello*, Op. 11. Amsterdam: Michele Carlo Le Cène, [1729].

Vivaldi, Antonio. *Sei concerti a violino principale, violino primo e secondo, alto viola, organo e violoncello*, Op. 12. Amsterdam: Michele Carlo Le Cène, [1729].

Whitmore, Philip. "Towards an Understanding of the Capriccio." *Journal of the Royal Musical Association* 113, no. 1 (1988): 48–56.

Wilk, Piotr. "Poetical Mottos in Tartini's Concertos – the Latest Concordances and Questions." *Musica Iagellonica* 9 (2018): 81–99.

Wilk, Piotr. *The Venetian Instrumental Concerto During Vivaldi's Time.* Translated by John Comber. Berlin: Peter Lang, 2020.

Chiara Casarin

University of Padua

A Contribution to the Devotional Music of the Eighteenth Century: Giuseppe Tartini's Spiritual *laude*

Abstract: The chapter explores a small part of Giuseppe Tartini's vocal repertoire: the 18 spiritual *laude* for one, two and three voices. These compositions represent a *unicum* within Tartini's sacred output: not only do they constitute the only group of devotional compositions in the Italian language but are also transmitted by the only surviving autograph of the composer's religious music. The research on these miniature compositions highlights their relevance. First of all, Tartini contributes to the ancient genre of *lauda* destined for personal devotion and often the work of anonymous musicians. The dual nature of the autograph materials – fair copy and composing score – also allows us an insight into Tartini's *modus componendi*: on one hand, an affinity emerges between the *laude* and the slow movements of the violin sonatas and, on the other, possible self-borrowings and connections with Istro-Venetian folk traditions emerge. This repertoire thus reveals another facet of Tartini's artistic identity.

Keywords: Giuseppe Tartini, vocal music, *lauda*, creative process, musical analysis

The fame of Giuseppe Tartini, one of the most eclectic personalities in the eighteenth-century European music scene, is linked, on the one hand, to his extensive instrumental output and, on the other, to the intense didactic mission that earned him the epithet *Maestro delle Nazioni* (Master of the Nations). Tartini's compositional activity mainly revolves around a single instrument, the violin, and a limited number of music genres. In this context, the contribution of the Piranese to the sacred and devotional music of the eighteenth century is analysed with interest. This chapter aims to promote knowledge of a small part of this vocal repertoire, namely the 18 spiritual *laude* for one, two, and three voices also called *Canzoncine sacre* (Sacred Songs) as per Tebaldini's definition.[1]

---

1 "Quite diverse significance [compared to *Miserere* and *Salve Regina*] reveal the *Canzoncine sacre*, created according to Benedetto Marcello's style" ("Ben diverse per importanza [rispetto al *Miserere* e alla *Salve Regina*] ne appaiono invece le *Canzoncine sacre* concepite con idealità marcelliana"). See Giovanni Tebaldini, *L'Archivio musicale della Cappella antoniana in Padova. Illustrazione storico-critica con cinque eliotipie* (Padova: Tipografia e Libreria Antoniana, 1895), 79. I believe I should clarify why I have used the name *spiritual laude*. Though Tartini didn't give a name to these

This *corpus* of compositions represents a *unicum* within the sacred music of the "primo violino e capo di concerto":[2] not only does it account for the only set of devotional works in Italian but it also comes from the only existing autograph ever received concerning the composer's religious music. Although these *laude*, which were consigned to oblivion until the end of the nineteenth century,[3] were considered, knowingly or not, as a minor production, their analysis points out their relevance in many respects. First of all, Tartini

compositions, Pietro Revoltella, who rediscovered Tartini's *laude* in the 1990s, gave them this name: this definition was then also used by David Di Paoli Paulovich (see note 4). In the eighteenth-nineteenth century devotional sources that I have consulted, the terms *lauda, canzone, canzoncina, canzonetta, cantico, aria musicale* coexist (with the predominance of the first term) and are employed without any apparent stylistic-formal difference. Owing to such considerations I decided to keep the name given by Revoltella. Below you will find a numbered list of the text *incipit* of the eighteen *laude* followed by the catalogue code adopted in Guido Viverit, Alba Luksich, Simone Olivari, eds., *Catalogo tematico online delle composizioni di Giuseppe Tartini* (tARTini-Turismo culturale all'insegna di Giuseppe Tartini, 2019–2020), http://catalog.discovertartini.eu/dcm/gt/navigation.xq: I. *Vedi Signor ch'io piango* (Canst thou see I'm crying, my Lord) (g1); II. *Iddio ti salvi Vergine bella* (May God save you fair Vergin) (G1); III. *Vergine bella del ciel regina* (Fair Vergin, queen of Heaven) (Bb1); IV. *Dio ti salvi* (May God save you) (G2); V. *Caro Signor amato* (My beloved God) (g2); VI. *Mio Gesù con tutto il core* (My God, with all my heart) (g3); VII. *Dolce mio Dio* (My sweet God) (a1); VIII. *Crocefisso mio Signor* (My crucified Lord) (a2); IX. *Amare lagrime* (Bitter tears) (g4); X. *No che terreno fallace* (No earthly fallacious love) (G3); XI. *Voglio amar Gesù* (I want to love Jesus) (G4); XII. *Chi cerca l'innocenza* (The one who looks for innocence) (G5); XIII. *O peccator che sai* (Oh sinner, thou who knowest) (g5); XIV. *E m'ami ancora* (You still love me) (D1); XV. *Infrangiti mio core* (Break, my heart) (d1); XVI. *Rimira o peccator* (Look, oh sinner) (a3); XVII. *Vergine bella e pietosa* (Fair and merciful Vergin) (F1); XVIII. *Alma pentita* (Regretful soul) (G6).

2 Tartini produced a limited number of vocal compositions. Besides the eighteen spiritual *laude* we can count twelve more works. For a list of Tartini's sacred vocal compositions, see the entry "vocal music" in Viverit et al., *Catalogo tematico online*. This production is considered of minor importance in the context of Tartini's work and consequently little studied by scholars. See contributions by Leonardo Frasson, *Giuseppe Tartini. L'uomo e l'artista* (Padova: Basilica del Santo, 1974), 9–10; Pietro Revoltella, "Giuseppe Tartini. La musica sacra," in *Tartini 1692–1992. Manifestazioni per il terzo centenario della nascita (13–29 ottobre 1992)* (Padova: Comune di Padova. Assessorato allo Spettacolo, 1992), 26–28; Pietro Revoltella, "Lo 'Stabat Mater' di Giuseppe Tartini," in *Tartini. Il tempo e le opere*, ed. Andrea Bombi and Maria Nevilla Massaro (Bologna: Il Mulino, 1994), 81–96.

3 The first to deal with them, in music literature, was Tebaldini, *L'Archivio musicale*, 79. In the 1990s Tartini's *laude* were slowly rediscovered, thanks to the contributions by Pietro Revoltella, "Le laude spirituali di Giuseppe Tartini," *Il Santo* 32, nos. 2–3 (1992): 265–289; David Di Paoli Paulovich, "Tartini e il suo impegno vocale-sacro: inediti e sopravvivenze nella tradizione istriana," *La Ricerca* 21, no. 60 (2011): 14–16; David Di Paoli Paulovich, "Giuseppe Tartini e le laudi spirituali nella

personally contributes to the ancient genre of *lauda*, destined to personal devotion and traditionally the work of anonymous musicians, and/or *contrafacta*.[4] Besides, compared to the eighteenth and nineteenth centuries, the current knowledge on the newly composed *laude* is very limited, so the interest of one of the main musicians of the time in this centuries-old tradition is quite relevant.

1 Remarks on the Paduan Autograph

The 18 *laude* are preserved in the music archive of the Cappella Antoniana in Padua.[5] The autograph source, sized 310 × 235 mm, consists of 12 sheets of paper in upright format grouped into three *bifolios*. Each sheet was probably numbered, using a blue pencil, in more recent times, but the numbering is not consistent with the structure of the manuscript material[6] which shows a dual nature. Sheets 5, 6, 7, and 8 look like a fair copy, characterized by extreme calligraphic care in the drafting of the poetical-musical texts, fluid and regular handwriting, precise text references and tempo marks for each composition. These elements suggest they are the final versions – or at least the latest draft – of the 18 *laude* (Figure 1).

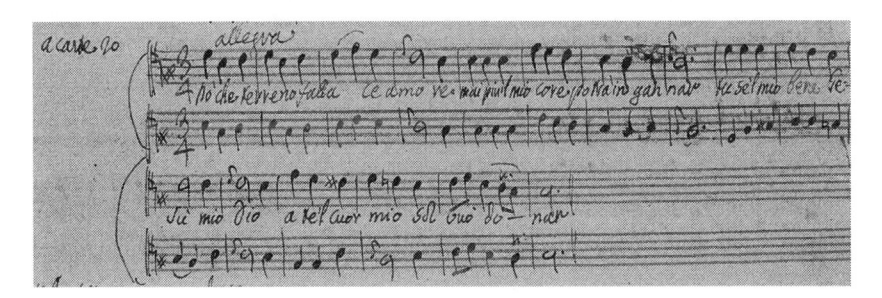

Figure 1: X. *No che terreno fallace* (G3), fair copy. (Tartini, "Canzoncine Sacre," f. 6.)

---

tradizione istriana," *Atti e memorie della Società istriana di archeologia e storia patria* 114 (2014): 215–229; Chiara Casarin, "Per un'edizione delle laude polifoniche di Giuseppe Tartini," (Bachelor's thesis, University of Padua, 2016–2017); Chiara Casarin, "Alla riscoperta della musica sacra di Giuseppe Tartini: le diciotto laudi spirituali," *Il Santo* 61, no. 3 (2021): 455–473.

4 The most common way of setting the *laude* to music was the *contrafactum*, an intertextual practice according to which the original literary text of a vocal composition is changed or replaced with another one without any relevant change to the music. *Contrafacta* were popular in the thirteenth century, when the *lauda* appeared, and continued to be produced until the end of the eighteenth century.

5 Giuseppe Tartini, "Canzoncine Sacre," autograph score, 1760–1770, I-Pca, D.VI.1894/08. Music archive of the Cappella Antoniana, Pontificia Biblioteca Antoniana, Padua, Italy.

6 All the articles concerning the *laude*, which have been written until now, have maintained this numbering. To avoid future misunderstanding, I have decided to use it in this chapter as well.

The other sheets, instead, show many erasures, rewrites, revision marks, and handwritten annotations such as "meglio" ("better"), "questa" ("this"), and "va bene" ("all right") which indicate the temporary preference of the composer for a given draft: these materials make up the "composing score" (Figure 2). These leaves contain previous versions such as sketches, drafts, and fragments. They are particularly interesting since it is possible to retrace the composer's different musical choices, thanks to the identification and interpretation of the rejected texts and the comparison with the latest versions.

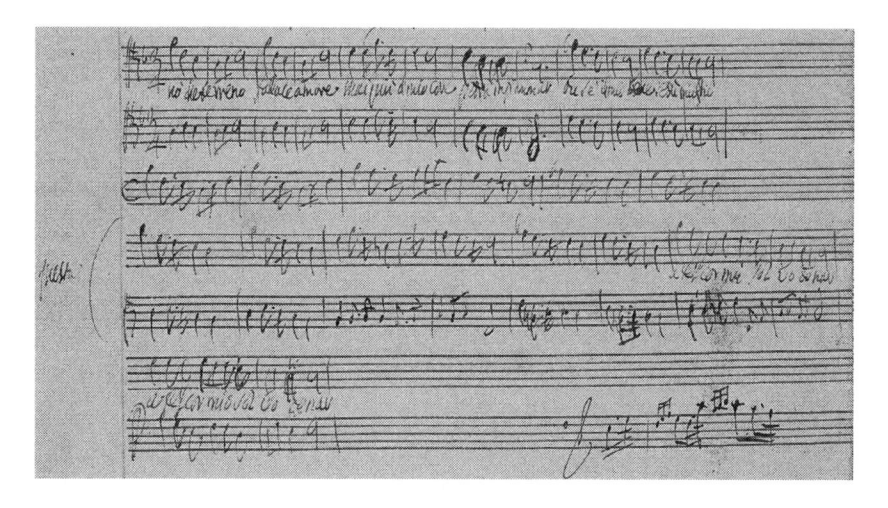

Figure 2: X. *No che terreno fallace* (G3), fragments and sketches. (Tartini, "Canzoncine Sacre," f. D2. For the use of the term "composing score", see Pierluigi Petrobelli, *Tartini, le sue idee e il suo tempo* (Lucca: LIM, 1992), 119.)

As far as the dating of the manuscript is concerned, the analysis of the watermarks[7] does not allow us to place in time the compositions with absolute

---

7 The bifolio, consisting of sheets 1, 2 and 11, 12 shows the three moons in the centre (selenometry mm. 73/14). The bifolio made of sheets 3, 4 and 9, 10 presents a watermark showing a cross and sagittarius while folios 5, 6 and 7, 8 have an unclear watermark. With regard to watermarks in Tartini's autograph, see Sofia Bisi et al., "Le filigrane in autografi di Tartini e Vallotti conservati nell'Archivio musicale dell'Arca di S. Antonio di Padova. Contributo per una cronologia dell'opera di Giuseppe Tartini," *Il Santo* 32, nos. 2–3 (1992): 307–333; Jolanda Dalla Vecchia, "Rilievi e prime ipotesi a margine degli studi sulle filigrane in autografi di Tartini e Vallotti," *Il Santo* 32, nos. 2–3 (1992): 335–343; Contributi dei Seminari di studio di Padova e Roma "Le filigrane degli autografi tartiniani: questioni di cronologia," in *Tartini. Il tempo e le opere*, ed. Andrea Bombi and Maria Nevilla Massaro (Bologna: Il Mulino,

certainty. However, the firmness and steadiness in writing suggest at least that these *laude* were not written at a very old age, the period to which Tartini's sacred compositions are supposed to date.[8]

2 For an Analysis of Poetical Texts and Their Narrative Content

The 18 poetical texts, of which Tartini only sets the first stanza to music,[9] should have been contained in a single source, maybe a printed collection or, more likely, a lost manuscript. The composer refers to it in the Paduan autograph using notes like "a carte..." ("turn to folio..."), "la emendata a carte..." ("amended on folio..."), and "questa è nel libretto" ("this is in the booklet"). The loss of the literary source used by Tartini entails both philological problems and performance practice difficulties. First of all, it is not possible to establish whether the texts set to music are the result of a choice of the composer or a possible commissioner or whether they are part of some anthology. Moreover, as seen after the analysis of concordant copies of eighteen-nineteen century prints, the content and structure of devotional collections depended on the function and purpose they were created for. The "libretto" would have been a useful tool to investigate these aspects about which it is only possible to make assumptions.

The analyses carried out thus far have led to the identification of 9[10] out of 18 poems contained in printed collections published between 1672 and 1878:[11] it was

---

1994), 377–387; Guido Viverit, "Catalogo ragionato dei libri-parte tartiniani presso l'Archivio musicale della Veneranda Arca del Santo," (Master's thesis, University of Padua, 2007–2008).

8   On the basis of stylistic considerations, Dounias claims that Tartini's devotional compositions were created towards the end of his life since the "last, abstract compositions of the almost 80-year-old composer are more than just an exterior expression of his religious feeling. Rather, they are the last, inexorable consequences of his ideas. His search for simplification of the means and dematerialization of the sound reaches here its outermost limits of possibility" ("[queste] ultime, astratte composizioni del quasi ottantenne sono più di una esteriore espressione del suo sentimento religioso. Sono piuttosto le ultime, inesorabili conseguenze delle sue concezioni. Il suo tendere verso la semplificazione dei mezzi, verso la smaterializzazione del suono raggiunge qui gli estremi limiti del possibile"). See Revoltella, "Giuseppe Tartini. La musica sacra," 26. If not otherwise stated in a footnote, English translations have been made by the author.

9   It was common practice: the following stanzas were sung on the same melody.

10 The following texts were found: II. *Iddio ti salvi Vergine bella* (G1); III. *Vergine bella del ciel regina* (Bb1); IV. *Dio ti salvi* (G2); VI. *Mio Gesù con tutto il core* (g3); VII. *Dolce mio Dio* (a1); VIII. *Crocefisso mio Signor* (a2); IX. *Amare lagrime* (g4); XVI. *Rimira o peccator* (a3); XVIII. *Alma pentita* (G6).

11 An incomplete list of literary sources concordant with Tartini's autograph is in Casarin, "Per un'edizione delle laude," 31–39. The list was then expanded by the writer.

therefore a repertoire with a wide circulation. For example, the text *Dio ti salvi*, also called "La Salve Regina volgarizzata" ("The vulgarized Salve Regina"), was found in 24 different anthologies besides the Paduan autograph. This is not surprising since, in the eighteenth century, pious practices, pilgrimages, devotions, the teaching of the Christian Doctrine and personal efforts at asceticism become more important and widespread and so paraliturgical singing becomes the privileged means for the understanding and spread of the Christian message. The Ecclesiastical Institution plays the important social role of the people's tutor and, aware of the evocative intensity of devotional chant, it promotes and regulates its use, associating it to solemn liturgical practices.[12]

Despite the widespread diffusion of this textual repertoire, the information on its performance modality is very limited. While, on the one hand, the references to "tono" ("tone") and "melodie" ("melodies") suggest a sung performance – perhaps even accompanied by musical instruments[13] – on the other hand, the almost total absence[14] of musical texts in the eighteenth-nineteenth-century anthologies

---

The volume about Tartini's sacred and devotional music, in "Edizione nazionale delle opere musicali di Giuseppe Tartini (ENGT)", will provide an updated list.

12 "Man too often forgets the great truth that he can only be happy when he aspires to heaven. He must often be reminded, in his thoughts and heart, of eternal things: this is what the Church, with preaching and external worship, does. Besides inspired psalms and sublime hymns, that it sings to this purpose during its sad or happy rites, holy men taught it was very useful to add the simplicity of the Christian lauds, in the language the people can understand" ("L'uomo troppo spesso dimentico della gran verità che solo può esser beato in terra, quando aspira al cielo, ha d'uopo d'esser chiamato sovente col pensiere e col cuore alle cose eterne: il che fa la Chiesa colla predicazione e col culto esteriore. Ai salmi inspirati, agl'inni sublimi che a tal fine ella fra' suoi riti or mesti or giulivi intuona, si sperimentò da uomini santi esser utile aggiugnere la semplicità della laude cristiana in lingua dal popolo intesa"). Giovanni Tommaso Ghilardi, *Nuovissima scelta di laude sacre approvate dal vescovo di Mondovì ad uso della sua Diocesi ed ora dal sommo pontefice Pio IX per tutto l'orbe cattolico ed arricchita di particolari indulgenze* (Mondovì: presso Pietro Rossi, 1855), 3–4.

13 Unfortunately, today we possess only a late evidence on the use of musical instruments in the singing of the lauds: "These *Sacred Laudi* are one of the most effective tools for the correct use of musical notes that are often used to excite passions. The songs are already known texts: the music is simple, easy, generally pleasant, as it should be for those melodies that must become popular [...]. And if you are an amateur and want to accompany them with an instrument, the same ease of writing guides your hand." ("Queste *Laudi Sacre* somministrano uno dei mezzi più efficaci per rivolgere a santo uso quelle note che servono a tanti a blandimento ed incentivo di passioni. Le canzoncine sono poesia già conosciuta: la musica è semplice, facile, generalmente piacevole, quale appunto conviene in melodie che debbono divenire popolari [...]. E se foste dilettante e voleste accompagnarvele con qualche strumento, la stessa facilità, con cui sono notate, vi condurrebbe la mano nell'accompagnarvi."). See *La civiltà cattolica. Anno Decimo* (Roma: coi tipi della Civiltà Cattolica, 1859), 93.

14 The only exception is the musical text *Dio ti salvi* found in *Istruzioni in forma di catechismo per la pratica della Dottrina cristiana spiegate nel Gesù di Palermo da*

leads to the assumption that these poems were sung on well-known, easily memorized melodies that could also be performed by people with no musical knowledge. As early as the eighteenth century, singing was recognized with multiple benefits: "Singing is praiseworthy when it is directed to a good end; it lifts the soul; it removes melancholy and sadness, which often oppresses the heart, and prevents us from doing well."[15]
The *lauda*, thanks to its simple and immediate language, thus meets spiritual, educational, and evangelical needs in both religious and secular contexts. This poetical-musical form becomes the symbol of the *pietas fidelium* since it allows the Christian believer to approach and feel the presence of God.

As far as the narrative content of Tartini's *laude* is concerned, it is part of the poetical-literary tradition which has characterized this form since its origins: the compositions have a pietistic-devotional, meditative, penitential, and exhortative character.

Deep spiritual sensitivity emerges from the 10 poems aimed at contrition and characterized by insistent references and exhortations to virtue, honesty, and perseverance in the fight for the achievement of the good.[16] Lyrical inspiration and warm humanity distinguish the 4 compositions to the Virgin Mary[17] while the 12th *lauda*, *Chi cerca l'innocenza*,[18] celebrates St Luigi Gonzaga, protector and symbol of the innocent and penitent. Intense drama emerges from two Lenten-time texts,[19] while the last poem, *Alma pentita*,[20] develops the Eucharistic theme.

Predominant is the theme of the anxiety to be forgiven in which the worshipper repeatedly asks to be cleared of any fault which causes his exhausting suffering. In the poems that Tartini put into music, the theme of penance is associated with the theme of sin, which the preacher Ambrogio Maria Barsotti defines as:

> Great evil [...] as hateful to God as detrimental for the soul! God is much more offended by just one mortal sin, may He be honoured by the praise of all righteous Men,

---

Pietro-Maria Ferreri (Bassano: a spese Remondini, 1768), 309, which will be discussed in the last section of this chapter.
15 "Il canto è lodevole quando è diretto a buon fine; solleva l'animo; scaccia la malinconia, e la tristezza, la quale molte volte opprime il cuore, e impedisce il ben fare [...]" *Divote istruzioni per conservare il frutto de' santi esercizj dedicate alla Madre di Dio Maria SS. con alcune canzoncine, ed altre orazioni* (Lucca: presso Filippo Maria Benedini, 1791), 115–116.
16 See: I. *Vedi Signor ch'io piango* (g1); V. *Caro Signor amato* (g2); VI. *Mio Gesù con tutto il core* (g3); VII. *Dolce mio Dio* (a1); VIII. *Crocefisso mio Signor* (a2); IX. *Amare lagrime* (g4); X. *No che terreno fallace* (G3); XI. *Voglio amar Gesù* (G4); XIII. *O peccator che sai* (g5); XIV. *E m'ami ancora* (D1).
17 II. *Iddio ti salvi Vergine bella* (G1); III. *Vergine bella del ciel regina* (Bb1); IV. *Dio ti salvi* (G2); XVII. *Vergine bella e pietosa* (F1).
18 (G5).
19 XV. *Infrangiti mio core* (d1); XVI. *Rimira o peccator* (a3).
20 (G6).

and all the Saints in Heaven. Mortal sin makes man incapable and unworthy of any grace [...].[21]

Penance is the means through which the sinner can get back into a state of grace by retracing the lost path. The reunion with God means humility, charity, and suffering: only through these virtues can the faithful heal the spirit. Repentance is associated with the literary image of the heart, which, besides symbolizing the seat of feelings and emotions, is the place of human inner reality, where final decisions are taken and where the most relevant experiences of our worldly and spiritual existence are lived. The heart is the organ of *religio*, the dimension in which God and man meet, the sanctuary where man donates himself entirely to God. Offering our heart means donating our life entirely to God because the heart constitutes all that a sinner possesses and can therefore give to restore the sacrifice of Christ who died on the cross for the salvation of humanity.[22]

Four of the 18 *laude* are concerned with the theme of the Virgin. Since the thirteenth century, the Mother of God has been a central character of popular devotion which found in Her a certain and privileged reference for the deliverance of the soul and hope in eternal life.[23] She is the protagonist of artistic creation – poetry, literature, painting, sculpture, architecture, and music – and Her presence is considerable in invocations and devotional prayers, both individual and collective.

Nowadays there is no devotional book that does not preach about Her. From the first centuries of the Church to the present day, all the Holy Fathers and Doctors, and

---

21 "[...] gran male [...] quanto odioso a Dio, quanto dannoso ad un'anima! Rimane Dio assai più vilipeso con un solo peccato mortale di quello, che resti onorato dalle lodi di tutti gli Uomini giusti, e da tutti i Santi del Paradiso. Il peccato mortale rende incapace, e indegno di qualunque grazia [...]" Ambrogio Maria Barsotti, *L'impurità abbattuta, e lo spirito immondo superato con varj mezzi, e specialmente colla divozione del sagro cingolo dell'angelico S. Tommaso D'Aquino* (Bologna: per Girolamo Corciolani, 1750), 69–70.

22 "What I have, I give to You [Mary], my poor heart, my soul. I always think of You, and I weep for the sorrows I have given You for my sins, for which I killed in Your holy arms Your dear and beloved Son Jesus, my beloved Redeemer." ("Quello ch'io ho, dono qui a Voi [Maria] il mio povero cuore, quest'anima mia. Sicché non pensi, che a Voi, e sempre pianga i disgusti, che una volta vi diedi per le mie colpe, per le quali uccisi nelle vostre ss. braccia l'amoroso, e caro vostro figlio Gesù, e mio amabilissimo redentore.") See *Divote istruzioni per conservare il frutto de' santi esercizj dedicate alla Madre di Dio Maria S[antissima] con alcune canzoncine, ed altre orazioni* (Lucca: presso Filippo Maria Benedini, 1791), 96.

23 About interesting considerations on the figure of the Virgin Mary from cultural and theological perspectives, see Stefano De Fiores, "L'immagine di Maria dal Concilio di Trento al Vaticano II (1563–1965)," in *La Vergine Maria dal Rinascimento a oggi*, ed. Ermanno M. Toniolo (Roma: Centro di cultura mariana "Madre della Chiesa", 1999), 9–62.

all-wise Men have recognized true devotion to Mary as a clear sign of predestination, and a way to Heaven.[24]

The texts Tartini set to music are rich in references to Marian theology. The Virgin has been exalted as a saving woman, since the birth of Christ to Her glory in Heaven: on Her we rely for the protection of humanity; she is a "shield" ("scudo") against evil forces, help against worldly dangers and guide for the souls on the way to the "harbour of Heaven" ("gran lido del ciel"). Mary is invoked as *mediatrix Dei et hominum*: the sinner addresses Her in the first person to meditate on his existential problems or his sufferings in an atmosphere dominated by subjectivism and intimism.

As for the stylistic profile, the texts are characterized by formal, lexical, and thematic essentiality. Syntax, mainly paratactic, is at the service of simplicity and immediacy, emphasized by the use of an everyday and humble register. From some poems, high tension develops, reached by the anonymous poets through wise lexical choice aimed at evoking a dramatic effect. The simplicity and transparency of these poems are not the consequence of a lack of expressive means but represent an effect aimed at involving and educating the faithful. This transparency is also reflected in the musical language.

3 Musical Texts as a Tool for Investigating the Creative Process

The lyricism and essentiality of the musical texts are the results of a continuous review process evidenced by the drafts. Tartini aims at the intelligibility of the poetic text, at an effective rhythmic-syllabic scansion, and the search for a "natural" melody, full of spirituality and intimacy. Each *lauda* is preceded by the handwritten expression "a carte ..." and tempo marks.[25] Of the 18 compositions, 3 are one-voice songs, 1 *lauda* is a 3-voice song, and all the others are 2-voice songs; furthermore, 16 are for male voices – tenor and bass – 2 are for alto. The melodies mainly proceed by adjoining notes; there is also a particular insistence on parallel motion in thirds and sixths between the voices, a typical feature of folk music. Vocal range is limited and accessible to performers with no great musical knowledge: Tartini carefully avoids decorative effects, melismas, or intervals[26] which would have proved difficult to perform. The composer also leaves us with vocal parts with no instrumental accompaniment, so we do not know whether instrumental parts were lost (like the poems) or the melodies were only created for vocals.

---

24 "Oramai non si trova più libro divoto, che non predichi di Lei. Da' primi secoli della Chiesa sino a qui con ragione tutti i Santi Padri, e Sacri Dottori, e tutti gli Uomini savj hanno riconosciuta la vera divozione a Maria Santissima un segno chiaro di predestinazione, e una via regia per andare al Cielo." See *Divote istruzioni*, 79.
25 Only in III. *Vergine bella del ciel regina* (Bb1) and XVI. *Rimira o peccator* (a3) Tartini omits tempo marks.
26 There are appoggiaturas which embellish notes with long rhythmic values and trills before final cadenzas.

The analysis of the sheets containing the sketches and drafts of these musical miniatures has revealed some meaningful aspects of Tartini's *modus componendi*. Comparing the *laude* with his instrumental production, some similarities between the *laude* and the slow movements of his sonatas emerge. For example, the beginning of the *Grave* of the *Sonata* in G major G32[27] (Example 1) compared with the first draft, identified as "Draft a",[28] written for the 16th *lauda Rimira o peccator* (Example 2).

Example 1: Violin and bass sonata (G32), I mov, *Grave*, mm. 1–2.

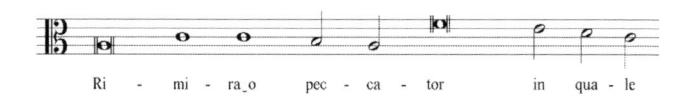

Example 2: XVI. *Rimira o peccator* (a3), Draft a. (Tartini, "Canzoncine Sacre," f. 9.)

The melodic *incipit* of the first movement of the sonata, in the *lauda*, is transposed one tone above, from G major to A minor. The sense of enthusiasm and grandeur conveyed by the major third interval is replaced by a melancholic atmosphere – provided by the third minor – which best suits the purpose and content of the literary text:

> Look oh sinner, how pale his skin
> how deep the wounds and huge the grief
> our sweet Jesus, our only Good,
> eventually, endure, but because of thy sin.[29]

---

27 G33 in the catalogue by Paul Brainard, *Le sonate per violino di Giuseppe Tartini. Catalogo tematico* (Padova: Accademia tartiniana di Padova, 1975), 88.
28 The comparison can also be made with the second draft in which the composer gives the *lauda* the same rhythm as in the fair copy.
29 "Rimira o peccator in quale stato,/tra quali piaghe, in mezzo a quante pene,/il buon Gesù, l'unico nostro bene,/hai ridotto alla fin col tuo peccato." The poetic text comes from the fair copy of the *lauda* in Tartini, "Canzoncine Sacre," f. 8. To date, the only literary source in concordance with the Paduan autograph is *Canzonette ed ariette sacre e morali su quasi tutte le migliori arie e musicali e correnti* (Vicenza: per Francesco Modena, 1786), 229. This print bears the following caption before the text: *Peccator invitato a mirar Gesù Crocifisso* (*Sinner invited to see Jesus Crucified*).

One more difference is the replacement of the rest, at the beginning of the second measure, with an A in correspondence to the central syllable of "peccator". The same happens with the *Andante cantabile* in G minor of *Sonata* g3[30] (Example 3) and the first three measures of the second draft of *Alma pentita* in G major (Example 4).

Example 3: Violin and bass sonata (g3), I mov, *Andante cantabile*, mm. 1–4.

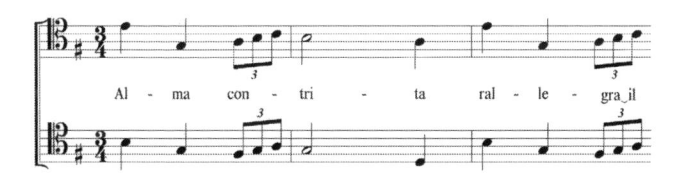

Example 4: XVIII. *Alma pentita* (G6), Draft b, mm. 1–3. (Tartini, "Canzoncine Sacre," f. 9.)

Besides changing the mode and so the character of the theme, from tender and sorrowful to sweet and brilliant, Tartini replaces the initial interval of descending fifth with a major sixth one. The following measure shows other changes: the composer prefers to simplify the melodic line which sweetly turns back to A in correspondence to the final syllable of "contrita".

From the analysis of the sketches, it is also apparent that the composer tends to "economize" and "recycle" musical material, for example, the first draft of the *lauda Alma pentita* (Figure 3).

---

30 g3 also in the Brainard catalogue. See Brainard, *Le sonate per violino*, 91. This similarity had already been discovered in Revoltella, "Le laude spirituali," 282.

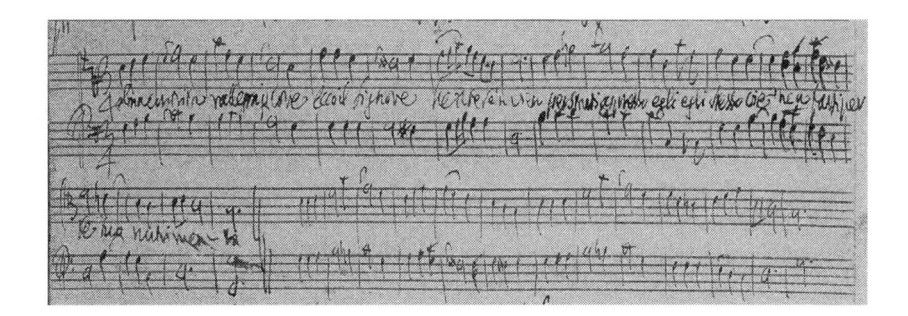

Figure 3: XVIII. *Alma pentita* (G6), Draft a. (Tartini, "Canzoncine Sacre," f. 1.)

It is a complete composition in which the only revisions, overwritten, are in bars 13–14 and the final one. Moreover, Tartini entirely writes the first stanza of the text for the *Santissimo Sacramento* ("Blessed Sacrament"). Notwithstanding, both in the sketch of sheet 1 and in the fair copy of sheet 5, the previously composed melody is given a new text, *Iddio ti salvi Vergine bella* ("May God save you fair Vergin") (Figure 4).

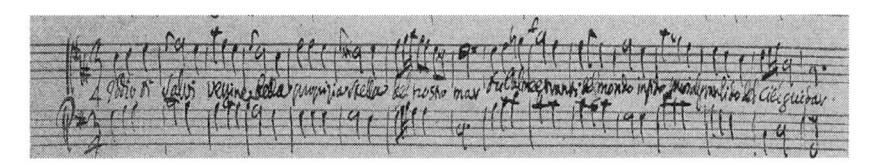

Figure 4: II. *Iddio ti salvi Vergine bella* (G1), Draft a. (Tartini, "Canzoncine Sacre," f. 1.)

This leads us to assume that Tartini's priority is the production of an essential, simple musical language, devoid of any decorations but lacking a direct text-music relationship. We could even argue that, sometimes, the composer tries to "adapt" the poetic text to a pre-existing musical composition. For example, in the first draft of *Vedi Signor ch'io piango* – which went through a long development – the tonic accent does not always coincide with the rhythmic-musical one[31] (Example 5).

---

31 See Tartini's considerations in Chapter 4 of *Trattato di musica secondo la vera scienza dell'armonia* (Treatise on Music according to the True Science of Harmony) about the organization of the melody in relation to the number of rhythmic stresses. Giuseppe Tartini, *Trattato di musica secondo la vera scienza dell'armonia* (Padova: Stamperia del Seminario, 1754), 115–117.

[Musical notation]

Example 5: I. *Vedi Signor ch'io piango* (g1), Draft a. (Tartini, "Canzoncine Sacre," f. 1.)

In the second draft, written in the following system, Tartini corrects the rhythmic-musical phrasing by adapting the rhythm of the melody to the rhythm of the literary text. He also gives the two vocal lines more delicacy and lyricism (Example 6).

[Musical notation]

Example 6: I. *Vedi Signor ch'io piango* (g1), Draft b. (Tartini, "Canzoncine Sacre," f. 1.)

The two drafts maintain the G minor key while the rhythm changes from 4/4 time to 3/4 time. From the structural point of view, we can notice a certain similarity: both versions are made of two sections. In the first draft (Example 5) each section consists of two bars and the composer provides continuity to the two parts using the repetition of a very similar rhythmic pattern in bars 2–3.[32] The first draft is also characterized by the predominance of short rhythmic values (quavers and semiquavers) and the concentration of the melodic-musical material in which Tartini fits, with some efforts, the first stanza of *Vedi Signor ch'io piango*. In the second draft (Example 6) the same text is distributed in 13 bars divided into two sections: the first part consists of bars 1–6 while the second one comprises bars 7–13. In this case, the connection between the two sections is marked by the repetition of the first three measures of the melody at the beginning of the second musical phrase. The search for more lyricism is also highlighted both from the more natural rendering of the melodic line and the bass structure.

---

32 The only difference is in the third beat.

These elements allow us to make some considerations about Tartini's creative process: there is a frequent attempt at simplification due to the need of composing an understandable, simple, lyric melodic line, without any technical difficulties. We can assume that the creation process is based on two steps: the horizontal development of the musical idea and then the creation of the bass line which is the counter melody or accompaniment. Moreover, the analysis of the drafts reveals the search for consistency and unity which the composer achieves, thanks to the repetition of rhythmic-musical structures.

The interest in investigating this repertoire, which allows us to reveal some aspects of Tartini's figure and compositional activity, is also stimulated by the discovery of anonymous musical intonations of the *laude Crocefisso mio Signor* and *Dio ti salvi* that enable us to make an interesting comparison with Piranese's production.

4 Two Texts for Two Stories: *Crocefisso mio Signor* and *Dio ti salvi*

The survival and reception of two anonymous compositions of the text *Crocefisso mio Signor* arouse our interest because they show remarkable rhythmic-melodic similarities with Tartini's *lauda* (Example 7). One of the two folk songs was still present in the oral tradition of the Veneto region until the nineties of the last century, the other until the 1940s in the Basilica of Sant'Eufemia in Rovigno.[33]

Example 7: VIII. *Crocefisso mio Signor* (a2), fair copy. (Tartini, "Canzoncine Sacre," f. 6.)

---

33 A systematic list of folk songs widespread in Istria can be found in Giuseppe Radole, *Canti popolari istriani* (Firenze: Leo S. Olschki Editore, 1965).

Tartini's *lauda*, originally written in the tenor clef, shows a 3/2 time signature and the key of A minor. From the structural point of view, it is divided into two sections: the first (bars 1–16) – used for the setting of the stanzas made up of quatrains of septenaries – repeats the same musical phrase twice, while the second (bars 17–26) sets the refrain. There are also some melodic elements, such as cadenzas, melodic progressions, and notes of anticipation, which give coherence and cohesion to the two parts. A comparison between the draft and the fair copy also shows as Tartini, in the drafting of the composition, had no uncertainty or rethinking: there is no variation between the two versions of the text.

Below is the *lauda* transmitted by the oral tradition of the Veneto region (Example 8):

Example 8: *Crocifisso mio Signor*, oral tradition of the Veneto region. (The musical transcription is taken from Dino Coltro, *Cante e cantàri. La vita, il lavoro, le feste nel canto veneto di tradizione orale* (Venezia: Marsilio, 1988), 152–153.)

The *lauda* is written in ¾ time signature and D major. From the structural point of view, this composition is also divided into two sections. The connection between the two parts is even more apparent since the second musical phrase repeats the beginning of the composition in bars 20–25 (only the first beat). Moreover, the descending third pattern that moves by adjoining notes – first used in bar 2 – is repeated nine times within the composition. From the rhythmic-melodic point of view, Tartini's composition is characterized by more variety and liveliness, thanks both to the variations of the melodic line and the use of the dotted notes.

The Rovigno version, written in E minor and 6/8 time signature, shows different interconnected musical segments. Moreover, as in the previous examples, it reveals a limited melodic extension in which the voices mainly move by adjoining notes, the use of the diatonic scale, and the absence of modulating sections.[34]

---

34 For the musical text, see Paulovich, "Giuseppe Tartini e le laudi spirituali," 225.

The apparent similarity between the compositions leads to two possible assumptions: "[...] either Tartini drew inspiration from a pre-existing music tradition or the two songs are a corruption of Tartini's original score."[35] The first hypothesis is supported by two reasons. The first is the interest in the folk-music repertoire shown by Tartini in his theoretical-musical works. Tartini considers traditional folk music as a spontaneous product of Nature[36] and therefore not subject to the corruption of artistic artifice. So, Tartini's approach to folk music is "experimental and eclectic" ("di natura sperimentale ed eterogenea").[37] According to Pierluigi Petrobelli, Tartini learns the traditional folk melodies – later employed in his compositions – from direct oral experience.[38] Petrobelli suggests that the folk melodies not only come from the nearby city of Venice but also from the town of Piran, or at least from Istria. Tartini only spent his childhood in his hometown, Piran. This experience would therefore have been crucial for his later and most important works.

The *lauda Crocefisso mio Signor* is not the only evidence of Tartini's relationship with the music of the oral tradition. Pierpaolo Ponzonetti found out:

> Two concerto movements [...], a group of sonata movements in MS I-Pca 1888 (started in the '40s) show features, in the name and text, of their popular origin: the "Aria del Tasso" in sonatas B.G2, B.D2, B.A11; the "Furlana" from sonata B.D2; the "Canzone veneziana" from sonata B.G2 and the movement with no tempo markings written in the Veneto dialect, "Senza de ti mia cara/no che no posso star/la pena é così amara / che mi fa delirar", in sonata B.G5.[39]

---

35 "[...] o il Piranese si è ispirato ad una tradizione preesistente o i due canti in questione sono una corruzione dell'originale tartiniano." See Paulovich, "Giuseppe Tartini e le laudi spirituali," 226.
36 "According to Tartini, 'Nature' is the source of Truth, with the term 'Nature' he means all the phenomena that we can perceive with our senses, which have not been modified by man. 'Nature' is in contrast with 'Art': any human activity which modifies facts, natural phenomena, above all in the field of music." ("Per Tartini, la 'Natura' è la fonte di ogni verità, intendendo con il termine 'Natura' l'insieme dei fenomeni che cadono sotto i nostri sensi, fenomeni non ancora modificati dall'intervento umano. Di fronte alla 'Natura' Tartini colloca l''Arte', che deve essere intesa come ogni specie di attività umana che modifichi fatti, fenomeni naturali, soprattutto nel campo della musica."). See Petrobelli, *Tartini, le sue idee e il suo tempo*, 102.
37 Pierpaolo Polzonetti, introduction to *Tartini e la musica secondo natura* (Lucca: LIM, 2001), XXVII.
38 "Everybody must listen to each other, in Venice I paid my traìro to those blind violin players, because I also learnt from them." ("Tutti e poi tutti devono ascoltarsi, ed io in Venezia pagavo il mio traìro a que' tali ciechi suonatori di violino, perché anche da quelli ho imparato."). This passage from the letter addressed to Angelo Gabrielli, dated 6th February 1760, is taken from Petrobelli, *Tartini, le sue idee e il suo tempo*, 104.
39 "[...] due movimenti di concerto [...], un gruppo di movimenti di sonata del MS I-Pca 1888 (redatto anch'esso a partire dagli anni Quaranta), i quali recano nel titolo o nel testo la prova della loro origine extra-colta: l''Aria del Tasso' presente nelle sonate

The second reason supporting the influence of a pre-existing tradition on Tartini's *lauda* emerges from the comparison with the collection *Musica per la nuovissima scelta di laude sacre* by Giovanni Tommaso Ghilardi.[40] The anthology – which enjoyed wide circulation in the nineteenth century[41] – contains the musical texts of 67 *laude* and is accompanied by a booklet with the full text of the poems. Among the poems which were set to music are *Crucifisso mio Signor* (Example 9) and *Alma contrita*.

Example 9: Giovanni Tommaso Ghilardi, *Crucifisso mio Signor*. (See Ghilardi, *Musica per la nuovissima scelta di laude*, 11.)

Under the rhythmic-melodic aspect, the *incipit* of the *lauda* is the same as the Venetian version as well as the repetition of the same descending third pattern (see Example 8). Instead, *Alma contrita* differs from Tartini's version both from the structural and melodic points of view.[42] It's unlikely that both Giovanni Tommaso Ghilardi and the composer mentioned in the preface to the devotional anthology, Giuseppe Blanchi from Turin, drew on Tartini's *laude* for the composition of

---

B.G2, B.D2, B.A11; la 'Furlana' della sonata B.D2; la 'Canzone veneziana' della Sonata B.G2, e il movimento senza indicazioni di agogica contrassegnato dal testo in dialetto veneto, 'Senza de ti mia cara / no che no posso star / la pena è così amara / che mi fa delirar', nella Sonata in B.G5." Polzonetti, *Tartini e la musica secondo natura*, 54; for a detailed analysis of the aforementioned sources, see pp. 53–99.

40 Giovanni Tommaso Ghilardi, *Musica per la nuovissima scelta di laude sacre approvate dal Vescovo di Mondovì ad uso della sua diocesi* (Mondovì: Tipografia di Giovanni Issoglio e C., 1867).
41 See *Catalogo di opere ed opuscoli di Monsignor Ghilardi de' predicatori vescovo di Mondovì* (Mondovì: Tipografia di Gio. Issoglio e C., 1868), 10.
42 See Ghilardi, *Musica per la nuovissima scelta di laude*, 14.

Crocifisso mio Signor for two reasons. First of all, Tebaldini states in *L'Archivio musicale* that, until 1895, the only known sacred composition by Tartini was the *Miserere* performed in the Sistine Chapel, attended by Pope Clement XIII, on Holy Wednesday 1768.[43] The second reason is that in the preface the Bishop of Mondovì claims he included "those *laude* he had long before chosen here and there, with their melody".[44] These are "lodi" that Ghilardi had heard – and probably made notes of – during his apostolic office. This detail suggests the Bishop might have drawn from the same folk song which Tartini, almost one century before, had transformed into a form of art. As can be seen from the Bishop's biography, his apostolic office began in 1840 and involved numerous centres, especially in central and northern Italy and Austria.[45] It must not be forgotten that in 1840, both Lombardo-Veneto and the Istrian peninsula were part of the Habsburg Empire and it is likely Ghilardi had listened to one of the songs which survived until the previous century in the Veneto-Istrian tradition during his preaching missions.

Finally, we examine the text *Dio ti salvi* dedicated to the Virgin Mary and attributed to the Jesuit Francesco De Geronimo. This poem was very celebre and was included in numerous devotional anthologies as early as the second half of the seventeenth century. Among these, the collection *Istruzioni in forma di catechismo*[46] captures our interest because it provides a literary text accompanied by a musical score, which is quite unusual in the context of eighteenth-century devotional books. The anthology, written by the Jesuit Pietro Maria Ferreri, exposes – according to the usual form of questions and answers – the principles of Christian

---

43 "Historians have so far told of only one vocal composition by Tartini; namely, the only *Miserere* performed in the Sistine Chapel on Holy Wednesday 1768 in the presence of Pope Clement XIII (Rezzonico), the original of which is preserved in the Library of the Academy of Music in Paris. Apparently it is such a poor composition that, according to Fétis, it would no longer be performed even in Rome." ("Gli storici finora hanno detto di una sola composizione vocale del Tartini; e cioè del solo *Miserere* cantato nella Cappella Sistina il mercoledì Santo del 1768 presente papa Clemente XIII (Rezzonico) di cui l'originale si conserva nella Biblioteca dell'Accademia di musica a Parigi. Pare sia desso una composizione scadente talché, stando a quanto dice il Fétis, non si sarebbe più eseguita neppure a Roma."). See Tebaldini, *L'Archivio musicale*, 78.
44 "[...] quelle lodi, che già da tempo scelto avea qua e là col rispettivo tono", see Ghilardi, preface to *Musica per la nuovissima scelta di laude*.
45 For a list of the countries where the Bishop of Mondovì was active, see: Alvaro Rulla, *Una gloria dell'episcopato italiano: mons. Giovanni Tommaso Ghilardi* (Alba: Pia Società San Paolo, 1942), 62; Ghilardi, preface to *Musica per la nuovissima scelta di laude*.
46 The devotional collection has gone through numerous editions and has been a good publishing success. The melody in this study is taken from the 1768 edition, as the previous versions I consulted did not contain any musical text.

doctrine. As regards the general organization of the doctrinal matter within the work, the preface states that:

> [...] the Work is thus divided [...] into Four Parts. The First Part contains six Proemial Doctrines, thirty Doctrines concerning the Virtue of Faith, and the Symbol of the Apostles. The Second Part contains in seven Doctrines the explanation of the Virtue of Hope, of the Sunday Prayer, and the Angelic Salutation. The Third Part contains in twenty-five Doctrines the explanation of the Virtue of Charity and the Precepts of the Decalogue. In the Fourth Part, the Seven Sacraments of the Church are explained in thirty-three Doctrines: and an Appendix of seven other Doctrines explains everything about the Moral Virtues and other works against the Capital Vices and Sins.[47]

The fourth part of the anthology features the setting of the composition *Dio ti salvi* (Example 10).

Example 10: *Dio di salvi. Istruzioni in forma di catechismo*, 309.

This is a composition for solo voice originally written in the soprano key. The melodic line is developed around three phrases, each of which is repeated twice within the composition with micro-variations. The musical incises are separated by rests that give the composition a fragmentary character. The predominant use of short rhythmic values – quavers and semiquavers – also suggests a rather agile melodic flow with a confidential tone. Regarding the reasons that led Ferreri to "print the musical notes, to which these songs are sung", the notice to readers shows that singing was used by numerous Jesuit preachers during their missions to memorize "the things of our Holy Faith" and at the same time avoid "the unworthy

---

47 "[...] vien tutta l'Opera adunque divisa [...] in Quattro Parti. La Prima Parte contiene VI. Dottrine Proemiali, ad altre XXX. Dottrine, in cui si spiega la Virtù della Fede, e tutto il Simbolo degli Apostoli. La Seconda Parte racchiude in VII. Dottrine la spiegazione della Virtù della Speranza, dell'Orazione Domenicale, e della Salutazione Angelica. La Terza Parte contiene in XXV. Dottrine la spiegazione della Virtù della Carità, e de' Precetti del Decalogo. Nella Quarta Parte si spiegano i Sette Sagramenti della Chiesa racchiusi in XXXIII. Dottrine: e in un'Appendice di altre VII. Dottrine si spiega tutto ciò che spetta alle Virtù Morali, ed altre Opere Buone, a' Vizj Capitali, e a' Peccati." Preface to *Istruzioni in forma di catechismo*, VI.

abuse of profane songs".[48] Therefore, singing was chosen by Ferreri as a privileged tool for his pastoral activity, thanks to its capacity to facilitate the memorization and dissemination of the Christian message.

The discovery of this *lauda* allows us to make a stylistic-formal comparison with Piranese's composition (Example 11).

Example 11: IV. *Dio ti salvi* (G2), fair copy. (Tartini, "Canzoncine Sacre," f. 5.)

Tartini's *lauda* is written for two tenors and is characterized by an essential and transparent musical language: the voices proceed mainly by adjoining notes except for an interval of a descending fifth and an interval of a descending minor third. The repetition of an ascending musical passage (anabasis) gives coherence and cohesion to the musical structure. Unlike the previous intonation, Tartini's melody has long rhythmic values (semiquavers).

The analysis of the short compositions shows the presence of some common aspects such as the immediacy of the musical language, the repetition of rhythmic-melodic patterns that facilitate both the performance and the eventual memorization of the compositions, and the intelligibility of the poetic text favoured by predominantly syllabic writing. Tartini, therefore, proves to be able to grasp the heritage of the past and the contemporary tradition and to be able to reinterpret it in unique musical creations.

Although these musical miniatures have long remained almost unknown – as most of Giuseppe Tartini's vocal and instrumental output – this chapter tries to highlight their multiple historical and cultural values. Tartini's *laude* are a privileged tool for understanding both the figure and the poetic of one of the most important composers of that time. These compositions are, on the one hand, the

---

48 The three quotations "imprimere le note musicali, con cui potranno cantarsi le dette canzonette", "meglio le cose della nostra Santa Fede", "l'indegno abuso delle canzoni profane" are taken from *Istruzioni in forma di catechismo*, VII.

result of an artistic personality that looks to the "aesthetics of simplicity" ("estetica della semplicità") and the "music of the humble" ("musica degli umili")[49] and, on the other hand, the product of an era defined, ungenerously and perhaps with some prejudice, as "transitional". The research on the *laude* was also an opportunity to shed light on the complex sacred-devotional context of the mid-eighteenth century. This field is still little explored today, although it is linked to the compositional activity of renowned composers. Therefore, it is meaningful as the knowledge and appreciation of Tartini's musical heritage thus allow us to look at the multi-faced cultural panorama of the eighteenth century with greater awareness.

Bibliography

Bisi, Sofia et al. "Le filigrane in autografi di Tartini e Vallotti conservati nell'Archivio musicale dell'Arca di S. Antonio di Padova. Contributo per una cronologia dell'opera di Giuseppe Tartini." *Il Santo* 32, nos. 2–3 (1992): 307–333.

Bombi, Andrea, and Maria Nevilla Massaro, eds. *Tartini: il tempo e le opere*. Bologna: Il Mulino, 1994.

Dalla Vecchia, Jolanda. "Rilievi e prime ipotesi a margine degli studi sulle filigrane in autografi di Tartini e Vallotti." *Il Santo* 32, nos. 2–3 (1992): 335–343.

De Fiores, Stefano. "L'immagine di Maria dal Concilio di Trento al Vaticano II (1563–1965)." In *La Vergine Maria dal Rinascimento a oggi*, edited by Ermanno M. Toniolo, 9–62. Roma: Centro di cultura mariana "Madre della Chiesa", 1999.

Di Paoli Paulovich, David. "Giuseppe Tartini e le laudi spirituali nella tradizione istriana." *Atti e memorie della Società istriana di archeologia e storia patria* 114 (2014): 215–229.

Di Paoli Paulovich, David. "Tartini e il suo impegno vocale-sacro: inediti e sopravvivenze nella tradizione istriana." *La Ricerca* 21, no. 60 (2011): 14–16.

Frasson, Leonardo. *Giuseppe Tartini. L'uomo e l'artista*. Padova: Basilica del Santo, 1974.

"Le filigrane degli autografi tartiniani: questioni di cronologia." In *Tartini. Il tempo e le opere*, edited by Andrea Bombi and Maria Nevilla Massaro, 377–387. Bologna: Il Mulino, 1994.

Petrobelli, Pierluigi. *Tartini, le sue idee e il suo tempo*. Lucca: LIM, 1992.

Polzonetti, Pierpaolo. *Tartini e la musica secondo natura*. Lucca: LIM, 2001.

Radole, Giuseppe. *Canti popolari istriani*. Firenze: Leo S. Olschki Editore, 1965.

Revoltella, Pietro. "Giuseppe Tartini. La musica sacra." In *Tartini 1692–1992. Manifestazioni per il terzo centenario della nascita (13–29 ottobre 1992)*. Padova: Comune di Padova. Assessorato allo Spettacolo, 1992.

---

49 The expressions are taken from Polzonetti, *Tartini e la musica secondo natura*, 70.

Revoltella, Pietro. "Le laude spirituali di Giuseppe Tartini." *Il Santo* 32, nos. 2–3 (1992): 265–289.

Revoltella, Pietro. "Lo 'Stabat Mater' di Giuseppe Tartini." In *Tartini. Il tempo e le opere*, edited by Andrea Bombi and Maria Nevilla Massaro, 81–96. Bologna: Il Mulino, 1994.

Tartini, Giuseppe. *Trattato di musica secondo la vera scienza dell'armonia*. Padova: Stamperia del Seminario, 1754.

Tebaldini, Giovanni. *L'Archivio musicale della Cappella antoniana. Illustrazione storico-critica*. Padova: Tipografia e libreria antoniana, 1895, 69–80.

Alan Maddox

University of Sydney

"A great commotion of spirit": Tartini's "Ancona experience" and the Power of Affective Performance

Abstract: Tartini famously recorded in his *Trattato di musica* (1754) that, as a young man playing the opera orchestra in Ancona, he heard a line of recitative that produced a remarkably chilling affective response in both audience and performers. In this chapter I reconsider the nature of this striking effect and how it was obtained. Treatises on singing and oratory make clear that apt delivery could move the passions powerfully, and if skilled recitation coincided with a compositional device which Tartini considered to have – even if accidentally – "hit upon the truth of nature", this is likely to have created a formidable expressive mix. Elucidating the link between expressive vocal performance practice and affective response may help us to understand how Tartini understood the projection of affect to work in his own compositions, understood not only as formal structures but also as performed, embodied sound.

Keywords: Giuseppe Tartini, affect, music and emotion, music and rhetoric, recitative, singing

1 Tartini in Ancona

Although Giuseppe Tartini is remembered primarily for his composition and pedagogy for the violin, he spent much of his career as a performer immersed in vocal music. Whether in theatre orchestras in his early career, or as a church musician, as he was in Padua for much of his maturity, vocal music was clearly important to him as a model for violin performance. Nowhere is this more evident than in his account of a remarkable formative experience which he underwent as a young man, when playing in the opera orchestra in Ancona.

Many people have had the experience of a sudden chill up the spine – a thrill of shock or fear – while in the theatre, watching a movie or listening to music. Something like this seems to have been what Tartini was setting out to describe in his account of the Ancona experience in his *Trattato di musica secondo la vera scienza dell'armonia* (Treatise on Music according to the True Science of Harmony).[1] The

---

1 Giuseppe Tartini, *Trattato di musica secondo la vera scienza dell'armonia* (Padova: Stamperia del Seminario, 1754; facs. ed., New York: Broude Brothers, 1966).

fact that there are several records of Tartini mentioning this incident, and the fact that it was important enough to him to include in a treatise published 40 years after the event, suggests that it was important to him in understanding how music creates its affective appeal.

The topic arises in the *Trattato di musica* in the context of his discussion of the ancient Greek modes and their fabled power over the passions. To demonstrate that such affective power is possible in modern music too, he asserted that "I myself am a witness to the possibility, which has happened to me in many instances, of which I will report just one:"[2]

> In the fourteenth year (if I am not mistaken) of the present century, in the drama which was presented in Ancona, there was at the beginning of the third act a line of recitative accompanied by no instruments other than the bass, by which, both in us professors and in the listeners, so great a commotion of spirit was raised that everyone was looking at one another because of the obvious mutation of color that was occurring in each of us. The effect was not one of lament (I recall very well that the words were of indignation), but of a certain severity, and cold bloodedness, that did indeed disturb the spirit. The drama was presented thirteen times, and the same effect always resulted, universally—a palpable sign of which was the complete silence beforehand, in which the entire audience prepared itself for enjoying the effect. I was too young to have the presence of mind to conserve this example, and now I regret it. I do not believe that the composer (although an excellent man of that time) knew by science that he had to pursue that effect; but I do believe that, being a man of excellent taste and of the highest judgment, he was led by good sense and by the words, and at that point accidentally came upon the truth of nature. Hence I conclude that if the beginning of emotion is given, there is no contrary reason against its progression and its fulfilment. The fact is that in small movements and for a short time, one often encounters from composers some fortunate point of similar strength. But there is no rule or science for obtaining it with certainty when it is desired, and far less of continuing it for many movements or for any considerable time.[3]

What produced this remarkable effect that stayed with Tartini throughout his life, and what historical evidence can we draw on to try to understand it? The episode has been the subject of considerable discussion, including notable studies by Luca Ferretti, who astutely investigated the archival evidence for Tartini's activities in the Marche, Candida Felici, who situated it in the context of Tartini's other writings on vocal music as a model for violin performance, and Pierpaolo Polzonetti, whose important study provides a reading of the incident in relation to

---

2   "[...] son testimonio io stesso della possibilità, per molti casi a me occorsi, de' quali ne riferirò un solo." Tartini, *Trattato di musica*, 135. English translation by the author.
3   Fredric Bolan Johnson, "Tartini's Trattato di musica seconda la vera scienza dell'armonia: An Annotated Translation with Commentary," (Doctoral dissertation, Indiana University, 1985), 343–344. Translation slightly adapted by the author.

Tartini's neo-platonic philosophical outlook and his aesthetic of "music according to Nature".[4] Sergio Durante has also reviewed the historical evidence for the event and its significance in relation to Tartini's concerns with words and music.[5] One theme that arises from these and other studies is that although Tartini composed no known theatre music and very little vocal music of any kind, vocal music and the expression of words were nevertheless fundamental to his aesthetic.[6] My focus in this chapter is on the mechanisms of affective musical expression, and in particular of vocal expression, that may be discerned in Tartini's account of the incident in Ancona. Although in the immediate context Tartini presents this paradigmatic episode as primarily a compositional achievement, it is clear in view of his broader ideas about vocal music and affective expression that in his mature thinking a confluence of carefully constructed verbal meaning; apt musical setting; skilful, engaged delivery; and actively embodied listening is essential to producing the most powerful expressive results.

In his own writings, Tartini never identified the opera in which the incident occurred, though Francesco Algarotti later reported that Tartini had told him it was by Gasparini and that the singer was "a certain Senesino, brother of the famous Senesino, a mediocre castrato",[7] surely a reference to Giovanni Carlo Bernardi of Siena, known as Senesino, brother of the illustrious Francesco Bernardi "Senesino", and also a castrato singer.[8] I will not review here all of the contradictory evidence about the operas performed in Ancona during Tartini's time there, which has been

---

4   Luca Ferretti, "Giuseppe Tartini e le Marche: Primi risultati di una ricerca," in *Tartini, il tempo e le opere*, ed. Andrea Bombi and Maria Nevilla Massaro (Bologna: Il Mulino, 1994), 37–65; Candida Felici, "'Non suona, canta su'l violino': From Aesthetics to Compositional and Performance Practice in Tartini's Instrumental Music," *Ad Parnassum* 11, no. 22 (2013), 127–141; Pierpaolo Polzonetti, *Tartini e la musica secondo natura* (Lucca: LIM, 2001).
5   Sergio Durante, *Tartini, Padova, l'Europa* (Livorno: Sillabe, 2018), 20–22.
6   Recent studies on Tartini's application of verbal mottos to his instrumental compositions include Sergio Durante, "Tartini and his Texts," in *The Century of Bach and Mozart. Perspectives on Historiography, Composition, Theory and Performance*, ed. Sean Gallagher and Thomas Forrest Kelly (Cambridge (MA): Harvard University Press, 2008), 145–186; Alessandro Zattarin, "'Vidi in sogno un guerrier': Tasso, Metastasio e altri fantasmi nelle sonate a violino solo di Giuseppe Tartini," *Ad Parnassum* 11, no. 22 (2013), 143–160; Piotr Wilk, "Poetical Mottos in Tartini's Concertos – the Latest Concordances and Questions," *Musica Iagellonica* 9 (2018), 81–100.
7   "Il Tartini mi ha detto che in Ancona in un'opera del Gasparini ci era un passo di recitativo (cantato da un Senesino fratello del famoso Senesino musico mediocre) senza strumenti e che faceva una commozione incredibile." Treviso, Biblioteca comunale, ms. 1257 A, fasc. VI, quoted in Durante, *Tartini*, 96. English translation by the author.
8   Melania Bucciarelli, "Senesino's Negotiations with the Royal Academy of Music: Further Insight into the Riva–Bernardi Correspondence and the Role of Singers in the Practice of Eighteenth-Century Opera," *Cambridge Opera Journal* 27, no. 3 (2015): 197, doi:10.1017/S0954586715000087.

assessed in detail by Ferretti and recently reviewed by Durante. Suffice to say that while there is currently no record of an opera which would meet both Tartini's and Algarotti's descriptions having been performed in Ancona in 1714 (or, indeed, in any of the seasons in which Tartini played in the orchestra of either Ancona or nearby Fano, between 1714 and 1718), Ferretti and Durante noted that Tartini's account could apply to Apostolo Zeno's *Faramondo* (Pharamond), a setting of which was performed in Ancona in 1714.[9] The composer is not identified in the libretto and no score is known to survive, but a setting of this libretto by Gasparini was performed in Rome in 1720, suggesting that the Ancona season could have been an earlier version of the same, or a related work.[10] In favour of *Faramondo*, too, is that the opening scene of its third act includes "words of indignation" which would fit Tartini's recollection of the relevant scene. The cast did not, however, include anyone who might be identified with Senesino's brother. In fact, the role of Gustavo, who delivers the fateful lines in Act 3, Scene 1, is assigned in the Ancona libretto not to a castrato (mediocre or otherwise) but to Michele Selvatici of Modena, who was variously described as a tenor or bass.[11]

It is possible, of course, that Tartini may simply have misremembered the singer, or that Algarotti confused the story, but Tartini's reported recollection seems very specific and even if he had mis-remembered the connection with Giovanni Carlo Bernardi, it would seem odd to confuse a castrato with a baritone. With that in mind, at least one other possibility is worth noting: in 2010, Colleen Reardon reported coming across reference to a libretto, sold at auction in the early 2000s, for an otherwise unknown *Tito Manlio* (Titus Manlius) given at the Teatro della Fenice in Ancona in 1715, a season in which Tartini was in the orchestra. Only scanty details of this work are known from the auction catalogue, which did not identify a composer and listed only two members of the cast, the castrati Giacinto Fontana, "il Farfallino" (the little butterfly) and Giovanni Battista Tamburini of Siena.[12] Could Tamburini have been the "Senesino" reported by Algarotti, or could Giovanni Carlo Bernardi also have been in the cast? There is no known setting of *Tito Manlio* by Gasparini to support such a hypothesis but if nothing else, the serendipitous discovery of this libretto suggests that the possibility of an opera in which Bernardi may have performed in Ancona in 1714 or 1715 – perhaps even one by Gasparini – cannot be entirely ruled out. Certainly the limited available

---

9 Ferretti, "Tartini e le Marche"; Durante, *Tartini*.
10 A score for Gasparini's 1720 setting survives, however it includes only arias. See Francesco Gasparini, "Faramondo," manuscript score, D-4340, Bibliothèque nationale de France, département Musique, https://imslp.org/wiki/Il_Faramondo_(Gasparini%2C_Francesco).
11 Claudio Sartori, *I libretti italiani a stampa dalle origini al 1800: Catalogo analitico con 16 indici*, 6 vols. (Cuneo: Bertola & Locatelli, 1990–1994).
12 Colleen Reardon, "Launching the Career of a Secondo Uomo in Late Seventeenth-Century Italy," *Journal of Seventeenth-Century Music* 16 no. 1 (2010), appendix, item 53, http://www.sscm-jscm.org/v16/no1/reardon.html.

information about Bernardi's career is not inconsistent with the possibility. After early performances in Siena and Florence, Giovanni Carlo worked in Palermo and Messina 1705–1713 but in 1715 he was back in Florence, and performed over the following 10 years across central and northern Italy, appearing at Livorno in 1716 (where he was described as "virtuoso of the Duke of Massa" ["virtuoso del duca di Massa"]), as well as in Massa, Rome, Genoa, Pesaro, Crema, Parma and Venice.[13] Sartori records no performances by him in 1714 but given his activity in central-northern Italy thereafter, his presence in Ancona during that season seems plausible. The fact that he appears to have made a long career primarily out of minor roles, including in casts in which his famous brother was the *primo uomo* (first man) also suggests that he was not a leading aria singer – perhaps meriting the description "mediocre castrato" – though perhaps nevertheless a good actor.

2 The Affective Power of Recitative: Composition, Performance, Listening

Although the current evidence does not allow us to identify with any certainty the opera, the composer or the singer to which Tartini was referring, we may still profitably consider how the dramatic effect that he described may have been created and its significance for him. How could a line of simple recitative – only voice and continuo without the resources of orchestration, regular melodic structure or metrical rhythm – have such affective power?

The immediate impression created by Tartini's account of the incident is that he understood the effect as entirely a compositional device: he described it as arising out of a conjunction of skill and luck through which the composer "was led by good sense and by the words, and at that point accidentally came upon the truth of nature".[14] He regretted not having recorded the example, yet he comments that "there is no rule or science for obtaining [the effect] with certainty when it is desired, and far less of continuing it for many movements or for any considerable time".[15] This seems contradictory: if the stimulus for his experience were purely a compositional device, presumably it *could* reliably be reproduced by copying the score. And his failure to do so when he had the chance, despite the impressive intensity of the experience, suggests that he did not think of it at the time as exclusively a compositional product. In addition, the fact that he appears not to have thought the name of the composer, librettist, or even the title of the opera significant enough to record publicly in the *Trattato di musica* again suggests that he may not have attributed the effect only to the musical composition of the passage.

Indeed, several clues suggest that he was conscious that other components of the experience were also essential to its powerful effect. The librettist's words

---

13 Sartori, *I libretti italiani*, Indici II, 80.
14 Johnson, "Tartini's Trattato," 344.
15 Slightly adapted from Johnson, "Tartini's Trattato," 343–344.

expressing indignation provided the vehicle for the musical setting and for the singer's delivery of it with voice and gesture, reinforced by the theatrical apparatus of costume and set design, props and lighting, while the audience, including the members of the orchestra, actively participated in anticipating and then enjoying the moment when it arrived. As Bettina Varwig has argued in relation to modern performances of historical music, "perceived expressiveness is necessarily embodied, or instantiated, through a set of human bodily actions".[16] What such an intensely embodied experience of the connection between composition, performance and "audiencing" felt like to an eighteenth-century sensibility is perhaps also captured by Johann Adolf Scheibe, who described musical expressivity as producing "in its listeners a motion which takes hold of the heart, bewitches the senses, freezes the blood and finally, upon recovery, induces wonder, thereupon reflection and ultimately a quiet sense of awe towards the infinite and eternal love of the Creator".[17]

In fact, listeners are central to the story. Like Scheibe's "freezing the blood", Tartini's feeling of "cold-blooded grimness", which "really shook one's feelings", was clearly an intensely physical experience. It seems likely to be related to the phenomenon that David Huron and Elizabeth Margulis call "music-induced frisson: the 'chills' or 'thrills' characterized by a sensation of the hair standing up on the back of one's neck, accompanied by sensations of coldness and pleasure", and perhaps goes beyond that to what Patrik Juslin characterizes as a "mixed emotions" response.[18]

How, then, might such intense experiences of musically induced emotions have been generated in performance? Even if the passage of recitative Tartini heard in Ancona may have struck him then as a miracle of composition, it surely depended substantially for its effect on the singer's flexible, emotive, vocal and gestural delivery of the line, aptly supported by the continuo players. At the very least, the interaction

---

16 Bettina Varwig, "Musical Expression: Lessons from the Eighteenth Century?" *Eighteenth Century Music* 17, no. 1 (2020): 60.
17 "[…] eine so nachdrückliche Erfindung zeiget, daß sie die Zuhörer auf das empfindlichste rühret, daß sie bey ihnen eine Bewegung verursachet, welche das Herz einnimmt, die Sinne bezaubert, das Geblüte erstarren macht, und wodurch endlich bey der Erholung eine Bewunderung, hieraus eine Ueberlegung, und endlich eine stille Ehrfurcht gegen die unendliche und ewige Liebe des Schöpfers entsteht". Johann A Scheibe, *Der Critische Musicus* (Leipzig: B. C. Breitkopf, 1745), 85, quoted (with translation) in Varwig, "Musical Expression," 68.
18 David Huron and Elizabeth Hellmuth Margulis, "Musical Expectancy and Thrills," in *Handbook of Music and Emotion: Theory, Research, and Applications*, ed. Patrik N. Juslin and John A. Sloboda (Oxford; New York: Oxford University Press, 2010), 576. Research on physiological and emotional responses to music from Charles Darwin to the present is discussed in Patrik N. Juslin, *Musical Emotions Explained: Unlocking the Secrets of Musical Affect* (Oxford: Oxford University Press, 2019); on "chills" see p. 217 ff; on "mixed emotions" responses, see p. 238–239.

between words and music was crucial to the effect and in this context, the fact that it was recitative rather than aria is particularly striking. It is in recitative that the words and their declamation are most foregrounded, and the musical composition ostensibly at its simplest. The fact that the compositional means in recitative are so limited – arguably as limited as anything in Western music apart from chant – suggests that delivery by both singer and continuo players must have been a significant element in the expressive effect. And in fact this impression is reinforced by Tartini's discussion, several pages further on in the *Trattato di musica*, of the importance for moving the passions of firstly, the conjunction of words and music, and secondly, flexibility of delivery, especially in relation to rhythm and timbre.

> When [human] discourse is joined to passion, the natural effect is (in accordance with the passion) greater and lesser inflection of the voice, greater and lesser sharpness and force of tone, greater and lesser prolongation of words and syllables, etc. When, in expressing a passion, one encounters a more significant word, this is spontaneously brought out more prominently than the others; hurriedly, if it expresses anger, prolonged, if of sadness etc., and so on in relation to all.[19]

Simple recitative, above all, exemplifies the truism that even an excellent composition can have a poor effect without good delivery; conversely, great delivery can raise an ordinary composition to be powerfully expressive. As Johann Joachim Quantz famously put it in his almost exactly contemporary *Versuch einer Anweisung die Flöte traversière zu spielen* (Essay on Playing the Transverse Flute),

> [t]he good effect of a piece of music depends almost as much upon the performer as upon the composer himself. The best composition may be marred by poor execution, just as a mediocre composition may be improved and enhanced by good execution.[20]

Even in the absence of a surviving score, contemporary sources can provide considerable information about the resources of rhetorical delivery that a skilled

---

19 "Quando questo [umano discorso] sia congiunto a passione, l'effetto naturale è (a ragguaglio della passione) maggior, e minore inflessione di voce; maggior, e minor acume, e forza di tuono; maggior, e minor prolungamento di parole, e sillabe ec. Nella espressione della passione s'incontra quella parola, che più significa: questa (e senza studio) si pone in maggior vista delle altre, affrettandola, se d'ira, prolungandola, se di mestizia ec., e così tutto a ragguaglio." Tartini, *Trattato di musica*, 139–140. Translation by the author, adapted from Johnson, "Tartini's Trattato," 357–358.
20 "Die gute Wirkung einer Musik hängt fast eben so viel von den Ausführern, als von dem Componisten selbst ab. Die beste Composition kann durch einen schlechten Vortrag verstümmelt, eine mittelmäßige Composition aber durch einen guten Vortrag verbessert, und erhoben werden." Johann Joachim Quantz, *Versuch einer Anweisung die Flöte traversière zu spielen* (Berlin: Johann Friedrich Voss, 1752; facs. ed., München: Deutscher Taschenbuch Verlag, 1992), 101. English translation in Johann Joachim Quantz, *On Playing the Flute*, trans. Edward R. Reilly (London: Faber and Faber, 1966), 119–120.

singer-actor would have been likely to deploy in creating the striking effect experienced in Ancona; some of these are discussed below. Like many of his contemporaries, however, Tartini also emphasized the need for the performer to personally feel the passions in order to convey them to the audience. After arguing in his Treatise that the expression of the passions will spontaneously disrupt a strictly metrical declamation of poetry, he continued,

> In simple narration the equality of motions can have a place, and in consequence the beat has strictness. But if the proposition is true, that *to move others one must be moved in oneself, (and I hold this to be true)* there are few narrations which according to nature can be regulated by equal motions, because few of them are entirely free of any passion.[21]

Certainly recitative, though often badly delivered, could have powerful effects when done well and some singers were noted as much for their recitative delivery as for their aria singing. For instance, Giambattista Mancini commented that the soprano Vittoria Tesi "by her voice alone, and her singing alone, however perfect this was, would never have acquired the celebrity which was hers, but for her sublime manner of declamation".[22] Later in the century the affecting recitative delivery of Gasparo Pachierotti was also particularly praised.[23]

What, then, of the singer who delivered the "words of indignation" with such "severity and cold-bloodedness that did indeed disturb the spirit"? If the 1715 *Tito Manlio* libretto resurfaces, or a yet unknown source for the 1714 Ancona season is discovered, the hypothesis that it was indeed Giovanni Carlo Bernardi might be tested further. In the meantime the most plausible hypothesis must remain that the gripping line was performed by Michele Selvatici, in *Faramondo*, set by Gasparini. It is perhaps surprising in this context that Selvatici spent much of his career specializing in buffo roles. Reinhard Strohm describes him as "an intermezzo specialist and thus probably a good actor",[24] and he was famous enough that a role appears to have been created especially for him to exhibit his comic powers in Alessandro

---

21 "Nella semplice narrazione può aver luogo la eguaglianza de' moti, e in conseguenza la battuta a rigore. Ma s'è vera la proposizione, che per muover altrui bisogna esser mosso in se stesso, (ed io la tengo per vera) poche saranno le narrazioni, che secondo natura possano esser regolate da moto eguale, perchè poche sono le affatto esenti da qualunque passione." Tartini, *Trattato di musica*, 140. English translation and emphasis by the author.
22 Giambattista Mancini, *Riflessioni pratiche sul canto figurato* (Milano: Giuseppe Galeazzi, 1777; facs. ed., Sala Bolognese: Arnaldo Forni, 1996), 29. English translation by the author.
23 Franz Haböck, *Die Kastraten und ihre Gesangskunst: Eine gesangsphysiologische, kultur- und musikhistorische Studie* (Berlin und Leipzig: Deutsche Verlags-Anstalt Stuttgart, 1927), 416 ff; Angus Heriot, *The Castrati in Opera* (London: Secker & Warburg, 1956), 163 ff.
24 Reinhard Strohm, *The Operas of Antonio Vivaldi* (Firenze: Leo S. Olschki, 2008), 348.

Scarlatti's *Telemaco* (Telemachus, Rome, 1718).[25] He also played many serious, if relatively minor "tenore" roles, however, and occasionally took on more substantial dramatic parts, such as when he appeared in the *secondo uomo* (second man) role of Teramene in *Il figlio delle selve* (The Son of the Forests, Florence, 1720).[26] Nevertheless, the role of Gustavo in *Faramondo* would have been one of the most prominent serious roles of his career.

A score for Gasparini's 1720 setting of *Faramondo* for Rome does survive, but it preserves only the arias, and therefore no musical setting of this scene which, as Tartini noted, was in simple recitative;[27] however, in the absence of a score for this scene, we can consider the libretto, which provides a sense of the kind of affect it may have conveyed.[28] As Durante has noted, the scene plays out the conflict of love and duty so common in opera libretti of this time. Rosimonda, who is in love with Faramondo, has set him free even though he is an enemy of the kingdom. Her father Gustavo persuades her to confess, and promises just retribution. Scenes similar to this appear in many such libretti, and we cannot be certain that this is the one to which Tartini was referring but certainly the words, particularly of the final two lines, are of anger and cold distain which would match Tartini's description.

Atto III	**Act III**
Scena Prima	**First Scene**
Galleria nel Palazzo di Villa.	**Gallery in the palace.**
Gustavo, e Rosimonda	*Gustavo and Rosimonda*
Gustavo: Tu, contumace al padre,	*Gustavo*: You, shunning your father,
al fratello spergiura,	deceiving your brother,
tu salvar Faramondo?	you save Faramondo?
Rosamonda: Ei s'era posto	*Rosamonda*: He put himself
volontario ne' ceppi.	voluntarily in fetters.
Gus: Anzi ve 'l trasse	*Gus*: Indeed, he was led to it
l'orror del suo delitto.	by the horror of his crime.
Te chi mosse a salvarlo?	Who moved you to save him?

---

25 Wendy Heller and Eleonora Stoppino, eds., *Performing Homer: The Voyage of Ulysses from Epic to Opera* (London: Taylor & Francis, 2019), 135.
26 Carlo Sigismondo Capece, *Il figlio delle selve*, libretto (Firenze: Anton Maria Albizzini, 1720).
27 In any case, the role of Gustavo was taken in Rome by the castrato Gaetano Berenstadt, for whom any pre-existing baritone recitatives would presumably have been rewritten. Sartori, *I libretti italiani*, 3:113.
28 Apostolo Zeno, *Faramondo drama per musica da rappresentarsi nel teatro della Fenice in Ancona il carnevale dell'anno 1714*, libretto (Ancona: Nicola Belelli, [1714]). A copy of this libretto is kept in the collection of Fondazione Giorgio Cini (collocazione: ROLANDI ROL.0717.02).

Ros: A lui non volli dover la mia vendetta.	*Ros*: I did not want to have to take my revenge on him.
Gus: Odio ch'è giusto, non ha tanti rispetti. Ah figlia, tu arrossisci richiesta, e colpevole se' di maggior fallo.	*Gus*: Hatred which is just does not consider such things. Ah, daughter, well may you blush; you are guilty of great fault.
Ros: Io, padre?	*Ros*: I, father?
Gus: A un vile affetto, senz'aver al tuo sangue, a' dèi patri, al mio sdegno alcun riguardo, consegnarti te stessa. Svela pur la tua colpa. Non la devi temer, se l'hai commessa.	*Gus*: To a base affection, without having regard for your blood, your ancestral gods, or my indignation, you surrender yourself. Reveal your fault, then. You must not fear to, if you have committed it.
Ros: Padre, un affetto è amore di noi più forte, e tu medesimo il sai. Nel suo poter discolpe pur non cerco al mio fallo. Amo, sì, Faramondo.	*Ros*: Father, love is an affection stronger than us, and you yourself know it. In its power it excuses, though I do not seek to do wrong. Yes, I love Faramondo.
Gus: E tanto ascolto?	*Gus*: What do I hear?
Ros: Ma l'amo da nemica, e da tua figlia.	*Ros*: But I love him as an enemy, and as your daughter.
Gus: Non dovea una mia figlia salvar mai Faramondo.	*Gus*: A daughter of mine should never have saved Faramondo.
Ros: Il voglio estinto.	*Ros*: I want him dead.
Gus: Ma libertà gli desti.	*Gus*: But you gave him freedom.
Ros: Per punirlo più giusta.	*Ros*: To punish him all the better.
Gus: Vattene; a me si aspetta di te far, e di lui giusta vendetta.	*Gus*: Begone! From me you can expect, on yourself and on him, just vengeance.[29]

If a singer who specialized in comic roles seems an unlikely candidate to have consistently delivered a line of such cold menace, Selvatici's buffo prowess suggests that he was a good actor, alive to the control of timing and vocal variation to convey emotion, and his continued casting in serious as well as comic roles suggests that he was versatile and able to deploy these skills in dramatic as well as comic situations.

3 Rhetorical Delivery

Important clues to the way this kind of expressive recitation was done by skilled actors can be found in sources on rhetoric and oratory which describe the use of

---

29 Libretto excerpt reproduced in Durante, *Tartini*, 21–22. English translation by the author.

the voice. Tartini was educated in rhetoric at the Scuole Pie ("Pious Schools") in Koper,[30] so it is not surprising that an understanding of communicative strategies grounded in classical rhetoric is reflected in his discussions of performance and expression throughout the *Trattato di musica*. The tenets of rhetorical delivery do not amount to a detailed method or "how-to" manual, but they do facilitate understanding of the principles which guided singers in managing those "intangible" vocal parameters of recitative that are not directly specified in the score, to create both variety and expression.

This requirement for variety of delivery, using variation of pacing, timbre, loudness and pitch to aptly project the meaning of the words, reflected the virtue of *decorum*, or appropriateness to the subject matter, one of the essential "virtues of delivery" defined by the Roman rhetorician Quintilian on the basis of his predecessor Cicero's four "virtues of style".[31]

For instance, according to Cicero,

> [t]here are as many variations in the tones of the voice as there are in feelings, which are especially aroused by the voice. Accordingly the perfect orator [...] will use certain tones according as he wishes to seem himself to be moved and to sway the minds of his audience [...][32]
>
> Anger requires the use of one kind of voice, high and sharp, excited, breaking off repeatedly [...] Lamentation and grief require another kind of voice, wavering in pitch, sonorous, halting, and tearful [...] Fear again has another kind of voice, subdued, hesitating, and downcast [...][33]

Apt and expressive variation was also advocated by Quintilian, who wrote:

> [W]hen we deal with a lively theme, the flow of the voice is characterised by fullness [...] but when it is roused to battle, it puts forth all its strength and strains every nerve. In anger it is fierce, harsh and intense [...] in flattery, admission, apology or question it will be gentle and subdued.[34]

---

30 Then known as Capodistria. Pierluigi Petrobelli, "Tartini, Giuseppe," in *Grove Music Online*, Oxford Music Online, accessed January 6, 2022, https://doi.org/10.1093/gmo/9781561592630.article.27529.
31 Alan Maddox, "The Rhetorical Virtues of Delivery and the Performance of Italian Recitative," in *Re-Visions: Proceedings of the 2010 Joint Conference of the MSA and NZMS*, ed. Marian Poole (Dunedin: New Zealand Music Industry Centre, University of Otago, 2012), 132–140.
32 Marcus Tullius Cicero, *Brutus, Orator*, trans. G. L. Hendrickson and H. M. Hubbell (London: W. Heinemann, 1962), xvii.55–56, 347.
33 Marcus Tullius Cicero, *On the Ideal Orator*, trans. James M. May and Jakob Wisse (New York: Oxford University Press, 2001), III.216–219, 292–293.
34 Marcus Fabius Quintilianus, *The Institutio Oratoria of Quintilian*, trans. H. E. Butler, 4 vols. (London: William Heinemann, 1920–1922), 341–342.

These principles were reproduced and paraphrased in many early modern rhetoric textbooks which were used by generations of Italian schoolboys from the sixteenth to the eighteenth centuries. For example, Jesuit schoolmaster Franciscus Lang noted in his 1727 treatise on acting:

> Care should be taken to vary the voice, so that it is used vigorously, then immediately mildly, now strongly, now softly, now precipitately, now calmly, according to what reason and nature seem to ask of one.[35]

The same principles are also reflected in the major treatises on singing of the eighteenth century, notably Pierfrancesco Tosi's *Opinioni de' cantori antichi, e moderni o sieno osservazioni sopra il canto figurato* (Opinions on Ancient and Modern Singers, or Observations on the Florid Song, 1723) and Giambattista Mancini's *Riflessioni pratiche sul canto figurato* (Practical Reflections on Figural Singing, 1777).[36] Tosi, in particular, highlighted the special qualities of theatrical recitative. Because of its intimate connection with acting, "the Master is obliged to teach the Scholar a certain natural Imitation, which cannot be beautiful if not expressed with that Decorum with which Princes speak, or those who know how to speak to Princes".[37] We should note here that declaiming with *decorum* does not necessarily imply a delivery that is "polite" or restrained. Princes may speak with vehement indignation like that described by Tartini when it is appropriate to the situation.

Mancini made the model of oratory explicit, advising aspiring singers to

> [l]isten to the speech of a good orator, and hear how many rests, what variety of tones, how many different emphases he uses to express its meanings. Now he raises

---

35 "Hunc in finem curanda est vocis immutatio, ut hæc subinde intensa, subinde remissa, jam fortis, jam lenis, jam præceps, jam lenta instituatur, prout ipsa ratio & natura videntur requirere. Utraque harum inspirat homini aliquem dicendi modum affectui conformem; qui si artis magisterio ritè perficiatur, sperandum, obtineri effectum posse, quem Actor intendit." Franciscus [Franz] Lang, *Dissertatio de actione scenica, cum Figuris eandem explicantibus, et Observationibus quibusdam de arte comica* (Monachii: Typis Mariae Magdalenae Riedlin, Viduae, 1727), 58. Translation by Adam Harris in Alan Maddox, "'On the Knowledge Necessary for One Who Wishes to Recite Well in the Theatre': The Rhetorical Tradition of Delivery and the Performance Practice of Recitativo Semplice in Eighteenth-Century Dramma Per Musica" (Ph.D., University of Sydney, 2006), 71.
36 Pierfrancesco Tosi, *Opinioni de'cantori antichi, e moderni o sieno osservazioni sopra il canto figurato* (Bologna: L. dalla Volpe, 1723). English edition as Pier Francesco Tosi, *Observations on the Florid Song, or, Sentiments on the Ancient and Modern Singers*, trans. Johann Ernest Galliard (London: J. Wilcox, 1743). Mancini, *Riflessioni*.
37 "[...] obbliga il Maestro d'istruir lo Scolaro d'una certa imitazione naturale, che non può esser bella se non è rappresentata con quel decoro col quale parlano i Principi, e quegli che a Principi sanno parlare." Tosi, *Opinioni*, 41. English translation by Galliard, in Tosi, *Observations*, 67.

his voice, now he lowers it; now he hurries a bit, now he grows harsh and now gentle, according to the various passions that he wishes to stir in the listener.[38] But expressive use of the voice is not sufficient in itself. Delivery was universally defined as consisting of the combination of voice and gesture. For instance, Cypriano Soarez, in his rhetoric textbook *De arte rhetorica* which was mandated throughout the Jesuit college system in the seventeenth and eighteenth centuries, introduced the topic of delivery as follows:

> Since [...] delivery has two elements, voice and gesture, one of which influences the eye and the other the ear – both senses through which all feeling enters the soul – we must first consider voice, and then gesture, the latter often being adapted to the voice.[39]

In this way, with skill and luck, the delivery of a line of simple recitative could be heightened far beyond the ordinary by the apt concurrence of words, music, vocal variation and gesture.

4 Conclusion

Tartini's views on vocal music and its performance practice and on the delivery of recitative, in particular, clearly reflect this rhetorical framework and reinforce the indications in sources on acting and singing that the best performers used a wide range of vocal timbre, flexible timing and contrasts of loud and soft to create genuinely thrilling dramatic moments. Even if the singer who performed the passage which so affected listeners in Ancona was, as Algarotti reported, a "mediocre castrato", or for that matter a *buffo* specialist such as Michele Selvatici, he may well have been a good actor and in the context of recitative, acting with voice and gesture is at least as important as sheer singing ability. If skilled delivery of even poor compositions could move the passions, where skilful recitation coincided with a composition which, even if accidentally, "came upon the truth of nature", how much more moving would such a performance have been!

---

38 "Attenti pure al discorso d'un buon Oratore, e sentire quante pose, quante varietà di voci, quante diverse forze adopra per esprimere i suoi sensi; ora innalza la voce, or l'abbassa, or l'affretta, or l'incrudisce, ed or la fa dolce, secondo le diverse passioni, che intende muovere nell'uditore." Mancini, *Riflessioni*, 220. English Translation by Wye J. Allanbrook in Leo Treitler, ed., *Strunk's Source Readings in Music History* (New York: Norton, 1998), 867.
39 Cipriano Soarez, *De arte rhetorica libri tres: Ex Aristotele, Cicerone, et Quintiliano praecipue deprompti* (Hispali: Ex officina Alphonsi Escriuani. Expensis Andreae Pescioni, 1569), 74r–74v. English translation in Lawrence Flynn, "The 'De Arte Rhetorica' (1568) by Cyprian Soarez, S. J.: A Translation with Introduction and Notes" (Ph.D., University of Florida, 1955), 425–426.

Studies of vocal performance practice, including for recitative as well as aria singing, may also provide insight into how a composer like Tartini understood the projection of affect to work in his instrumental compositions. For him, as a famous player and teacher, composition was after all the creation of performed, embodied sound, perhaps particularly in his "third period" when, in older age and perhaps in response to the *galant* sensibility of the mid-century, he settled on a style which was compositionally simpler but arguably musically and affectively more demanding than that of his heroic youth, when he played in the orchestra in Ancona.

Bibliography

Bucciarelli, Melania. "Senesino's Negotiations with the Royal Academy of Music: Further Insight into the Riva–Bernardi Correspondence and the Role of Singers in the Practice of Eighteenth-Century Opera." *Cambridge Opera Journal* 27, no. 3 (2015): 189–213.

Capece, Carlo Sigismondo. *Il figlio delle selve*. Libretto. Firenze: Anton Maria Albizzini, 1720.

Cicero, Marcus Tullius. *Brutus, Orator*. Translated by G. L. Hendrickson and H. M. Hubbell. London: W. Heinemann, 1962.

Cicero, Marcus Tullius. *Cicero on the Ideal Orator*. Translated by James M. May and Jakob Wisse. New York: Oxford University Press, 2001.

Durante, Sergio. "Tartini and his Texts." In *The Century of Bach and Mozart. Perspectives on Historiography, Composition, Theory and Performance*, edited by Sean Gallagher and Thomas Forrest Kelly, 145–186. Cambridge, MA: Harvard University Press, 2008.

Durante, Sergio. *Tartini, Padova, L'Europa*. Livorno: Sillabe, 2018.

Felici, Candida. "'Non suona, canta su'l violino': From Aesthetics to Compositional and Performance Practice in Tartini's Instrumental Music." *Ad Parnassum* 11, no. 22 (2013): 127–141.

Ferretti, Luca. "Giuseppe Tartini e le Marche: Primi risultati di una ricerca." In *Tartini, il tempo e le opere*, edited by Andrea Bombi and Maria Nevilla Massaro, 37–65. Bologna: Il Mulino, 1994.

Flynn, Lawrence. "The 'De Arte Rhetorica' (1568) by Cyprian Soarez, S. J.: A Translation with Introduction and Notes." Ph.D., University of Florida, 1955.

Gasparini, Francesco. "Faramondo." Manuscript score, D-4340. Bibliothèque nationale de France, département Musique. Accessed October 16, 2020. https://imslp.org/wiki/Il_Faramondo_(Gasparini%2C_Francesco).

Haböck, Franz. *Die Kastraten und ihre Gesangskunst: Eine gesangsphysiologische, kultur- und musikhistorische Studie*. Berlin und Leipzig: Deutsche Verlags-Anstalt Stuttgart, 1927.

Heller, Wendy, and Eleonora Stoppino, eds. *Performing Homer: The Voyage of Ulysses from Epic to Opera*. London: Taylor & Francis, 2019.

Heriot, Angus. *The Castrati in Opera*. London: Secker & Warburg, 1956.

Huron, David, and Elizabeth Hellmuth Margulis. "Musical Expectancy and Thrills." In *Handbook of Music and Emotion: Theory, Research, and Applications*, edited by Patrik N. Juslin and John A. Sloboda, 575–604. Oxford; New York: Oxford University Press, 2010.

Johnson, Fredric Bolan. "Tartini's Trattato di musica seconda la vera scienza dell'armonia: An Annotated Translation with Commentary." Doctoral dissertation, Indiana University, 1985.

Juslin, Patrik N. *Musical Emotions Explained: Unlocking the Secrets of Musical Affect*. Oxford: Oxford University Press, 2019. doi:10.1093/oso/9780198753421.001.0001.

Lang, Franciscus [Franz]. *Dissertatio de actione scenica, cum Figuris eandem explicantibus, et Observationibus quibusdam de arte comica*. Monachii: Typis Mariae Magdalenae Riedlin, Viduae, 1727.

Maddox, Alan. "'On the Knowledge Necessary for One Who Wishes to Recite Well in the Theatre': The Rhetorical Tradition of Delivery and the Performance Practice of Recitativo Semplice in Eighteenth-Century Dramma Per Musica." Ph.D., University of Sydney, 2006.

Maddox, Alan. "The Rhetorical Virtues of Delivery and the Performance of Italian Recitative." In *Re-Visions: Proceedings of the 2010 Joint Conference of the MSA and NZMS*, edited by Marian Poole, 132–140. Dunedin: New Zealand Music Industry Centre, University of Otago, 2012.

Mancini, Giambattista. *Riflessioni pratiche sul canto figurato*. Milano: Giuseppe Galeazzi, 1777; facsimile edition, Sala Bolognese: Arnaldo Forni, 1996.

Petrobelli, Pierluigi. "Tartini, Giuseppe." In *Grove Music Online*. Oxford Music Online. Accessed January 6, 2022. https://doi.org/10.1093/gmo/9781561592630.article.27529.

Polzonetti, Pierpaolo. *Tartini e la musica secondo natura*. Lucca: LIM, 2001.

Quantz, Johann Joachim. *On Playing the Flute*. Translated by Edward R. Reilly. London: Faber and Faber, 1966.

Quantz, Johann Joachim. *Versuch einer Anweisung die Flöte traversière zu spielen*. Berlin: Johann Friedrich Voss, 1752; facsimile edition, München: Deutscher Taschenbuch Verlag, 1992.

Quintilianus, Marcus Fabius. *The Institutio Oratoria of Quintilian*. Translated by H. E. Butler. 4 vols. London: William Heinemann, 1920–1922.

Reardon, Colleen. "Launching the Career of a Secondo Uomo in Late Seventeenth-Century Italy." *Journal of Seventeenth-Century Music* 16, no. 1

(2010). Accessed October 23, 2020. http://www.sscm-jscm.org/v16/no1/rear don.html.

Sartori, Claudio. *I libretti italiani a stampa dalle origini al 1800: Catalogo analitico con 16 indici.* 6 vols. Cuneo: Bertola & Locatelli, 1990–1994.

Scheibe, Johann A. *Der Critische Musicus.* Leipzig: B. C. Breitkopf, 1745.

Soarez, Cipriano. *De arte rhetorica libri tres: ex Aristotele, Cicerone, et Quintiliano praecipue deprompti.* Hispali: Ex officina Alphonsi Escriuani. Expensis Andreae Pescioni, 1569.

Strohm, Reinhard. *The Operas of Antonio Vivaldi.* Firenze: Leo S. Olschki, 2008.

Tartini, Giuseppe. *Trattato di musica secondo la vera scienza dell'armonia.* Padova: Stamperia del Seminario, 1754; facsimile edition, New York: Broude Brothers, 1966.

Tosi, Pier Francesco. *Observations on the Florid Song, or, Sentiments on the Ancient and Modern Singers.* Translated by Johann Ernest Galliard. London: J. Wilcox, 1743.

Tosi, Pier Francesco. *Opinioni de'cantori antichi, e moderni o sieno osservazioni sopra il canto figurato.* Bologna: L. dalla Volpe, 1723.

Treitler, Leo, ed., *Strunk's Source Readings in Music History.* New York: Norton, 1998.

Varwig, Bettina. "Musical Expression: Lessons from the Eighteenth Century?" *Eighteenth Century Music* 17, no. 1 (2020): 53–72.

Wilk, Piotr. "Poetical Mottos in Tartini's Concertos – the Latest Concordances and Questions." *Musica Iagellonica* 9 (2018): 81–100.

Zattarin, Alessandro. "'Vidi in sogno un guerrier': Tasso, Metastasio e altri fantasmi nelle sonate a violino solo di Giuseppe Tartini." *Ad Parnassum* 11, no. 22 (2013): 143–160.

Zeno, Apostolo. *Faramondo. Drama per musica da rappresentarsi nel teatro della fenice in Ancona il carnevale dell'anno 1714.* Libretto. Ancona: Nicola Belelli, [1714].

In Search of Perfect Harmony in Musical Thought: Tartini's Theory and Beyond

Nejc Sukljan

University of Ljubljana

Tartini and the Ancients: Traces of Ancient Music Theory in the Tartini–Martini Correspondence

Abstract: This chapter discusses various questions of music theory in the correspondence between Giuseppe Tartini (1692–1770) and Giovanni Battista Martini (1706–1784). After a general presentation of the correspondence, three groups of letters are discussed: (1) Letters from the early 1730s, in which Tartini presents his proposal for a tonal system and is critical of earlier authors, especially Zarlino. (2) Letters from the early 1750s discussing the manuscript treatise *Quadratura del circolo*, in which Tartini attempts to solve the ancient problem of squaring the circle with the means of physical harmonic science. (3) Late letters in which Tartini approaches the metaphysical and mainly discusses Plato's famous dialogue *Timaeus*.

Keywords: Tartini, Martini, Zarlino, music theory, tone systems, history of science

In the famous engraving by Carlo Calcinotto from 1761 (made after a drawing by Vincenzo Rota), Tartini is depicted with several objects that indicate the maestro's main interests and models. Besides a violin resting on a Corelli score, there are books by Plato and Zarlino (see Figure 1). These items not only confirm the well-known fact that Tartini was a man of many interests and qualities but also suggest that he was interested in ancient music theory and perhaps even made it the model for his own theorems. As is commonly known, Pythagorean-Platonic musical thought formed one of the most important ancient theoretical traditions; meanwhile Gioseffo Zarlino (c. 1520–1590), the leading Italian music theorist of the sixteenth century, largely adopted the ancient models and made them a cornerstone on which he built his own theoretical system, which he set out in detail in his famous treatise *Istitutioni harmoniche* (Harmonic Institutions, 1558).

Figure 1: Calcinotto's engraving of Tartini's portrait. (*Https://it.wikipedia.org/wiki/ Giuseppe_Tartini#/media/File:Giuseppe_Tartini.jpg.*)

Tartini, however, formed his music-theoretical views not only through the private study of theoretical and philosophical treatises but also by discussing many of his theoretical concepts and hypotheses in a lively correspondence with some of the most prominent contemporary European scientists and humanists, with whom he formed a kind of personal informal scientific academy. In this respect, the correspondence with the well-known composer, theorist, historian and erudite Giovanni Battista Martini (1706–1784) seems to be of particular importance, as the extant letters date from the early 1730s to the late 1760s, thus allowing us to trace the flow of Tartini's theoretical thought over a longer period of time. Now a wider audience has the opportunity to study Tartini's letters, thanks to a recently published edition with Slovenian and English translations.[1]

Given the framework just outlined, several questions can be posed about the role of the ancient theoretical tradition in the letters between Tartini and Martini: What is ancient music theory in the correspondence between Tartini and Martini, and how does it manifest itself? With what aim and in what way does Tartini take it up? How does he represent it, how does he use it, and what does he ultimately derive from it?

1 The Letters

The correspondence with Martini undoubtedly occupies an important place within the extant epistolary of Tartini.[2] If we consider only the letters written by Tartini (excluding the extant answers), they are 196, of which 91 were written to Martini. With 46.4 %, this group has by far the largest share, compared to the second largest group of "only" 26 letters Tartini wrote to the music theorist and mathematician Count Giordano Riccati (1709–1790) with a share of 13.2 %. On the one hand, these figures may not tell us much, since we do not know how many letters may have been lost or are still waiting to be found in some archive. On the other hand, however, these letters undoubtedly are of great importance, especially in view of the fact that the two men exchanged them over quite a long period, which is not the case with any of the other known correspondents with whom Tartini discussed his theoretical concepts. The fact that the group of letters Tartini wrote to Martini is the one that has survived in such large numbers should not surprise us: Martini was a historian who was used to handling and archiving documents.

---

1 Giorgia Malagò, ed., *Giuseppe Tartini: Lettere e documenti/Pisma in dokumenti/Letters and Documents*, 2 vols., trans. Jerneja Umer Kljun and Roberto Baldo (Trieste: Edizioni Università di Trieste, 2020).
2 The "extant epistolary of Tartini" refers to the letters published in the above-mentioned edition by Giorgia Malagò and to those edited by Luca Del Fra. See Luca Del Fra, ed., *Commercio di lettere intorno ai Principj dell'Armonia fra il Signor Giuseppe Tartini; ed il Co. Giordano Riccati* (Lucca: LIM, 2007). The complete list is included in Malagò, *Tartini: Lettere*, 2:483–503.

The contents of Tartini's letters to Martini cover various topics. In general, they can be divided into "personal" and "professional" (although many of them could easily be assigned to both of these categories). Most of the personal letters are about various favours: Tartini asks for or sends all kinds of goods, e.g. chocolate, sausages, ladies' stockings, tobacco and even money, which indicates that he must have had at least some kind of trusting if not close relationship with Martini.[3] In the professional letters, Tartini writes about students, lessons, compositions, treatises and – for the most part – theoretical topics. Mostly, these topics are only mentioned in passing and not really discussed: Tartini often asks Martini, for example, whether he and the mathematician Paolo Battista Balbi (1693–1772) had already had the opportunity to study the texts he sent them.[4] Finally, there is a group of about 15 letters in which theoretical questions are discussed in detail. These letters will be the focus of this chapter, as they offer a fair insight into Tartini's theoretical thought.

Given that Tartini and Martini corresponded for about 40 years, it is not surprising that Tartini's theoretical thought would evolve. Consequently, the discussed letters could be further divided into three groups:

(1) The letters from the early 1730s (no. 5 in the Malagò edition).[5]
(2) The letters from the early 1750s (nos. 83, 85, 93, 94, 96–102, 105 in the Malagò edition).[6]
(3) The letters from the late 1760s (nos. 172, 175, 176 in the Malagò edition).[7]

2 Early Letters to Martini: Building a System

Although the first surviving letter from Tartini to Martini is dated 10 December 1730,[8] it is clear from its contents that the two musicians had already been corresponding for some time. It is also evident that Tartini had already been studying the field of music theory in depth and had even attempted to construct a system of his own, the discussion of which seems to be the main subject of this letter. In his answers to Martini's questions (*difficoltà*), Tartini criticizes both the ancient theoretical tradition and modern theoretical views. In addition to mentioning some other authors, he refers directly to Gioseffo Zarlino, and an attentive reader might get the impression that he could have become acquainted with the ancient theorems in question precisely through Zarlino's *Istitutioni*.

---

3 For example, letters nos. 13–15, 33 and 77 in Malagò edition. Malagò, *Tartini: Lettere*, 2:271–273, 288, 332–333.
4 For example, letters nos. 75, 76 and 79 in Malagò edition. Malagò, *Tartini: Lettere*, 2:331–332, 334–335.
5 Malagò, *Tartini: Lettere*, 2:256–264.
6 Malagò, *Tartini: Lettere*, 2:338–342, 350–357, 359–376, 380–383.
7 Malagò, *Tartini: Lettere*, 2:455, 456, 459–461.
8 Malagò, *Tartini: Lettere*, 2:256.

The tuning question (i.e. the theoretical construction of an acoustic system within which practical music exists) is one of the main themes in Zarlino's treatise. Instead of the Pythagorean system, which he believed had been used in the past[9] and was based on perfect consonances whose ratios could be described by the first four numbers,[10] Zarlino advocated a system based on Ptolemy's syntonic diatonic tetrachord (see Musical example 1).[11]

$$16:15 \quad 9:8 \quad 10:9$$

Musical example 1: Ptolemy's syntonic diatonic tetrachord.

According to Zarlino, of all the ancient tetrachords, only Ptolemy's syntonic diatonic is suitable, since it was created by nature and is based on true harmonic numbers (*veri numeri armonici*) derived from the system of the *senario*;[12] consequently, it is the only one that contains perfect harmony.[13] The latter is also confirmed by the division of the octave, which according to Zarlino is the principle

---

9 Gioseffo Zarlino, *Istituzioni armoniche*, ed. Silvia Urbani (Treviso: Diastema, 2011), 190.
10 Double octave (4:1), octave plus fifth (3:1), octave (2:1), fifth (3:2), and fourth (4:3). For a more detailed description of the Pythagorean system, see André Barbera, "Pythagoras," in *Grove Music Online*, Oxford Music Online, accessed January 8, 2022, https://doi.org/10.1093/gmo/9781561592630.article.22603; Mark Lindley, "Pythagorean Intonation," in *Grove Music Online*, Oxford Music Online, accessed January 8, 2022, https://doi.org/10.1093/gmo/9781561592630.article.22604.
11 Ptolemy (second century AD) presented various species of tetrachords in Chapters 12–16 of his *Harmonika* (Harmonics). See Andrew Barker, *Greek Musical Writings II: Harmonic and Acoustic Theory* (Cambridge: Cambridge University Press, 1989), 301–314.
12 As is well known, Zarlino in *Istitutioni* also defines thirds and sixths as consonant intervals (albeit imperfect) in addition to the Pythagorean consonances. However, the thirds and sixths did not sound good in the Pythagorean system since their ratios are quite complex (32:27, 81:64, 128:81, and 27:16). Therefore, instead of number four (*numero quaternario*), Zarlino advocates the importance of number six (*numero senario*). In addition to the ratios of perfect consonances, from the first six numbers the simpler ratios of better-sounding major (5:4) and minor (6:5) third and major sixth (5:3) can be derived. Since the ratio of minor sixth (8:5), which was also considered to be consonant, remains outside the first six numbers, along with the number six, Zarlino also argues for the importance of number eight. For a more detailed description of the *senario* see Nejc Sukljan, "Renaissance Music between Science and Art: The Case of Gioseffo Zarlino," *Muzikološki zbornik/Musicological Annual* 56, no. 2 (2020): 183–206, 10.4312/mz.56.2.183-206.
13 Zarlino, *Istituzioni armoniche*, 230–233, 255.

of all other intervals,[14] into seven parts (tones) by means of the harmonic mean:[15] Let us divide an octave between two strings, A and B. First we divide the given octave (2:1) harmonically with the string C into fifth (3:2) and fourth (4:3).[16] We must now take the larger of the obtained parts (the fifth) and divide it further: if we tried to harmonically divide the fourth, the terms of the resulting intervals would not belong to the numbers of the *senario*, warns Zarlino.[17] Therefore, the resulting fifth must be further divided harmonically with the string D to obtain the ratios of the two-thirds, major (5:4) and minor (6:5).[18] The resulting thirds are exactly those found in the tones of the syntonic diatonic tetrachord.[19] Next, the major third must

---

14 Zarlino believed that smaller intervals are a product of the division of larger intervals and not vice versa. See, for example, Zarlino, *Istituzioni armoniche*, 295–297, 313–316.
15 Zarlino, *Istituzioni armoniche*, 255–259. In the *Istitutioni*, an interval is defined as the distance between two different tones, lower and higher. Mathematically speaking, these distances are expressed by numerical ratios, but not by any ratios, only by *unequal ratios of comparison of the larger with the smaller, which are closer to simplicity*, explains Zarlino. (See Zarlino, *Istituzioni armoniche*, 81–83, 185, 300–305.) Because intervals are expressed by numerical ratios, they are inevitably subject to all of their laws, including the arithmetic operations between them. And since they are divided the same way as ratios, their division can generally be irrational (musical science does not deal with this) or rational, and the latter can be arithmetic, geometric or harmonic. (See Zarlino, *Istituzioni armoniche*, 207–208.) Actually, the division of a given interval determines the arithmetic, geometric or harmonic mean of the ratio by which the divided interval is expressed; the mathematical formula for the harmonic mean is $m = \dfrac{2xy}{x+y}$.
16 The aim is to find the harmonic mean of the ratio 2:1 (transformed into 6:3 to avoid fractions), which is 6:4:3, and to derive from this result the ratios of fifth (6:4 = 3:2) and fourth (4:3).
17 The harmonic mean of the ratio 4:3 (transformed into 28:21 to avoid fractions) is 28:24:21, from which the ratios 7:6 (28:24) and 8:7 (24:21) can be derived; these ratios are not found in the syntonic diatonic intervals, since there is no number 7 among the numbers of the *senario*.
18 The aim is to find the harmonic mean of the ratio 3:2 (transformed into 15:10 to avoid fractions), which is 15:12:10, and to derive from this result the ratios of major third (15:12 = 5:4) and minor third (12:10 = 6:5).
19 The major third is composed of the major tone (9:8) and the minor tone (10:9): $\dfrac{9}{8} \times \dfrac{10}{9} = \dfrac{5}{4}$. The minor third is composed of the major tone (9:8) and the semitone (16:15): $\dfrac{9}{8} \times \dfrac{16}{15} = \dfrac{6}{5}$.

be divided harmonically with the string E to obtain the ratios of major tone (9:8) and minor tone (10:9);[20] see the Musical example 2.

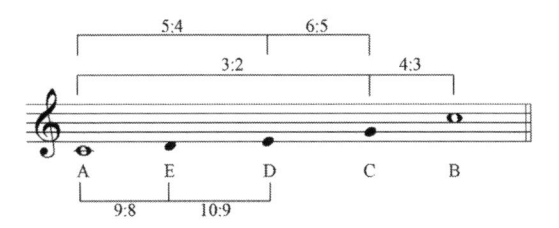

Musical example 2: The harmonic division of the octave: fifth, fourth, thirds, tones.

At this stage of the division, we encounter a problem: the major semitone (16:15) cannot be obtained by harmonic division. Zarlino tries to solve the problem by dividing the original octave AB again, but this time with the arithmetic mean instead of the harmonic mean; the result is the string F, which divides the octave into a fourth and a fifth.[21] The resulting tone falls between the tones of the minor third DC, dividing it into two parts, the major semitone DF (16:15) and the major tone FC (9:8). The next step, Zarlino continues, is to place the tone G a fourth above the string D. This new tone will divide the fourth CB into CG (10:9) and GB (6:5) and at the same time a major sixth (5:3) will be formed between AG. Finally, a tone H must be placed a fifth above D and the octave is divided into seven intervals, according to the nature of the harmonic numbers: three major tones (AE, FC, GH), two minor tones (ED, CG) and two major semitones (DF, HB). In addition, a syntonic diatonic tetrachord is formed between the tones DFCG. Since all intervals in Ptolemy's syntonic diatonic tetrachord are obtained by the harmonic division of the octave, Zarlino concludes that the tetrachord itself is in accordance with the nature of harmonic numbers. The final result of the procedure is shown in Musical example 3.

---

20 The aim is to find the harmonic mean of the ratio 5:4 (transformed into 45:36 to avoid fractions), which is 45:40:36, and to derive from this result the ratios of major tone (45:40 = 9:8) and minor tone (40:36 = 10:9).

21 The mathematical formula of the arithmetic mean is $m = \dfrac{x+y}{2}$. The aim is to find the arithmetic mean of the ratio 2:1 (transformed into 4:2 to avoid fractions), which is 4:3:2, and to derive from this result the ratios of fourth (4:3) and fifth (3:2). Therefore, the octave is divided into fourth + fifth, instead of fifth + fourth, as was the case when it was divided by the harmonic mean.

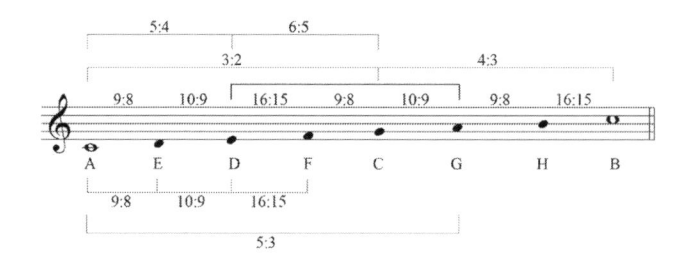

Musical example 3: The division of the syntonic diatonic octave.

Zarlino's advocacy of the perfection of the syntonic diatonic system and the intervals within it is purely speculative. He uses the mathematical tool of the harmonic mean but quickly encounters problems: some of the intervals cannot be obtained by harmonic division, including the major semitone (16:15), which is part of the very core of the system, the syntonic diatonic tetrachord. Zarlino is aware of this and draws attention to the problem, but he does not believe that this undermines his argument. The result – though not entirely correct – is clear: the syntonic diatonic system is perfect because its intervals are the result of the harmonic division of the octave and because the terms of their ratios are among the true harmonic numbers of the *senario*. Consequently, perfect harmony can only be achieved in this system.

Like Zarlino, Tartini wanted his system to reflect some kind of a firm natural order. And like Zarlino, he believed that the octave was the first and most important interval and the principle of all the others.[22] But unlike Zarlino, he did not divide it by the harmonic mean to prove the perfection of the syntonic diatonic system. In fact, in his letter to Martini, he rejected this system completely. One of his main arguments was that the old (Zarlino's) system did not correspond to the – natural order.[23]

At the beginning of his discussion of the system, Tartini is harsh: "The ancient system never knew the true division of tones."[24] With this he refers to the problem of the division of the major tone in the ratio of 9:8, which Zarlino encountered in his harmonic division of the octave: Tartini wonders why, after dividing the major third (5:4) into the major tone (9:8) and the minor tone (10:9), the former was not divided, even though the "reason then would want one to take (when continuing to divide) the greater proportion of the ditone".[25] He suggests that the major tone,

---

22 Malagò, *Tartini: Lettere*, 2:261–263.
23 Malagò, *Tartini: Lettere*, 2:259–260.
24 "Il sistema antico non ha mai conosciuto la vera radical divisione de'tuoni." Malagò, *Tartini: Lettere*, 1:117. English translation in Malagò, *Tartini: Lettere*, 2:257.
25 "La raggione dunque voleva che si prendesse (seguitando a dividere) la proporzione maggiore del ditono [...]" Malagò, *Tartini: Lettere*, 1:118. English translation in Malagò, *Tartini: Lettere*, 2:258.

like all other intervals, could simply be divided into two semitones, major (17:16) and minor (18:17).[26] Tartini goes on to discuss an even greater problem: the ancient system did not follow the natural order of number (*l'ordine naturale del numero*), which is completely opposite to the order in the syntonic diatonic tetrachord (16:15, 9:8, 10:9).[27] Tartini is clear:

> Number requires that after 10, 11 follows, and after that 12. And if until 10 we have counted correctly: 1, 2, 3, 4, 5, 6, 7, 8, 9, 10, what reason for continuing obliges us to prefer the above order, and instead of counting 10, 11, 12, 13, 14, 15, 16, to decide to count inappropriately 16:15 9:8:10:9:8 16:15 and to do that arbitrarily, for no reason, and, what is worse, repeating those same proportions that nature avoids repeating as the enemy of the superfluous?[28]

Tartini therefore argues for a new system that follows "the natural order of the number and the necessity of nature, which leads imperceptibly from the more to the less by degrees that are certain and fixed in their quantity".[29] Instead of the traditional series of tetrachords, Tartini's system is based on a series of octaves in double ratios: 1:2:4:8:16. These octaves are then divided simply by inserting the missing natural numbers between the terms of their ratios, thus achieving the desired natural order with fixed quantities: "The first duple 1/2 is indivisible. The second duple 2/4 is divisible by 3, but is perfected in the 4. The third 4/8 is divisible by 5, 6, 7, but ends and is perfected in the 8, and so on for all the others."[30]

---

26 According to Tartini, in order to divide the major tone (9:8) into two semitones, major (17:16) and minor (18:17), the terms of the original ratio would first have to be doubled into 18:16, and then the number 17 could be inserted in between them (18:17:16). Malagò, *Tartini: Lettere*, 2:257. It is clear that this solution was out of the question for Zarlino for two reasons: (1) the number 17 cannot be obtained by a harmonic mean (which is approximately 16.94); (2) 16:15 semitone was needed to fit into the syntonic diatonic system.
27 Malagò, *Tartini: Lettere*, 2:259.
28 "Il numero vuole che dopo il 10 segua l'11, e dopo questo il 12. E se sino al 10 abbiamo contato giustamente: 1, 2, 3, 4, 5, 6, 7, 8, 9, 10 qual raggione per proseguire ci obbliga a preferire il suddetto ordine, e invece di contare, 10, 11, 12, 13, 14, 15, 16, voler contare a sproposito, 16:15 9:8: 10:9:8 16:15 e ciò per puro arbitrio, non per alcuna raggione, e quel ch'è peggio, replicando quelle stesse proporzioni, che la natura fugge di replicare, come nemica del superfluo?" Malagò, *Tartini: Lettere*, 1:119. English translation in Malagò, *Tartini: Lettere*, 2:259.
29 "[...] l'ordine naturale del numero, e la necessità della natura, che conduce insensibilmente dal più al meno per gradi certi, e determinati nella quantità." Malagò, *Tartini: Lettere*, 1:119. English translation in Malagò, *Tartini: Lettere*, 2:259.
30 "La prima dupla 1/2 è indivisibile. La seconda dupla 2/4 è divisibile da 3, ma si perfeziona nel 4. La terza 4/8 è divisibile dal 5, 6, 7, ma termina e si perfeziona nell'8, e così di tutte le altre." Malagò, *Tartini: Lettere*, 1:120. English translation in Malagò, *Tartini: Lettere*, 2:260.

The system obtained from this division is actually the overtone series (see Musical example 4), although Tartini did not understand it that way at all.[31]

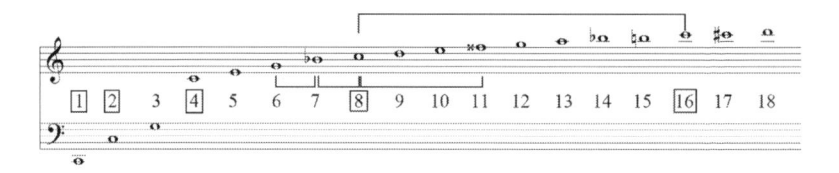

Musical example 4: Tartini's system.

It is clear that the ratios between the tones in the octave c″–c‴ follow the series of natural numbers: 8:9, 9:10, 10:11, 11:12, 12:13, 13:14, 14:15, 15:16. Although both Tartini and Zarlino constructed their systems according to the criterion of *nature*, there are obviously significant differences between them. A comparison between the two octave systems and the modern equal temperament is shown in Table 1, which also gives the size of the intervals in cents.

Table 1: Comparison between the systems of Zarlino, Tartini, and the modern system.

Interval	Zarlino (ratios)	Zarlino (cents)	Tartini (ratios)	Tartini (cents)	Modern (cents)
c–d	9:8	203,89	8:9	203,89	200
d–e	10:9	182,39	9:10	182,39	200
e–f	16:15	111,72	10:11	164,99	100
f–g	9:8	203,89	11:12	150,63	200
g–a	10:9	182,39	12:13	138,56	200
a–b flat	–	–	13:14	128,29	100
b flat–b	–	–	14:15	119,43	100
a–b	9:8	203,89	13:15	247,72	200
b–c	16:15	111,72	15:16	111,72	100

---

31 It would be wrong to think that while Zarlino's ratios referred to the parts of the string, Tartini (in this letter to Martini) used them to denote the vibrations of the string (frequency). He too divided a single monochord string into parts, but he did so by a different method: instead of dividing it traditionally according to the ratios of the individual intervals, he divided it according to harmonic progression (1, 1/2, 1/3, 1/4, 1/5, etc.) and thus obtained the ratios of his "natural" scale (1:2, 2:3, 3:4, 4:5, etc.). See Malagò, *Tartini: Lettere*, 2:261–262, 264.

It is hard to imagine Tartini's system actually being used in practice,[32] although he advocates it as such: "For the practical aspect there is the correct understanding of the placing of the notes when we want them to create the best harmony between them, whether they be consonances or dissonances. [...] There is a better understanding about modulations, and many other things which we shall see."[33] Of these things, he first draws attention to the ratios of 6:7 and 7:8, which, according to him, are "true and legitimate consonances unknown to both Greeks and Latins, and even less known to those Italians who referred back to the Greek institution. In Nature nothing is superfluous and missing."[34] Then the fact is highlighted that the natural scale (*fatta della natura*) comprises nine tones, one more than the traditional scale, which is consequently faulty. Finally, Tartini lists the differences between the ratios of the individual tones and particularly emphasizes the fourth in the ratio 11:8 between the first and fourth tone: with this ratio, nature clearly shows us that this interval is dissonant and should not be used, whereas in the ordinary system the dissonance of the fourth in the ratio 4:3 is not so clear.[35]

Conforming to the postulates of the Enlightenment, Tartini also wants to confirm his theoretical findings with practical proof. In fact, one of his main arguments against the existing system is that it is completely incompatible with the rules of physical nature (*la natura fisica è affatto contraria*). He therefore proposes to Martini to carry out a simple experiment with weights to confirm the order of his system.[36] He also refers to various *natural* instruments, namely trumpet marine, hunting horn and trumpet, which only operate according to the laws of nature and clearly advocate the validity of his system.[37]

3 Letters from the 1750s: Squaring the Circle

It seems that in the following years, in the 1730s, Tartini devoted himself to an even deeper theoretical study. He reported the results of this study in a letter to Balbi, dated 14 April 1741:

---

32 This was also emphasized by some *Signori Maestri* who, together with Martini, must have studied Tartini's system. Tartini contradicts them by saying that even if the purpose of his system were mere speculation, it would still be useful, but in this case the system is also useful in practice. See Malagò, *Tartini: Lettere*, 2:260.
33 "Vi è per la prattica la retta cognizione del sito delle note quando vogliamo che facciano la meglior armonia tra loro, siano le consonanti, o le dissonanti. [...] Vi è meglior cognizione per le modulazioni, e molte altre cose, che andremo vedendo." Malagò, *Tartini: Lettere*, 1:120. English translation in Malagò, *Tartini: Lettere*, 2:260.
34 "[...] vere e legitime consonanze non conosciute né da Greci, né da Latini, e molto meno da quegli italiani, che si sono riportati alla istituzione greca. La natura non fa cos'alcuna di superfluo, o di mancante." Malagò, *Tartini: Lettere*, 1:122. English translation in Malagò, *Tartini: Lettere*, 2:263.
35 Malagò, *Tartini: Lettere*, 2:263–264.
36 Malagò, *Tartini: Lettere*, 2:259–260.
37 Malagò, *Tartini: Lettere*, 2:256–257, 260.

Led on by my fortunate simplicity of thought, infinitely helped by the harmonic science, into which no great man has until now considered immersing himself, although in it alone the key of nature is to be found, I have discovered many phenomena and much physical proof; enlightened by these and led from music in universal physical nature, I have clearly seen the solution to all those difficulties that have hitherto been unsolvable for mathematicians; and these are all the immeasurables made measurable by means of a common measure, be it the diagonals, be it the squaring of the circle, the law of falling bodies, forces, resistance, etc. The nature of continuous, the nature of centres, and in a word the measure of one as one: something that seems contradictory but which is absolutely true, as we are dealing with demonstrations and physical proof. All of this stems from the discovery of a most evident error, in the first mathematical elements, hitherto believed to be undisputable truth, and an error of such importance that there is no greater. The geometric progression is wrong. May this be sufficient for you to grasp the importance of the error. [...]
I have proposed this discovery to the Académie Royale of Paris, if I shall be sufficiently rewarded. I am waiting for the reply to come soon, but then things will be quite complicated because, given that I do not know the terms of the mathematical sciences, I shall not be able to express myself if not in my own way. [...] What does Your Most Illustrious Lordship say to me on the matter? Could it happen that your customary devotion to St Anthony could receive an effective inducement from what I'm writing to you, sufficient for you to come here for eight or ten days [...]?[38]

Apparently, in the early 1740s, Tartini was convinced that he had made some very important discoveries, and he asks Balbi to help him present them appropriately. He speaks of a new kind of science, harmonic science, which enabled him to

---

38 "Condotto a mano dalla mia fortunata semplicità di pensare, aiutato infinitamente dalla scienza armonica, in cui sinora niun uomo grande si è degnato internarsi, sebben in essa solamente vi e la chiave della natura, ho scoperto molti fenomeni e fisiche demostrazioni, dalle quali illuminato, e dalla musica portato nella natura fisica universale, ho veduto chiaramente la soluzione di tutte quelle difficoltà, che sinora sono insolubili appresso li matematici; e sono tutte le incomensurabili riddotte mensurabili a misura commune, siano le diagonali, sia la quadratura del circolo; la legge de' gravi, forze, resistenza etc. La natura del continuo, la natura de' centri, e in una parola sola la misura dell'uno come uno: cosa che pare contraddittoria, ma ch'è vera verissima perché si tratta di demostrazioni, e di prove fisiche. Tuttociò procede dalla scoperta di un fallo evidentissimo, ne' primi elementi matematici, creduto sinora verità incontrastabile, e fallo di tal rimarco, che niente più. È fallata la progressione geometrica. Questo le basti per conoscer la importanza del fallo. [...] Ho proposto tale scoperta all'Accademia reale di Parigi, se mi sarà dato premio conveniente. Attendo la risposta in breve, ma allora sarò imbrogliatissimo, perché non sapendo io li termini delle scienze matematiche, non saprò spiegarmi se non a modo mio. [...] Cosa dunque mi dice vostra signoria illustrissima in tal caso? Potrebbe mai essere, che la solita sua devozione a san Antonio ricevesse uno stimolo efficace da quanto le scrivo, perché lei se ne venisse qui per otto o dieci giorni [...]?" Malagò, *Tartini: Lettere*, 1:150. English translation in Malagò, *Tartini: Lettere*, 2:289–290.

penetrate the innermost mysteries of nature and solve difficulties that had troubled mankind for centuries. What exactly did Tartini discover? What is this new kind of science and how did he solve all the problems mentioned? At least some answers to these questions can be found in Tartini's letters to Martini from the early 1750s. It is not clear from the extant correspondence whether Balbi decided to travel to Padua to help Tartini. However, in early 1751 Tartini informed Martini and Balbi that he had written a short but rather difficult treatise and would be glad if they (especially the mathematician Balbi) could examine it.[39] Although Martini and Balbi agreed,[40] they did not immediately begin studying the text,[41] so the main part of the discussion took place in a group of letters from 1752.[42]

Several Tartini scholars who have studied this group of letters in the past and more recently have been of the opinion that the treatise in question is the *Trattato di musica secondo la vera scienza dell'armonia* (Treatise on Music according to the True Science of Harmony, 1754), which was actually printed some years later.[43] However, a careful examination of letters and archival material has shown that these assumptions were wrong and that the treatise in question is actually an unedited manuscript entitled *Quadratura del circolo* (Squaring the circle, ms. 232), which is kept in the Piran archives.[44] The evidence supporting this claim is strong. First of all, there is circumstantial information in some of Tartini's statements. For example, in the letter to Martini of 2 April 1751, Tartini says that the treatise in question is not long[45] (the manuscript contains 50 handwritten pages, while the *Treatise on music* is far more voluminous), and in the letter of 14 April 1752 he

---

39 Malagò, *Tartini: Lettere*, 2:329–331.
40 Malagò, *Tartini: Lettere*, 2:332.
41 At first Tartini is patient and even encourages Martini and Balbi to take as much time as they need. But after several months he becomes restless and when he finally gets some answers from Martini, he doubts that Balbi was actually involved in the examination of the treatise. See Malagò, *Tartini: Lettere*, 2:330, 334, 335, 343–345, 353, 359, 363–365.
42 These are mainly letters nos. 93–102 and 105 from the Malagò edition. See Malagò, *Tartini: Lettere*, 2:350–376, 380–383.
43 See, for example, Pierluigi Petrobelli, "Tartini, Giuseppe," *Grove Music Online*, Oxford Music Online, accessed January 8, 2022, https://doi.org/10.1093/gmo/9781561592630. article.27529; Daniel Pickering Walker, *Studies in musical science in the late Renaissance* (London: The Warburg institute, University of London, 1978), 145–146; Patrizio Barbieri, *Quarrels on Harmonic Theories in the Venetian Enlightenment* (Lucca: Libreria musicale italiana, 2020), 150–156.
44 "Quadratura del circolo," by Giuseppe Tartini, SI-Pit, SI PAK PI 334, box 3, ms. 232, *Collection Giuseppe Tartini*, Regional archives Koper, Piran Unit, Slovenia. Although this manuscript treatise was written with a completely different aim, a substantial part of it was later included in the first three chapters of the *Trattato di musica*. See Giuseppe Tartini, *Trattato di musica secondo la vera scienza dell'armonia* (Padova: Stamperia del seminario, 1754), 10–93.
45 Malagò, *Tartini: Lettere*, 2:329.

clearly affirms that his "treatise is not for publication, nor for practical music".[46] Moreover, in the letter of 21 December 1752 he reports that in the autumn of 1751 he had to write a musical treatise (obviously a different one from the one he had previously sent to Balbi and Martini for examination) for "a patron and student" (*padrone e scolare*) of his who then decided to finance its printing in August 1752;[47] the report that the book was finally printed is not to be found until the letter of 9 August 1754, the year in which *Trattato di musica* was published.[48] These and other similar indications should already raise at least some doubts, but there is also more precise evidence.

In addition to the general content of the correspondence, which can clearly be linked to the content of the manuscript treatise *Quadratura del circolo*, there are several places in the individual letters where Tartini and Martini refer to the manuscript in question with direct quotations. In letters of 5 and 19 November 1571, for example, Tartini says that about 30 lines before the first proposition in his treatise, the following words can be read:

> [...] è cosa meravigliosa, ch'essendosi osservati li tre suoni che si sentono in una sola corda tesa sopra il monocordo, cioè 1, 1/3, 1/5 non si abbia dedotto, che la unità è in se stessa di natura armonica, quando 1, 1/3, 1/5 è progressione armonica [...][49]

If we examine the manuscript, on f. 8r (Figure 2), exactly the same words can be found 25 lines above the chapter "Propositione prima":

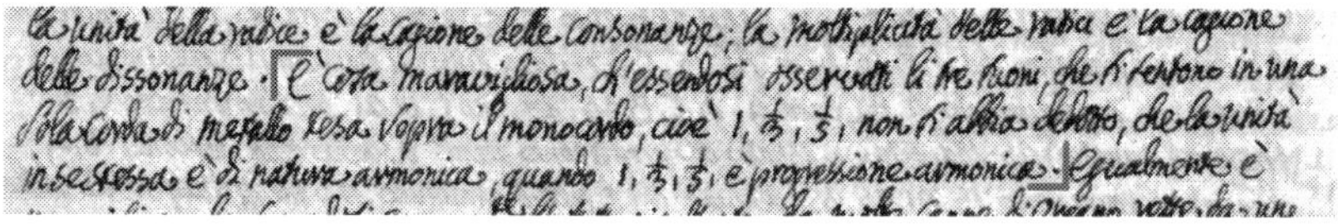
la unità della radice è la ragione delle consonanze; la moltiplicità delle radici è la ragione
delle dissonanze. È cosa maravigliosa, ch'essendosi osservati li tre suoni, che si sentono in una
sola corda di metallo tesa sopra il monocordo, cioè 1, 1/3, 1/5, non si abbia dedotto, che la unità
in se stessa è di natura armonica, quando 1, 1/3, 1/5, è progressione armonica. Egualmente è

Figure 2: Tartini, "Quadratura del circolo," ms., f. 8r (excerpt).

Another example is found in Martini's letter of 4 April 1752, where Martini refers to the contents of the manuscript in question following the words "Ma come che &" on page 4.[50] On the f. 7r of the manuscript[51] (Figure 3), exactly the same words are found, followed by the content to which Martini refers:

---

46 "[...] trattato non è per la stampa, né per la musica prattica." Malagò, *Tartini: Lettere*, 1:215. English translation in Malagò, *Tartini: Lettere*, 2:353.

47 Malagò, *Tartini: Lettere*, 2:383.

48 Malagò, *Tartini: Lettere*, 2:393. Confirmation that it was in fact the *Trattato di musica* that was printed is also found in Tartini's letter to Gian Rinaldo Carli (1720–1795) of 1 June 1754. Malagò, *Tartini: Lettere*, 2:392.

49 Malagò, *Tartini: Lettere*, 1:199, 203.

50 Malagò, *Tartini: Lettere*, 1:210.

51 After several blank pages, the text actually begins on f. 6r of the manuscript.

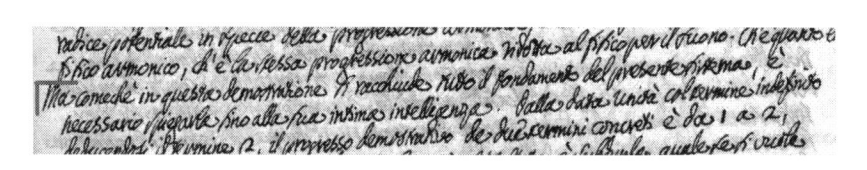

Figure 3: Tartini, "Quadratura del circolo," ms., f. 7r (excerpt).

Let us now turn to the content of the letters (and the manuscript treatise *Quadratura del circolo*), which may give us some clues to the questions about Tartini's discovery. From the title of the treatise it is clear that Tartini was concerned with solving the well-known ancient geometrical problem of squaring the circle (i.e. constructing a square with exactly the same area as that of the given circle, using only geometrical tools, namely ruler and compass). The solution of this problem alone, which many scholars have been trying to solve for centuries, would be a spectacular discovery. But it seems that for Tartini the new *approach* to the ancient problem, suggested already at the very beginning of the treatise, was of even greater importance:

> A harmonic phenomenon has been discovered by which the squaring of the circle is said to have been achieved. Not in the usual way, but in a particular way that is much more important: derived from the physical harmonic science of which we have no knowledge at present.[52]

Obviously, Tartini approached the ancient problem not through geometry but through the physical harmonic science, which, according to him, was known to the ancient philosophers (but carefully concealed, even by Plato), was later forgotten and which he now rediscovered.[53] Tartini described this rediscovered science most precisely in a letter to Francesco Algarotti (1712–1764) of 12 November 1750:

> This science is founded entirely on physical things, for nothing is, or could be, determined by the will of man. Its subject is physical-acoustic phenomena, and demonstrations inseparably accompany the phenomena, so that nothing can be deduced from these unless demonstratively. The demonstrations are in part deduced from geometry, and specifically from the circle, and in general from a demonstrative science founded on the arithmetic common number. This is the true science of the

---

52 "Si è scoperto un fenomeno armonico, per di cui mezzo si pretende ottenuta la quadratura del circolo. Non già nel modo comune, ma in modo particolare, che significa molto più: dedotto dalla scienza fisicoarmonica, di cui presentemente non si hà cognizione." Tartini, "Quadratura del circolo," ms., f. 6r. English translation by the author.
53 Malagò, *Tartini: Lettere*, 2:325, 456, 461.

proportions, for hitherto it has been most imperfect, because restricted within narrow boundaries and because the proportions have never been properly regulated.[54]

In the letters to Martini of 4 August 1752 and 9 June 1769, Tartini even placed the physical harmonic science above all other sciences of quantity and defined it as a prime principle (*principio primo*):

> The physical harmonic science assigns the causes, and when the cause is known to me, it is impossible that the effect should be unknown to me; and to say everything in one word, the physical harmonic science is the metaphysics of the known sciences of quantity.[55]

> Music, or better said, the science of harmonics, is not otherwise subordinate to arithmetic and geometry; it is actually that prime principle which allows no other principle before it. As a consequence, arithmetic is subordinate to this science, and geometry, which is its minister, is a composite resulting from the conjunction of the two measures of harmonic and arithmetic quantity. Your Reverence can readily see, and immediately understand, that making such statements on the most highly accredited common sciences is the same as uttering as many heresies, whereas for certain ancient philosophers they were inconvertible truths.[56]

In relation to the physical harmonic science, two things should be mentioned that are clearly new and crucial to Tartini's attempt to solve the squaring of the circle. Firstly, the *third tone* (*terzo suono*), the harmonic phenomenon to which Tartini

---

54 "Questa scienza è fondata intieramente sopra le cose fisiche: nulla essendovi né potendovi essere di arbitrio umano. Li fenomeni fisicoarmonici sono il suo soggetto e le demostrationi accompagnano inseparabilmente li fenomeni, cosiché nulla si possa dedurre da questi, se non demostrativamente. Le demostrationi si desumono in parte dalla geometria, in precisione dal circolo, e in genere da una scienza demostrativa fondata sopra il numero commune aritmetico. Questa è la vera scienza delle proportioni, quale sinora è imperfettissima, perché ristretta a miserabili confini, e perché non ridotte mai le proportioni a sistema." Malagò, *Tartini: Lettere*, 1:186. English translation in Malagò, *Tartini: Lettere*, 2:325. Text underlined by the author.
55 "La scienza fisico-armonica assegna le cagioni, e quando mi sia nota la cagione, è impossibile, che mi sia ignoto l'effetto; e per dir tutto in una parola, la scienza fisico-armonica è la metafisica delle scienze note di quantità." Malagò, *Tartini: Lettere*, 1:229. English translation in Malagò, *Tartini: Lettere*, 2:368–369.
56 "La musica, o per dir meglio, la scienza armonica non è altrimenti subalterna dell'aritmetica, e della geometria: è anzi quel tal principio primo che non ammette altro principio avanti sé. Per conseguenza l'aritmetica è subalterna di questa scienza, e la geometria ch'è la sua ministra, è un composto che risulta dalla congiunzione delle due misure di quantità, armonica e aritmetica. V*ostra* r*iverenza* vede, e comprende subito, che l'enunciare tali proposizioni è lo stesso ch'enunciare tante eresie rispetto alle accreditat*issi*me scienze comuni, rispetto poi a qualche antico filosofo erano verità incontrastabili." Malagò, *Tartini: Lettere*, 1:325. English translation in Malagò, *Tartini: Lettere*, 2:461.

refers at the very beginning of the *Quadratura del circolo*[57] and which is well known to Tartini scholars and violinists: when two high tones are played simultaneously, a third tone is also heard, usually below them.[58]

Secondly, there is a new category of mean, the *discrete geometric proportion* (*proporzione geometrica discreta*).[59] In addition to the harmonic and arithmetic means already mentioned, the geometric mean was also used in ancient music theory.[60] However, this mean is often irrational and, in such cases, useless for harmonic science which only operates with rational numbers. Therefore, Tartini tries to approach it by determining the other two means (the harmonic and the arithmetic) of a given ratio, thus obtaining an approximation to the irrational geometric mean that lies between them (and is actually also their geometric mean).[61]

Let us illustrate what we have just said with an example and try to determine the geometric means of a double octave (in the ratio 4:1) and an octave (in the ratio 2:1). The geometric mean divides a given ratio into two equal ratios. This can easily be done with the ratio of the double octave (4:1):

$$m = \sqrt{4 \times 1} = 2$$

The result is the proportion 4:2:1, the geometric mean dividing the given ratio (4:1) into two equal ratios (4:2 = 2:1). Tartini refers to the proportion with a rational geometric mean as to the *continuous geometric proportion* (*proporzione geometrica continua*).[62] Let us now try to divide the ratio of the octave (2:1) by the harmonic mean:

$$m = \sqrt{2 \times 1} = \sqrt{2}$$

The result is clearly irrational, leading Tartini to first transform the ratio into 12:6 (to avoid fractions) and then determine the other two means, arithmetic[63]

---

57 See the quotation above.
58 The phenomenon of the third tone has already been studied in detail from various aspects. For a basic description of the phenomenon and some suggestions for further reading see Margherita Canale Degrassi's chapter in this volume. Margherita Canale Degrassi, "The Orchestral Accompaniments of Giuseppe Tartini's Concertos for Violin and Orchestra and the Third-Tone Theory: Hyphoteses for an Analysis," in *In Search of Perfect Harmony: Tartini's Music and Music Theory in Local and European Contexts*, ed. Nejc Sukljan (Berlin: Peter Lang, 2022), 55–75.
59 Tartini attempts to describe it in the Foreword (*Trattato premesso*) to the *Trattato di musica*. See Tartini, *Trattato di musica*, 1–9.
60 The mathematical formula for the geometric mean is $m = \sqrt{ab}$.
61 Zarlino and other earlier theorists made no attempt to approach the irrational geometric mean arithmetically but merely tried to determine it by means of geometric procedures or even special geometric tools such as the *mesolabe*. (See Zarlino, *Istituzioni armoniche*, 208–213.)
62 See, for example, Tartini, *Trattato di musica*, 30.
63 The aim is to find the arithmetic mean of the ratio 12:6, which is 12:9:6.

and harmonic.[64] The resulting proportion is 12:9:8:6, where the geometric mean ($m = \sqrt{12x6} = \sqrt{72} \cong 8.49$) lies between the arithmetic and harmonic means (and is also their geometric mean: $m = \sqrt{9x8} = \sqrt{72} \cong 8.49$). Since the resulting proportion is only an approximation to the exact geometric mean and there is a gap between nine and eight (where the actual geometric mean lies), Tartini calls this proportion *discrete geometric proportion* (there is no exact mean that would continuously link the two extremes of the divided ratio).

After what has just been presented, we can see that Tartini's physical harmonic science is based, on the one hand, on sensual, auditory experience and, on the other, on concrete mathematical calculations: he tries to solve the actual problem of squaring the circle by the phenomenon of the third tone and by various mathematical tools such as discrete geometric proportion. Since the *Quadratura del circolo* is primarily a mathematical treatise and only indirectly related to ancient theory, and since Tartini's mathematical speculations are far beyond the scope of this chapter and have already been discussed in more detail elsewhere,[65] only a few key points that are also discussed in the letters to Martini will be highlighted here.

Tartini begins by explaining the phenomenon of the third tone and quickly points out an interesting fact he had discovered: the third tone between the tones in the harmonic series is always the same (constant) and can be expressed mathematically as ½ (see Musical example 5).[66]

Musical example 5: A constant third tone between the tones of a harmonic series. (Tartini, *Trattato di musica*, 18.)

---

64 The aim is to find the harmonic mean of the ratio 12:6, which is 12:8:6.
65 The manuscript treatise *Quadratura del circolo* was translated into Slovenian language and examined in Vladimir Bensa, "Tartinijeva kvadratura kroga," (BSc dissertation, University of Ljubljana, 2007). Among others, the studies of Patrizio Barbieri and Daniel Pickering Walker should be highlighted: Barbieri, *Quarrels on Harmonic Theories*, above all 61–161; Walker, *Studies in musical science*, 124–170.
66 Tartini, "Quadratura del circolo," ms., f. 6r–v.

This discovery is fundamental to the whole discussion, Tartini affirms in his letters to Martini,[67] explaining that string instruments must be used to prove his claim, since each tone represents a string and these in turn can be understood as *sounding physical lines* (*linea fisica che sia sonora*).[68] From sounding physical lines it is only a step to geometric lines and thus a connection is made between the sound phenomenon of the third tone and the geometric figures, namely the square and the circle, as Tartini also explains in several letters to Martini:

> Here then is the fundamental principle of my system. The physical sounding lines, from which I infer by harmonic series the third sound always constant in ½, are equal to the lines in the plane of the diameter harmonically divided, and the third sound is a physical sounding line unfailingly equal to the semidiameter [...][69]
>
> My method consists in comparing square and circle. In the comparison I find the harmonic circle constantly: the square being either arithmetic or counter-harmonic respectively. Having established the harmonic circle, I find the infinite harmonic root by means of the third sound, which is an effect inseparable from two sounding lines played at the same time. [...] the root determined in ½ is the same.[70]

Having discovered that the third tone between the tones of the harmonic series is always constant ½, Tartini used the same harmonic ratios in his treatment of the square and the circle, where he also tried to define constant values as he had found them in the third tone, and finally the number π,[71] which led him to the solution of the problem of squaring the circle.

If Tartini was quite confident of his discovery, Martini and Balbi were not:

> For geometers obtaining the squaring of the circle means finding a rectilinear figure which is demonstrated to be equal to the given circle. Until now it has not been possible to obtain such a demonstration, indeed there are many geometers that prove it to be impossible, hence it is greatly doubted that the physical-harmonic art may

---

67 See, for example, Malagò, *Tartini: Lettere*, 2:338, 355.
68 Malagò, *Tartini: Lettere*, 1:217. Although Tartini uses the term *line* (*linea*), what is actually meant is a *line segment* (delimited by two different endpoints).
69 "Ecco dunque il principio fondamentale del mio sistema. Le linee fisiche sonore, dalle quali per serie armonica deduco il terzo suono sempre costante in ½ sono eguali alle linee in piano del diametro diviso armonicamente, e il terzo suono è una linea fisica sonora infallibilmente eguale al semidiametro." Malagò, *Tartini: Lettere*, 1:235–236. English translation in Malagò, *Tartini: Lettere*, 2:375.
70 "Il mio metodo è di comparare quadrato, e circolo. Nella comparatione trovo il circolo armonico costantemente, il quadrato o aritmetico, o controarmonico rispettivamente. Stabilito il circolo armonico, scuopro la radice armonica infinita per mezzo del terzo suono, ch'è un effetto inseparabile da due linee sonore suonate nello stesso tempo. [...] la radice determinata in 1/2 è la stessa." Malagò, *Tartini: Lettere*, 1:226–227. English translation in Malagò, *Tartini: Lettere*, 2:365–366.
71 Tartini, "Quadratura del circolo," ms., f. 15r–v.

achieve it, unless we should wish to achieve it by approximation, as indeed the mathematicians can do.[72] At first, Tartini was happy to address their concerns. But while he took the third tone completely for granted and wanted to discuss mathematical questions, Martini, on the other hand, persisted with questions about the sound phenomenon. More than once Tartini explained that the study of the treatise should be carried out by a mathematician and that the musician's role was only to assist him in musical matters,[73] but when Martini insisted, Tartini got impatient:

> My treatise is indeed founded upon the physical, but this is inseparable from the demonstrations, and the demonstrations are inseparable from the two figures, the square and the circle. What is the purpose, then, of raising objections against the phenomenon? [...] Even a deaf person can hear it, and I have at least two dozen students around Europe who show it to anyone who has the ear for it. [...] The phenomenon exists, and the phenomenon is joined to, and inseparable from, the demonstrations founded upon the two figures.[74]

Then, to answer with precision to what is asked to me, namely the physical explanation of the third sound as to be able to adapt it to linear figures, I shall say that I do not owe this explanation in any way, as it is unnecessary for the demonstration of my main proposition, which is the squaring. [...] If the harmonic root is demonstratively and physically determined in ½, I ask, what is the purpose in wanting to know the physical means of the third sound? Certainly not for my proposition in general, which is the squaring. [...] To sum up, my natural argument is this. There is the third sound (be it in any way); and it is the harmonic root. This being given, I demonstrate and form my treatise.[75]

---

72 "L'ottenere la quadratura del circolo significa presso i geometri ritrovare una figura rettilinea a cui si dimostri eguale un dato circolo. Fino ad ora non s'è tal dimostrazione potuta ottenere, anzi vi sono più geometri che la dimostrano impossibile, laonde si dubita assai, che l'arte fisico-armonica vi possa giungere; quando non volessimo giungervi per approssimazione, come appunto possono fare i matematici." Malagò, *Tartini: Lettere*, 1:196. English translation in Malagò, *Tartini: Lettere*, 2:335–336.
73 See, for example, Malagò, *Tartini: Lettere*, 2:359–360.
74 "Il mio trattato è fondato bensì sopra il fisico, ma questo è inseparabile dalle dimostrationi, e le dimostrationi sono inseparabili dalle due figure, quadrato, e circolo. A che serve dunque il produrre difficoltà sopra il fenomeno? [...] Si fa sentire anco da sordi, et io ho almeno due dozzine di scolari sparsi per la Europa, che lo fanno sentire a chiunque ha orecchio. [...] Il fenomeno è, e tal fenomeno è congiunto, et inseparabile dalle dimostrationi fondate sopra le due figure." Malagò, *Tartini: Lettere*, 1:221. English translation in Malagò, *Tartini: Lettere*, 2:360.
75 "Per rispondere poi in precisione a quanto mi si ricerca, et è la spiegatione fisica del terzo suono per poterla adattare alle figure lineari, dico, che non ho debito alcuno di tal spiegatione, perché non è necessaria alla dimostratione della mia propositione principale, ch'è la quadratura. [...] Quando sia dimostrativamente e fisicamente

When, after some months, they finally turned to mathematical questions, Martini and Balbi were still very critical and expressed many concerns. Although he constantly opposed and contradicted them, it seems that after Martini and Balbi had poked so many holes in his theories, Tartini finally had to admit that his attempt to solve the ancient problem of squaring the circle was too flawed. Thus, in *Trattato di musica*, which was published a few years later, he writes:

> After such proofs, you would not ever believe, Count, that I profess, by virtue of my system, to be going towards the squaring of the circle. I profess quite the contrary, and it is to demonstrate the impossibility of squaring the circle, precisely by virtue of my system. [...]
> With this premised, I state as impossible the squaring of the circle with regard to the idea, mode, and commonly known sciences of quantity. [...] And here, as regards the known sciences of quantity, the search for the squaring of the circle ends forever.[76]

4 Late Letters: Approaching Metaphysical

Although mathematical speculations are frequent in Tartini's earlier letters to Martini, they are always at least remotely connected to the actual audible music (for example, by making the sound phenomenon of the third tone the basis of his speculations). But it seems that in the late letters Tartini touches the roots of ancient music theory and turns to the purely metaphysical. In this respect, Tartini's letter of 28 April 1769,[77] in which he discusses one of the writings that had a most profound impact on ancient Greek musical thought, namely Plato's *Timaeus*, is of particular importance.

In the centre of Tartini's attention is the famous (and in many ways puzzling) passage on the creation of the world soul. Here Plato explains that the craftsman god (demiurge) first prepared a special mixture of identity, difference and substance

---

determinata la radice armonica in ½, domando a che serva il volersi sapere il modo fisico del terzo suono? Non certamente per la mia propositione in genere, ch'è la quadratura. Insomma il mio discorso naturale è questo. Vi è il terzo suono (sia in qualunque modo); et è la radice armonica. Ciò dato, dimostro, e formo il mio trattato." Malagò, *Tartini: Lettere*, 1:226–227. English translation in Malagò, *Tartini: Lettere*, 2:365–366.

76 "Dopo prove sì fatte ella non credesse mai Sig. Conte, che io pretendessi in forza del mio sistema di andar incontro alla quadratura del circolo. Pretendo bensì il contrario, ed è di dimostrare la impossibilità della quadratura del circolo in forza appunto del mio sistema. [...] Ciò premesso, dico impossibile la quadratura del circolo rispetto alla idea, modo, e scienze comunemente note di quantità. [...] E qui rispetto alle scienze note di quantità finisce per sempre la ricerca della quadratura del circolo." Tartini, *Trattato di musica*, 46–47. English translation in Fredric Bolan Johnson, "Tartini's Trattato di musica seconda la vera scienza dell'armonia: An Annotated Translation with Commentary," (Doctoral dissertation, Indiana University, 1985), 120, 123.

77 Malagò, *Tartini: Lettere*, 2:459–460.

and then constructed the world soul by distributing carefully measured portions of this mixture:

> He began the division by first taking a single portion [1] from the mixture; next he took a portion which was double the quantity of the first [2], and then a third portion, which was one-and-a-half times the quantity of the second and three times the quantity of the first [3]; then he took a fourth portion which was double the quantity of the second [4], and a fifth which was three times the quantity of the third [9], and a sixth which was eight times the quantity of the first [8], and then a seventh portion which was twenty-seven times the quantity of the first [27]. After this, he filled up the double and triple intervals by cutting off further portions from the mixture and inserting them into the gaps, so that in each interval there were two means, a mean that exceeded one of its extremes by the same fraction of the extremes as it was exceeded by the other extreme, and another mean that exceeded one of its extremes by the same number as it was exceeded by the other extreme. These links created, within the first set of intervals, further intervals of 3 : 2, 4 : 3, and 9 : 8, and then he filled up all the 4 : 3 intervals with the 9 : 8 interval, leaving in each case a portion, and the portion that remained was an interval whose terms, expressed numerically, were 256 : 243. And so at this point the mixture, from which he was cutting these portions, was all used up.[78]

The result of Plato's original construction was a series of seven quantities (1:2:3:4:8:9:27), which actually consists of two geometric series of four quantities: one with double intervals (1:2:4:8) and the other with triple intervals (1:3:9:27). These intervals were then filled up by taking additional portions from the mixture in such a way that the added quantities formed the harmonic ("exceeded one of its extremes by the same fraction of the extremes as it was exceeded by the other extreme") and arithmetic ("exceeded one of its extremes by the same number as it was exceeded by the other extreme") means of the extremes. The result of this process are the following proportions with harmonic and arithmetic means (that Tartini would call discrete geometric proportions):

Series **1:2:4:8**

E1	HM	AM	E2[79]
1	$\frac{4}{3}$	$\frac{3}{2}$	2
2	$\frac{8}{3}$	3	4
4	$\frac{16}{3}$	6	8

Series **1:3:9:27**

E1	HM	AM	E2
1	$\frac{3}{2}$	2	3
3	$\frac{9}{2}$	6	9
9	$\frac{27}{2}$	18	27

---

78 Plato, *Timaeus and Critias*, trans. Robin Waterfield (Oxford: Oxford University Press, 2009), 35b–36b, 23–24.
79 E = extreme, HM = harmonic mean, AM = arithmetic mean.

Tartini and the Ancients 163

In his letter to Martini, Tartini argues that Plato's craftsman god actually transforms continuous geometric proportions into discrete geometric proportions in the process of constructing the world soul:

I ask Your Reverence to observe in Plato's dialogue of the universe [...] the formation of the world soul. The doctrine contained there substantially says that parts are removed from a given continuous geometric proportion and are carried forward to the mean, so that a discrete geometric proportion is formed and deduced, which certainly can no longer preserve the ratio of the geometric extremes, because having had a part removed in order to place them in the mean, the extremes of the second discrete geometric proportion must be in a lesser ratio to the extremes of the continuous geometric ratio.[80]

According to Tartini, the reason for this transformation was the fact that Plato did not admit the continuous geometric proportion because it did not conform to the laws of the cosmos.[81] Tartini also gives some concrete examples of the procedure: if we reduce the extreme 4 of the continuous geometric proportion 1:2:4 by 1 (or take a part of it), the new extreme is 3 and the proportion becomes an arithmetic one (1:2:3). Next, the ratio between the original and the new extreme (3:4) "must be carried forward to the mean" of the new arithmetic proportion. This means that to the already existing mean (2) a second one is added (¾), giving us a discrete geometric series 1:¾:2:3 or in integers 2:3:4:6, which contains both harmonic and arithmetic means of the extremes. Tartini concludes:

[...] it will be generally accepted that the term subtracted from the continuous geometrical extreme and carried forward to the discrete geometrical mean is always the harmonic mean of the extremes of the discrete geometrical proportion, and that the geometric mean of the continuous proportion is always converted into the arithmetical mean of the discrete relation.[82]

---

80 "Osservi vostra riverenza nel dialogo dell'universo di Platone [...] la formazione dell'anima del mondo. La dottrina ivi contenuta sì è in sostanza, che da una data proposizione geometrica continua si taglino parti, e si riportino nel mezzo, sicché si formi, e deduca una proporzione geometrica discreta, la quale certamente non può più conservare la ragione degli estremi geometrici, perché da questi dovendosi tagliar qualche parte per riporla nel mezzo, è forza che gli estremi della seconda proporzione geometrica discreta siano in minor ragione degli estremi della geometrica continua." Malagò, *Tartini: Lettere*, 1:323. English translation in Malagò, *Tartini: Lettere*, 2:459.
81 Malagò, *Tartini: Lettere*, 1:324.
82 "[...] si verificherà per proposizione universale, che il termine sottratto all'estremo geometrico continuo, e riportato al mezzo geometrico discreto, è sempre il mezzo armonico degli estremi della proposizione geometrica discreta, e che il mezzo geometrico della proporzione continua si converte sempre nel mezzo aritmetico della discreta." Malagò, *Tartini: Lettere*, 1:323. English translation in Malagò, *Tartini: Lettere*, 2:459.

Tartini's discussion of the doctrine behind Plato's construction of the world soul is somehow unclear and confusing. It would be difficult to conclude from Plato's narrative that his craftsman god actually transforms continuous geometric proportions into discrete ones. Plato speaks only of filling in the gaps between the individual terms of the two series, while the terms themselves remain untouched: the portions added to the series are taken from the original mixture and not from the portions already distributed (the terms or extremes of the series). It is not clear from the extant correspondence how exactly Tartini substantiated his argument.

It seems, however, that Tartini was once again in search of some kind of fixed natural order expressed by the natural progression of numbers (1, 2, 3, 4, 5, 6 …), for his conclusion quoted above (namely, "that the geometric mean of the continuous proportion is always converted into the arithmetical mean of the discrete relation") is only true if the adjacent terms of the given continuous geometric proportions are in the ratios that follow the natural progression of the numbers and, at the same time, in their smallest integer values.

Let us illustrate what has just been said with some examples. Tartini claims that the geometric mean of the continuous geometric proportion and the arithmetic mean of the discrete geometric proportion (which is obtained from the continuous geometric proportion by reducing the extreme by 1) are the same number, which can be expressed as follows:[83]

If

x:GM:y (continuous geometric proportion) is transformed into

x:HM:AM:(y−1) (discrete geometric proportion)

and x:GM = GM:y = x:(x+1); x ∈ N, then

GM = AM.

Consider the continuous geometric proportion 1:2:4 with geometric mean 2. Its terms have their smallest integer values and the ratio of adjacent terms in both cases is 1:2 (1:2, 2:4 =1:2), where 1 and 2 are the first two numbers of the natural progression. If the given continuous geometric proportion 1:2:4 is transformed into a discrete proportion according to Tartini's method (1:¾:2:3), then 2 will be its arithmetic mean. Take the continuous geometric proportion 4:6:9 with geometric mean 6. Here the adjacent terms are in the ratio 2:3, where 2 and 3 are the next two numbers of the natural progression. When this continuous geometric proportion is transformed into a discrete proportion (4: ¹⁶/₃:6:8), 6 will be its arithmetic mean. We can observe the same pattern with the continuous geometric proportions 9:12:16 (where the ratio of adjacent terms is 3:4), 16:20:25 (where the ratio of adjacent terms is 4:5) and so on. However, if we take the continuous geometric proportion

---

83 GM = geometric mean, HM = harmonic mean, AM = arithmetic mean.

1:4:16, where the ratio between adjacent terms is 1:4 (and does not follow the natural progression of numbers), we cannot transform it into a discrete geometric proportion according to Tartini's instructions.

5 Conclusion

In view of all that has been set out above, it is clear that Tartini was familiar with various aspects of the ancient theoretical tradition and treated them in different ways. In doing so, he never simply adopted the ancient theorems uncritically but thought them through thoroughly and, when necessary, adapted them for his own use. His different approaches to ancient theoretical thought are evident in the three groups of letters presented.

Like many theorists before him (and especially Zarlino, to whom Tartini explicitly refers), in the first group, he took ancient theory as the basis for building his own theoretical system. However, considering some of his own theoretical discoveries, he is also critical of the earlier authors: he rejects some of the cornerstones of their system and constructs his own system in relation to this.

In the second group of letters, Tartini uses the elements of ancient music theory to describe a particular sound phenomenon (the third tone), and then attempts to solve the ancient problem of squaring the circle by the means of this phenomenon. He thus approaches this problem not with the help of geometry or arithmetic, as many before him did, but with the help of ancient *harmonike*, which he believes he has rediscovered: for him, arithmetic and geometry are merely (subordinate) tools that can help him achieve his goal, while the essential principle is the harmonic order of nature (which is also reflected in the third tone). In this way, Tartini even reversed the ancient paradigm to a certain extent: while ancient writers tried to describe musical (acoustic) phenomena with exact mathematical definitions, Tartini in this case strives for the opposite, namely to solve one of the most intriguing ancient mathematical problems with the help of a specific sound phenomenon, for which he even argued that its mathematical explanation and physical proof were insignificant and unnecessary, since everyone could clearly hear it.

The third group of letters is largely a commentary and an attempt to explain a passage from Plato's *Timaeus*, which is one of the most important writings on the ancient concept of universal harmony, which Boethius many centuries later defined as *musica mundana*.

Like many theorists before him, Tartini began from ancient theorems, but at the same time he transformed them, reinterpreted them, came to new insights and discoveries during his studies and adapted them to his time: Tartini's approach to antiquity, in which he always emphasized central concepts such as reason, nature, the pursuit of knowledge through rational and practical proofs, is closely linked to the key postulates of the Enlightenment. Judging by the content of his letters, it seems that in this context he undertook a long journey from the physical to the metaphysical.

Bibliography

Barbera, André. "Pythagoras." In *Grove Music Online*. Oxford Music Online. Accessed January 8, 2022. https://doi.org/10.1093/gmo/9781561592630.article.22603.

Barbieri, Patrizio. *Quarrels on Harmonic Theories in the Venetian Enlightenment*. Lucca: Libreria musicale italiana, 2020.

Barker, Andrew. *Greek Musical Writings II: Harmonic and Acoustic Theory*. Cambridge: Cambridge University Press, 1989.

Bensa, Vladimir. "Tartinijeva kvadratura kroga." BSc dissertation, University of Ljubljana, Faculty of Mathematics and Physics, 2007.

Canale Degrassi, Margherita. "The Orchestral Accompaniments of Giuseppe Tartini's Concertos for Violin and Orchestra and the Third-Tone Theory: Hyphoteses for an Analysis." In *In Search of Perfect Harmony: Tartini's Music and Music Theory in Local and European Contexts*, edited by Nejc Sukljan, 55–75. Berlin: Peter Lang, 2022.

Del Fra, Luca, ed. *Commercio di lettere intorno ai Principj dell'Armonia fra il Signor Giuseppe Tartini; ed il Co. Giordano Riccati*. Lucca: LIM, 2007.

Johnson, Fredric Bolan. "Tartini's Trattato di musica seconda la vera scienza dell' armonia: An Annotated Translation with Commentary." Doctoral dissertation, Indiana University, 1985.

Lindley, Mark. "Pythagorean Intonation." In *Grove Music Online*. Oxford Music Online. Accessed January 8, 2022. https://doi.org/10.1093/gmo/9781561592630.article.22604.

Malagò, Giorgia, ed. *Giuseppe Tartini: Lettere e documenti/Pisma in dokumenti/Letters and Documents*. 2 vols. Translated by Jerneja Umer Kljun and Roberto Baldo. Trieste: Edizioni Università di Trieste, 2020.

Petrobelli, Pierluigi. "Tartini, Giuseppe." In *Grove Music Online*. Oxford Music Online. Accessed January 8, 2022. https://doi.org/10.1093/gmo/9781561592630.article.27529.

Plato. *Timaeus and Critias*. Translated by Robin Waterfield. Oxford: Oxford University Press, 2009.

Sukljan, Nejc. "Renaissance Music between Science and Art: The Case of Gioseffo Zarlino." *Muzikološki zbornik/Musicological Annual* 56, no. 2 (2020): 183–206. 10.4312/mz.56.2.183-206.

Tartini, Giuseppe. Quadratura del circolo. SI-Pit, SI PAK PI 334, box 3, ms. 232, Collection Giuseppe Tartini, Regional archives Koper, Piran Unit, Slovenia.

Tartini, Giuseppe. *Trattato di musica secondo la vera scienza dell'armonia*. Padova: Stamperia del seminario, 1754.

Walker, Daniel Pickering. *Studies in musical science in the late Renaissance.* London: The Warburg Institute, University of London, 1978.

Zarlino, Gioseffo. *Istituzioni armoniche.* Edited by Silvia Urbani. Treviso: Diastema, 2011.

Walter Kurt Kreyszig

University of Saskatchewan, Saskatoon, Canada

Conservatory of Music Niccolò Paganini, Genoa, Italy

Giuseppe Tartini, the *philosophia naturae* and the *natura-ars* Dichotomy: In Defence of *natura* as the Key to His *Traité des agréments de la musique*[1]

Abstract: Giuseppe Tartini's preoccupation with the Platonic-Aristotelian *philosophia naturae* in his *Trattato di musica* (Padua, 1754), *De' principj* (Padua, 1767), and *Scienza platonica* (manuscript, ca. 1767–1770), accounts for the conscientious emulation of *natura* in his seminal contribution to the *practica musicae* in his *Traité des agréments de la musique* (Paris, 1771), the first treatise exclusively devoted to ornamentation. Tartini's scholarship and compositional practice left an undeniable impact on his contemporaries, especially Leopold Mozart, who in his *Versuch einer gründlichen Violinschule* (Augsburg, 1756) includes a number of (unacknowledged) references to Tartini's *Trattato di musica, Regole per arrivare a saper ben suonare il Violino* and his *Sonata* in G minor *Il trillo del diavolo* (B.G. 13). Tartini embarked on a path of scholarship that paved the way for related contemplations by Johann Wolfgang von Goethe in his pursuit of a *Tonlehre* and *Farbenlehre*, both of which were anchored in Goethe's conceptualization of the *Urpflanze*, a further extension of the *philosophia naturae*.

Keywords: ars, natura, philosophia naturae, scientia, third tone, *Traité des agréments de la musique*

> *Meanwhile, let us praise our Giuseppe [Tartini], who,*
> *with the acute subtlety of his rare talents*
> *and with untiring study,*
> *succeeded not only in copying Nature but in improving*
> *on her [...]*[2]

---

1 The author wishes to thank Prof. Dr. Nejc Sukljan (Department of Musicology, Faculty of Arts, University of Ljubljana; Ljubljana, Slovenia) for spearheading the *Tartini Project* and providing access to the primary sources on Giuseppe Tartini.
2 "Sia laude intanto del nostro Giuseppe [Tartini] l'esser giunto colla perspicace sotilità de'suoi rari talenti, et con instancabile studio non pur a rappresentare,

1

Next to the contemplation of the origin of music, a topic of prime importance even within the broader overall music historiographical discourse during the era of musical humanism (1400–1600), ancient music-theoretical thought beginning with the examination of the Greek *systema teleion*, is often framed within the overarching concept of the *natura*,[3] embedded within a *philosophia naturae*.[4] In fact, during Antiquity, the preoccupation with the *disciplina musicae* emanated from the *philosophia naturae*, generally serving as a point of departure for reflections on the natural world, specifically with a focus on the concepts of the proportion, perfection and beauty, and that from a teleological perspective as communicated by Plato (ca. 428 B.C.E.– 348–347 B.C.E.), who set forth the musical scale as an ordered cosmos in his *Timaeus*[5] and in his *De republica* (The Republic).[6] His student, Aristotle (384 B.C.E.– 322 B.C.E.), who in his *De rhetorica* (On Rhetoric), regarded the

---

ma a perferzionar la natura"; Francesco Fanzago, *Elogi di Giuseppe Tartini, primo violinista nella Cappella del Santo di Padova, e del P. Francesco Antonio Vallotti, maestro della medesima* (Padua: Conzatti, 1792), 18–19; English translation by Cuthbert Girdlestone, in Giuseppe Tartini, *Traité des agréments de la musique/Abhandlung über die Verzierung in der Musik/Treatise on Ornaments in Music*, ed. Erwin Reuben Jacobi (Celle: Moeck, 1961), 51.

3 Heidi Marguerite Northwood, "Harmony and Stability: Number and Proportion in Early Greek Conceptions of Nature," (Ph.D. Dissertation, University of Alberta, Edmonton, Alberta, 1997); Daniel A. Di Liscia, Eckhard Kessler and Charlotte Methuen, eds., *Method and Order in Renaissance Philosophy of Nature: The Aristotle Commentary Tradition* (Aldershot, Hants: Ashgate, 1997); see also John Torrance, ed., *The Concept of Nature* (Oxford: Clarendon Press, 1992).

4 Roger Kenneth French, *Ancient and Natural History: Histories of Nature* (London: Routledge, 1994); Karsten Friis Johansen, *A History of Ancient Philosophy: From the Beginnings to Augustine*, trans. Henrik Rosenmeier (London: Routledge, 1998); John Madison Cooper, *Knowledge, Nature and the Good: Essays on Ancient Philosophy* (Princeton, New Jersey: Princeton University Press, 2004); Gerard Naddaf, *The Greek Concept of Nature* (Albany, New York: State University of New York Press, 2005); Arie Johan Vanderjagt and Klaas van Berkel, *The Book of Nature in Antiquity and the Middle Ages* (Leeuven: Peeters, 2005); Edward Grant, *A History of Natural Philosophy: From the Ancient World to the Nineteenth Century* (Cambridge: Cambridge University Press, 2007); Paul Feyerabend, *Philosophy of Nature*, trans. Dorothea Lotter, ed. with an introduction by Helmut Heit and Eric Oberheim (Cambridge, UK: Polity, 2016); see also James Wilberding and Christoph Horn, eds., *Neoplatonism and the Philosophy of Nature* (Oxford: Oxford University Press, 2012).

5 Jacques Handschin, "The 'Timaeus' Scale," *Musica Disciplina* 4 (1950): 3–42; Thomas Kjeller Johansen, *Plato's Natural Philosophy: A Study of the Timaeus-Critias* (Cambridge: Cambridge University Press, 2004).

6 Plato, *The Republic*, 2 vols., ed. and trans. Paul Shorey (London: Heinemann and New York: Putnam, 1930); J.F. Mountford, "The Musical Scales of Plato's Republic," *Classical Quarterly* 17 (1923): 125–136.

"universal law as the law of *natura*",[7] began with the consideration of *musica* as a *scientia physicae*,[8] initially disclosed in his *Problemata* (Problems)[9] and subsequently explored in a number of his treatises, including his *De anima* (On the Soul)[10] and *De politica* (On Politics),[11] with a focus on the *ethos* (effect) of the Greek *tonoi*[12] and *harmoniai*.[13] Aristotle's *philosophia naturae* attracted the attention of pre-humanist scholarship in that his ideas received attention by Marchetto of Padua (flourished 1305–1319), both in his *Lucidarium in arte musice plane* (Explanation of the Art of Plainchant, 1317–1318)[14] and *Pomerium in arte musice mensurate* (The Orchard in the Art of Mensural Music, ca. 1318),[15] as well as in Pietro d'Abano's Commentary on Aristotle's *Problemata*,[16] with Padua emerging as a centre of pre-eminence for

7   Aristotle, *The Art of Rhetoric*, ed. and trans. John Henry Freese (London: Heinemann and New York: Putnam, 1926), 1373b 6–9.
8   Andrew James Hicks, *Composing the World: Harmony in the Medieval Platonic Cosmos* (New York: Oxford University Press, 2017).
9   Andrew Barker, ed., *Greek Musical Writings*, vol. 2, *Harmonic and Acoustic Theory* (Cambridge: Cambridge University Press, 1989), 85–97. Furthermore, on the transmission of Aristotle's *Problems* in the Latin West, see F. Alberto Gallo, "Greek Texts and Latin Translations of the Aristotelian *Musical Problems*: A Preliminary Account of the Sources," trans. Charles André Barbera, in *Music Theory and Its Sources: Antiquity and the Middle Ages*, ed. Charles André Barbera (Notre Dame, Indiana: University of Notre Dame Press, 1990), 190–196.
10 Aristotle, *On the Soul [...]*, ed. and trans. Walter Stanley Hett (Cambridge, Massachusetts: Harvard University Press and London: Heinemann, 1935); Michael Wittmann, *Vox atque sonus: Studien zur Rezeption der Aristotelischen Schrift "De anima" und ihre Bedeutung für die Musiktheorie*, 2 vols. (Pfaffenweiler: Centaurus, 1987).
11 Aristotle, *The Politics*, ed. and trans. Harris Rackham (London: Heinemann and New York: Putnam, 1932); Fred D. Miller, *Nature, Justice and Rights in Aristotle's Politics* (Oxford: Clarendon Press, and New York: Oxford University Press, 1996); Jonathan A. Jacobs, *Aristotle's Virtues: Nature, Knowledge, & Human Good* (New York: Lang, 2004).
12 Jon Solomon, "Towards a History of Tonoi," *The Journal of Musicology* 3 (1984): 242–251; Thomas J. Mathiesen, "Harmonia and Ethos in Ancient Greek Music," *The Journal of Musicology* 3 (1984): 264–279.
13 Andrew Barker, *The Science of Harmonics in Classical Greece* (Cambridge: Cambridge University Press, 2017).
14 Jan Herlinger, *The Lucidarium of Marchetto of Padua: A Critical Edition, Translation and Commentary* (Chicago, Illinois: University of Chicago Press, 1985).
15 Marchetto of Padua, *Pomerium in arte musicae mensuratae*, ed. Giuseppe Vecchi (Rome: American Institute of Musicology, 1961); Ralph Clifford Renner, "The Pomerium of Marchettus of Padua: A Translation and Critical Commentary," (M.A. Thesis, Washington University, 1980).
16 Petrus Aponensis [Petrus d'Abano]. *Expositio problematum Aristotelis cum textu* (Mantua: Paul von Butzbach, 1475); see also Nancy G. Siraisi, "The *Expositio Problematum Aristotelis* of Peter of Abano," *Isis* 61, no. 3 (Autumn 1970): 321–339; Pieter de Leemans, "Ego, Petrus Paduanus, philosophie minimus alumpnorum: Pietro d'Abano's Preface to His Expositio problematum Aristotilis," in *Between Text and*

the study of the Aristotelian *philosophia naturae*.[17] As a resident of Padua, Giuseppe Tartini was presumably inspired by and directly benefitted from this tradition in his own music-theoretical and practical discourse.[18]

2

Tartini's Franciscan upbringing accounts for his preoccupation with the *philosophia naturae* embedded within Franciscan-Platonic naturalism.[19] In 1714, during his collaboration with the orchestra of the *Teatro della Fenice* in Ancona,[20] Tartini made a path-breaking discovery in physics: the acoustic principle of the *terzo suono*,[21] also known as the third tone or the combination tone, a phenomenon of *natura*, resulting from two simultaneously vibrating tones that are in a relationship expressed by an arithmetic proportion, reflecting the number of the vibrations responsible for the generating of these two sounds.[22] According to Tartini, the third tone underscores the harmonic basis of each interval and thus of the chords, with

---

Tradition: Pietro d'Abano and the Reception of Pseudo-Aristotle's Problemata Physica in the Middle Ages, ed. Pieter de Leemans and Maarten J.F.M. Hoenen (Leuven: Leuven University Press, 2016), 21–52.

17 See the chapter "Aristotle and the Science of Music in Padua: Marchetto da Padova and Pietro d'Abano" in Eleonora M. Beck, *Giotto's Harmony: Music and Art in Padua at the Crossroads of the Renaissance* (Florence: European Press Academic Publishing, 2005), 51–77; Adriano Carugo, "Giuseppe Moleto: Mathematics and the Aristotelian Theory of Science at Padua in the Second Half of the Sixteenth Century," in *Aristotelismo Veneto et scienza moderna*, ed. Luigi Olivieri (Padua: Antenore, 1983), 509–517; Marcella Grendler, "A Greek Collection in Padua: The Library of Gian Vincenzo Pinelli (1535–1600)," *Renaissance Quarterly* 33 (1980), 386–416.

18 Sergio Durante, *Tartini, Padova, l'Europa* (Livorno: Sillabe, 2017); see also Martin Staehelin, "Giuseppe Tartini über seine künstlerische Entwicklung: Ein unbekanntes Selbstzeugnis," *Die Musikforschung* 35, no. 4 (1978): 251–274.

19 Giovanni Guanti, "La natura nel sogno platonizzante di Giuseppe Tartini," in *Tartini "maestro" narodov in kulturno življenje v obalnih mestih današnje Slovenije med 16. in 18. stoletjem/Tartini "maestro delle nazioni" e la vita culturale delle cittadine del Litorale tra i secoli XVI e XVIII*, ed. Metoda Kokole (Ljubljana: Znanstvenoraziskovalni center SAZU, 2001), 51–69.

20 Pierluigi Petrobelli, *Giuseppe Tartini: Le fonti biografiche* (Milan: Universal Edition, 1968), 55–56.

21 Giorgia Malagò, ed., *Giuseppe Tartini: Lettere e documenti/Pisma in dokumenti/Letters and Documents*, vol. 1, trans. Jerneja Umer Kljun and Roberto Baldo (Trieste: Edizioni Università di Trieste, 2020), 85; see also Patrizio Barbieri, "Tartinis Dritter Ton und Eulers Harmonische Exponenten, mit einem unveröffentlichten Manuskript Tartinis," *Musiktheorie* 7, no. 3 (1992): 219–234.

22 Angela Lohri, *Kombinationstöne und Tartinis "Terzo suono"* (Mainz: Schott, 2016); Patrizio Barbieri, "Die beiden Harmonie-Systeme der Paduaner Schule (1720–1820)," in *Die Musiktheorie im 18. und 19. Jahrhundert*, ed. Stefan Keym (Darmstadt: Wissenschaftliche Buchgesellschaft, 2021), 43–99: 61–76.

the diatonic scale as a whole having its origin in the horizontal arrangement of the sounds.[23] With these observations, Tartini argues for the "true science of harmony" rooted in *natura*.[24] While the third tone paved the way for his lifelong preoccupation with *natura*, including an examination of this phenomenon both from the point of view of *scientia* and *ars*, Tartini perhaps was not the first to engage in the study of the third tone, at least from the perspective of the *ars*. Presumably during his sojourn at Arnstadt (1703–1707), Johann Sebastian Bach (1685–1750) composed a *Praeludium et Partita del Tuono Terzo* (Prelude and Partita on the Third Tone), BWV 833, which was initially circulated in the *Möllersche Manuscript*,[25] copied prior to 1707/1708 by Bach's brother Johann Christoph Bach (1671–1721). Rich in ornamentation (by-and-large with recourse to traditional symbols for ornamentation) and in emulation of the French style of Nicolas Lebègue (ca. 1631–1702), the title of the work as transmitted in the *Möllersche Manuscript* appears to include an indirect reference to the third tone, which Bach explored within the overall melodic/harmonc frame of this composition and which he intended to draw to the attention of the performer and the listener.

In a letter dated Padua, 20 November 1749 to the Venetian philosopher and art critic, Count Francesco Algarotti (1712–1764), Tartini expressed his unabiding commitment to *natura* in that "I must say that I am at home as much as I can be with Nature, as little as I can with Art, having no other art if not the imitation of nature."[26] For Tartini, the third tone provided a vital proof for the presence and

---

23 Both Jean-Philippe Rameau and Friedrich Wilhelm Marpurg (1718–1795) also regard diatonicsm as directly related to *natura*; see Markus Waldura, "Zum Stellenwert der physikalischen Natur in den Musiktheorien Rameaus und Marpurgs – Ein Vergleich," in *Künste und Natur: In Diskursen der Frühen Neuzeit*, ed. Hartmut Laufhütte (Wiesbaden: Harrassowitz, 2000), 755–779.
24 Stewart Carter, "Giuseppe Tartini and the Music of Nature," in *Barocco Padano*, ed. Alberto Colzani, Andrea Luppi and Maurizio Padoan (Padua: Centro Studi Antoniani, 2018), 515–526.
25 *Manuscript Berlin, Staatsbibliothek Preussischer Kulturbesitz Mus. MS 40664 (Möllersche Handschrift)*. This anthology of keyboard pieces (both organ and clavier) includes pieces by Nicolaus Bruhns (1665–1697), Dieterich Buxtehude (1637–1707), Christian Flor (1626–1697), Petrus Heydorm (1660–1720), Nicolas Lebègue, Jean-Baptiste Lully (1632–1687), Johann Pachelbel (1653–1706), Johann Adam Reincken (1643–1722) and Friedrich Wilhelm Zachow (1663–1712); see also Heinrich Deppert, *Studien zum Frühwerk Johann Sebastian Bachs: Untersuchungen zur Chronologie auf der Grundlage der Kompositionstechnik in den Werken der Möllerschen Handschrift und der sogenannten Neumeister-Choräle* (Tutzing: Schneider, 2009).
26 "[…] devo dire che io sto di casa più che posso con la natura, meno che posso con l'arte: non avendo io altra arte, se non la imitazione della natura […]" Malagò, *Tartini: Lettere*, 1:179. For a partial English translation of this remark, see Pierluigi Petrobelli, "Tartini, Giuseppe," in *The New Grove Dictionary of Music and Musicians*, vol. 25, ed. Stanley Sadie (London: Macmillan, 2001), 108–114: 110. The date of 20 December 1749 provided for this letter is incorrect.

power of *natura*. Captivated by the *philosophia naturae* and within the *disciplina musicae* as part of the *quadrivium* and the *artes liberales*, by the concept of the *natura*, to which both Anicius Manlius Severinus Boethius (480–624/525 C.E.) in Chapter 1 of Book 1 of his *De institutione musica* (On the Fundamentals of Music)[27] and Saint Augustine (354–430 C.E) in his *De musica* (On Music)[28] had alluded, Tartini began his music-theoretical deliberations with a detailed examination of *musica* during Antiquity – a study which extended across three treatises. In the *Trattato di musica secondo la vera scienza dell'armonia* (Treatise on Music according to the True Science of Harmony, 1754),[29] the *De' principj dell'armonia musicale contenuta nel diatonico genere* (On the Principles of Musical Harmony Contained in the Diatonic Genus, 1767)[30] and in the *Scienza platonica fondata nel cerchio* (Platonic Science Founded in the Circle, manuscript, written between 1767 and 1770),[31] as well as in his copious correspondence with scholars,[32] Tartini devoted his attention to the study of *musica* from the perspectives of *scientia*, *ars* and *natura*.

27 *Anicii Manlii Torquati Severini Boetii: Institutione arithmetica libri duo e Institutione musica libri quinque [...]*, ed. Gottfried Friedlein (Leipzig: Teubner, 1867); Anicius Manlius Severinus Boethius, *Fundamentals of Music*, trans. Calvin Bower, ed. Claude V. Palisca, (New Haven, Connecticut: Yale University Press, 1989), 1–8; see also Calvin M. Bower, "Natural and Artificial Music: The Origins and Development of an Aesthetic Concept," *Musica Disciplina* 25 (1971): 17–33.

28 Saint Augustine, in his *De musica*, proposes a threefold division of the living being according to the *musicus* knowledgeable in theory and practice, the *cantor* conversant only in the practice of music and the *animal*, and the correlation of this division, respectively, in the terms *scientia*, specifically with reference to the *musica theorica*; *ars*, with attention to the *musica practica*, including both compositional practice and performance practice; and *natura*, as the overriding principle presenting a frame for both *scientia musicae* and the *ars musicae*, pillars of the educational system of Antiquity, the Middle Ages and the Renaissance; see Aurelius Augustinus, *De musica liber VI: A Critical Edition with a Translation and an Introduction*, trans. Martin Jacobsson (Stockholm: Almquist & Wiksell International, 2002).

29 Fredric Bolan Johnson, "Tartini's Trattato di musica seconda la vera scienza dell'armonia: An Annotated Translation with Commentary," (Doctoral Dissertation, Indiana University, 1985).

30 Giuseppe Tartini, *De' principj dell'armonia musicale contenuta nel diatonico genere* (Padua: Stamperia del Seminario, 1767); see also Giovanni Guanti, "Chi ha paura della 'Scienza platonica fondata nel cerchio' di Tartini?," *Rivista Italiana di Musicologia* 38, no. 1 (2003): 41–73.

31 Giuseppe Tartini, *Scienza platonica fondata nel cerchio*, ed. Anna Todeschini Cavalla (Padua: CEDAM, 1977); see also Giuseppe Tartini, "Trattato di musica: Music and Geometry – Scienza Platonica: Rediscovery of Ancient Harmonic Wisdom," in *The Harmony of the Spheres: A Sourcebook of the Pythagorean Tradition in Music*, ed. Joscelyn Godwin (Rochester, Vermont: Inter Traditions International, 1993), 314–361; Giovanni Guanti, "Giuseppe Tartini lettore di Platone," in *Florilegium Musicae: Studi in onore di Carolyn Gianturco*, vol. 2, ed. Patrizia Radicchi and Michael Burden (Pisa: ETS, 2004), 603–619.

32 Malagò, *Tartini: Lettere*, 1:109–364.

Already, in his *Trattato di musica*, Tartini, notwithstanding his treatment of *musica* as a *scientia* with recourse to *arithmetica* and *geometria*,[33] places particular emphasis upon *natura*, in claiming that "nature has more force than art"[34] – a statement which he makes in consecutive chapters of this treatise. Earlier in the same treatise, Tartini observes that "nature will have more force than human judgment"[35] – a remark which unequivocally positions *natura* ahead of any contemplation, notwithstanding the unabiding presence of *natura* in any examination, including *scientia* and *ars*, with the relationship between *natura* and *ars* serving as the focal point of Tartini's *Traité des agréments de la musique* (Treatise on Ornaments in Music, 1771).

3

The unprecedented interest in performance practices in the mid-1750s, with the publication of four major treatises on this broad topic covering the principal instrumentarium, that is, winds, keyboard, strings and voice – the *Versuch einer Anweisung die Flöte traviersiere zu spielen* (On Playing the Flute, 1752) of Johann Joachim Quantz (1697–1773),[36] the *Versuch über die wahre Art das Clavier zu spielen* (Essay on the True Art of Playing Keyboard Instruments, 1753–1762) of Carl Philipp Emanuel Bach (1714–1788),[37] the *Versuch einer gründlichen Violinschule* (Fundamental Principles of Violin Playing, 1756) of Leopold Mozart (1719–1787)[38] and the *Anleitung zur Singkunst* (Introduction to the Art of Singing, 1757) of Pier Francesco

---

33 Pierpaolo Polzonetti, *Tartini e la musica secondo natura* (Lucca: Libreria Musicale Italiana, 2001).
34 "La natura ha più forza dell'arte." Giuseppe Tartini, *Trattato di musica secondo la vera scienza dell'armonia* (Padova: Stamperia del Seminario, 1754), 129, 148; English translation in Johnson, "Tartini's Trattato," 102, 119.
35 "[...] la natura avrà più forza dell'arbitrio umano [...]," Tartini, *Trattato di musica*, 21; English translation in Johnson, "Tartini's Trattato," 60.
36 Johann Joachim Quantz, *Versuch einer Anweisung die Flöte traversière zu spielen [...]* (Berlin: Voß, 1752); Johann Joachm Quantz, *On Playing the Flute*, trans. with introduction and notes by Edward R. Reilly (New York: Schirmer, 1966).; see also the study "The Dissemination of the *Versuch*" in Edward R. Reilly, *Quantz and His Versuch: Three Studies* (New York: American Musicological Society, 1971), 40–92.
37 Carl Philipp Emanuel Bach, *Versuch über die wahre Art das Clavier zu spielen*, Erster Teil (Berlin: Henning, 1753), Zweiter Teil (Berlin: Winter, 1762); Carl Philipp Emanuel Bach, *Essay on the True Art of Playing Keyboard Instruments*, trans. and ed. William J. Mitchell (New York: Norton, 1949); Dieter Gutknecht, "Zur Rezeptionsgeschichte von Carl Philipp Emanuel Bachs 'Versuch' in den Verzierungslehren des 19. Jahrhunderts," in *Carl Philipp Emanuel Bach als Lehrer: Die Verbreitung der Musik Carl Philipp Emanuel Bachs in England und Skandinavien*, ed. Hans-Günter Ottenberg and Ulrich Leisinger (Frankfurt an der Oder: Musikgesellschaft Carl Philipp Emanuel Bach, 2005), 195–203.
38 Leopold Mozart, *Versuch einer gründlichen Violinschule [...]* (Augsburg: Lotter, 1756); Leopold Mozart, *A Treatise on the Fundamental Principles of Violin Playing*, trans. Editha Knocker (Oxford: Oxford University Press, 1948); see also Ulrich Leisinger, "Leopold Mozart's Violin Textbook: Genesis – Circulation – Significance," trans.

Tosi (1653–1732)/Johann Friedrich Agricola (1720–1774),[39] must have provided considerable inspiration for Tartini to put his own multifaceted experience as a scholar, violin virtuoso, pedagogue and composer in writing. This inner urge may have been all the more pronounced following his return from Prague, where he had met Quantz,[40] and the founding of his own famous School of Violin Playing in Padua in 1727 as a devoted teacher of violin and composition.[41] These multifaceted experiences and resultant accomplishments are collected in the *Regole per arrivare a saper ben suonare il Violino* (The Rule for Arriving at the Knowledge of Sounding the Violin Well)[42] which also survives in a number of variances,[43] and in the *Traité des agréments*, with the French translation of Tartini's original, prepared by Pietro Denis (1720–1790), the Paris Professor of Music and Mandoline, with this publication joining the already wide dissemination of the aforementioned performance practice treatises.

In his performance practice treatises, Tartini, unlike the authors of the principal performance practice documents published in the 1750s, justifiably leaves behind the *studia humanitatis* and with it the *scientia-ars* dichotomy, replacing

---

Elizabeth Mortimer, in *Leopold Mozart: Musiker – Manager – Mensch/Musician – Manager – Man*, ed. Anja Morgenstern (Salzburg: Pustet, 2019), 88–95.

39 *Anleitung zur Singkunst, aus dem Italiänischen von Herrn Peter Franz Tosi [...]* (Berlin: Winter, 1757); Johann Friedrich Agricola, *Introduction to the Art of Singing*, ed. and trans. Julianne Baird (New York: Cambridge University Press, 1995); Thomas Seedorf, "Die italienische Gesangslehre und ihre deutsche Rezeption im 17. und 18. Jahrhundert," in *Musica e storia* 10, no. 1 (June 2002): 259–270.

40 "Herrn Johann Joachim Quantzens Lebenslauf von ihm selbst entworfen," in Friedrich Wilhelm Marpurg, *Historisch-kritische Beyträge zur Aufnahme der Musik*, vol. 1 (Berlin: Schütz, 1754–1755), 197–250: 221.

41 Margherita Canale Degrassi, "Fonti per una ricostruzione della didattica di Tartini nella 'scuola delle nazioni'," *Muzikološki zbornik* 28 (1992): 15–24; Guido Viverit, "Dissemination and Tradition of Tartini's Compositions Within the 'School of Nations'," *Ad Parnassum* 11, no. 22 (2013): 87–98; Guido Viverit, "Giuseppe Tartini e l'aristocrazia: La formazione dei violinisti per le corti europee e per i mecenati practi," in *Music and Power in the Baroque Era*, ed. Rudolf Rasch (Turnhout: Brepols, 2018), 381–396.

42 Tartini, *Traité des agréments*, 53–58; see also Erwin Reuben Jacobi, "G.F. Nicolai's Manuscript of Tartini's 'Regole per ben suonar il violino'," *The Musical Quarterly* 47, no. 2 (April 1961): 207–223.

43 David Dodge Boyden, "The Missing Italian Manuscript of Tartini's *Traité des Agréments*," *The Musical Quarterly* 46, no. 3 (July 1960): 315–328; Leonella Grasso Caprioli, "Lessico tecnico e strutture linguistiche di Tartini didatta nelle Regole per ben suonar il violino," in *Tartini: Il tempo e le opere*, ed. Maria Nevilla Massaro and Andrea Bombi (Bologna: Società editrice il Mulino, 1994), 281–298; Erwin Reuben Jacobi, "Giuseppe Tartini's Regula per ben accordare il Violino," in *Music East and West: Essays in Honor of Walter Kaufmann*, ed. Thomas L. Noblitt (New York: Pendragon, 1981), 199–207; Danilo Vitali, "Il 'Trattato degli abbellimenti' di Giuseppe Tartini," (Ph.D. Dissertation, Sapienza Università di Roma, 1995).

the latter with the *natura-ars* dichotomy. Within the history of performance practices, Tartini's *Traité des agréments de la musique* represents a milestone within eighteenth-century treatise writing as the first written account exclusively focussed on the topic of ornamentation with some attention to the bowing technique (as an expression of and in response to *natura*) – a topic which Tartini takes up in greater detail in the *Regole per arrivare a saper ben suonare il Violino* as well as in the personal correspondence with his students, for example, in his letter of 1760 to Maddalena Laura Lombardini-Sirmen (1745–1818),[44] with the significance of this particular letter providing insight into Tartini's outstanding pedagogical skills on the violin gleaned from the published translations in English (1771) by the eminent traveller Charles Burney (1726–1814) and in German (1784) by the theorist Johann Adam Hiller (1728–1804).[45] Beyond this particular letter, the profound pedagogical insights of Tartini are also revealed in the overall layout of his *Traité des agréments*, especially in his juxtaposition of musical examples and explanatory text – an organizational feature that is present in the treatise of Tosi/Agricola, however not found in the treatises of Quantz, C.P.E. Bach and L. Mozart, who gather (at least some of) the musical examples at the end of the respective volumes, as disclosed in the full title of their publication. In the case of C.P.E. Bach, his *Probestücke* (Practice Pieces) to the *Versuch* were issued as separate publications.[46]

During the eighteenth century, the imitation of *natura*, with its lengthy history dating back to the era of musical humanism, gains a new impetus vis-a-vis a series of new terms, including *regula, le bon goût* and *galanterie*, common in courtly-aristocratic circles.[47] Tartini, in his exploration of the *natura-ars* dichotomy, the focal point of his deliberations in the *Traité des agréments*, attaches greater importance to *natura* than to *ars*. Within this treatise, he sets forward a hierarchical approach regarding the examination of ornamentation, with only those facets addressed that are of immediate relevance to *natura* and the expression thereof in addition to a clear demarcation of the boundaries between *natura* and *ars*, as shown in the Table below. In his reflections, Tartini is fully aware of the difficulties associated with the adjustment in the tuning of wind instruments, operations which fall squarely within the domain of the *ars artificialis* so that nearly all of

---

44 For a reproduction of the *Lettera de Defonto Signor Giuseppe Tartini alla Signora Maddalena Lombardini inserviente Ad una importante Lezione per i Suonatori di Violino*, see Malagò, *Tartini: Lettere*, 1:286–289; see also Jane L. Berdes, "L'ultima allieva di Tartini: Maddalena Lombardini Sirmen," in *Tartini: Il tempo e le opere*, ed. Maria Nevilla Massaro and Andrea Bombi (Bologna: Società editrice il Mulino, 1994), 213–228.
45 For a reproduction of both documents, see Tartini, *Traité des Agréements*, 131, 133–139.
46 Beverly Woodward, "The Probestücke and C.P.E. Bach's Versuch über die wahre Art das Clavier zu spielen," in *De clavichordo 2* (Magnano: Musica antica, 1995), 84–93.
47 Joachim Kremer, "'Regel' versus 'Geschmack': Die Kritik an musikalischen Regeln zwischen 1700 und 1752 als Paradigmenwechsel," in *Musikalische Norm um 1700*, ed. Rainer Bayreuther (Berlin: De Gruyter, 2010), 117–143.

his remarks are made with reference to the voice and the strings – an observation which also pertains to L. Mozart's *Versuch*.[48]

Table
The Practical Discourse of Giuseppe Tartini
The *natura-ars* Dichotomy in His *Traité des agréments de la musique*[49]

[*terzo suono*] natura	ars
Premier Partie [First Part]	
[natural ornamental figure] *petit note* [grace note] De la Pogiatura descendant [descending appoggiatura] **[65]**	[artificial ornamental figure] De la Pogiatura montant [ascending appoggiatura] **[65]**
les petites notes breves ou de passage en descendant [short or passing descending grace notes] **[69]**	*Des petits notes simples en moutant* [single grace notes ascending] **[71]**
... *de la petite note breve* [short passing grace note] **[70]**	
agrément naturel [natural ornamental figure] **[75]**	*agrément artificiel* [artificial ornamental figure] **[75]**
[*du trillo naturel*] [natural trill] **[74–83]**	[*du trillo artificiel*] [artificial trill] **[74–83]**
Du tremolo (tremblement) [tremolo (vibrato)] **[84–87]** [preferable on instruments]	
Du mordant descendant [descending turn] **[88–91]** [pertaining to vocal and instrumental music]	Du mordant montant [ascending turn] **[88–91]** [pertaining to vocal and instrumental music]
Du mordant descendant [mordent] **[91]**	
Deuxième Partie [Second Part]	
modes naturels [natural figures] **[94–105]** [pertaining to cadences and placement of ornaments]	*modes artificielles* [artificial figures] **[106–108]**
cadences naturelles [natural cadences] **[109–116]**	*cadences artificielles* [artificial cadences] **[117–125]**

48 Pierluigi Petrobelli, "La Violinschule di Leopold Mozart e la musica vocale," *Neues Musikwissenschaftliches Jahrbuch* 14 (2006): 11–15; see also Beate Hiltner, "Leopold Mozart: Der Versuch einer gründlichen Violinschule – Fundus für Singstil und Instrumentalstil," *Wiener Figaro* 53, no. 1 (1996): 7–10.
49 The page references in bold refer to edition of the treatise, ed. Jacobi.

In the *Traité des agréments*, Tartini places *natura* in bold relief to *ars*, thereby implicitly referring back to the beginning of his *Trattato di musica*. In commenting on the *Traité des agréments*, Francesco Fanzago (1749–1823) applauded Tartini "not only in copying nature but in improving on her"[50] – a praise that could have very well pertained also to Tartini's music-theoretical writings, in particular his *Trattato di musica*, in which he sets the stage for his reflections on the *philosophia naturae*. Tartini's focus on the *natura* in the *Traité des agréments* is reinforced by the *goût du chant*, which Pietro Denis included as a subtitle for the French translation of Tartini's treatise. With this subtitle, in reference to both singing and playing with appropriate ornamentation, obviously suitable to *natura*, Denis aimed at directing the reader's attention to Tartini's principal objective in his treatise. For Tartini, ornamentation in the broadest sense of the word, embracing dynamic variation, modes of articulation (the result of the bowing technique) and free cadenzas, is subordinate to the *affectus*,[51] which in turn is controlled by *natura*. Tartini groups and judges the various types of ornamentation according to the *natura-ars* dichotomy, with the particular ornament either imitating *natura*, such as in the case of a grace note associated with a scale-wise or diatonic progression or resulting from the intervention of an artificial process, as, for example, in the insertion of a grace note in melodic lines progressing by leap.[52] With his comment on the impact of the short and passing grace notes on the enhancement of the expression of the melodic line,[53] Tartini underscores the correlation between *affectus* and *natura*, specifically the dependence of the *affectus* upon the *natura*. In polyphonic repertoires, the insertion of grace notes needs to be judged against the *harmonia* as a further parameter of the particular passage.[54]

---

50 Fanzago, *Elogi*, 18–19; English translation in Tartini, *Traité des agréments*, 51.
51 Furthermore on the doctrine of the *affectus*, see David Lasocki, "Quantz and the Passions: Theory and Practice," *Early Music* 6, no. 4 (October 1978): 556–567; Ulrich Thieme, *Die Affektenlehre im philosophischen und musikalischen Denken des Barock: Vorgeschichte, Ästhetik, Physiologie* (Celle: Moeck, 1984); Ernest C. Harriss, "Johann Mattheson and the Affekten-, Figuren-, and Rhetoriklehren," in *La musique et le rite sacré et profane*, vol. 2, ed. Marc Honegger, Christian Meyer and Paul Prévost (Strasbourg: Association des Publications près les Universités de Strasbourg, 1986), 517–531; Claude V. Palisca, "Moving the Affections Through Music: Pre-Cartesian Psycho-Physiological Theories," in *Number to Sound: The Musical Way to the Scientific Revolution*, ed. Paolo Gozza (Boston, Massachusetts: Kluwer Academic Publishers, 2000), 289–308; Rudolf Pečman, "C.Ph.E. Bach und die Affektenlehre: Bemerkungen zur Aufführungspraxis," *Musicologica Brunensia* 50–51, H36–H37 (2001–2002): 17–22.
52 Tartini, *Traité des agréments*, 69.
53 Tartini, *Traité des agréments*, 70.
54 Tartini, *Traité des agréments*, 73; see also Beverly Scheibert, "New Information About Performing 'Small Notes'," in *The Harpsichord and Its Repertoire*, ed. Pieter Dirksen (Utrecht: STIMU Foundation for Historical Performance Practice, 1992), 99–118.

That Tartini displayed considerable expertise in the execution of trills was duly observed by Quantz, in that "the trills, even the double trills, he [Tartini] struck with all fingers equally well".[55] In the case of trills exceeding the prescribed semitone or tone, Tartini recommends its replacement by an *agrément naturel* or an *agrément artificiel*[56] – with the latter choice somewhat perplexing in light of Tartini's staunch adherence to *natura* as the ultimate arbitrator in musical decisions. Also factored in with the *affectus* and thus within the broader consideration of *natura* is the speed of trills, with Tartini recommending a slow path for the execution of the trill in mournful pieces.[57] With his cautionary note against the use of the *tremolo* in connection with the interval of the semitone, Tartini advocates the retention of a pure intonation induced by *natura*, here indirectly reflecting upon his detection of the third tone and their seminal importance in music theory, as discussed in the *Trattato di musica*[58] in the *De' principj*.[59] and in the *Scienza platonica*. In the examination of the *mordant*, with reference to both the *mordant* (English turn) and the *mordant* (English mordent), Tartini acknowledges the confluence of *natura* and *ars*,[60] with preference given to the descending *mordant* (English turn).[61] Here Tartini justifies his preference by invoking the *appoggiatura* in descending form which "sounds better" than the ascending form[62] – obviously in his justification relying on *natura*. In the case of the *mordant* (English turn), the *affectus* enters in the consideration of tempo designations *Andante* and *Allegro* best suited for the rendition of this ornament.[63] Likewise, the *mordant* (English mordent) is also associated with the *affectus*, especially with regard to lively pieces.[64]

In the second part of his *Traité des agréments*, Tartini considers the placement of ornaments in more detail, including examples of a polyphonic frame comprising melody and partly figured *basso continuo* lines, also a reflection of his

---

55 "Die Triller, so gar die Doppeltriller, schlug er mit allen Fingern gleich gut", as reproduced from "Herrn Johann Joachim Quantzens Lebenslauf", 221; also in Willi Kahl, with introductions and annotations, *Selbstbiographien deutscher Musiker des XVIII. Jahrhunderts* (Cologne: Staufen, 1948), 128; English translation by Walter Kurt Kreyszig.
56 Tartini, *Traité des agréments*, 75.
57 Tartini, *Traité des agréments*, 76.
58 Tartini, *Trattato di musica*, 13–19, 21, 30–32, 53–56, 61–62, 67–68, 72, 75, 88, 91, 93, 100, 102, 104, 126, 128, 163, 171, 173.
59 Giuseppe Tartini, *De' Principj dell'armonia musicale contenuta nel diatonico genere* (Padova: Stamperia del Seminario, 1767), 5–16, 20–28, 32, 34–38, 40–44, 46–47, 57–71, 73–76, 80–86, 88, 92, 96, 100–101, 108–109, 111–115.
60 Tartini, *Traité des agréments*, 88.
61 Tartini, *Traité des agréments*, 88–91.
62 Tartini, *Traité des agréments*, 88. Furthermore, on two different notations of the *appoggiatura* in Tartini's practical discourse, see Beverly Jerold, "Tartini and the Two Forms of Appoggiature," *Eighteenth-Century Music* 16, no. 1 (March 2019): 83–86.
63 Tartini, *Traité des agréments*, 89.
64 Tartini, *Traité des agréments*, 91.

compositional process,[65] with attention to both *ars* and *natura*, the latter in comparison with the former, not unexpectedly, receiving more attention. When Tartini states that "nature herself teaches us these figures, the place in the melody where they should be used must be noted with precision,"[66] he is obviously contemplating *natura* as a progenitor of *musica*. He justifies his assertion of the preeminence of *natura* and its infallibility in that

> nature never goes wrong over them [i.e. the figures], it is certain that she [i.e. nature] never goes wrong over where to put them. This is so true that experience shows it in any person who has no knowledge of music but has received this gift [of placing the natural figures] from nature. When a person uses this kind of figure, not only the figure itself but its position will be excellent.[67]

For the first time in his treatise, Tartini turns to a group of people previously unaccounted for in his remarks on ornamentation, with the impact of *natura* upon the novice underscoring the importance of this concept for the broader society and thus in this treatise as a whole. In the segment on the *modes naturels*, Tartini initially turns to a series of examples in authentic cadences, plagal cadences, on cadences with the fourth and the sixth, respectively, in root position and the fifth of the key, and finally on the sixth in first inversion and the fifth of the key. In each example, Tartini illustrates the correct voice leading in both melody and basses, with attention to both unfigured and figured basses, the latter with single suspensions (4–3 and 7–8) and double suspensions (6–5 and 4–3 in superimposition).[68] Unlike earlier music examples, Tartini refrains from written explanations for each example of the various cadence types included but instead merely offers a few cursory remarks on the 34 examples, before proceeding immediately to the actual topic of this segment, an illustration of the *modes naturels* in another 34 examples, grouped according to four distinctly different contexts, that is, authentic cadences (unidentified), "endings of medial or retarded cadences which do not conclude the strain with their last notes,"[69] "[natural] figures fall[ing] on the second note"[70] and "ending of medial or retarded cadences which do not conclude the strain with their first note".[71] Unlike the previous examples of polyphony capturing numerous examples of basic cadence types, with melody and *basso continuo* shown on two staves grouped together, Tartini resorts to three staves for inserting the *modes*

---

65 Examples of Tartini's compositional process are found in *Manuscript Padua, Cappella Antoniana, MS 1888*, Fascicle 1, 13, 32–33, as reproduced in facsimile in Paul Brainard, "Tartini and the Sonata for Unaccompanied Violin," *Journal of the American Musicological Society* 14, no. 3 (Fall 1961): 383–394, especially after 390.
66 Tartini, *Traité des agréments*, 94–95.
67 Tartini, *Traité des agréments*, 95.
68 Tartini, *Traité des agréments*, 96–97.
69 Tartini, *Traité des agréments*, 98.
70 Tartini, *Traité des agréments*, 98–99.
71 Tartini, *Traité des agréments*, 99.

naturels on the staff in the middle, with the plain unornate melody on the top staff and the *basso continuo* on the bottom staff, in order to provide the proper melodic harmonic context for the passage in question in addition to placing the *modes naturels* in bold relief from the original. Tartini is not the first author to resort to the separation of the *compositio* and the *diminutiones*, a practice which dates back to the early eighteenth century, with an analogous disposition of notated lines used by Georg Philipp Telemann (1681–1767) in his *Zwölf Methodische Sonaten für Violine oder Querflöte und Basso continuo* (Twelve Methodical Sonatas for Violin or Transverse Flute and Basso continuo, 1728, 1732), TWV 41, undoubtedly with a pedagogical intent, and subsequently by Quantz, perhaps under the influence of Telemann,[72] in the notation of his *Adagio in C-Dur für Flöte und Basso continuo* (Adagio in C Major for Flute and Basso continuo), QV 1:7, included in his *Versuch*.[73] Again these examples are nearly devoid of any written explanations. In a number of musical examples Tartini attests to the inclusion of the trill as a genuine exemplar of the *modes naturels*.[74] Towards the end of the second part of his *Traité des agréments*, Tartini, in his comments on another ornament, the turn, briefly touches on the expression of this *modes naturels*, suggesting a sustaining of the initial note as an enhancement of *natura*.[75] Theorists traditionally conclude chapters or segments of treatises with a few (often general) suggestions for the performer, directly relating to the topic of the particular chapter. For example, Quantz, in his Chapter 13 entitled "Von den willkührlichen Veränderungen über die simpeln Intervalle" (Of Extempore Variations on Simple Intervals), states that

> all the rules just given for variations are designed chiefly for the Adagio, since it is there that you have the greatest time and opportunity to introduce variations. You will, however, be able to use many of them in the Allegro too. Those suitable for the Allegro I leave to the consideration of each individual. [...][76]

---

72 Walter Kurt Kreyszig, "Zur Beziehung zwischen *compositio* und *diminutio* im Kontext der Telemann-Rezeption: Georg Philipp Telemanns 'Methodische Sonaten' (Hamburg, 1728, 1732) als Vorbild für den 'Versuch' (Berlin, 1752) von Johann Joachim Quantz?" in *Vom Umgang mit Telemanns Werk einst und jetzt: Telemann-Rezeption in drei Jahrhunderten*, ed. Carsten Lange and Brit Reipsch (Hildesheim: Olms, 2017), 33–57.
73 Stephen E. Hefling, "'Of the Manner of Playing the Adagio': Structural Levels and Performance Practice in Quantz's *Versuch*," *Journal of Music Theory* 31, no. 2 (1987): 205–223; Walter Kurt Kreyszig, "Quantz's *Adagio in C-Major for Flute and Basso continuo* (QV 1:7) in His *Versuch* (1752): Baroque Ornamentation in the Context of the Mid-18th Century Music Theoretical Discourse and Compositions in the *stilus mixtus*," *Ad Parnassum* 10, no. 22 (2012): 139–171.
74 Tartini, *Traité des agréments*, 100–102.
75 Tartini, *Traité des agréments*, 103.
76 "Alle diese von den Veränderungen gegebenen Regeln nun, sind zwar hauptsächlich nur auf das Adagio gerichtet, weil man in demselben die meiste Zeit und Gelegenheit

In comparison with Quantz's observation, Tartini leaves the reader of his segment on the *modes naturels* with a far more provocative observation when he writes that

> [...] if we note the simple figures of each of the two notes and by practice learn to master them, there will arise in our playing many composite figures drawn from the first which, in many other places, are simple and taught by Nature, and we shall come to do them without study, application, practice or thought.[77]

Here, Tartini places emphasis on *natura* as the advantageous point of entry into the study of the *modes naturels*, even eliminating the consultation of written documentation on the *modes naturels*, obviously in anticipation of the performer's improvisatory skills,[78] closely linked to *natura* as an expression thereof.[79]

Commensurate with the focus on *natura* in his *Traité des agréments*, Tartini's lesser interest in the *modes artificiels* is self-explanatory. On the one hand, he concedes to the existence of innumerable *modes artificiels*,[80] which in turn explains his immediate deflection from providing specific examples of this category of ornamentation. Instead he turns to 15 examples of bass progressions at cadences, with a brief reference to the identification of the authentic cadence and the plagal cadence, respectively, as harmonic [cadence] and arithmetic [cadence][81] – terminology to which Tartini first resorted in connection with the discussion of the harmonic cadence and arithmetic cadence in his *Trattato di musica*.[82] Since Tartini in the aforementioned 15 examples of bass progressions has refrained from the use of figured bass symbols, with the exception of the raised third in the second penultimate and penultimate examples, he is obviously referring to succession of root progressions, that is, progressions of the *basse fondamentale*, as outlined by Jean Philippe Rameau (1683–1764) in his *Traité de l'harmonie* (Treatise on Harmony, 1722),[83] and that without placing any of these bass progressions into the broader context of the application of the *modes artificiels*.

---

zu verändern hat. Dessen ungeachtet wird man doch auch viele davon im Allegro brauchen können. Die im Allegro überlasse ich eines jeden seinem eigenen Nachdenken. [...]" Quantz, *Versuch*, 135; English translation in Quantz, *On Playing the Flute*, 160.
77 Tartini, *Traité des agréments*, 105.
78 Minnie A. Elmer, "Tartini's Improvised Ornamentation," (Ph.D. Dissertation, University of California at Berkeley, 1962).
79 Gregorio Carraro, "Natura e arte nell'improvvisazione di Giuseppe Tartini," in *Beyond Notes: Improvisations in Western Music of the Eighteenth and Nineteenth Centuries*, ed. Rudolf Rasch (Turnhout: Brepols, 2011), 97–108.
80 Tartini, *Traité des agréments*, 106.
81 Tartini, *Traité des agréments*, 107.
82 Johnson, "Tartini's Trattato," 262–266.
83 Jean-Philippe Rameau, *Treatise on Harmony*, trans. with an introduction and notes by Philip Gossett (New York: Dover, 1971); see also Thomas Christensen, "Rameau's 'L'Art de la Basse fondamentale'," *Music Theory Spectrum* 9 (Spring 1987): 18–41.

Notwithstanding the discussion of the harmonic cadence in the segment on *modes artificiels*, Tartini returns to this particular cadence in his consideration of the *cadences naturelles*,[84] initially as a two-note figure (i.e. simple figure), consisting of the move from the dominant (V) to the tonic (I) [109], and subsequently as a three-note figure (i.e. composite figure), embracing either the subdominant (IV), dominant (V) and tonic (I) [110], or the supertonic (II), dominant (V) and tonic (I) [111], or the submediant (VI), dominant (V) and tonic (I) [111]. He uses the cadences based on composite figures, with an increase in movement in the bass, as a point of departure for rather elaborate ornamentation in the melody line [112–116], again with little connecting text and surprisingly no reference to the concept of *natura*.

Tartini concludes his *Traité des agréments* with a segment on *cadences artificielles*, also known as *Point d'Orgue*, where the composer, in the case of a two-note figure in the bass outlining the cadential move, inserts a fermata over the first note, suggesting a free extemporization, possibly of such dimension that Tartini finds the use of the term *cadence* inappropriate, to be replaced by the term *capriccio*[85] – a designation that commonly refers to entire movements, often conceived independently of one another unfolding in a strict adherence to the *tactus*[86] in the idiom of the *stile galante* and meant to develop and test the performer's virtuosity, alongside an etude, with both these designations surfacing in volumes designed by the composer with the pedagogical intention of training the emerging professional *musicus*.[87] Tartini provides a number of smaller solo passages abounding with ornamentation and a display of virtuosity that reflect more closely the style of an eighteenth-century *cadenza* rather than a *capriccio*. Even the final two extended

---

84 Tartini, *Traités des agréments*, 109–116.
85 Tartini, *Traité des agréments*, 117; Philip J. Whitmore, "Towards an Understanding of the Capriccio," *Journal of the Royal Musical Association* 113, no. 1 (1988): 48–56.
86 Aleksej Anatol'evič and Ivan Vasil'evič Rozanov, "Towards the Tact and Tactus in German Baroque Treatises," *Musiqi dünyasi* 3, no. 60 (2014): 7157–7180; Ruth I. DeFord, "Mensural Theory in Early German Music Textbooks," *Musiktheorie: Zeitschrift für Musikwissenschaft* 31, no. 1 (2016): 11–28; Wilhelm Seidel, "Der Tactus, die Taktarten und der Takt," in *Musikedition als Vermittlung und Übersetzung: Festschrift für Petra Weber zum 60. Geburtstag*, ed. Christian Speck (Bologna: Ut Orpheus, 2016), 11–22.
87 For example, Quantz wrote capricces for his students, pieces that presumably attracted his most famous student, Frederick the Great (1712–1786). For a modern edition of Quantz's Caprices, see Johann Joachim Quantz, *Capricen, Fantasien und Anfangsstücke für Flöte solo und mit B.c./Caprices, Fantasias and Beginner's Pieces for Flute solo and with Basso continuo*, ed. Wilfried Michel and Hermien Teske (Winterthur: Amadeus, 1980); see also Walter Kurt Kreyszig, "Oltre il *Versuch einer Anweisung die Flöte traversière zu spielen* (Berlino, 1752) di Johann Joachim Quantz (1697–1773): I suoi *Capricci* per flauto solo contenuti nel manoscritto di Copenaghen (Collezione Giedde I,17) nel contesto del suo approccio pedagogico," *Il Paganini* 5 (2019): 113–117. Furthermore, on Tartini's submission of hitherto lost sonatas to Frederick the Great, see Gregorio Carraro, "Hidden Affinities: Accompanied Solo, Tartini and Germany," *Ad Parnassum* 11, no. 22 (2013): 113–126.

examples – one in C Major with modulations to various keys and tonicizations (without clear modulations),[88] the other *en tierce mineure*[89] – adhere more closely to the idiom of the *cadenza* than to the *capriccio*. These examples, placed within the realm of *ars*, concluding Tartini's treatise, attest to his skills both as a composer and a performer, with his own sonatas[90] and concertos[91] also underscoring his pedagogical virtues. Beyond that, these *cadenzas* provide a forceful illustration regarding the differentiation between two distinct performance traditions, that is, the *sonabile* of the instrumental tradition and the *cantabile* of the vocal tradition,[92] both of which were first identified in Tosi's *Opinioni de' cantori antichi e moderni* (Opinions of the Old and Modern Cantors, 1723)[93] and later echoed in the treatises of Quantz, L. Mozart and Tartini.

4

For Tartini, the underlying precept of all his treatises is the *disciplina musicae* firmly rooted in the *imitatio* of *natura*, with *natura* reduced to specific mathematical formulas in his *Trattato di musica, De' principj* and *Scienza platonica* and *natura* delineated from *ars* in his *Traité des agréments*. This approach in turn accounts for the intrinsic workings of the various parameters of *musica*, such as *harmonia*, also known as *melos*, and *rhythmos*, within the confines of *natura*, such as the third tone, as opposed to the overtone series of Gioseffo Zarlino (1517–1590) – who in his *Istitutioni harmoniche* (Harmonic Institutions, 1558) on the whole shows

---

88 Tartini, *Traité des agréments*, 122–123.
89 Tartini, *Traité des agréments*, 124–125.
90 Paul Brainard, *Le sonate per violino di Giuseppe Tartini: Catalogo tematico* (Padua: Accademie tartiniana di Padova, 1975); see also Candida Felici, "La disseminazione della musica di Giuseppe Tartini in Francia: Le edizioni settecentesche di sonate per violino e basso," *De musica disserenda* 10, no. 1 (2014): 57–75.
91 Margherita Canale Degrassi, "The Solo Concertos by Giuseppe Tartini: Sources, Tradition and Thematic Catalogue," *Ad Parnassum* 11, no. 22 (2013): 11–49; see also Sergio Durante, "Tartini and His Texts," in *The Century of Bach and Mozart: Perspectives on Historiography, Composition, Theory, and Performance*, ed. Sean Gallagher and Thomas Forrest Kelly (Cambridge, Massachusetts: Harvard University, Department of Music, 2008), 145–186.
92 For an overview of these traditions, see Blaise David Bryski, "Cantabile vs. Sonabile: The Difference Between Singing and Playing," (D.M.A. Thesis, Cornell University, 2006); see also Candida Felici, "'Non suona, canta su'l violino': From Aesthetics to Compositional and Performance Practice in Tartini's Instrumental Music," *Ad Parnassum* 11, no. 22 (2013): 127–141; Alessandro Cazzato, "Eclettismo e modernità delle 26 piccole sonate di Giuseppe Tartini, all'incrocio tra musica e poesia," in *Musica storia, analisi e didattica*, ed. Augusta Dall'Arche and Francesco di Lernia (Foggia: Claudio Grenzi, 2016), 43–59.
93 In English translation: John Ernest Galliard, *Observations on the Florid Song, or Sentiments on the Ancient and Modern Singers* [...] (London: J. Wilcox, 1743).

vehement opposition to the Pythagorean monochord division[94] in favour of the *senario*[95] – and the *mezzo geometrico*, the latter with reference to the mathematical means, discussed in Chapter 2 of Book 3 of Franchino Gaffurio's *Theoricum opus musice discipline* (The Theoretical Work on the Discipline of Music, 1480), the first publication in music theory in Western culture, as well as in Chapter 7 of Book 3 of his *Theorica musice* (The Theory of Music, 1492)[96] and *De harmonia musicorum instrumentorum opus* (The Work on the Harmony of the Instrumental Musicians, 1518),[97] and in Zarlino's *Istitutioni harmoniche*,[98] with this knowledge of physical/mathematical concepts gleaned from theorists of Greek Antiquity in their examination of the *systema teleion*, among them Aristides Quintilianus in his *De musica* (On Music).[99] *Natura* here serves as a source of the *harmonia perfecta*, and as such an expression of the genuine *ars musicae*, the topic of Tartini's music-theoretical deliberations in his three principal treatises, that is, the *Trattato di musica*, the *De' principj* and the *Scienza platonica*.

That Tartini left an undeniable impact on Leopold Mozart, who like Tartini displayed considerable interest in and commitment to musical humanism,[100] is seen

---

94 Claude V. Palisca, "Introduction," in: Gioseffo Zarlino, *The Art of Counterpoint: Part Three of Le Istitutioni harmoniche (1558)*, trans. Guy A. Marco and Claude V. Palisca (New Haven, Connecticut: Yale University Press, 1968), xx.
95 Zarlino, *Le istitutioni harmoniche*, 25–28; Gioseffo Zarlino, *Theorie des Tonsystems: Das erste und zweite Buch der Istitutioni harmoniche (1573)*, translated with remarks, commentary and a postscript by Michael Fend (Berlin: Lang, 1989), 87–96; see also Guido Mambella, "La musica fuori del numero in Zarlino," in *Musico perfetto: Gioseffo Zarlino, 1517–1590: La teoria musicale a stampa nel Cinquecento*, ed. Luisa Maria Zanoncelli (Venice: Biblioteca Nazionale Marciana, 2017), 61–66; Nejc Sukljan, "Renaissance Music Between Science and Art: The Case of Gioseffo Zarlino," *Muzikološki zbornik* 56, no. 2 (2020): 183–206.
96 Franchino Gaffurio, *The Theory of Music*, trans. with introduction and notes by Walter Kurt Kreyszig (New Haven, Connecticut: Yale University Press, 1993), 108, 110.
97 *Franchinus Gaffurius: De harmonia musicorum instrumentorum opus*, trans. Clement A. Miller (n.p.: American Institute of Musicology, 1977), 155–177.
98 Zarlino, *Theorie des Tonsystems*, 146–152.
99 Aristides Quintilianus, *De musica libri tres/Peri mousikes*, ed. Reginald Pepys Winnington-Ingram (Leipzig: Teubner, 1963), 1.6–12; Aristides Quintilianus, *On Music in Three Books*, trans. Thomas J. Mathiesen (New Haven, Connecticut: Yale University Press, 1983), 77–93.
100 Walter Kurt Kreyszig, "'Leopold Mozart ... a man of much ... sagacity': The Revival of Humanist Scholarship in His Gründliche Violinschule (Augsburg, 1789)," in *Music's Intellectual History*, ed. Zdravko Blažeković and Barbara Dobbs Mackenzie (New York: Répertoire International de Littérature Musicale, 2009), 43–156; Walter Kurt Kreyszig. "Humanistische Tendenzen im *Versuch einer gründlichen Violinschule* (1756) von Leopold Mozart, im *Versuch einer Anweisung die Flöte traversiere zu spielen* (1752) von Johann Joachim Quantz und im *Notenbuch* (1785) von Thomas Attwood," in *Leopold Mozart: Chronist und Wegbereiter – Dokumentation einer*

in a number of comments of Tartini on *theorica musicae* and *practica musicae*, although unacknowledged by L. Mozart, that guided the latter in the writing of his *Versuch*.[101] In his commentary to the third edition of the *Versuch* (1789), Hans Rudolf Jung identified five points of contact between L. Mozart and Tartini,[102] both of whom in their respective treatises were striving for the singing instrumental style, and with that in the insistence on the exact intonation of pairs of strings.[103] In this edition, L. Mozart, in his discussion of the double stop on the violin, that is, in the simultaneous sounding of two tones, refers to the acoustical phenomenon of setting another string of an analogous tuning in motion, thereby producing the sounds of the third, subsequently the fifth, the octave and so forth,[104] though, in the case of the sounding third, not identifying Tartini's third tone but rather, in the further detailed reflection upon this phenomenon of *natura* in a footnote, crediting Aristides Quintilianus, with reference to Book 2 of his *De musica*.[105] In light of Tartini's expertise in the execution of trills, here recalling the aforementioned comment of Quantz, it is hardly surprising that L. Mozart in his discussion of this ornament in the *Versuch* includes copious illustrations with recourse to music examples, especially in Paragraphs 3–6,[106] directly taken from the manuscript of Tartini's *Regole per arrivare*.[107] Beyond that, L. Mozart changes the abbreviation of the trill from "t" in the first edition of his *Versuch* to the "tr" in the third edition, with this adjustment in emulation of Tartini's sign for the trill. Furthermore, with regard to a number of examples illustrating the execution of the tremolo,[108]

Tagung, ed. Thomas Hochradner and Michaela Schwarzbauer (Vienna: Hollitzer, 2022), 119–153; see also Thomas Irvine, "Der belesene Kapellmeister: Leopold Mozart und seine Bibliotheken," *Acta Mozartiana* 55, nos. 1–2 (June 2008): 6–15.

101 Eugenia Angelucci, "Le Regole per ben suonar il violino di Tartini e la Violinschule di Leopold Mozart," in *Tartini: Il tempo e le opere*, ed. Maria Nevilla Massaro and Andrea Bombi (Bologna: Società editrice il Mulino, 1994), 299–320.

102 Leopold Mozart, *Gründliche Violinschule* (Wiesbaden: Breitkopf & Härtel, 1983), 26–27.

103 Pierluigi Petrobelli, "La scuola di Tartini in Germania e la sua influenza," in *Studien zur italienisch-deutschen Musikgeschichte*, ed. Friedrich Lippmann (Cologne: Böhlau, 1968), 1–17; also in Pierluigi Petrobelli, *Tartini, le sue idee e il suo tempo* (Lucca: Libreria Musicale Italiana, 1992), 81–99.

104 Mozart, *Violinschule*, 191.

105 L. Mozart's reference to Book 2 of Aristides Quintilianus's *De musica* is incorrect, as Book 2 does not contain any comment on sound (*sonus*). Books 1 and 3 of the *De musica* include references to sound, but none of the passages agree with the alleged comments of L. Mozart in his footnote to Chapter 8, Paragraph 20; see Mozart, *Violinschule*, 191.

106 Mozart, *Violinschule*, 221–223.

107 Tartini, *Le regole*, 10–12; also included in Tartini, *Traité des agréments*, 74–77.

108 Mozart, *Violinschule*, 245–246; English translation in Leopold Mozart, *A Treatise on the Fundamental Principles of Violin Playing*, trans. Editha Knocker (Oxford: Oxford University Press, ²1951), 204–205.

L. Mozart is indebted to Tartini.[109] In addition to the aforementioned examples, L. Mozart also includes a lengthier passage from Tartini's *Sonata in g minor for solo violin 'Il trillo del diavolo'* (Devil's Trill Sonata, B.G. 13)[110] in his *Versuch*,[111] and that as an exemplification of Tartini's contribution to the bravura tradition.[112] In their preoccupation with the two strands of the *disciplina musicae*, Tartini and L. Mozart follow a rather widespread tradition in the overall eighteenth-century discourse,[113] with their profound knowledge in the *theorica musicae* and the *practica musicae* providing full justification for their designation as "musicus",[114] and that as an integral part of their professional identification.[115] That the prominent ties with *natura* in the eighteenth century extend beyond the narrower confines of the *theorica musicae* and *practica musicae* dichotomy is readily gleaned from the direct preoccupation and involvement of composers with horticulture and botany – a trend and its effect on the musical creativity that can be traced back to the sixteenth century.[116] Even in the era of Tartini's music

109 Tartini, *Le regole*, 13–15; also included in Tartini, *Traité des agréments*, 79–83.
110 Agnese Pavanello, "Il Trillo del diavolo di Giuseppe Tartini nell'edizione di Jean Baptiste Cartier," *Recercare* 11 (1999): 265–279.
111 Mozart, *Violinschule*, 241.
112 Susan Murphree Wallace, "The 'Devil's Trill Sonata': Tartini and His Teachings," (D.M.A. Thesis, University of Texas at Austin, 2003); Gregorio Carraro, "'Ah!, vous dirai-je Tartini!': Per la definizione di un contesto europeo delle 'Piccole sonate' di Giuseppe Tartini (I-Pca 1888/I)," in *Locatelli and the Violin Bravura Tradition*, ed. Fulvia Morabito (Turnhout: Brepols, 2015), 123–130.
113 Furthermore on the exploration of both *theorica musicae* and *practica musicae* by an individual *musicus*, see, for example, Walter Kurt Kreyszig, "The Eminent Pedagogue Johann Joachim Quantz as Instructor of Frederick the Great During the Years 1728–1741: The 'Solfeggi', the 'Versuch einer Anweisung die Flöte traversière zu spielen', and the 'Capricen, Fantasien und Anfangsstücke' of Quantz, the 'Flötenbuch' of Frederick the Great and Quantz, and the 'Achtundzwanzig Variationen' über die Arie 'Ich schlief, da träumte mir' of Quantz (QV 1:98)," in *Kolloquium "Krisen- und Blütezeiten: Die Entwicklung der Königlich-Preußischen Hofkapelle von 1713 bis 1806"*, ed. Lena van der Hoven and Jürgen Luh (Elektronische Publikationsplattform der Max Weber Stiftung, 2017), 41 pages, accessed 2 January 2022, https://perspectivia.net/rsc/viewer/plonei mport_derivate_00010462/kreyszig_quantz.doc.pdf?page=1&q=kreyszig.
114 For an overview of the dichotomy between the *musicus* and the *cantor*, the latter with reference to those only familiar with the *practica musicae* see Dagmar Hoffmann-Axthelm, "David musicus, or: On the Consoling Power of String Music," trans. Roger Harmon, in *Bonjour, bon mois et bonne estrenne: Essays on Renaissance Music in Honour of David Fallows*, ed. Fabrice Fitch and Jacobijn Kiel (Woodbridge, Suffolk: Boydell Press, 2011), 326–337.
115 Gabriele Busch-Salmen, "'Geübter Spieler, Musicus, Virtuos, Instrumentist von Profession, Meister': Anmerkungen zur Beziehungsvielfalt des Berufsmusikers in der zweiten Hälfte des 18. Jahrhunderts," in *Professionalismus in der Musik*, ed. Christian Kaden and Volker Kalisch (Essen: Die Blaue Eule, 1999), 98–104.
116 Jürgen Neubacher, "Einflüsse der Gartenkultur auf die Musik im 16. und 17. Jahrhundert," *Die Blumenbücher des Hans Simon Holtzbecker und Hamburgs*

theoretical discourse and compositional practice, the cultivation of the garden as a natural space for the observation of the process of growth – curiously in anticipation of Goethe's *Urpflanze* as a model for his theories of growth[117] – exclusively within the control of *natura*, must have caught the interest of Telemann, who, as the owner of a garden in the inner court of the *Gruson Gewächshäuser* (Gruson Greenhouses) in Magdeburg,[118] may have transferred the inspiration gleaned from *natura*, unlike Tartini, to his compositional oeuvre that is invariably inspired by phenomena observed in *natura*, which provide the stimulus for musical creativity, as for example, in the case of his *Wasser-Ouverture* (Water-Ouverture), also known as the *Hamburger Ebb und Fluth* (Hamburg Low Tide and High Tide, TWV 55 C3, 1723).[119]

Unlike L. Mozart, Tartini in his discussion of *natura* displays a penchant for folk music,[120] that repertory which, in his opinion was not affected by *ars*, bears a particularly close reflection of *natura*. For Tartini, his quest for *natura* as the prime criterion for the judgment of *musica* from the perspective of the *practica musicae* accounts for his reliance in four movements from his violin sonatas upon the *Aria del Tasso* (Aria of Tasso)[121] – the theme which had caught the attention of both Jean Jacques Rousseau (1712–1778), during his appointment as secretary to the French ambassador in Venice from September 1743 until August 1744, and Johann Wolfgang von Goethe (1749–1832) during their sojourn in Venice in October 1816.[122] Notwithstanding the latter's lack of a formal training in music,

---

Lustgärten: Hans Simon Holtzbecker, Hamburger Blumenmaler des 17. Jahrhunderts – Botanische, garten- und kunsthistorische Aspekte, ed. Dietrich Roth (Kellern-Weiler: Goecke & Evers, 2003), 155–174.

117 Gary W. Don, "Music and Goethe's Theories of Growth," (Ph.D. Dissertation, University of Washington, 1991).

118 Ralph-Jürgen Reipsch, "Dokumente zu Georg Philipp Telemanns 'Blumen-Liebe'," in *Das Moller-Florilegium des Hans Simon Holtzbecker*, ed. Dietrich Roth (Berlin: Kulturstiftung der Länder, 2001), 60–79; see also Eckart Kleßmann, *Der Blumenfreund Georg Philipp Telemann* (Hamburg; Saucke, 1996).

119 Adolf Hoffmann, *Die Orchestersuiten Georg Philipp Telemanns TWV 55, mit thematisch-bibliographischem Werkverzeichnis* (Wolfenbüttel: Möseler, 1969).

120 Pierluigi Petrobelli, "Tartini e la musica popolare," *Chigiana* 26–27, nos. 6–7 (1971): 443–452; see in Petrobelli, *Tartini, le sue idee e il suo tempo*, 101–108; see also Polzonetti, *Tartini e la musica secondo natura*.

121 On the inclusion of the *Aria di Tasso* in Tartini's *Sonata G2 in G-Major* and *Sonata D2 in D-Major*, see Alessandro Zattarin, "'Vidi in sogno un guerrier': Tasso, Metastasio e altri fantasmi nelle sonate a violino solo di Giuseppe Tartini," *Ad Parnassum* 11, no. 22 (2013): 143–159; see also Ivano Cavallini, "Natura e alterità: Ancora sull'Aria del Tasso di Giuseppe Tartini," *De musica disserenda* 10, no. 1 (2014): 77–94; Ivano Cavallini, "Artificio e natura: Alcune osservazioni sull'Aria del Tasso di Giuseppe Tartini," in *Barcarola: Il canto del gondoliere nella vita quotidiana e nell'immaginazione artistica*, ed. Sabine Meine (Rome: Viella, 2016), 89–104.

122 Cavallini, "Artificio e natura"; see also Paolo Fabbri, "Tasso e la sua fortuna musicale a Venezia," in *Formazione e fortuna del Tasso nella cultura della Serenissima*, ed.

Goethe, as a result of his longstanding involvement with music throughout his life,[123] in particular in connection with his directorship of the Weimar Theatre and Weimar Opera, was able to develop and formulate his own *Tonlehre*,[124] results of his profound reflection on *musica* and *scientia*[125] from the vantage point of a philosopher[126] based not on aesthetic theories related to methods and techniques of composition but rather on the sensual experience of the listener[127] – as a counterpart to his *Farbenlehre*[128] – centred around the dichotomy of major and minor keys, and the distinction between a *Naturwahren* (the preservation of *natura* in the sense of *musica naturalis*) and *Kunstwahren* (the preservation of *ars* in the sense of *musica artificialis*)[129] – topics which had been addressed by composers of the common-practice era, including Tartini. A first-hand experience with opera enabled Goethe to crystallize the differentiation between *ars* and *natura*, with the pre-eminence of the latter underscored by his theoretical model of the *Urpflanze*,[130] thereby achieving the culmination of a debate that had been at the forefront of Tartini's all-embracing discourse on the *disciplina musicae*.

Luciana Borsetto and Bianca Maria De Rif (Venice: Istituto Veneto di Scienze, Lettere ed Arti, 1997), 251–258.
123 Edgar Istel, "Goethe and Music," *The Musical Quarterly* 14, no. 2 (1928): 218–254.
124 Anny von Lange, *Mensch, Musik und Kosmos: Anregungen zu einer goetheanistischen Tonlehre* (Freiburg im Breisgau: Novalis, 1956).
125 Annemarie M. Sauerlander, "Goethe's Relation to Music," in *Essays on German Language and Literature in Honor of Theodore B. Hewitt*, ed. Jay Alan Pfeffer (Buffalo, New York: University of Buffalo, 1952), 39–55.
126 John Neubauer, "On Goethe's Tonlehre," in *Music and German Literature: Their Relationship Since the Middle Ages*, ed. James M. McGlathery (Columbia, South Carolina: Camden House, 1992), 132–141.
127 Further on this facet, see Andreas Eichhorn, "'Die Musik wirkt nur gegenwärtig und unmittelbar': Goethe als Musikhörer," *Österreichische Musikzeitschrift* 54, no. 2 (1999): 16–24.
128 Hilmar Dressler, "Die Farbe-Ton-Analogien im historischen Teil von Goethes Farbenlehre," *Freiburger Universitätsblätter* 35, no. 133 (1996): 97–108. On the affinity between Goethe's *Farbenlehre* and *Tonlehre*, see Anneliese Liebe, "Goethes Klang- und Tonvorstellung als Grundlage seiner Musikanschauung," in *Festschrift Heinz Becker: Zum 60. Geburtstag am 26. Juni 1982*, ed. Jürgen Schläder and Reinhold Quandt (Laaber: Laaber, 1982), 405–416.
129 Dieter Borchmeyer, "'Götterwert der Töne': Goethes Theorie der Musik," *Freiburger Universitätsblätter* 35, no. 133 (September 1996): 109–134; also in *Ein unteilbares Ganzes – Goethe: Kunst und Wissenschaft*, ed. Gottfried Schramm and Günter Schnitzler (Freiburg im Breisgau: Rombach, 1997), 117–172.
130 Further on the notion of Goethe's *Urpflanze*, in connection with his *Farbenlehre* and the reflection on the philosophies of Plato, see Barbara Zuber, "Reihe, Gesetz, Urpflanze, Nomos: Anton Weberns musikalisch-philosophisch-botanische Streifzüge," in *Anton Webern II*, ed. Heinz-Klaus Metzger and Rainer Riehn (Munich: Edition Text & Kritik, 1984), 304–336.

Bibliography

Agricola, Johann Friedrich. *Introduction to the Art of Singing*. Edited and translated by Julianne Baird. New York: Cambridge University Press, 1995.

Anatol'evič, Aleksej and Ivan Vasil'evič Rozanov. "Towards the Tact and Tactus in German Baroque Treatises." *Musiqi dünyasi* 3, no. 60 (2014): 7157–7180.

Angelucci, Eugenia. "Le Regole per ben suonar il violino di Tartini e la Violinschule di Leopold Mozart." In *Tartini: Il tempo e le opere*, edited by Maria Nevilla Massaro and Andrea Bombi, 299–320. Bologna: Società editrice il Mulino, 1994.

Aristides Quintilianus. *De musica libri tres/Peri mousikes*. Edited by Reginald Pepys Winnington-Ingram. Leipzig: Teubner, 1963.

Aristides Quintilianus. *On Music in Three Books*. Translated by Thomas J. Mathiesen. New Haven, Connecticut: Yale University Press, 1983.

Aristotle. *The Art of Rhetoric*. Edited and translated by John Henry Freese. London: Heinemann and New York: Putnam, 1926.

Aristotle. *On the Soul [...]*. Edited and translated by Walter Stanley Hett. Cambridge, Massachusetts: Harvard University Press and London: Heinemann, 1935

[Aristotle. *The Politics*. Edited and translated by Harris Rackham. London: Heinemann and New York: Putnam, 1932.

[Augustinus, Aurelius]. *Aurelius Augustinus, De musica liber VI: A Critical Edition with a Translation and an Introduction*. Translated by Martin Jacobsson. Stockholm: Almquist & Wiksell International, 2002.

[Bach, Carl Philipp Emanuel]. *Essay on the True Art of Playing Keyboard Instruments by Carl Philipp Emanuel Bach*. Edited and translated by William J. Mitchell. New York: Norton, 1949.

Bach, Carl Philipp Emanuel. *Versuch über die wahre Art das Clavier zu spielen [...]*, Erster Teil. Berlin: Henning, 1753; Berlin: Winter, ²1759; Leipzig; Schwickert, ³1780, ⁴1787, Zweiter Teil. Berlin: Winter, 1762; Leipzig: Schwickert, ²1780, ³1797.

Barbieri, Patrizio. "Die beiden Harmonie-Systeme der Paduaner Schule (1720–1820)." In *Die Musiktheorie im 18. und 19. Jahrhundert*, edited by Stefan Keym, 43–99. Darmstadt: Wissenschaftliche Buchgesellschaft, 2021.

Barbieri, Patrizio. "Tartinis Dritter Ton und Eulers Harmonische Exponenten, mit einem unveröffentlichten Manuskript Tartinis." *Musiktheorie* 7, no. 3 (1992): 219–234.

Barker, Andrew, ed. *Greek Musical Writings*, vol. 2, *Harmonic and Acoustic Theory*. Cambridge: Cambridge University Press, 1989.

Barker, Andrew. *The Science of Harmonics in Classical Greece*. Cambridge: Cambridge University Press, 2017.

Beck, Eleonora M. *Giotto's Harmony: Music and Art in Padua at the Crossroads of the Renaissance*. Florence: European Press Academic Publishing, 2005.

Berdes, Jane L. "L'ultima allieva di Tartini: Maddalena Lombardini Sirmen." In *Tartini: Il tempo e le opere*, edited by Maria Nevilla Massaro and Andrea Bombi, 213–320. Bologna: Società editrice il Mulino, 1994.

[Boethius]. *Anicii Manlii Torquati Severini Boetii: Institutione arithmetica libri duo e Institutione musica libri quinque accedit Geometria quae fertur Boetii*. Edited by Gottfried Friedlein. Leipzig: Teubner, 1867.

Boethius, Anicius Manlius Severinus. *Fundamentals of Music*. Translated by Calvin Bower, edited by Claude V. Palisca. New Haven, Connecticut: Yale University Press, 1989.

Borchmeyer, Dieter. "'Götterwert der Töne': Goethes Theorie der Musik." *Freiburger Universitätsblätter* 35, no. 133 (September 1996): 109–134; also in *Ein unteilbares Ganzes – Goethe: Kunst und Wissenschaft*, edited by Gottfried Schramm and Günter Schnitzler, 117–172. Freiburg im Breisgau: Rombach, 1997.

Bower, Calvin M. "Natural and Artificial Music: The Origins and Development of an Aesthetic Concept." *Musica Disciplina* 25 (1971): 17–33.

Boyden, David Dodge. "The Missing Italian Manuscript of Tartini's *Traité des Agréments*." *The Musical Quarterly* 46, no. 3 (July 1960): 315–328.

Brainard, Paul. *Le sonate per violino di Giuseppe Tartini: Catalogo temático*. Padua: Accademie tartiniana di Padova, 1975.

Brainard, Paul. "Tartini and the Sonata for Unaccompanied Violin." *Journal of the American Musicological Society* 14, no. 3 (Fall 1961): 383–394.

Bryski, Blaise David. "Cantabile vs. Sonabile: The Difference Between Singing and Playing." D.M.A. Thesis, Cornell University, 2006.

Busch-Salmen, Gabriele. "'Geübter Spieler, Musicus, Virtuos, Instrumentist von Profession, Meister': Anmerkungen zur Beziehungsvielfalt des Berufsmusikers in der zweiten Hälfte des 18. Jahrhunderts." In *Professionalismus in der Musik*, edited by Christian Kaden and Volker Kalisch, 98–104. Essen: Die Blaue Eule, 1999.

Canale Degrassi, Margherita. "Fonti per una ricostruzione della didattica di Tartini nella 'scuola delle nazioni'." *Muzikološki zbornik* 28 (1992): 15–24.

Canale Degrassi, Margherita. "The Solo Concertos by Giuseppe Tartini: Sources, Tradition and Thematic Catalogue." *Ad Parnassum* 11, no. 22 (October 2013): 11–49.

Carraro, Gregorio. "'Ah!, vous dirai-je Tartini!': Per la definizione di un contesto europeo delle 'Piccole sonate' di Giuseppe Tartini (I-Pca 1888/I)." In *Locatelli and the Violin Bravura Tradition*, edited by Fulvia Morabito, 123–130. Turnhout: Brepols, 2015.

Carraro, Gregorio. "Hidden Affinities: Accompanied Solo, Tartini and Germany." *Ad Parnassum* 11, no. 22 (October 2013): 113–126.

Carraro, Gregorio. "Natura e arte nell'improvvisazione di Giuseppe Tartini." In *Beyond Notes: Improvisations in Western Music of the Eighteenth and Nineteenth Centuries*, edited by Rudolf Rasch, 97–108. Turnhout: Brepols, 2011.

Carter, Stewart. "Giuseppe Tartini and the Music of Nature." In *Barocco Padano*, edited by Alberto Colzani, Andrea Luppi and Maurizio Padoan, 515–526. Padua: Centro Studi Antoniani, 2018.

Carugo, Adriano. "Giuseppe Moleto: Mathematics and the Aristotelian Theory of Science at Padua in the Second Half of the Sixteenth Century." In *Aristotelismo Veneto e scienza moderna*, edited by Luigi Olivieri, 509–517. Padua: Antenore, 1983.

Cavallini, Ivano. "Artificio e natura: Alcune osservazioni sull'Aria del Tasso di Giuseppe Tartini." In *Barcarola: Il canto del gondoliere nella vita quotidiana e nell'immaginazione artistica*, edited by Sabine Meine, 89–104. Rome: Viella, 2016.

Cavallini, Ivano. "Natura e alterità: Ancora sull'Aria del Tasso di Giuseppe Tartini." *De musica disserenda* 10, no. 1 (2014): 77–94.

Cazzato, Alessandro. "Eclettismo e modernità delle 26 piccole sonate di Giuseppe Tartini, all'incrocio tra musica e poesia." In *Musica storia, analisi e didattica*, edited by Augusta Dall'Arche and Francesco di Lernia, 43–59. Foggia: Claudio Grenzi, 2016.

Christensen, Thomas. "Rameau's 'L'Art de la Basse fondamentale'." *Music Theory Spectrum* 9 (Spring 1987): 18–41.

Cooper, John Madison. *Knowledge, Nature and the Good: Essays on Ancient Philosophy*. Princeton, New Jersey: Princeton University Press, 2004.

[d'Abano, Petrus]. Aponensis, Petrus [d'Abano, Petrus]. *Expositio problematum Aristotelis cum textu*. Mantua: Paul von Butzbach, 1475.

DeFord, Ruth I. "Mensural Theory in Early German Music Textbooks." *Musiktheorie: Zeitschrift für Musikwissenschaft* 31, no. 1 (2016): 11–28.

de Leemans, Pieter. "Ego, Petrus Paduanus, philosophie minimus alumpnorum: Pietro d'Abano's Preface to His Expositio problematum Aristotilis." In *Between Text and Tradition: Pietro d'Abano and the Reception of Pseudo-Aristotle's Problemata Physica in the Middle Ages*, edited by Pieter de Leemans and Maarten J.F.M. Hoenen, 21–52. Leuven: Leuven University Press, 2016.

Deppert, Heinrich. *Studien zum Frühwerk Johann Sebastian Bachs: Untersuchungen zur Chronologie auf der Grundlage der Kompositionstechnik in den Werken der Möllerschen Handschrift und der sogenannten Neumeister-Choräle*. Tutzing: Schneider, 2009.

Di Liscia, Daniel A., Eckhard Kessler and Charlotte Methuen, eds. *Method and Order in Renaissance Philosophy of Nature: The Aristotle Commentary Tradition*. Aldershot, Hants: Ashgate, 1997.

Don, Gary W. "Music and Goethe's Theories of Growth." Ph.D. Dissertation, University of Washington, 1991.

Dressler, Hilmar. "Die Farbe-Ton-Analogien im historischen Teil von Goethes Farbenlehre." *Freiburger Universitätsblätter* 35, no. 133 (September 1996): 97–108.

Durante, Sergio. "Tartini and His Texts." In *The Century of Bach and Mozart: Perspectives on Historiography, Composition, Theory, and Performance*, edited by Sean Gallagher and Thomas Forrest Kelly, 145–186. Cambridge, Massachusetts: Harvard University, Department of Music, 2008.

Durante, Sergio. *Tartini, Padova, l'Europa*. Livorno: Sillabe, 2017.

Eichhorn, Andreas. "'Die Musik wirkt nur gegenwärtig und unmittelbar': Goethe als Musikhörer." *Österreichische Musikzeitschrift* 54, no. 2 (March 1999): 16–24.

Elmer, Minnie A. "Tartini's Improvised Ornamentation." Ph.D. Dissertation, University of California at Berkeley, 1962.

Fabbri, Paolo "Tasso e la sua fortuna musicale a Venezia." In *Formazione e fortuna del Tasso nella cultura della Sernissima*, edited by Luciana Borsetto and Bianca Maria De Rif, 251–258. Venice: Istituto Veneto di Scienze, Lettere ed Arti, 1997.

Fanzago, Francesco. *Elogi di Giuseppe Tartini, primo violinista nella Cappella del Santo di Padova, e del P. Francesco Antonio Vallotti, maestro della medesima*. Padua: Conzatti, 1792.

Felici, Candida. "La disseminazione della musica di Giuseppe Tartini in Francia: Le edizioni settecentesche di sonate per violino e basso." *De musica disserenda* 10, no. 1 (2014): 57–75.

Felici, Candida. "'Non suona, canta su'l violino': From Aesthetics to Compositional and Performance Practice in Tartini's Instrumental Music." *Ad Parnassum* 11, no. 22 (October 2013): 127–141.

Feyerabend, Paul. *Philosophy of Nature*. Translated by Dorothea Lotter, edtited with an introduction by Helmut Heit and Eric Oberheim. Cambridge: UK: Polity, 2016.

French, Roger Kenneth. *Ancient and Natural History: Histories of Nature*. London: Routledge, 1994.

[Gaffurio, Franchino]. *Franchinus Gaffurius: De harmonia musicorum instrumentorum opus*. Translated by Clement A. Miller. n.p.: American Institute of Musicology, 1977.

Gaffurio, Franchino. *The Theory of Music*. Translated with introduction and notes by Walter Kurt Kreyszig. New Haven, Connecticut: Yale University Press, 1993.

Galliard, John Ernest. *Observations on the Florid Song, or Sentiments on the Ancient and Modern Singers [...]*. London: J. Wilcox, 1743.

Gallo, F. Alberto. "Greek Texts and Latin Translations of the Aristotelian *Musical Problems*: A Preliminary Account of the Sources," translated by Charles André Barbera. In *Music Theory and Its Sources: Antiquity and the Middle Ages*, edited by Charles André Barbera. Notre Dame, 190–196. Indiana: University of Notre Dame Press, 1990.

Grant, Edward. *A History of Natural Philosophy: From the Ancient World to the Nineteenth Century.* Cambridge: Cambrige University Press, 2007.

Grasso Caprioli, Leonella. "Lessico tecnico e strutture linguistiche di Tartini didatta nelle Regole per ben suonar il violino." In *Tartini: Il tempo e le opere*, edited by Maria Nevilla Massaro and Andrea Bombi, 281–298. Bologna: Società editrice il Mulino, 1994.

Grendler, Marcella. "A Greek Collection in Padua: The Library of Gian Vincenzo Pinelli (1535–1600)." *Renaissance Quarterly* 33 (1980): 386–416.

Guanti, Giovanni. "Chi ha paura della 'Scienza platonica fondata nel cerchio' di Tartini?" *Rivista Italiana di Musicologia* 38, no. 1 (2003): 41–73.

Guanti, Giovanni. "Giuseppe Tartini lettore di Platone." In *Florilegium Musicae: Studi in onore di Carolyn Gianturco*, 2 vols., edited by Patrizia Radicchi and Michael Burden, vol. 2, 603–619. Pisa: ETS, 2004.

Guanti, Giovanni."La natura nel sogno platonizzante di Giuseppe Tartini." In *Tartini "maestro" narodov in kulturno življenje v obalnih mestih današnje Slovenije med 16. in 18. stoletjem/Tartini "maestro delle nazioni" e la vita culturale delle cittadine del Litorale tra i secoli XVI e XVIII*, edited by Metoda Kokole, 51–69. Ljubljana: Znanstvenorazikovalni center SAZU, 2001.

Gutknecht, Dieter. "Zur Rezeptionsgeschichte von Carl Philipp Emanuel Bachs 'Versuch' in den Verzierungslehren des 19. Jahrhunderts." In *Carl Philipp Emanuel Bach als Lehrer: Die Verbreitung der Musik Carl Philipp Emanuel Bachs in England und Skandinavien*, edited by Hans-Günter Ottenberg and Ulrich Leisinger, 195–203. Frankfurt an der Oder: Musikgesellschaft Carl Philipp Emanuel Bach, 2005.

Handschin, Jacques. "The 'Timaeus' Scale." *Musica Disciplina* 4 (1950): 3–42.

Harriss, Ernest C. "Johann Mattheson and the Affekten-, Figuren-, and Rhetoriklehren." In *La musique et le rite sacré et profane*, 2 vols., edited by Marc Honegger, Christian Meyer and Paul Prévost, vol. 2, 517–531. Strasbourg: Association des Publications près les Universités de Strasbourg, 1986.

Hefling, Stephen E. "'Of the Manner of Playing the Adagio': Structural Levels and Performance Practice in Quantz's *Versuch*." *Journal of Music Theory* 31, no. 2 (Fall 1987): 205–223.

Herlinger, Jan. *The Lucidarium of Marchetto of Padua: A Critical Edition, Translation and Commentary.* Chicago, Illinois: University of Chicago Press, 1985.

Hicks, Andrew James. *Composing the World: Harmony in the Medieval Platonic Cosmos*. New York: Oxford University Press, 2017.

Hiltner, Beate. "Leopold Mozart: Der Versuch einer gründlichen Violinschule – Fundus für Singstil und Instrumentalstil." *Wiener Figaro* 53, no. 1 (March 1996): 7–10.

Hoffmann, Adolf. *Die Orchestersuiten Georg Philipp Telemanns TWV 55, mit thematisch-bibliographischem Werkverzeichnis*. Wolfenbüttel: Möseler, 1969.

Hoffmann-Axthelm, Dagmar. "David musicus, or: On the Consoling Power of String Music," translated by Roger Harmon. In *Bonjour, bon mois et bonne estrenne: Essays on Renaissance Music in Honour of David Fallows*, edited by Fabrice Fitch and Jacobijn Kiel, 326–337. Woodbridge, Suffolk: Boydell Press, 2011.

Irvine, Thomas. "Der belesene Kapellmeister: Leopold Mozart und seine Bibliotheken." *Acta Mozartiana* 55, nos.1–2 (June 2008): 6–15.

Istel, Edgar. "Goethe and Music." *The Musical Quarterly* 14, no. 2 (April 1928): 218–254.

Jacobi, Erwin Reuben. "G.F. Nicolai's Manuscript of Tartini's 'Regole per ben suonar il violino'." *The Musical Quarterly* 47, no. 2 (April 1961): 207–223.

Jacobi, Erwin Reuben. "Giuseppe Tartini's Regula per ben accordare il Violino." In *Music East and West: Essays in Honor of Walter Kaufmann*, edited by Thomas L. Noblitt, 199–207. New York: Pendragon, 1981.

Jacobs, Jonathan A. *Aristotle's Virtues: Nature, Knowledge, & Human Good*. New York: Lang, 2004.

Jerold, Beverly. "Tartini and the Two Forms of Appoggiature." *Eighteenth-Century Music* 16, no. 1 (March 2019): 83–86.

Johansen, Karsten Friis. *A History of Ancient Philosophy: From the Beginnings to Augustine*. Translated by Henrik Rosenmeier. London: Routledge, 1998.

Johansen, Thomas Kjeller. *Plato's Natural Philosophy: A Study of the Timaeus-Critias*. Cambridge: Cambridge University Press, 2004.

Johnson, Fredric Bolan. "Tartini's Trattato di musica seconda la vera scienza dell'armonia: An Annotated Translation with Commentary." Doctoral Dissertation, Indiana University, 1985.

Kahl, Willi, with introductions and annotations, *Selbstbiographien deutscher Musiker des XVIII. Jahrhunderts*. Cologne: Staufen, 1948.

Kleßmann, Eckart. *Der Blumenfreund Georg Philipp Telemann*. Hamburg; Saucke, 1996.

Kremer, Joachim. "'Regel' versus 'Geschmack': Die Kritik an musikalischen Regeln zwischen 1700 und 1752 als Paradigmenwechsel." In *Musikalische Norm um 1700*, edited by Rainer Bayreuther, 117–143. Berlin: De Gruyter, 2010.

Kreyszig, Walter Kurt. "Humanistische Tendenzen im *Versuch einer gründlichen Violinschule* (1756) von Leopold Mozart, im *Versuch einer Anweisung die Flöte traversiere zu spielen* (1752) von Johann Joachim Quantz und im *Notenbuch* (1785) von Thomas Attwood." In *Leopold Mozart: Chronist und Wegbereiter – Dokumentation einer Tagung*, edited by Thomas Hochradner and Michaela Schwarzbauer, 119–153. Vienna: Hollitzer, 2022.

Kreyszig, Walter Kurt. "'Leopold Mozart ... a man of much ... sagacity': The Revival of Humanist Scholarship in His Gründliche Violinschule (Augsburg, 1789)." In *Music's Intellectual History*, edited by Zdravko Blažeković and Barbara Dobbs Mackenzie, 43–156. New York: Répertoire International de Littérature Musicale, 2009.

Kreyszig, Walter Kurt. "Oltre il *Versuch einer Anweisung die Flöte traversière zu spielen* (Berlino, 1752) di Johann Joachim Quantz (1697–1773): I suoi *Capricci* per flauto solo contenuti nel manoscritto di Copenaghen (Collezione Giedde I,17) nel contesto del suo approccio pedagogico." *Il Paganini* 5 (2019): 113–117.

Kreyszig, Walter Kurt. "Quantz's *Adagio in C-Major for Flute and Basso continuo* (QV 1:7) in His *Versuch* (1752): Baroque Ornamentation in the Context of the Mid-18th Century Music Theoretical Discourse and Compositions in the *stilus mixtus*." *Ad Parnassum* 10, no. 22 (October 2012): 139–171.

Kreyszig, Walter Kurt. "The Eminent Pedagogue Johann Joachim Quantz as Instructor of Frederick the Great During the Years 1728–1741: The 'Solfeggi', the 'Versuch einer Anweisung die Flöte traversière zu spielen', and the 'Capricen, Fantasien und Anfangsstücke' of Quantz, the 'Flötenbuch' of Frederick the Great and Quantz, and the 'Achtundzwanzig Variationen' über die Arie 'Ich schlief, da träumte mir' of Quantz (QV 1:98)." In *Kolloquium "Krisen- und Blütezeiten: Die Entwicklung der Königlich-Preußischen Hofkapelle von 1713 bis 1806"*, edited by Lena van der Hoven and Jürgen Luh, perspectivia. net Elektronische Publikationsplattform der Max Weber Stiftung, 2017, 41 pages; accessed 2 January 2022, https://perspectivia.net/rsc/viewer/ploneimport_derivate_00010462/kreyszig_quantz.doc.pdf?page=1&q=kreyszig

Kreyszig, Walter Kurt. "Zur Beziehung zwischen *compositio* und *diminutio* im Kontext der Telemann-Rezeption: Georg Philipp Telemanns 'Methodische Sonaten' (Hamburg, 1728, 1732) als Vorbild für den 'Versuch' (Berlin, 1752) von Johann Joachim Quantz?" In *Vom Umgang mit Telemanns Werk einst und jetzt: Telemann-Rezeption in drei Jahrhunderten*, edited by Carsten Lange and Brit Reipsch, 33–57. Hildesheim: Olms, 2017.

Lasocki, David. "Quantz and the Passions: Theory and Practice." *Early Music* 6, no. 4 (October 1978): 556–567.

Leisinger, Ulrich. "Leopold Mozart's Violin Textbook: Genesis – Circulation – Significance." In *Leopold Mozart: Musiker – Manager – Mensch/Musician – Manager – Man*, edited by Anja Morgenstern, trans. Elizabeth Mortimer, 88–95. Salzburg: Pustet, 2019.

Liebe, Anneliese. "Goethes Klang- und Tonvorstellung als Grundlage seiner Musikanschauung." In *Festschrift Heinz Becker: Zum 60. Geburtstag am 26. Juni 1982*, edited by Jürgen Schläder and Reinhold Quandt, 405–416. Laaber: Laaber, 1982.

Lohri, Angela. *Kombinationstöne und Tartinis "Terzo suono"*. Mainz: Schott, 2016.

Malagò, Giorgia, ed. *Giuseppe Tartini: Lettere e documenti/Pisma in dokumenti/Letters and Documents*. 2 vols. Translated by Jerneja Umer Kljun and Roberto Baldo. Trieste: Edizioni Università di Trieste, 2020.

Mambella, Guido. "La musica fuori del numero in Zarlino." In *Musico perfetto: Gioseffo Zarlino, 1517–1590 – La teoria musicale a stampa nel Cinquecento*, edited by Luisa Maria Zanoncelli, 61–66. Venice: Biblioteca Nazionale Marciana, 2017.

Marchetto of Padua. *Pomerium in arte musicae mensuratae*. Edited by Giuseppe Vecchi. Rome: American Institute of Musicology, 1961.

Mathiesen, Thomas J. "Harmonia and Ethos in Ancient Greek Music." *The Journal of Musicology* 3 (1984): 264–279.

Miller, Fred D. *Nature, Justice and Rights in Aristotle's Politics*. Oxford: Clarendon Press, and New York: Oxford University Press, 1996.

Mountford, J. F. "The Musical Scales of Plato's Republic." *Classical Quarterly* 17 (1923): 125–136.

[Mozart, Leopold]. *A Treatise on the Fundamental Principles of Violin Playing by Leopold Mozart*. Translated by Editha Knocker. Oxford: Oxford University Press, ²1951.

Mozart, Leopold. *Versuch einer gründlichen Violinschule [...]*. Augsburg: Lotter, 1756, ²1769/1770, ³1787, ⁴1800; facsimile reprint of third edition, with a preface by David Oistrach; explained with commentary by Hans Rudolf Jung. Wiesbaden: Breitkopf & Härtel, 1983.

Naddaf, Gerard. *The Greek Concept of Nature*. Albany, New York: State University of New York Press, 2005.

Neubacher, Jürgen. "Einflüsse der Gartenkultur auf die Musik im 16. und 17. Jahrhundert." In *Die Blumenbücher des Hans Simon Holtzbecker und Hamburgs Lustgärten: Hans Simon Holtzbecker, Hamburger Blumenmaler des 17. Jahrhunderts – Botanische, garten- und kunsthistorische Aspekte*, edited by Dietrich Roth, 155–174. Kellern-Weiler: Goecke & Evers, 2003.

Neubauer, John. "On Goethe's Tonlehre." In *Music and German Literature: Their Relationship Since the Middle Ages*, edited by James M. McGlathery, 132–141. Columbia, South Carolina: Camden House, 1992.

Northwood, Heidi Marguerite. "Harmony and Stability: Number and Proportion in Early Greek Conceptions of Nature." Ph.D. Dissertation, University of Alberta, Edmonton, Alberta, 1997.

Palisca, Claude V. "Moving the Affections Through Music: Pre-Cartesian Psycho-Physiological Theories." In *Number to Sound: The Musical Way to the Scientific Revolution*, edited by Paolo Gozza, 289–308. Boston, Massachusetts: Kluwer Academic Publishers, 2000.

Pavanello, Agnese. "Il Trillo del diavolo di Giuseppe Tartini nell'edizione di Jean Baptiste Cartier." *Recercare* 11 (1999): 265–279.

Pečman, Rudolf. "C.Ph.E. Bach und die Affektenlehre: Bemerkungen zur Aufführungspraxis." *Musicologica Brunensia* 50–51, H36–H37 (2001–2002): 17–22.

Petrobelli, Pierluigi. *Giuseppe Tartini: Le fonti biografiche*. Milan: Universal Edition, 1968.

Petrobelli, Pierluigi. "La scuola di Tartini in Germania e la sua influenza." In *Studien zur italienisch-deutschen Musikgeschichte*, edited by Friedrich Lippmann, 1–17. Cologne: Böhlau, 1968.

Petrobelli, Pierluigi. "La Violinschule di Leopold Mozart e la musica vocale." *Neues Musikwissenschaftliches Jahrbuch* 14 (2006): 11–15.

Petrobelli, Pierluigi. "Tartini e la musica popolare." *Chigiana* 26–27, nos. 6–7 (1971): 443–452.

Petrobell, Pierluigi. "Tartini, Giuseppe." In *The New Grove Dictionary of Music and Musicians*, 29 vols., edited by Stanley Sadie,vol. 25, 108–114. London: Macmillan, 2001.

Petrobelli, Pierluigi. *Tartini, le sue idee e il suo tempo*. Luca: Libreria Musicale Italiana, 1992.

Plato. *The Republic*, 2 vols. Edited and translated by Paul Shorey. London: Heinemann and New York: Putnam, 1930.

Polzonetti, Pierpaolo. *Tartini e la musica secondo natura*. Lucca: Libreria Musicale Italiana, 2001.

Quantz, Johann Joachim. *Capricen, Fantasien und Anfangsstücke für Flöte solo und mit B.c./Caprices, Fantasias and Beginner's Pieces for Flute solo and with Basso continuo*. Edited by Wilfried Michel and Hermien Teske. Winterthur: Amadeus, 1980.

[Quantz, Johann Joachim] "Herrn Johann Joachim Quantzens Lebenslauf von ihm selbst entworfen." In Friedrich Wilhelm Marpurg, *Historisch-kritische Beyträge zur Aufnahme der Musik*, 5 vols. Berlin: Schütz [vol. 1], and Berlin: Lange [vols. 2–5], 1754–1762, vol. 1 (1754–1755), 197–250.

Quantz, Johann Joachim. *On Playing the Flute*. Translated with introduction and notes by Edward R. Reilly. New York: Schirmer, 1966.

Quantz, Johann Joachim. *Versuch einer Anweisung die Flöte traversière zu spielen [...]*. Berlin: Voß, 1752.

Rameau, Jean-Philippe. *Treatise on Harmony*. Translated with an introduction and notes by Philip Gossett. New York: Dover, 1971.

Reilly, Edward R. *Quantz and His Versuch: Three Studies*. New York, American Musicological Society, 1971.

Reipsch, Ralph-Jürgen. "Dokumente zu Georg Philipp Telemanns 'Blumen-Liebe'." In *Das Moller-Florilegium des Hans Simon Holtzbecker*, edited by Dietrich Roth, 60–79. Berlin: Kulturstiftung der Länder, 2001.

Renner, Ralph Clifford. "The Pomerium of Marchettus of Padua: A Translation and Critical Commentary." M.A. Thesis, Washington University, 1980.

Sauerlander, Annemarie M. "Goethe's Relation to Music." In *Essays on German Language and Literature in Honor of Theodore B. Hewitt*, edited by Jay Alan Pfeffer, 39–55. Buffalo, New York: University of Buffalo, 1952.

Scheibert, Beverly. "New Information About Performing 'Small Notes'." In *The Harpsichord and Its Repertoire*, edited by Pieter Dirksen, 99–118. Utrecht: Foundation for Historical Performance Practice, 1992.

Seedorf, Thomas. "Die italienische Gesangslehre und ihre deutsche Rezeption im 17. und 18. Jahrhundert." *Musica e storia* 10, no. 1 (June 2002): 259–270.

Seidel, Wilhelm. "Der Tactus, die Taktarten und der Takt." In *Musikedition als Vermittlung und Übersetzung: Festschrift für Petra Weber zum 60. Geburtstag*, edited by Christian Speck, 11–22. Bologna: Ut Orpheus, 2016.

Siraisi, Nancy G. "The *Expositio Problematum Aristotelis* of Peter of Abano." *Isis* 61, no. 3 (Autumn 1970): 321–339.

Solomon, Jon. "Towards a History of Tonoi." *The Journal of Musicology* 3 (1984): 242–251.

Staehelin, Martin. "Giuseppe Tartini über seine künstlerische Entwicklung: Ein unbekanntes Selbstzeugnis." *Die Musikforschung* 35, no. 4 (1978): 251–274.

Sukljan, Nejc. "Renaissance Music Between Science and Art: The Case of Gioseffo Zarlino." *Muzikološki zbornik* 56, no. 2 (2020): 183–206.

Tartini, Giuseppe. *De' principj dell'armonia musicale contenuta nel diatonico genere*. Padova: Stamperia del seminario, 1767.

Tartini, Giuseppe. *Scienza platonica fondata nel cerchio*. Edited by Anna Todeschini Cavalla. Padua: CEDAM, 1977.

Tartini, Giuseppe. *Traite des agremens de la musique/Abhandlung über die Verzierung in der Musik/Treatise on Ornaments in Music*. Edited by Erwin Reuben Jacobi, with English translation by Cuthbert Girdlestone. Celle: Moeck, 1961.

Tartini, Giuseppe. "Trattato di musica: Music and Geometry – Scienza Platonica: Rediscovery of Ancient Harmonic Wisdom." In *The Harmony of the*

Spheres: A Sourcebook of the Pythagorean Tradition in Music, edited by Joscelyn Godwin, 314–361. Rochester, Vermont: Inner Traditions International, 1993.

Tartini, Giuseppe. *Trattato di musica secondo la vera scienza dell'armonia*. Padova: Stamperia del Seminario, 1754.

Thieme, Ulrich. *Die Affektenlehre im philosophischen und musikalischen Denken des Barock: Vorgeschichte, Ästhetik, Physiologie*. Celle: Moeck, 1984.

Torrance, John, ed. *The Concept of Nature*. Oxford: Clarendon Press, 1992.

[Tosi, Peter Franz and Johann Friedrich Agricola]. *Anleitung zur Singkunst, aus dem Italiänischen von Herrn Peter Franz Tosi [...]*. Berlin: Winter, 1757.

Vanderjagt, Arie Johan and Klaas van Berkel, *The Book of Nature in Antiquity and the Middle Ages*. Leeuven: Peeters, 2005.

Vitali, Danilo. "Il 'Trattato degli abbellimenti' di Giuseppe Tartini." Ph.D. Dissertation, Sapienza Università di Roma, 1995.

Viverit, Guido. "Dissemination and Tradition of Tartini's Compositions Within the 'School of Nations'." *Ad Parnassum* 11, no. 22 (October 2013): 87–98.

Viverit, Guido. "Giuseppe Tartini e l'aristocrazia: La formazione dei violinisti per le corti europee e per i mecenati practi." In *Music and Power in the Baroque Era*, edited by Rudolf Rasch, 381–396. Turnhout: Brepols, 2018.

von Lange, Anny. *Mensch, Musik und Kosmos: Anregungen zu einer goetheanistischen Tonlehre*. Freiburg im Breisgau: Novalis, 1956.

Waldura, Markus. "Zum Stellenwert der physikalischen Natur in den Musiktheorien Rameaus und Marpurgs – Ein Vergleich." In *Künste und Natur: In Diskursen der Frühen Neuzeit*, edited by Hartmut Laufhütte, 755–779. Wiesbaden: Harrassowitz, 2000.

Wallace, Susan Murphree. "The 'Devil's Trill Sonata': Tartini and His Teachings." D.M.A. Thesis, University of Texas at Austin, 2003.

Whitmore, Philip J. "Towards an Understanding of the Capriccio." *Journal of the Royal Musical Association* 113, no. 1 (1988): 48–56.

Wilberding, James and Christoph Horn, eds. *Neoplatonism and the Philosophy of Nature*. Oxford: Oxford University Press, 2012.

Wittmann, Michael. *Vox atque sonus: Studien zur Rezeption der Aristotelischen Schrift "De anima" und ihre Bedeutung für die Musiktheorie*, 2 vols. Pfaffenweiler: Centaurus, 1987.

Woodward, Beverly. "The Probestücke and C.P.E. Bach's Versuch über die wahre Art das Clavier zu spielen." In *De clavichordo 2*. Magnano: Musica antica, 1995, 84–93.

Zarlino, Gioseffo. *The Art of Counterpoint: Part Three of Le Istitutioni harmoniche (1558)*. Translated by Guy A. Marco and Claude V. Palisca. New Haven, Connecticut: Yale University Press, 1968.

Zarlino, Gioseffo. *Theorie des Tonsystems: Das erste und zweite Buch der Istitutioni harmoniche (1573)*. Translated with remarks, commentary and a postscript by Michael Fend. Berlin: Lang, 1989.

Zattarin, Alessandro. "'Vidi in sogno un guerrier': Tasso, Metastasio e altri fantasmi nelle sonate a violino solo di Giuseppe Tartini." *Ad Parnassum* 11, no. 22 (October 2013): 143–159.

Zuber, Barbara. "Reihe, Gesetz, Urpflanze, Nomos: Anton Weberns musikalisch-philosophisch-botanische Streifzüge." In *Anton Webern II*, edited by Heinz-Klaus Metzger and Rainer Riehn, 304–336. Munich: Edition Text & Kritik, 1984.

Bella Brover Lubovsky

Jerusalem Academy of Music and Dance

"No Other Art than the Imitation of Nature": Tartini, Algarotti, and the Hermeneutics of Modal Dualism

Abstract: This chapter explores the notion of pairing the parallel major and minor triads in Giuseppe Tartini's compositions vis-à-vis in his theoretical writings, using a conceptual link between his harmonic theories and the ideological syncretism promulgated by Francesco Algarotti. Algarotti's famous bestseller *Il newtonianismo per le Dame* (1737) and other works greatly contributed to the connection between the optical and acoustical theories and to their domestication within the cultural consciousness of his time. Tartini, in his remarkable correspondence with Algarotti, deployed his views in a mode similar to that of his renowned interlocutor. One of the issues that arose in the wake of this discussion was the crucial explanation of the minor triad as a direct "gift of nature." An analysis of main patterns of Tartini's usage of the parallel minor in his music demonstrates a unity with his theories, attesting what he conceived as the most natural way of pairing the major and minor triads.

Keywords: Giuseppe Tartini, Francesco Algarotti, Newtonian sciences, optical theories, modal dualism, parallel keys

> *These arts [...] are not only true imitations of Nature, but of the best nature; of that which wrought up to a nobler pitch. They present us with images more perfect than the life in any individual: and we have the pleasure to see all the scattered beauties of Nature united.*[1]
>
> From Francesco Algarotti's *Saggio sopra la pittura*

> *I seek the greatest possible affinity with nature and am least at home in the matter of art: for if I possess any art at all, it is that of imitating nature.*[2]
>
> Giuseppe Tartini

---

1 Francesco Algarotti, *Opere. Edizione novissima*, vol. 3, *Saggio sopra la pittura* (Venice: Palese, 1791–1794), 99.

2 "[...] devo dire che io sto di casa più che posso con la natura, meno che posso con l'arte; non avendo io altra arte, se non la imitazione della natura." Giorgia Malagò, ed., *Giuseppe Tartini: Lettere e documenti/Pisma in dokumenti/Letters and documents*,

This chapter explores the epistemological roots of one of Tartini's stylistic idiosyncrasies – namely, his theoretical view and practical use of the parallel minor key within his compositions. It is true that abrupt flashes of the minor triads instead of their expected major-third counterpart on the same root are a signature device of Tartini's style, their occurrence being virtually compulsory in his major-key concerto and sonata movements in an impressive diversity of patterns, starting from a momentary touch of the minor third in the triad and up to deploying passages built on extended harmonic progressions and whole protracted episodes in the parallel minor key. Tartini's creative response to such a vital problem as establishing the system built on the dualism of the major and minor thirds, triads and scales, will be viewed within the cultural and intellectual climate of the mid-eighteenth century and, more specifically, within his dialogue with one of the leading savants of this time, Francesco Algarotti (1712–1764).

Pierluigi Petrobelli's pioneering essay explored Tartini's link to the prince-elector of Saxony and the cultural and intellectual activity at court in Dresden.[3] Since then much has been written on Tartini's communication with European rulers, conducted via Algarotti, their accomplished courtier and confidant.[4] Further examination of the personal and ideological link between these two figures will possibly outline their shared views on one of the pivotal notions of mid-eighteenth-century European science and culture and enable a conceptual framework to be drawn up in order to examine their implications in Tartini's compositions.

Tartini's epistolary communication with Algarotti mostly took place during the latter's stay at German courts – as a counsellor of Frederick II, King of Prussia, in Berlin, and of Augustus III, King of Poland and Elector of Saxony, in Dresden (1740–1753). Tartini was the only composer with whom the savant exchanged letters during the entire decade (1746–1756), strengthening our assumption of their personal interaction after Algarotti's return to Venice in 1754 (even if no documentary evidence of such meetings has been found until now).[5] Apart from this, the

---

vol. 1, trans. Jerneja Umer Kljun and Roberto Baldo (Trieste: Edizioni Università di Trieste, 2020), 179. English translation in Malagò, *Tartini: Lettere*, 2:318.
3 Pierluigi Petrobelli, "Tartini, Algarotti e la corte di Dresda," *Analecta Musicologica* 2 (1965): 72–84.
4 See Domenico Michelessi, *Memorie intorno alla vita ed agli scritti del conte Francesco Algarotti* (Venice: Pasquali, 1770); Vincenzo C. Alberti, *De vita, et scriptis Francisci Algarotti commentarius* (Lucca: Riccomini, 1771); Franco Arato, *Il secolo delle cose: Scienza e storia in Francesco Algarotti* (Genoa: Marietti, 1991).
5 See Malagò, *Tartini: Lettere*. Algarotti's letters are also reproduced in Francesco Algarotti, *Opere. Edizione novissima*, vol. 9, *Lettere varie* (Venice: Palese, 1791–1794), 267–272; Francesco Algarotti, *Lettere filologiche del conte Francesco Algarotti* (Venice: Alvisopoli, 1826), 122–126; *Opere varie del Conte Francesco Algarotti Ciamberlano di S. M. il Re di Prussia e cavaliere dell'Ordine del Merito*, vol. 1 (Venice: Pasquali, 1757): 421–425.

violinist occupies a solid physical presence in Algarotti's prose, being frequently mentioned in his essays and letters as the "incomparable" Tartini – as an exemplar of naturalness of style and as a violin player and teacher of outstanding reputation: "The famous Tartini deserves all his attention, and he alone is well worth a musician going to Padua to hear him."[6]

Algarotti was a true polymath, whose exuberant writings embrace virtually any field of human activity: arts and languages, anatomy and natural philosophy, history and military science, etc.; all gravitate towards the quest for the systematic commonality between various domains, revealing a fervent zeal to link scientific endeavours to their cultural outcome. His famous bestseller, *Il newtonianismo per le dame* (*Newton's Theory [...] for the Use of the Ladies*), completed in 1737, based on his own earlier replication of the Newtonian optical *experimentum crucis* in the *Istituto delle Scienze e delle Arti* in Bologna, focused on the cultural and artistic implications of this prismatic performance. These had led the savant to merge the disciplines of optics and acoustics: "This sound and this light [...] seem so faithfully copied one from another, as if they were the portrayals of Nature."[7]

Algarotti pays tribute to various aspects of the similarity of light and pitch and their shared physical characteristic, extensively elaborating on the consanguinity between them: "The different Quickness of the Vibrations on the Air, or the auditory Nerve, produces different Sounds, as Bass, Treble, and their different Degrees. In the same manner the different Quickness of the Vibrations raises in the ethereal Matter or the Optic Nerve produces different Colours, as red, yellow, and the like, which may be considered as the *Tones* of Light."[8]

---

6 "Le célèbre Tartini merite toute son attention, et lui seul vaut bien qu'un musicien aille à Padoue pour l'écouter." Quoted from a letter to Prince of Prussia Frederick Henry Louis (1726–1802), a younger brother of Frederick II, of 6 July 1761. See Francesco Algarotti, *Opere. Edizione novissima*, vol. 15, *Carteggio inedito del conte Algarotti: parte quinta* (Venice: Palese, 1791–1794), 282–283. English translation by the author.

7 "Questo suono e questa luce [...] mi pajono così fedelmente copiati gli uni dagli altri, com' erano i ritratti [...] da Natura." Francesco Algarotti, *Il Newtonianismo per le dame ovvero Dialoghi sopra la Luce e i Colori* (Naples [Milan], 1737), 136. English translation by the author.

8 "La differenza della prontezza delle vibrazioni nell'aria o nel nervo dell'orecchio produce la differenza de' toni, come, il basso, l'acuto, e i loro differenti gradi: è la differenza della prontezza delle vibrazioni nella materia eterea o nel nervo ottico, non produce ella la differenza de' colori, come il rosso, il giallo, e gli altri, che si ponno in certa maniera considerare come i toni della luce?" Algarotti, *Il Newtonianismo*, 135, quoted and translated in Francesco Algarotti, *Sir Isaac Newton's Philosophy explain'd for the Use of the Ladies in Six Dialogues on Light and Colours*, vol. 1, trans. Elisabeth Carter (London: Cave, 1739): 217. See also Bella Brover Lubovsky, "Venetian Clouds and Newtonian Optics. Modal Polarity in Early Eighteenth-Century Music," in *Music Theory and Interdisciplinarity*, ed. Christian Utz (Saarbrücken, PFAU Verlag, 2010), 191–202.

Reverberations of such implications of optical theories are prominent in the entire period, including the bold stance in writings of another of Tartini's famous interlocutors – mathematician and physicist Leonhard Euler (1707–1783), Algarotti's colleague at the Berlin court. Euler's fascination with this kinship is revealed in his *Lettres à une Princesse d'Allemagne* (Letters to a German Princess): "The parallel between sound and light is so perfect, that it holds even in the minutest circumstances. [...] It is exactly the same as with light and colours, for the different colours correspond to the different musical sounds."[9] And further: "Diversity of colours is occasioned by this difference [i.e., the number of the vibrations produced in every body during a second]; and that difference of colour is to the organ of vision what sharp or flat sounds are to the ear."[10]

Consonant with Algarotti's credo that "nature, in multiple effect, is *unitary*,"[11] Tartini's philosophy also lies within the context of a longed-for unity and his firm belief that Nature as an all-embracing phenomenon is the source of every truth, as expressed in one of his letters to his learned interlocutor:

> This science is founded entirely on physical things, for nothing is, or could be, determined by the will of man. [...] But, my Most Revered Count, if this is true, then the whole science is true; and if the whole science is true, in spite of the presumptions of today's philosophy, and in spite of the prejudices against the author of the discovery (that violin player, ignoramus, etc., etc.), one must necessarily conclude, with the force of physical and demonstrative evidence, that not enough was known and that much more will be known thanks to this science;[12]

Tartini's *sistema mundi* reciprocates his correspondent's zeal for the systematic unity of all natural and cultural phenomena.[13] His concept of the unity of Nature

---

9 David Brewster, ed., *Letters of Euler on Different Subjects in Natural Philosophy, addressed to a German Princess*, vol. 1, trans. Henry Hunter (New York: Harper, 1837), 112.
10 Brewster, *Letters of Euler*, 1:110.
11 "[...] la natura, negli effetti moltiplice, è unitaria." Francesco Algarotti, *Opere. Edizione novissima*, vol. 2, *Dialoghi sopra l'ottica neutoniana* (Venice: Palese, 1791–1794), 299. English translation by the author.
12 "Questa scienza è fondata intieramente sopra le cose fisiche: nulla essendovi né potendovi essere di arbitrio umano. [...] Ma signor conte mio veneratissimo, se questa è vera, è vera tutta la scienza; se vera tutta la scienza, a dispetto della presuntione della presente filosofia, [...] e a dispetto de' pregiudicij, che porta seco l'autore della sopra scoperta, suonator di violino, ignorante, etc. etc., bisognerà concludere per forza fisica e demostrativa che non si sapeva a bastanza, e che in gratia di questa scienza si saprà molto di più." Quoted from a letter of Tartini to Algarotti of 12 November 1750. See Malagò, *Tartini: Lettere*, 1:186–187. English translation in Malagò, *Tartini: Lettere*, 2:325–326.
13 See Pierluigi Petrobelli, *Tartini, le sue idee e il suo tempo* (Lucca: LIM, 1992); Pierpaolo Polzonetti, *Tartini e la musica secondo natura* (Lucca: LIM, 1998).

that reveals its universal laws via various tracks was paradigmatic for the entire intellectual landscape. Algarotti responds to Tartini in a letter, sent from Venice to Padua in early 1754, declaring the priority of Nature:

"[...] those verses of mine have only caused in you [...] that motion which is of nature, and not of study. I pay more attention to your natural response than to the study of many academies. [...] Conversely, it will be the greatest delight of gentle souls if we take nature as a subject and are capable of painting those aspects that it presents to us, and those combinations among which we were born."[14]

Tartini's city, Padua, was an epicentre of north-Italian intellectual life, and the reverberations of new sciences were emblematic of its entire intellectual climate: here the local physicist Giovanni Rizzetti (1675–1751) replicated Newtonian experiments at the University; the famous mathematician Jacopo Riccati (1676–1754), the humanist educator Scipione Maffei (1675–1755), the writer and physicist Antonio Conti (1677–1749), Tartini's countryman, professor of history and economics at the University, Gianrinaldo Carli (1720–1795), and the mathematician and antiquarian Giovanni Poleni (1683–1761) participated in a public discussion on the truth of Newtonian optics and their pertinence to local scientific activity.[15] Tartini, having studied at the famous University, proved to be in frequent contact with this intellectual milieu, as he mentions in a letter to Paolo Battista Balbi of 14 April 1741: "I have worked for Polleni, for *Abate* Conti, for Riva, for Riccati, for Suzzi, but none of them, albeit most excellent men, are suitable for me."[16] His exposure to this debate and his acquaintance with Algarotti's *magnum opus* becomes explicit in one of the letters to the author, in which he mentions with genuine warmth Algarotti's "dissertation" (most likely, one of the later versions of *Il newtonianismo*) that has been sent to him, accompanied by his acknowledgment of his interlocutor's love and patronage.[17]

---

14 "[...] que' miei versi abbiano solamente cagionato in lei, secondo ch'ella pur dice, quel moto che è di natura, e non di studio. Io fo più caso del suo naturale che dello studio di parecchie accademie. [...] laddove sarà tuttavia la maggior delizia delle anime gentili, se noi piglieremo la natura per obbietto, e sapremo ben dipingere quegli aspetti, ch'ella ci va presentando, e quelle combinazioni, in mezzo alle quali noi siamo nati [...]" Malagò, *Tartini: Lettere*, 1:249–250. English translation in Malagò, *Tartini: Lettere*, 2:385–390.

15 See Paolo Casini, *Newton e la conscienza europea* (Bologna: Mulino, 1983), 173–227; Vincenzo Ferrone, *The Intellectual Roots of the Italian Enlightenment: Science, Religion and Politics in the Early Eighteenth Century*, trans. Sue Brotherton (Atlantic Highlands, NJ: Humanities Press, 1995); Brendan M. Dooley, *Science, Politics, and Society in Eighteenth-Century Italy: The Giornale de' letterati d'Italia and Its World* (New York: Garland, 1991).

16 "Ho servitù col Polleni, con l'abate Conti, col Riva, col Riccati, col Suzzi, ma niuno di questi per altro eccellentissimi fa per me." Malagò, *Tartini: Lettere*, 1:150. English translation in Malagò, *Tartini: Lettere*, 2:290.

17 See Tartini's letter of 18 November 1746 in Malagò, *Tartini: Lettere*, vol. 1:171–172.

It is equally noteworthy that Tartini's close acquaintance with contemporary optical theories and his exposure to the latest discoveries were reported by contemporaries, such as the following observation by Tartini's follower and fervent enthusiast, Benjamin Stillingfleet:

> [He] proves the harmony of the universe to be true in a literal sense; there is another instance totally new, discovered also by Newton, equally striking, and equally extensive. He found that the breadths of the seven original colours, were in same proportion as the seven musical intervals that compose an octave. [...] we cannot avoid believing that it tends some way or other to the perfection of the universe, either as to the use or beauty; and that the proportions cannot be altered.[18]

Tartini's major acoustical discovery – the recognition of the phenomenon of the *terzo suono* (difference or combination tone) – prior to being offered for public discussion was sent for approval to a number of intellectuals, including Leonhard Euler, Frederick the Great himself (for both these communications Algarotti served as a conduit), the music theorist, acoustician, and architect Giordano Riccati (1709–1790), and other leading European minds, receiving, as is known, an unfavourable response, even derision.[19] Algarotti, however, was not inclined to discuss and express his opinion on the essence of Tartini's theories, but rather preferred to pick up the notions that reverberated with his own views and his inclination to bold and imaginative metaphorical methods of representation.

The conceptual and rhetorical similarities between the ideological battles deployed in concurrent optical and acoustical theories of the arrangement of pitch phenomena are obvious; one of the crucial issues raised in contemporaneous discussion was the attempt to explain the dualism of the major and minor thirds and triads as a "direct gift of nature." Natural measuring and pairing of the major and minor thirds in a triad was expressed via rhetoric and metaphorical language similar to terms discussing light and shade and their shared characteristics in optics. Algarotti, for example, often uses the expression "the harmonization of colours" in painting, similar to Tartini's deployment of colour-oriented *chiaroscuro* parallels

---

18 Benjamin Stillingfleet, *Principles and Power of Harmony* (London: Hughs, 1771), 146.
19 *Risposta all'esame di Eulero*, by Giuseppe Tartini, Ms. D.VI.1894, pp. 17a–f. Cappella Antoniana Musical Archive, Padua; *Risposta di Giuseppe Tartini alla Critica del di lui Trattato di Musica di Mons. Le Serre di Ginevra* (Venice: De Castro, 1767); *Risposta di un'anonimo al celebre Sig. Rousseau* (Venice: De Castro, 1769); etc. See also Patrizio Barbieri, "Il sistema armónico di Tartini nelle 'censure' di due celebri fisico-matematici: Eulero e Riccati," in *Tartini: Il tempo le opere*, ed. Andrea Bombi and Maria Nevilla Massaro (Bologna: Il Mulino, 1994), 321–344; Luca Del Fra, *Commercio di Lettere intorno di Principj dell'Armonia fra il Signor Giuseppe Tartini ed il Co. Giordano Riccati* (Lucca: LIM, 2007); Patrizio Barbieri, *Quarrels on Harmonic Theories in the Venetian Enlightenment* (Lucca: LIM, 2020).

when discussing tuning systems in acoustics.[20] Art historian Michael Baxandall shows that the contemporaneous "discovery" of a shadow in painting was also a corollary of Newtonian optics and its epistemological repercussions, synchronically with the formation of the concept of modal dualism in music.[21] A figure of speech of the anonymous Marchioness – the interlocutor of the author in Algarotti's *Newtonianismo* – "We need only consult the Thirds of this Harpsichord, and we shall be sure never to make any Discord in the Shading"[22] – was thus fully comprehensible in this intellectual environment.

Following Gioseffo Zarlino (1517–1590) and other authors since the sixteenth century to his time, Tartini endeavoured to prove that the minor triad must be integral to any harmonic system. Hugo Riemann claimed that Zarlino was the founder of this concept, asserting, however, that his "splendid idea remained whether unnoticed or misunderstood for a full two hundred years, until it was recovered from oblivion and rediscovered by Tartini."[23] Tartini's basic approach, expressed as unity in multiplicity, was to establish the concept of modal dualism based on the premise that both the major and the minor triad are two aspects of the same harmonic system. He attempted to maintain the systematic unity of his dualistic conception by deriving both triads from a hierarchy of relationships based on harmonic versus arithmetic proportions in dividing a string. Tartini concluded that, while every facet of music theory was an inseparable part of the whole, major harmony, generated from the natural basic acoustical phenomena (harmonic division of a string), is therefore perfect; minor harmony, produced as a result of the arithmetical division of a string, leans on mathematical rather than physical proof, and is imperfect and deficient.

In his *Trattato di musica secondo la vera scienza dell'armonia* (Treatise on Music according to the True Science of Harmony, 1754), and even more in *De'principj dell'armonia musicale contenuta nel diatonico genere* (On the Principles of Musical Harmony Contained in the Diatonic Genus, 1767), Tartini considers the minor triad as extrapolated from the unity of the *tuone differenze* (combination tones) in the

---

20 "Di accordo nel dipinto." See, for example, Algarotti, *Opere*, 3:113; Giuseppe Tartini, *Trattato di musica secondo la vera scienza dell'armonia* (Padova: Stamperia del seminario, 1754), 100.
21 Michael Baxandall, *Shadows and Enlightenment* (New Haven and London: Yale University Press, 1995), 20–31.
22 "Noi non avremo che a consultar le terze, [...] di questo Cembalo per esser sicure di non metterne insieme di quegli, che poi scordino e si faccian guerra l'un altro." Algarotti, *Il Newtonianismo*, 138–139; english translation in Algarotti, *Sir Isaac Newton's Philosophy*, 1:224.
23 William C. Michelsen, trans. and ed., *Hugo Rieman's Theory of Harmony and History of Music Theory, Book III* (Lincoln: University of Nebraska Press, 1977), 3. See also Bella Brover Lubovsky, "Concepts of Modal Dualism in the Time of Vivaldi," in Alessandro Borin and Jasmin M. Cameron, eds., *Fulgeat sol frontis decorate. Studi in onore di Michael Talbot* (Venice: Fondazione Cini, 2016), 65–84.

major triad; by arranging the intervals of the harmonic series in the order of their appearance, and deriving the combination tones of the first order, he demonstrated the "natural" origin of the C minor triad paired with its parallel C major triad:

Our musical practice embraces two different kinds of harmony: that which is called the major-third type, and which arises from harmonic division of the sonorous string into unequal parts, 1/2, 1/3, 1/4, 1/5, 1/6; and that which is called the minor-third type, and which arises from arithmetic division of the same string into equal parts 1, 2, 3, 4, 5, 6.

It is certain that everything established up to now belongs solely to the major-third kind of harmony, which means to harmonic division; in no way to the minor-third kind of harmony, which means to arithmnetic division. And although it is admitted that minor-third harmony, as deduced from arithmetical division, is almost borrowed from arithmetical science, and it is admitted that the harmonic system (which is major-third harmony) is by nature the only kind, the first par excellence, nonetheless anyone who proposes to form a universal system has the duty to embrace the two different kinds of the system and to reduce them to a single kind, which is the universal. Otherwise, in the same system there will be two different principles, which is absurd, and opposed to the very idea of system. The inquiry is not only reasonable but necessary because, in fact, our music is based equally upon the two above-mentioned kinds of harmony. [...] It is understood between us that both the major-third kind of harmony and the minor-third kind of harmony extend to the sextuple, and nothing more. [...]

It is said that minor-third harmony has been borrowed from arithmetical science, and is almost foreign and accidental to music: this I deny absolutely; and on the contrary, I say that the system of minor-third harmony is not only inseparable from the major-third system of harmony, but indeed is the same identical system, which in itself, and independently of any different principle, includes the two kinds of harmony. [...]

Therefore, the arithmetic system (which is minor-third harmony) not only is inseparable from the harmonic system (which is major-third harmony); but indeed, is the same identical system, which, in itself and independently of any other principle, includes both kinds of harmony.[24]

---

24 "La nostra musica pratica abbraccia due generi diversi di armonia: quello, che si chiama di terza maggiore, e nasce dalla divisione armonica della corda sonora in parti ineguali 1/2, 1/3, 1/4, 1/5, 1/6; E quello, che si chiama di terza minore, e nasce dalla divisione aritmetica della stessa corda in parti equali 1, 2, 3, 4, 5, 6.
È certo, che tutto il fin'ora stabilito appartiene unicamente al genere di armonia di terza maggiore, che vuol dire alla divisione armonica; in niun modo al genere di armonia di terza minore, che vuol dire alla decisione aritmetica. E benchè si confessi, che l'armonia di terza minore, come dedotta dalla divisione Aritmetica, sia quasi presa in prestito dalla scienza aritmetica; e si confessi, che il sistema armonico (ch'è l'armonia di terza maggiore) sia per natura l'unico, e per eccellenza il primo, nullandimeno vi è il debito in chi si propone di formare un sistema universale di abbracciare i due generi diversi del sistema, e ridurli ad un genere solo, che sia l'universale. Altrimenti nello stesso sistema vi saranno due principj diversi, il che è assurdo, e si oppone alla vera idea di sistema.

In addition and corollary to this, Tartini demonstrates that if the first six intervals engendered by the harmonics are successfully counted above the same pitch, the resulting combination tones for the *sestupla armonica* series will provide the F minor triad – the subdominant minor triad in its relation to the root C.[25]

So, as Tartini shows, various subdivisions of the string create the symmetrically placed major ascending triad, produced by the fundamental harmonic series *sestupla armonica*; the desired parallel-minor descending triad naturally occurs as a result of the arithmetic series, consisting of the remainder of the previous series. Tartini thus considers the minor triad as an intrinsically inseparable physical and mathematical consequence of its parallel major triad and thus a product of Nature.

Even if not always viewed as such nowadays, these theories were embodied in Tartini's compositional strategies and performance practice, resonating with Algarotti's plea for a unity of scientific and cultural phenomena. In his (undated, probably 1757) response to a letter by Leonhard Euler, Tartini emphasizes that such a manifestation of theoretical concepts via their artistic demonstration proves essential for testing their correctness and fidelity: "I firstly grant the great difficulty *of uniting in a single subject all the needs of physics, geometry and music with the aim of establishing a foundation of the science of harmony sought after by musical practice.*"[26]

Indeed, an examination of Tartini's compositional output proves that his contemplation of the parallel minor within its major-key context is deemed an incarnation of Nature: various procedures of introducing the parallel-minor triad as the most "natural" step in developing his musical ideas occur in most of Tartini's works throughout his long compositional career. Even the obvious changes in melodic idiom, texture, syntax, and overall treatment of form around 1740, "from

---

La ricerca è non solo ragionevole, ma necessaria. Perchè di fatto la nostra musica è fondata egualmente sopra i due suddetti generi d'armonia; [...] Si conviene tra noi, che tanto il genere di armonia di terza maggiore, quanto il genere di armonia di terza minore si estenda sino alla sestupla, e nulla piu'. [...]
[D]dico, che il sistema dell'armonia di terza minore non solo è inseparabile dal sistema dell'armonia di terza maggiore, ma anzi è lo stesso identico sistema, che per se, e indipendentemente da qualunque principio diverso include i due generi di armonia. [...]
Dunque il sistema aritmetico (ch'è l'armonia di terza minore) non solo è inseparabile dal sistema armonico (ch'è l'armonia di terza maggiore); ma anzi è lo stesso identico sistema, che per se, e indipendentemente da qualunque altro principio include i due generi di armonia." Tartini, *Trattato di musica*, 65–66, 68–69. English translation in Fredric Bolan Johnson, "Tartini's Trattato di musica seconda la vera scienza dell'armonia: An Annotated Translation with Commentary," (Doctoral dissertation, Indiana University, 1985), 165–167, 171–172, 176.. See also Alejandro E. Planchart, "A Study of the Theories of Giuseppe Tartini," *Journal of Music Theory* 4 (1960): 32–61.
25 Tartini, *Trattato di musica*, 71.
26 "Accordo primieramente la somma difficoltà di *unire in un solo soggetto tutto il bisogno di fisica, geometria, e musica per stabilire quel tal fondamento di scienza di armonia, che si ricerca dalla pratica musicale.*" Malagò, *Tartini: Lettere*, 1:264–265; italics by the author. English translation in Malagò, *Tartini: Lettere*, 2: 404.

the elaborate and virtuosic early concertos, very much in Vivaldi's footsteps, through the more elegant galanterie of the middle period (marked by efflorescence rather than technical show), to the extreme simplicity and sensitive cantabile of the latest works, supported by the lightest two-violin accompaniment"[27] notwithstanding, his most preferred patterns remain equally valid in different stages of his creative activity, as will be further demonstrated.[28]

Perhaps the G major *Concerto* D. 73 that opens Opus 2 (*VI concerti à 5*), published in 1734 in Amsterdam, shows the most "Vivaldian" fashion in treating the overall ritornello structure, with its textural contrasts, spinning out of unrelated syntactical units, and mimicking of the Red Priest's favourite treatment of the parallel minor triads. This genuinely galant music demonstrates a true virtuosity in a combination of eccentric rhythmic modules; the preparation of the cadence that crowns the framing ritornellos in the tonic (bb. 14–15 and 102–103) and in the key of the dominant major (bb. 39–40) is shaded by brief parenthetical lyrical motives in their parallel minor.[29] (See Example 1a.) In addition, bars 70–77 display the clever interplay with minor-third triads; here, the G minor chords are subsumed as a subdominant minor in the context of the tonal centre D major. The basic idea of the boisterous bourrée finale of this concerto elaborates on Tartini's much preferred "Fonte" voice-leading schema (V6/5/ii–ii / V6/5–I);[30] it keeps playing with the shadings of the dominant and subdominant major triads by their minor-third counterparts, demonstrating another of Tartini's signature patterns – that of a chromatic descent within the species of fourth, harmonized by a chain of seventh chords over the bass falling by fifths. (bb. 12–27, repeated at the end, bb. 111–116). (See Example 1b.)

---

27 Simon McVeigh and Jehoash Hirshberg, *The Italian Solo Concerto, 1700–1760. Rhetorical Strategies and Style History* (Woodbridge: The Boydell Press, 2004): 285.

28 Minos Dounias, in his *Die Violinkonzerte Giuseppe Tartinis als Ausdruck einer Künstlerpersönlichkeit und einer Kulturepoche* (Wolfenbüttel and Berlin: Möseler, Georg Kallmeyer Verlag, 1935), identified three broad stylistic layers: period 1 (1721–1735), period II (c. 1735–1750) and period III (c. 1750–1760). See as well George W. Thompson, "I primi concerti di Giuseppe Tartini: Fonti, abozzi e revisioni," in Andrea Bombi and Maria Nevilla Massaro, *Tartini: Il tempo e le opera* (Bologna: Il Mulino, 1994), 347–362; Margherita Canale Degrassi, "I concerti di Giuseppe Tartini. Problematiche proposte per un nuovo catalogo tematico," *De musica disserenda* 10, no. 1 (2014), 41–55.

29 See Bella Brover Lubovsky, "*Die schwarze Gredel* or the Parallel Minor Key in Vivaldi's Instrumental Music," *Studi vivaldiani*, 3 (2003), 105–132, especially 108–110. Similar flashes of the parallel-minor chords appear in some of Tartini's short movements in binary form, such as in both movements of the *Trio sonata* in D major, D. 12, from Giuseppe Tartini, *XII Sonatas for two Violins and a Bass* (London, 1750).

30 Robert O. Gjerdingen, *Music in the Galant Style* (Oxford: Oxford University Press, 2007), 61–63.

Example 1a: *Violin Concerto* in G major D. 73, Opus 2 no. 1, I movement, bars 12–17.

Example 1b: *Violin Concerto* in G major D. 73, Opus 2 no. 1, III movement, bars 13–20.

Concertos à 5, published in three volumes as Op. 1 by Le Cène in Amsterdam around 1730, despite their chronological and certain stylistic proximity to Vivaldi's model, follow an entirely different pattern, including the treatment of the parallel minor interjections. The sparkling opening *Allegro* of the D major concerto D. 15 (Op. 1/I no. 4), styled as a regal minuet, elaborates on descending arpeggios on the tonic triad, answered by the first and second violins in imitation. This modest and chaste musical idea is reiterated in both the ritornellos and most of the solos, gaining new hues in the keys of the tonic, dominant, and minor-third degrees: supertonic (bb. 175–197), submediant (bb. 236–248), and mediant (bb. 264–299), alternating with a contrasting lyrical *tasto solo* motive of stepwise ascending minor thirds (bb. 9–14). In the opening ritornello (bb. 1–46) an alternation of the ripieno arpeggio with *tasto solo* casts emphasis on C natural – the dominant seventh to the subdominant degree (bb. 28–31), aptly emphasized in the further shift into the dominant minor key in which the new lyrical material (bb. 63–70) appears. (See Example 2.) A similar unexpected switch to the key of the dominant minor (with the same accentuated pitch, C natural) occurs within the second solo (bb. 134–136). The third solo as well features a protracted digression into A minor (dominant minor) that eventually leads the motion towards the tonicized supertonic degree. Here Tartini deploys a chromatic descent from the high to medial A, embellished by a *martellato* with the high strings (bb. 332–345). The last reminiscence of the parallel tonic and dominant triads casts in the virtuosic solo violin capriccio (bb. 371–375), where switches into the parallel D minor expose its peripheral degrees: the low submediant B flat major and minor subdominant G minor triads. Various appearances of the minor triads in places of their expected major-third counterparts thus form a consistent harmonic idea of this piece.

Example 2: *Violin Concerto* in D major D. 15, Opus 1/I no. 4, I movement, bars 63–70.

Another ceremonial minuet – the opening *Allegro assai* of the *Concerto* D. 24 in the same key – is a typical example of Tartini's middle period. Its first solo demonstrates Tartini's favourite "turn of phrase": after arriving at the half-cadence (unison on the dominant A), he suddenly lowers the third, introducing the A minor triad that starts an auxiliary progression to the key of the supertonic minor (iv–V–V65/ii in bb. 49–52), with the entire manoeuvre repeated one tone lower (leading to the tonic in bars 53–56), after which the interchange between the major and minor triads of the dominant continues (bb. 57–61). (See as well Examples 1b and 4a, bb. 8–12.) Tartini's propensity for the supertonic that "sometimes occurs as part of a larger grouping of peripheral keys, but usually [...] leads directly to the tonic, reflecting a general fondness for sequential patterns falling by a tone," is mentioned as well by McVeigh and Hirshberg.[31] This composer's use of the parallel minor triad of the dominant as a trigger for initiating either the falling-fifths or "Fonte" schemata, expanded to four harmonic events in each chain, appears one of the truly bold traits of his syntactical concept and harmonic idiolect: its overwhelming preponderance throughout Tartini's whole stylistic journey, in both concerto and sonata movements, shows the crucial role of the parallel minor triad as a turning point in circumscribing the tonal space in his compositions, additionally contributing to the effect of "naturalness" due to the syntactical regularity and prediction of phrase structure it creates.[32] In the bourrée-finale (*Presto*) of the same concerto, a chromatic descent within the species of fourth evokes the interplay with the major- and minor-third chords at the stage leading to the cadence in both the ritornello and solo sections (such as bb. 206–212 in the last solo, bb. 224–228 in the concluding ripieno). In general, preparation for cadences in a variety of structural conditions is typical of embracing such enclaves of the parallel minor, as appears, for example, in the *Andante* from his *Trio sonata* in F major, F. 2, from *XII Sonatas* (London, 1750), reprinted in the same place as Op. 3 (1756) and in Amsterdam one year earlier. Here, after arriving at the unison on the tonic f', the violins rocket to the high a'' flat, over the bass digressing to D flat – A flat – and the augmented sixth (Italian) chord, leading to an additional cadence. (See Example 3.) The same device occurs in the following Allegro.

---

31 McVeigh and Hirshberg, *The Italian Solo Concerto*, 292.
32 Tartini's predilection for this pattern becomes obvious when examining his trio and solo sonatas: *Trio sonata* in D major, D. 11, Op. 8 no. 6, second movement *Andante* (bb. 10–12). Bars 24–28 of the same movement cast an enclave in the parallel minor tonic, including an emphasis on the subdominant minor and its alternation with the diatonic species of the same chord, as well as a chromatic descending within the species of fourth.

[musical notation]

Example 3: *Trio sonata* in F major, F. 2, *XII Sonatas* (London, 1750), Andante, bars 23–24.

The finale of the *Volin concerto* in B flat major D. 119 – a sweet and innocent *siciliana* – demonstrates a delightful example of the composer's vision and treatment of the parallel minor as the main musical idea's *alter ego*: each consequent phrase of its opening period (both in the ritornellos and solos) responds in the parallel minor on the antecedent phrases in the original key. (See Example 4a–b.)

[musical notation]

Example 4a: *Violin concerto* in B flat major, D. 119, III movement, bars 1–8.

Example 4b: *Violin concerto* in B flat major, D. 119, III movement, bars 13–15.

An additional *siciliana* – this time a virtuosic solo cadenza in the finale of the D-major *Concerto* D. 38, bearing the title *Pastorale*, accompanied with tempo and metric changes – displays a whole episode in the parallel D minor (bb. 248–260), strengthening the assumption that for Tartini, the naturalness of the topos is intrinsically coupled with syntactical regularity and parallel-minor interjections. (See Example 5.)

Example 5: *Violin concerto* in D major D. 38, III movement, bars 248–260.

Another of Tartini's idiosyncrasies, a frequent touch of the subdominant minor chord, or a minor tonic triad in the guise of the subdominant minor within the domain of the dominant key, also has resonance with his observation on the combination tones of the *sextupla armonica*.

As the analysis of his music shows, an interplay with parallel triads, used in an impressive variety of ways, enables the composer to build a long-term tonal-harmonic coherence and to maintain a circular concept of tonal space. In so doing, Tartini gradually departs from the juxtaposition of motivic cells in major and its parallel minor in alternation, paired with dynamic and textural contrast, as became typical in the music of Vivaldi and his numerous followers. It is also important to note that Tartini's notion of harmonic dualism on the level of the parallel triads is interwoven with his broad concept of the relationships between major and minor scales, according to which, the relative keys create the closest relationships.[33] Even a brief exploration of Tartini's strategies regarding the dualism of major and minor

---

33 Tartini, *Trattato di musica*, 94.

triads in his music shows conceptual coherence in the way the violinist-virtuoso employs this resource, advocated by himself in a guise of a learned *Musicus*: "One passes from major-third harmony to the minor-third harmony (and vice versa in the same way), not only by means of the changed third, but also through the changed order of the ratios."[34] Tartini's comprehension of the concomitance of the parallel triads over the same pitch as most "natural" and indeed innate for his stylistic procedure certainly became one of the reasons his music was conceived a specimen of neoclassical chastity and noble expression by Francesco Algarotti and his many other contemporaries.

Bibliography

Alberti, Vincenzo C. *De vita, et scriptis Francisci Algarotti commentarius.* Lucca: Riccomini, 1771.

Algarotti, Francesco. *Il Newtonianismo per le Dame ovvero Dialoghi sopra le Luce e i Colori.* Naples [Milan]: n.p., 1737.

Algarotti, Francesco. *Lettere filologiche del conte Francesco Algarotti.* Venice: Alvisopoli, 1826.

Algarotti, Francesco. *Opere: Edizione novissima.* Vol. 2, *Dialoghi sopra l'ottica neutoniana.* Venice: Carlo Palese, 1791.

Algarotti, Francesco. *Opere: Edizione novissima.* Vol. 3, *Saggio sopra la pittura.* Venice: Carlo Palese, 1791.

Algarotti, Francesco. *Opere: Edizione novissima.* Vol. 9, *Lettere varie.* Venice: Carlo Palese, 1794.

Algarotti, Francesco. *Opere: Edizione novissima.* Vol. 15, *Carteggio inedito, Parte quinta. Lettere Francesi.* Venice: Carlo Palese, 1794.

Algarotti, Francesco. *Sir Isaac Newton's Philosophy explain'd for the Use of the Ladies in Six Dialogues on Light and Colours,* 2 vols. Translated by Elisabeth Carter. London: Edward Cave, 1739.

Arato, Franco. *Il secolo delle cose: Scienza e storia in Francesco Algarotti.* Genoa: Marietti, 1991.

Barbieri, Patrizio. "Il sistema armónico di Tartini nelle 'censure' di due celebri fisico-matematici: Eulero e Riccati." In *Tartini: Il tempo le opera,* edited by Andrea Bombi and Maria Nevilla Massaro, 321–344. Bologna: Il Mulino, 1994.

Barbieri, Patrizio. *Quarrels on Harmonic Theories in the Venetian Enlightenment.* Lucca: LIM, 2020.

---

[34] "[…] si passa dall'armonia di terza maggiore all'armonia di terza minore (e così pel contrario) non solamente per la terza cambiata, ma per l'ordine cambiato delle ragioni." Tartini, *Trattato di musica,* 87. English translation in Johnson, "Tartini's Trattato," 223.

Baxandall, Michael. *Shadows and Enlightenment.* New Haven and London: Yale University Press, 1995.

Brewster, David, ed. *Letters of Euler on Different Subjects in Natural Philosophy, addressed to a German princess.* vol. 1. Translated by Henry Hunter. New York: Harper, 1837.

Brover Lubovsky, Bella. "Concepts of Modal Dualism in the Time of Vivaldi." In *Fulgeat sol frontis decorate. Studi in onore di Michael Talbot,* edited by Alessandro Borin and Jasmin Melissa Cameron, 65–84. Venice: Fondazione Cini, 2016.

Brover Lubovsky, Bella. "*Die schwarze Gredel* or the Parallel Minor Key in Vivaldi's Instrumental Music." *Studi vivaldiani* 3 (2003), 105–132.

Brover Lubovsky, Bella. "Newtonian Optics and Modal Polarity in Eighteenth-Century Venetian Music." In *Music Theory and Interdisciplinarity,* edited by Christian Utz, 145–158. Saarbrücken: PFAU Verlag, 2010.

Canale Degrassi, Margherita. "I concerti di Giuseppe Tartini. Problematiche proposte per un nuovo catalogo tematico." *De musica disserenda* 10, no. 1 (2014), 41–55.

Casini, Paolo. *Newton e la conscienza europea.* Bologna: Mulino, 1983.

Del Fra, Luca. *Commercio di Lettere intorno di Principj dell'Armonia fra il Signor Giuseppe Tartini ed il Co. Giordano Riccati.* Lucca: LIM, 2007.

Dooley, Brendan Maurice. *Science, Politics, and Society in Eighteenth-Century Italy: The Giornale de' letterati d'Italia and Its World.* New York: Garland, 1991.

Dounias, Minos. *Die Violinkonzerte Giuseppe Tartinis als Ausdruck einer Künstlerpersönlichkeit und einer Kulturepoche.* Wolfenbüttel and Berlin: Georg Kallmeyer Verlag, 1935.

Ferrone, Vincenzo. *The Intellectual Roots of the Italian Enlightenment: Science, Religion and Politics in the Early Eighteenth Century.* Translated by Sue Brotherton. Atlantic Highlands, NJ: Humanities Press, 1995.

Gjerdingen, Robert O. *Music in the Galant Style.* Oxford: Oxford University Press, 2007.

Johnson, Fredric Bolan. "Tartini's Trattato di Musica seconda la vera scienza dell'armonia: An Annotated Translation with Commentary." Doctoral dissertation, University of Indiana, 1988.

Malagò, Giorgia, ed. *Giuseppe Tartini. Lettere e documenti/Pisma in dokumenti/ Letters and Documents,* 2 vols. Translated by Jerneja Umer Kljun and Roberto Baldo. Trieste: Edizioni Università di Trieste, 2020.

McVeigh, Simon, and Jehoash Hirshberg. *The Italian Solo Concerto, 1700–1760. Rhetorical Strategies and Style History.* Woodbridge: The Boydell Press, 2004.

Michelessi, Domenico. *Memorie intorno alla vita ed agli scritti del conte Francesco Algarotti.* Venice: Pasquali, 1770.

Michelsen, William C., ed. and trans. *Hugo Rieman's Theory of Harmony and History of Music Theory, Book III*. Lincoln: University of Nebraska Press, 1977.

Opere varie del Conte Francesco Algarotti Ciamberlano di S. M. il Re di Prussia e cavaliere dell'Ordine del Merito. Vol. 1. Venice: Pasquali, 1757.

Petrobelli, Pierluigi. "Tartini, Algarotti e la corte di Dresda." *Analecta Musicologica* 2 (1965): 72–84.

Petrobelli, Pierluigi. *Tartini, le sue idee e il suo tempo*. Lucca: LIM, 1992.

Planchart, Alejandro Enrique. "A Study of the Theories of Giuseppe Tartini." *Journal of Music Theory* 4 (1960): 32–61.

Polzonetti, Pierpaolo. *Tartini e la musica secondo natura*. Lucca: LIM, 1998.

Stillingfleet, Benjamin. *Principles and Power of Harmony*. London: Hughs, 1771.

Tartini, Giuseppe. *De'principj dell'armonia musicale contenuta nel diatonico genere*. Padova: Stamperia del Seminario, 1767.

Tartini, Giuseppe. *Risposta all'esame di Eulero*, by Giuseppe Tartini, Ms. D.VI.1894, pp. 17a–f. Cappella Antoniana Musical Archive, Padua.

Tartini, Giuseppe. *Risposta di Giuseppe Tartini alla Critica del di lui Trattato di Musica di Mons. Le Serre di Ginevra*. Venice: De Castro, 1767.

Tartini, Giuseppe. *Risposta di un'anonimo al celebre Sig. Rousseau*. Venice: De Castro, 1769.

Tartini, Giuseppe. *Trattato di musica secondo la vera scienza dell'armonia*. Padova: Stamperia del Seminario, 1754.

Thompson, George W. "I primi concerti di Giuseppe Tartini: Fonti, abozzi e revisioni." In *Tartini: Il tempo e le opera*, edited by Andrea Bombi and Maria Nevilla Massaro, 347–362. Bologna: Il Mulino, 1994.

Roberta Vidic

University of Music and Theater Hamburg (HfMT)

Tartini's "Musical Inference" between Epistemology and History of Harmony

Abstract: The current convention in interdisciplinary informal logic is to postulate, besides deduction and induction, a variously named third category of inference. This generally happens in practice, where uncertainty additionally comes into play. The proposed term of musical inference is therefore likely to be appeared at those moments in the history of music theory when theory is closely related to musical practice, and these collide in musical controversies. A telling example for such a controversy is the role played by the introduction of rule of the octave in the origin and foundation of modern harmony. After a discussion of the theoretical and historical background, the so-called demonstration of the scale is analysed in dispute writings of Francesco Antonio Calegari (1732) and Giuseppe Tartini (1767). In this, Tartini also introduces an explicit concept of musical fundament (*fondamento musicale*) for his epistemological and historical discussion of the principles of harmony.

Keywords: informal logic, epistemology, history of harmony, rule of the octave, Francesco Antonio Calegari, Giuseppe Tartini

Giuseppe Tartini published two larger theoretical works during his lifetime: the *Trattato di musica secondo la vera scienza dell'armonia* (Treatise on Music according to the True Science of Harmony, Padua, 1754) and *De' Principj dell'Armonia Musicale contenuta nel Diatonico genere* (On the Principles of Musical Harmony Contained in the Diatonic Genus, Padua, 1767). In the latter work, the first three chapters are dedicated to a physical fundament (*Del fisico fondamento*), a demonstrative fundament (*Del fondamento dimostrativo*), and a musical fundament (*Del fondamento musicale*). The three *fondamenti* are finally combined in the fourth chapter (*Della congiunzione dei tre fondamenti*) that literally serves the scientific foundation of Tartini's system of harmony. Besides fundament (*fondamento*), Tartini also uses principle (*principio*) as synonym, as we can read in the following passage from the preface, where he explains the general structure of his work:

> And is it not for almost two centuries that the most distinguished modern philosophers have been searching for the true principles (*principi*) of musical harmony? Were these principles ever established, or do they remain controversial more than ever? That is a sure proof, because their nature is, in fact, very difficult to detect. What the author has

been able to do here to facilitate understanding, he has done by joining the necessary principal notions of modern and ancient Music to the respective physical discoveries of the moderns, and to the demonstrative institutions of the ancients. But from this good has become inseparable the evil of having to pour at the same time, and place on three different fundaments (*fondamenti*), which are the physical, the demonstrative, and the practical musical: something, for which the author could not force himself to a rigorous method, but rather obliges the reader to pay particular attention.[1]

Briefly, the main topic for Tartini is proving the basic principles of harmony or, in other words, of music as a science. Although the issue is nothing but new in the history of music theory, Tartini announces to adopt an approach that includes not only discoveries in modern physics and ancient demonstration techniques but also notions of musical practice. Coming to the point – a question arises whether the fundament in the headings indicates only the destination or also the journey. For it makes a big difference whether Tartini's third chapter concerns only an investigation of *matters* from musical practice by usual means of scientific method, such as induction and deduction, or whether a third and specific category of *reasoning* on musical practice becomes somehow discernible. In this case, it could be possible to speak of musical inference as an integral part of the Tartinian method.

This chapter will consider Tartini's reasoning on musical matters from both a theoretical and a historical perspective. As we will see, the debate about the scientific method in the Age of the Enlightenment leaves some questions open until our times. Moreover, it is important to consider Tartini's theoretical and polemic writings in the context of his networks in the fields of music and the arts, no less than in relation to the remarkable reception of his theories in the circles of Venetian and French Enlightenment. The proposed example from *De' Principj* and the comparison with an additional source from Tartini's immediate surroundings, will finally give an insight into a certainly multi-layered field of research.

The discussion is divided into four parts:

1. Theoretical discourse
2. Historical discourse

---

1 "E poi non sono forse due secoli da che si cercano i veri principi della musical armonia dai più insigni Filosofi moderni? Si sono per anco accertati questi principi, o sono attualmente in disputa piucchè mai? Quella è ben prova sicura, perchè di fatto, che la loro natura è assai difficile da rilevarli. Quanto qui ha potuto far l'autore per facilitarne la intelligenza, lo ha fatto, congiungendo le necessarie principali nozioni della odierna, e antica Musica alle rispettive fisiche scoperte de' moderni, ed alle dimostrative istituzioni degli antichi. Ma da questo bene si è poi reso inseparabile il male di dover versare nello stesso tempo, e luogo su tre diversi fondamenti, quali sono il fisico, il dimostrativo, e il pratico musicale: cosa, per cui l'autore non ha potuto obbligarsi ad un metodo rigoroso, ma obbliga bensì chi legge a particolar attenzione." Giuseppe Tartini, *De' Principj dell'Armonia Musicale contenuta nel Diatonico genere* (Padova: Stamperia del seminario, 1767), iv. English translation by the author.

3. Calegari and Tartini in comparison
4. Conclusions

1 Theoretical Discourse

With the physical, demonstrative, and musical fundament, Tartini introduces three different fundaments "for easier understanding". For the same reason, he can, however, "not force himself to a rigorous method". To understand his position in general, it is necessary to go deeper into the theoretical discourse. Thomas Christensen examines the question in his book *Rameau and Musical Thought in the Enlightenment* (1993) obviously from a French perspective and with a focus on Jean-Philippe Rameau (1683–1764). In this context, the much-received theory of Étienne Bonnot de Condillac, Abbé of Mureau (1714–1780), plays a central role. The philosopher-epistemologist defines a scientific system in the following terms:

> A system is nothing but the disposition of the different parts of an art or science in an order in which they all mutually sustain one another and where the last are explained by the first. Those parts which give reason to the others are called *principles,* and the system is so much the more perfect as the principles are few in number. It is even to be hoped that they may be reduced to a single one.[2]

As Christensen comments, a well-ordered system implies a strict hierarchically structure fulfilling two conditions, such as the reduction to a single governing principle, and induction or deduction as means of descending or ascending from one point to another.[3] This gives already a hint about what Tartini could have more-or-less mean when he speaks of a less rigorous method, in the frame of the contemporary discourse about the scientific method.

1.1 The Merging of Physical and Demonstrative Fundament in the 1754 *Trattato di musica*

Patrizio Barbieri has considered some aspects of Tartini's methodological approach in his recent book *Quarrels on Harmonic Theories in the Venetian Enlightenment* (2020), which includes, among others, a comparison of Tartini with Rameau as well as an analysis of his correspondence with major music-interested scientists of the time, such as Leonhard Euler (1707–1783) and, here, Count Giordano Riccati

---

2 Étienne Bonnot de Condillac, *Traité des systems, où en démêle les inconvéniens at les avantages* in *Oeuvres de Condillac*, vol. 2 (Paris, 1778), 1, quoted in Thomas Christensen, *Rameau and Musical Thought in the Enlightenment* (Cambridge: Cambridge University Press, 1993), 36.
3 Thomas Christensen, *Rameau*, 37–38.

(1709–1790).[4] Accordingly, both Tartini and Rameau follow a "rigid Cartesian approach"[5] while pursuing their physical foundation of harmony – Rameau in the acoustical phenomenon of the overtone series (*réssonance du corps sonore*), Tartini in the combination tones or third tone (terzo suono). A weakness of the Cartesian approach becomes very clear in the comparison of Rameau with Riccati's adoption of the Galileo-Newton method, as Barbieri states: "In substance, Rameau starts from the vibrating string and, by means of induction, establishes which laws should be obeyed by an ear not spoilt by custom (an approach that will oblige him to revise his theories frequently). Riccati, on the other hand, starts from the sound just as it is perceived by the ear, i.e. from a truly experimental fact."[6]

Apart from this, a major difference between Tartini and Rameau is found in the application of a physical discovery to the own system of harmony. The first problem is well known: Rameau uses the overtone series to explain the origin of the major mode and tries also to introduce a merely hypothetical undertone series for justifying the minor mode. Tartini, however, goes far beyond this, in a way that Barbieri explains in terms of a methodological problem: "Tartini starts by declaring that when 'a system is to be established, it is necessary to merge the two genres, physical and demonstrative, so that they are inseparable and form a single principle'. To this end however, his choice of 'demonstrative' method was based on a set of highly debatable considerations that are not always easy to decipher [...]."[7] The historical quotation is taken from the second chapter of the *Trattato di musica*, in which Tartini introduces the harmonic circle (*circolo armonico*). This geometric-acoustic construction coincides with Tartini's ambitious attempt to establish a general theory for harmony, before extending it to the minor mode and the dissonances. The harmonic circle and its defence will remain a highly problematic issue in Tartini's harmonic theories, as it has already been described in detail by Barbieri.[8] On the other hand, it is interesting to observe which role musical practice played in Tartini's system, when he largely left out his favourite construct.

1.2 The Emerging of a Musical Fundament in the 1767 *De' Principj*

A cursory comparison between *Trattato di musica* and *De' Principj* (Table 1) shows, in this sense, how the emerging musical fundament in Tartini's theoretical work first results from editorial work. Although the order of chapters and key issues

---

4   The volume is largely based on long-standing research, with substantial revision work and some new chapters.
5   Patrizio Barbieri, *Quarrels on Harmonic Theories in the Venetian Enlightenment* (Lucca: Libreria Musicale Italiana, 2020), 84.
6   Barbieri, *Quarrels on Harmonic Theories*, 18.
7   Barbieri, *Quarrels on Harmonic Theories*, 84.
8   Barbieri, *Quarrels on Harmonic Theories*, 83–110.

is broadly maintained, two main editorial interventions are particularly remarkable: First, the chapter about the harmonic circle remains excluded from the later publication. Despite of this, the circle itself remains essential for the connection of all three fundaments at the end of the *De' Principj*.[9] Second, a separate chapter about the distinction between modal and tonal system is suppressed. Without going into greater detail here, these two editorial choices lead also to a new weighting of topics and chapters within Tartini's theoretical work. The physical fundament regards in any case not only the third tone for its own but also in relation to Rameau's overtone series.[10] The demonstrative fundament is henceforth centred on the matter of musical consonance and dissonance. After that, the musical fundament results altogether from a reordering of material concerning musical practice and the scale. If the closing chapters then fulfil an important task within the overall work, such as that of showing – in addition to the goal of the entire discussion – a prioritization of topics in context of a contemporary debate, we observe a significant change between *Trattato di musica* to the *De' Principj*: that is, the preference for theoretical discourse on the scientific foundation of harmony – over the previous historical discourse about the practice in ancient or modern style.

---

9 Tartini, *De' Principj*, 110. This is because he was publishing on it his forthcoming *Risposta di Giuseppe Tartini alla Critica del di lui Trattato di Musica di Mons. Le Serre di Ginevra* (Venice: A. De Castro, 1767).
10 Tartini, *De' Principj*, 27.

Table 1: Structure of Tartini's *Trattato di musica* and *De' Principj* in comparison

Trattato di musica (1754)	*De' Principj* (1767)
1. On the Harmonic Phenomena, Their Nature and Significance [De' Fenomeni Armonici, loro natura, e significazione]	1. On the Physical Fundament [Del fisico fondamento]
2. On the Circle, its Nature and Significance [Del circolo, sua natura, e significazione]	2. On the Demonstrative Fundament [Del fondamento dimostrativo]
3. On the Musical System Consonances, Dissonances, Their Nature and Definition [Del Sistema musicale Consonanze, Dissonanze, loro Natura, e Definizione]	3. On the Musical Fundament [Del fondamento musicale]
4. On the Scale, and on Musical Practice, Origin, Use, and Consequences [Della Scala, e del Genere pratico Musicale, Origine, Uso, e Conseguenze]	4. On the Conjunction of the three Fundaments [Della congiunzione dei tre fondamenti]
5. On the Musical Modes, or Tones, Ancient and Modern [De' Modi, o siano Tuoni musicali, antichi, e moderni]	
6. On the Particular Intervals and Modulations of Modern Music [Degl'Intervalli, e Modulazioni particolari della Musica moderna]	

Tartini not only faces the task to reduce his own system of harmony to a few or even a single principle, but, as we have seen, he also attaches an increasing importance to a practice-oriented musical fundament. The inclusion of practice does not make his task any easier for reasons that are inherent in the field of scientific demonstration. A demonstration generally presupposes to go over hypothesis construction and furnishing a proof of given principles, in which a science must be established. The scientific method, in its basic definition, is the technique used in both the construction and testing of a scientific hypothesis. In this, the adoption of induction and deduction has been considered differently in the course of time, while the validity of other settings was bound to remain controversial until our days.

This also applies to the emergence of an informal logic in the North American teaching of logic in the 1970s, regarding no less than the fundamental distinction between *real* demonstration and *mere* argumentation – and their respective theories. On this basis, it is possible to draw a parallel between contemporary and historical problems concerning scientific method in the fields of logic and beyond that also in epistemology. As Frans van Eemeren resumes, "[t]he label informal logic covers a collection of normative approaches to the study of reasoning in ordinary language that remain closer to the practice of argumentation than formal logic."[11] A current convention within informal logic is then to postulate, besides deduction and induction, a variously named "third category" of inference – Charles Sanders Peirce (1839–1914) added abduction, as an example.[12] Considering that inferences are generally steps in reasoning, moving from premises to logical consequences, this "third category" of inference is relevant more specifically in practice, where uncertainty additionally comes into play.[13] Uncertain and tentative reasoning is nowadays known as defeasible reasoning, but its origin can be traced back to a standard reference of logic, such as Aristotle's *Posterior Analytics*. Common areas of applications of defeasible reasoning include everyday thinking as well as scientific hypothesis construction.[14]

Summing up, a central issue in the *Trattato di musica* is the merging of the physical and the demonstrative fundament alongside with the introduction of the harmonic circle as a geometric-acoustic construction. In the *De' Principj*, the emerging of a musical fundament from musical practice coincides with the revision of a chapter about the scale as a music-specific construction. Therefore, Tartini should have at least three good reasons for warning the readers about the risk of his enterprise in the preface, as he is expected no less than (1) to furnish a valid proof of the principles of harmony, (2) to reduce three different principles to possibly one, and (3) to justify the adoption of practice-based reasoning in a scientific context. Musical practice is a historically variable practice, whereas Tartini is aware of the difference among ancient and modern practice. If the object of the musical science is already problematic, the adoption of a practice-based reasoning, or even

---

11 Frans H. van Eemeren, "The Study of Argumentation," in *The SAGE handbook of rhetorical studies*, ed. Andrea A. Lunsford, Kirt H. Wilson, Rosa A. Eberly (Thousand Oaks, CA: SAGE, 2009), 117.
12 Douglas N. Walton, "Abductive, presumptive and plausible arguments," *Informal Logic* 21, no. 2 (2001): 142–143, https://doi.org/10.22329/il.v21i2.2241; John R. Josephson and Susan G. Josephson, *Abductive Inference. Computation, philosophy, technology* (Cambridge: Cambridge University Press, 1994), 28.
13 Christoph Lumer, "Walton's Argumentation Schemes," *OSSA Conference Archive* 110 (2016): 142, http://scholar.uwindsor.ca/ossaarchive/OSSA11/papersandcommentaries/110.
14 Robert Koons, "Defeasible Reasoning," in *The Stanford Encyclopedia of Philosophy*, Stanford University, accessed February 12, 2022, https://plato.stanford.edu/archives/fall2021/entries/reasoning-defeasible/.

of a practice-oriented kind of reasoning – what we will call a *musical inference* in a narrow sense – is nothing but self-evident in historical and current theories of demonstration.

2 Historical Discourse

Tartini perceived the search for the "true principles of musical harmony" as an ongoing process for about two centuries. This corresponds with the time of Gioseffo Zarlino (1517–1590) and Giovanni Pierluigi da Palestrina (1525/1526–1594), who have long been seen as major exponents for theory and practice in *stile antico*. Like other composers, theorists, and church musicians in the Venetian area, Tartini is highly interested in the tradition – also in relation or in reaction to further developments in theory and practice of his time. The proposed description of his context here is deliberately left a little bit vague, as current historiography can adopt – as it can only be touch upon here – different criteria to embed his musical, theoretical, and didactic work.

2.1 The General Context of Tartini's Theoretical Work

If we depart from the school concept, the definition of a *Scuola delle nazioni* (School of nations) and a *Scuola dei rivolti* (School of inversions) with a main centre in Padua and the discussion about Antonio Lotti (1666–1740) and the Palestrinian style in early eighteenth-century Venice are almost equally important for understanding the genesis and successive development of Tartini's theoretical work. The *Scuola delle Nazioni* indicates Tartini's circle of pupils and his own teaching in Padua. According to Margherita Canale, contemporaries already spoke of a real school in this connection. Tartini followed, in fact, a precise method and a well-defined curriculum. The two years of instruction could include either violin lessons only or the study of composition and counterpoint as well.[15] The Paduan School or *Scuola dei Rivolti*, on the other hand, refers to a group of theorists and composers with whom Tartini is also associated, and to the formulation and application of their innovations in the field of harmony. For Barbieri, these innovations essentially "derive from license harking back to the sixteenth century" and met with great opposition. Nevertheless, they were adopted in the following of Francesco Antonio Calegari (1656–1742) by "several eminent maestri di cappella", such as Francesco Antonio Vallotti (1697–1780).[16]

The current classification of the Paduan theorists has been mostly based on contemporary accounts. Not surprisingly, judgements can partly or even strongly

---

15 Margherita Canale, "Fonti per una ricostruzione della didattica di Tartini nella 'Scuola delle Nazioni'," *Muzikološki Zbornik/Musicological Annual* 28 (1992), 16, 20, and 22.
16 Barbieri, *Quarrels on Harmonic Theories*, 3 and 33–37.

diverge. This becomes evident in the analysis of the role played by Lotti, who was long-term organist and then maestro at St. Mark's Basilica, in Venice in the reform of church music on the model of Palestrina. For instance, both Calegari and Giuseppe Saratelli (1714–1762) studied under Lotti in Venice: Calegari at least in 1700,[17] Saratelli at least in 1732, when he was appointed a substitute organist at St. Mark.[18] If we follow Barbieri's reconstruction, Saratelli must have learnt the rules of the *Scuola dei rivolti* before 1732, when he was still organist at St. Anthony's Basilica in Padua under Vallotti.[19] In 1733, the new school had probably just four adherents: Calegari, Vallotti, Saratelli, and Tartini, while Lotti would have strongly refused to join them.[20] According to Claudia Valder-Knechtges, it was Lotti who gave decisive impulses for a turn to the tradition of the old masters that began around 1700 and later had a major influence on Saratelli. From this point of view, Saratelli was eventually regarded as a leading follower of Lotti's school, whereas even Riccati was concerned, together with Vallotti, with a church music renewal that had been essentially begun by Lotti.[21]

Instead of the volatile concept of school, it is also possible to take formal institutions – such as chapels and scientific academies – into account. Compared with the remaining early adherents of the *Scuola dei rivolti*, Tartini is then the sole theorists, who eventually succeeded in publishing a complete treatise or system of harmony. Indeed, Calegari delivered a series of unfinished manuscript versions, Vallotti left his treatise with exception of the first book finally unpublished, Saratelli's teaching might has handed down exclusively in didactic materials. Most interestingly, several theoretical writings are strictly related or even coincide with didactic writings. Conversely, treatises and dissertations of Calegari, Vallotti, and Tartini are not merely the result of teaching activity in and outside the chapel,

---

17 Daniele Gambino, "Il trattato teorico-pratico di Francesco Antonio Calegari ovvero *l'Ampla dimostrazione degli armoniali musicali tuoni*," in *Barocco padano e musici francescani 2*, ed. Alberto Colzani, Andrea Luppi, Maurizio Padoan (Padua: Centro Studi Antoniani, 2018), 543–544.
18 Claudia Valder-Knechtges, "Giuseppe Saratelli. Ein Venezianischer Musiker des 18. Jahrhunderts," *Musikforschung* 37, no. 2 (1984), 112.
19 Barbieri, *Quarrels on Harmonic Theories*, 32–33.
20 See the letter of Giovanni Antonio Riccieri to Giovanni Battista Martini (Padua, March 1733), published in Giancarlo Zanon, "Il P. M.° Francescantonio Vallotti del giudizio dei contemporanei e dei posteri," introduction to *Trattato della moderna musica*, by Francesco Antonio Valotti (Padua: Il Messaggero di S. Antonio/Basilica del Santo, 1950), xxvii–xxviii, quoted in Barbieri, *Quarrels on Harmonic Theories*, 34.
21 Valder-Knechtges, "Giuseppe Saratelli," 113–114. This position has remained substantially undisputed. See Benjamin Byram-Wigfield, "The Sacred Music of Antonio Lotti: Idiom and Influence of a Venetian Master," (Doctoral dissertation, The Open University, 2016), 33, https://doi.org/10.21954/ou.ro.0000bc4c; Irene Maria Caraba, "I Bassi per esercizio d'accompagnamento all'antico," *Rivista Italiana di Musicologia* 53 (2018), 61–62.

but they originated in the frame of larger and partly public controversies over the origin and foundation of harmony. In this regard Tartini is again the sole theorist of this group, who was not only interested but then also somehow able to maintain an exchange with music theorists and scientists of his time at an international level.

2.2 The 1767 *De' Principj* in Context of Historical Controversies

A series of controversies over the *true* modes (ca. 1730–1736) goes back to Vallotti at the time he was working on his (historical) treatise on the modes. Before he unsuccessfully tried to involve the famous Johann Joseph Fux (1660–1741) in Vienna,[22] he disputed with his older colleague Calegari, who was also member of the Franciscan Order. At the end, the dispute most likely remained limited to a local context. Calegari was well acquainted with both Vallotti and Tartini[23] since he served as a *maestro di cappella* at St Antony's Basilica from 1705 to 1727, after which he resigned and changed back to the Venetian Basilica de' Frari. Vallotti, who succeeded him as *maestro* at the Paduan Basilica after an interim phase on 22 February 1730,[24] is credited just from about 1730 to have intensified his study of modes and keys.[25] The dispute with Calegari over the *true* Minor mode in D or A must have begun at least in the following year; thus, a *Raggionamento* (Reasoning) in dialogic form between the two Franciscan *maestri* is dated 24 November 1731.[26] Henceforth, Calegari delivered various manuscripts, including the *Ampla Dimostrazione degli Armoniali Musicali Tuoni* (Large Demonstration of the Harmonic Musical Modes,

---

22 Othmar Wessely, "Johann Joseph Fux und Francesco Antonio Vallotti. Vortrag gehalten vor der Jahreshauptversammlung der Johann-Joseph-Fux-Gesellschaft am 17. März 1966," *Jahresgabe 1966 der Johann-Joseph-Fux-Gesellschaft* (1967), 14.
23 Vallotti arrived in Padua in November 1721 and was appointed third organist at St. Anthony Basilica in Padua only one year later. See Wolfgang Hochstein, "Vallotti, Francesco Antonio," in *MGG Online*, Bärenreiter, accessed February 12, 2022, https://www.mgg-online.com/mgg/stable/50871. Tartini joined the orchestra as *primo violino e capo di concerto* from 1721–1723, before returning definitively to Padua in 1726. See Matteo Giuggioli, "Tartini, Giuseppe," in *MGG Online*, Bärenreiter, accessed February 12, 2022, https://www.mgg-online.com/mgg/stable/12743.
24 Zanon, "Il P. M.° Francescantonio Vallotti," xvi.
25 Wessely, "Johann Joseph Fux und Francesco Antonio Vallotti," 10.
26 Raggionamenti del Padre Francescantonio Calegari che servono per sostenere il di lui sistema del Tuono minore musicale armoniale nella corda, ed Ottaua di D. la sol re contro il Padre Vallotti che lo vuole fondato nella corda, ed ottaua di A la mi re per le raggioni che si vedranno in risposta alle obbiezioni del sudetto Padre, senza considerare di presente gli altri validissimi fondamenti, che mirabilmente accordando in teorica, non meno che in prattica lasciano la mente libera da qualunque, benche menoma confusione con grande sensibilissimo vantaggio di chiunque si accinge alla pratica, by Francesco Antonio Vallotti, manuscript, 24th November 1731, I-Pca, A.VI.537, f. <i>, Music Archive, Pontifical Antoniana Library (Pontificia Biblioteca Antoniana con Archivio Musicale), Padua.

Venice, 15 August 1732),[27] from which the example in the next chapter is taken. The dispute was later resolved without a settlement, with Vallotti justifying his choice for A minor in a further writing of 1736. In the meantime, we will see how he provided an important premise for the next quarrels, in which Tartini was more significantly involved.

Another series of controversies, to which Tartini refers in the initial quotation, concerns the *true* principles of harmony and is strictly related with Rameau's and Tartini's attempts to achieve recognition by various academies of science. Although its origin can be differently traced back to the 1730s, the dispute reached its peak from 1750s to 1760s, assuming over a long period an international dimension. As part of the international discourse, the Paduan involvement (ca. 1750s–1779) essentially encompassed the time span and writings from the publication of Tartini's *Trattato di musica* to its public critique and defence.[28] In this frame, especially the *De' Principj* allows us, almost chapter by chapter, to summarize some events, which had a major influence on the successive development of Tartini's theoretical work. The first chapter on the *physical fundament* is preceded, among others, by various reactions from Berlin and Paris. As Barbieri reports, Tartini came up at all with the idea of writing a shorter version or dissertation during the correspondence with Euler, whose critique is documented in an *Esame del Trattato di Giuseppe Tartini* (Examination of the *Trattato* of Giuseppe Tartini, 1754–1756). Euler was the director of the physics and mathematics class at the Berlin Academy of Sciences.[29] From 1757 a rather French-Italian quarrel was sparked by Jean le Rond d'Alembert (1717–1783), starting with the publication of the article on "Fondamental". The polymath and co-editor of the *Éncyclopedie* had progressively distanced himself from Rameau, showing now, by contrast, some interest in Tartini's *Trattato di musica*.[30] The second chapter on the *demonstrative fundament* then partly results from a debate between Tartini and his own student Giuseppe

---

27 "Ampla dimostrazione degli armoniali musicali tuoni. Trattato teorico-pratico," by Francesco Antonio Calegari, 1732, 9r–126r, manuscript copy, A-Wn, 19103, Music Department, Austrian National Library, Vienna. Manuscript treatise also available in Walter William Schurr, "Francesco Antonio Calegari (d. 1742): Music Theorist and Composer," 2: 17–251.
28 The precise date given for the end of the Paduan involvement refers here to a late statement by Vallotti, as most parties to the dispute were already no longer alive. See Roberta Vidic, "Rameau und die italienische Tradition. Zum Vergleich zwischen der rameauschen und der paduanischen Umkehrungslehre," in *Rezeption und Kulturtransfer. Deutsche und französische Musiktheorie nach Rameau*, ed. Birger Petersen (Mainz: ARE, 2016), 70.
29 For a detailed survey about an early connection of the *De' principj* with Euler see Barbieri, *Quarrels on Harmonic Theories*, 116 and 122–124.
30 Jonathan W. Bernard, "The Principle and the Elements: Rameau's 'Controversy with d'Alembert'," *Journal of Music Theory* 24, no. 1 (1980); Christensen, *Rameau*, 252–290; Barbieri, *Quarrels on Harmonic Theories*, 113.

Michele Stratico (1728–1783) that took place in March 1756. A persisting point of disagreement regarded, in this case, the limit of consonant proportions.[31] After that, the third chapter on the *musical fundament* contains, as anticipated, one of the most important links between the achievements of the 1730s and the 1750s–60s, when it comes to the correlation of theory and musical practice: that is, the rule of the octave[32] with the 6-4-chord on the second and fifth degree. As Barbieri found out, Vallotti and Riccati used this scale in January 1735 for explaining the origin of the diatonic scale from the first, fourth, and fifth degrees. On the contrary, Rameau did not introduce this fundamental concept of modern harmony until 1737.[33] As we will see in the next part of the discussion, this peculiar accompaniment is a central argument in Tartini's demonstration of the scale.

Overall, already this brief survey reveals how complex it is to embed Tartini's theoretical writings in the eighteenth-century discourse. In this, at least three aspects are particularly remarkable: (1) the importance of different networks, such as schools, chapels, and scientific academies, as well as the role of controversies in the development of theories and the formation of texts; (2) the (inter)relationship of theoretical and didactical writings; (3) the division of the *Scuola dei rivolti* into a more practical and a more scientific direction. All three fields of research will benefit considerably from further exploration of the Venetian archives.

3 Calegari and Tartini in Comparison

The discussion about the adoption of a practice-based reasoning – or even of a third, practice-oriented category of reasoning – is relevant for both the epistemology and the history of harmony. Musical inference is therefore likely to appear at those moments in the history of music theory when theory is closely related to musical practice and this association leads to musical controversies. Originally developed as a useful pedagogical tool for continuo practice, the rule of the octave turned into a central argument in dispute writings and is used here as exemplary topic in the comparison of Calegari and Tartini. Calegari's "large demonstration" has like the Latin word *demonstrare* the twofold meaning of showing and demonstrating the modern Major and Minor mode. After an historical excursus on counterpoint and previous tonal systems, his theoretical and practical treatise continues with a series of quasi-logical demonstrations followed by musical examples and practical exercises in the form of figured basses (*bassi*). His introduction of the rule survives, however, in two versions, both contained in the manuscript source jointly known under the title of *Ampla dimostrazione*:

---

31 The correspondence is dated 6th–13th March 1756. See Barbieri, *Quarrels on Harmonic Theories*, 122–123.
32 The rule of the octave (*regola dell'ottava, règle d'octave, Oktavregel*) is in basso continuo a scale – or part of it – with figures showing the standard harmonization for each scale degree.
33 Barbieri, *Quarrels on Harmonic Theories*, 20 and 51–52.

- I: *Ampla Dimostrazione | Degli Armoniali Tuoni | Trattato teorico-pratico* (1732)[34]
- II: *Origine | De' Corali | Modali Tuoni* (1732?)[35]

In comparison, Tartini's demonstration of the Major mode is present in the following chapters:

- *Trattato di musica*, Fourth Chapter: On the Scale, and on Musical Practice, etc.
- *De' Principj*, Third Chapter: On the musical fundament.

To put it simple, the discussion of their argumentation scheme (Table 2) is here limited to the reasoning steps immediately before the introduction of the rule. More generally, Calegari's versions were unified and compared only with Tartini's *De' Principj* more directly. Calegari and Tartini both come from different premises to comparable conclusions and from tentative conclusions to allegedly best explanations. For this, their argumentations are interpreted as two *competing stories* in terms of defeasible reasoning. Typical for all abductive argumentation schemes is generally to focus on the result and to search for an explanation from given premises. Therefore, this kind of reasoning is not conclusive, leading only to a provisional conclusion. Especially in case of two competing stories, we speak of a subsequent process of inference to best explanation.

Table 2: Key elements of Calegari's and Tartini's demonstrations in comparison

Calegari, *Ampla dimostrazione* (1732 I/II)	Tartini, *De' Principj* (1767)
Two important premises	
Practical discovery (continuo/composition)	Physical discovery (overtones/combination tones)
Palestrinian practice	Greek theory
Introduction of the rule of the octave	
1. Origin of the Major and Minor scale	1. Origin of the (Major) diatonic scale
2. Solmization	2. Just intonation
3. Rule of the octave (standard)	3. Rule of the octave (scientific)
–	4. Physical and musical foundation

---

34 Title page (I) in Calegari, "Ampla dimostrazione," f. 9r.
35 Title page (II) in Calegari, "Ampla dimostrazione," f. 94r.

3.1 Calegari's Introduction of the Rule[36]

Two important premises for Calegari's demonstration of the modern Major and Minor modes are derived from seventeenth-century practice: that is, the introduction of continuo practice and the study of sixteenth-century masterworks. These premises are, respectively, embodied by keyboard players and modern composers. As Calegari explains, keyboard players discovered the modern modes, putting their hands on the instrument and examining, how the octave can be accompanied in harmony. Modern composers observed, instead, how sixteenth-century masters could not achieve true harmony, because their composition were still based on the modes of the Gregorian chant and had no continuo part. Alongside with continuo practice, it became also necessary to correct this "mistake" introducing the Major and Minor mode into modern composition. At a further analysis, Calegari's premises are interrelated because they coincide with the accompaniment practice of original works of Palestrina and further sixteenth-century masters, the so-called called *Palestrinesca pratica* (Palestrinian practice). Moreover, keyboard players and composer of church music were often the same person.

3.1.1 The Origin of the Major and Minor Scale

The Major and Minor modes originate in the *consonante complesso* (consonant complex) and in the two principal octaves in C and D, which have almost the same reading in solmization. When the scales are considered in their *natural condition*, each scale degree or, in other words, each bass motion has a consonant accompaniment.[37] Although Calegari does not comment on it, the best explanation for the voice disposition in the consonant complex is the symmetrical disposition of the two hands on the keyboard.

Figure 1: F. A. Calegari, example II *Origine di ambedue Armoniali Musicali Tuoni* (Origin of both Harmonic Musical Modes). (Calegari, "Ampla dimostrazione," (II), f. 95v.) There is no example for the "complesso consonante" in the first version.

---

36 Calegari, "Ampla dimostrazione," (I), f. 14v; (II), f. 91v.
37 Calegari, "Ampla dimostrazione," (I), f. 14v; Calegari, "Ampla dimostrazione," (II), f. 91v-92r.

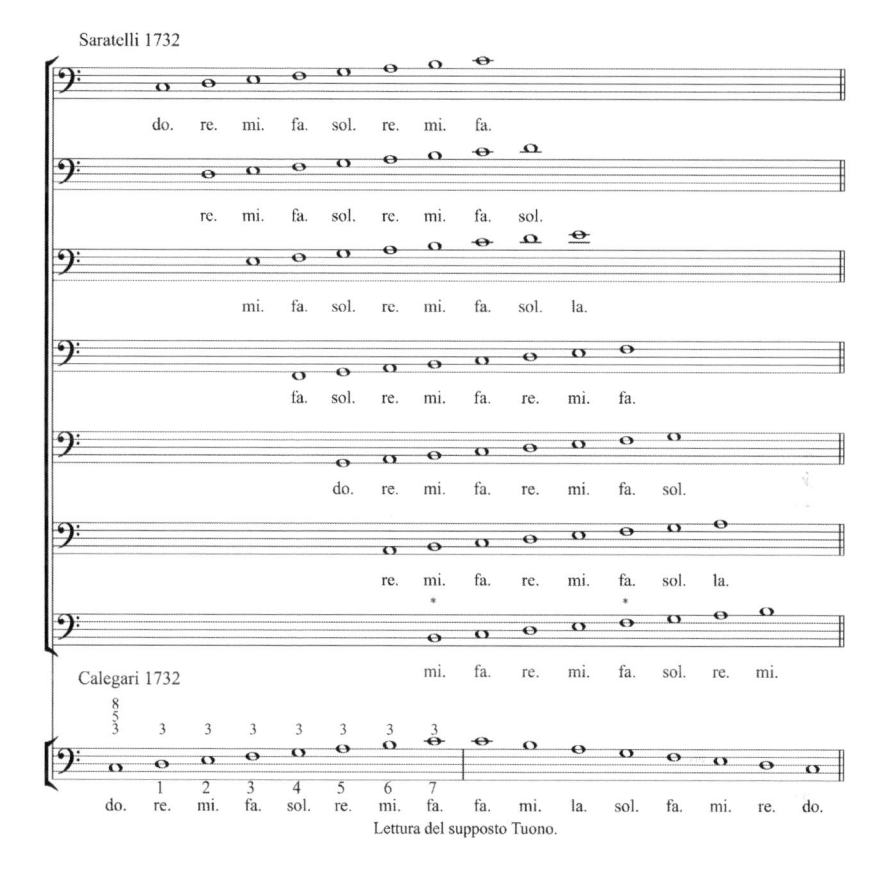

Tartini's "Musical Inference" between Epistemology and History of Harmony 237

Figure 2: F. A. Calegari (below), example I *Principale Ottava Dell'Armonia| Tuono Maggiore nello stato suo naturale considerate* (Principal octave of the Major mode considered in its natural condition). (Calegari, "Ampla dimostrazione," (I), f. 18r.) The example in the second version was used for Figure 1. G. Saratelli (above), example *Dimostrazione delle Sette Ottave di lettura e specie diverse* (Demonstration of the Seven different Readings, and Genre of the Octave). ("Ammaestramenti Prattici dal lume de quali si apprende il vero modo di perfettamente accompagnare la parte soppra lo Stromento da tasto del Sig.r Giuseppe Saratelli Maestro della Ducal Capella di S. Marco 1732," by Giuseppe Saratelli, 1732, manuscript copy, I-Vc, Giust. B. 45 n. 5, f. 9. *Fondo Giustiniani*, Library of the Conservatory of Music "Benedetto Marcello" (Biblioteca, Conservatorio di Musica Benedetto Marcello), Venice.)

3.1.2 Solmization[38]

Far from being outdated, solmization practice serves as link between modal and tonal harmony. In the accompaniment of the octave, Calegari formulates the correspondence of harmony and scales in terms of interdependence between consonant accompaniment and the seven different scales built on each scale degree. (see Figure 2 on previous page). Such "natural" modes are suggested for a modal accompaniment, even in a discourse about Major and Minor tonal music.[39]

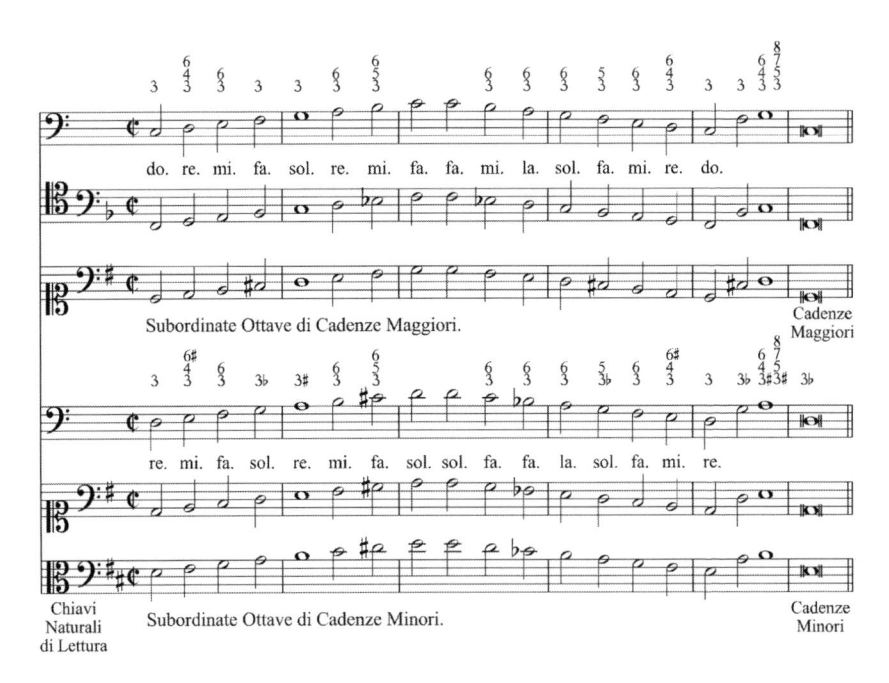

Figure 3: F. A. Calegari, example *Prima Pratica Dell'Armonial Tuono Maggiore* (I, First Practice of the Harmonic Major Mode) or *Principale Ottava, del Tuono Maggiore* (II, Principal Octave, of the Major mode). (Calegari, "Ampla dimostrazione," (I), f. 21r; Calegari, "Ampla dimostrazione," (II), f. 98r. The indications about keys and cadences were added to the second version.)

---

38 Calegari, "Ampla dimostrazione," (I), f. 17; Calegari, "Ampla dimostrazione," (II), f. 96 r–v.
39 It is remarkable, how Baroque theory can remember aspects of jazz.

3.1.3 The Rule of the Octave[40]

The rule of the octave represents for Calegari the natural immutable condition of the principal octave. Accordingly, it is necessary to establish the "first (accompaniment) practice" of a mode, for better understanding any artful (*artificioso*) motion of the bass in composition. What he calls the perfect integrity of the Major and Minor mode is then only reached, when a series of conditions are satisfied. These include the ascending and descending scales and the addition of subordinate octaves, which follows the same rule of the principal octaves (see Figure 3).

Calegari's reasoning is not conclusive, because it offers a *best explanation* only for the rule according to his current practice. The analogy between principal and subordinate octaves is, however, not only essential for the classification of principal and subordinate cadences, but it also lays the grounds for the "co-participation" of the Major and Minor modes – towards a modern concept of relative keys.

3.2 Tartini's Introduction of the Rule

Two general premises for Tartini's demonstration of the diatonic scale come from Greek Theory and from the discovery in the field of acoustics. These primarily includes Rameau's *réssonance* and his own *third tone*. Against this background, in the third chapter about the musical fundament, there are especially two immediate premises, which are related to the introduction of the rule of the octave. The first is the difference between the only three consonances of the Greeks – fourth, fifth, and octave – and the modern addition of the major and minor thirds. The second is the discussion of the major and minor triad in Rameau and in the own system of harmony. Another important issue regards the definition of three kinds of cadences, departing from bass motion. In own words, Tartini calls the section about the rule of the octave a *Dimostrazione della suddetta scala come conseguenza necessaria dei premessi necessarj principj* (Demonstration of the mentioned scale as a necessary consequence from the previous necessary principles).[41] The aim of the following description is to outline the main differences with Calegari and Vallotti.

3.2.1 The Origin of the (Major) Diatonic Scale[42]

From the very beginning of his demonstration of the scale, Tartini follows Vallotti rather than Calegari. This implies that he does not add a fundamental accompaniment to each scale degree, while he makes a point of explaining that the "applicazione attuale" (current application) of the consonant triad regards only the

---

40 Calegari, "Ampla dimostrazione," (I), f. 20v; (II), f. 96v–97r.
41 Tartini, *De' Principj*, 118.
42 Tartini, *De' Principj*, 76–77. The *Trattato di musica* does not contain this music example. See Giuseppe Tartini, *Trattato di musica secondo la vera scienza dell'armonia* (Padova: Stamperia del seminario, 1754), 98.

three main degrees C, F, and G. In this way, the successive harmony of the diatonic scale is expected to originate from the simultaneous harmony of the first, fourth, and fifth degrees.

Figure 4: G. Tartini, example of the three main triads in their "current application" to the scale. (Tartini, *De' Principj*, 77.)

3.2.2 Just Intonation[43]

As Tartini's reasoning essentially departs from natural intervals, the following introduction of just intonation is strictly necessary to his demonstration. On the contrary, solmization would be here totally useless. In own words, Tartini underlines that he deduced the tuning from first principles, while the Greek theorists Ptolemy focused on the best possible intervals. Overall, this is a telling example of Tartini's rigid separation of deduction and induction.

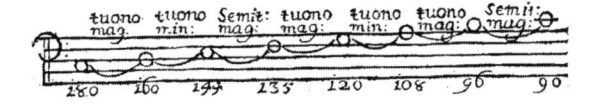

Figure 5: G. Tartini, example "scala diatonica sintona di Tolomeo" (Ptolemy's sintonic diatonic scale). (Tartini, *De' Principj*, 77, and *Trattato di musica*, 99.)

3.2.3 The Rule of the Octave[44]

Other than Calegari, Tartini does not regard the scale as an axiom. Rather, he seeks to demonstrate a correlation between the number of degrees and the order of three different cadences – harmonic, arithmetic, and mixed – by resorting to the Euclidean axiomatic method. In detail, his scheme works as follows: (1) the diatonic scale necessarily consists of eight terms; (2) the order of the three cadences necessarily resulted in eight musical notes; (3) Therefore, scale and cadences are exactly interrelated. More broadly, they have a common origin in the simultaneous and successive harmony. The scheme corresponds to a syllogism.

---

43   Tartini, *De' Principj*, 77–78. Compare with Tartini, *Trattato di musica*, 99.
44   Tartini, *De' Principj*, 78. Compare with Tartini, *Trattato di musica*, 107.

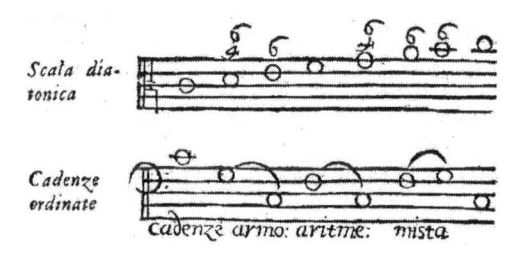

Tartini's "Musical Inference" between Epistemology and History of Harmony   241

Figure 6: G. Tartini, scale with the three different cadences in a well-ruled order. (Tartini, *De' Principj*, 78, and *Trattato di musica*, 107.)

3.2.4 The Physical and Musical Foundation[45]

In the end, Calegari was unable to move from the standard rule of the early eighteenth-century practice to the demonstration of the fundamental bass. Tartini departs, instead, from the *scientific* rule of Vallotti and Riccati in the 1730s, adding a further step to the reasoning: with the help of the physical principle of the *third tone*, he can finally transform the well-ruled order of cadences into a fundamental bass that generates the accompaniment of the scale in accordance with the rule. Nevertheless, Tartini is forced, however, to put two notes under the seventh and eighth degree, for avoiding consecutive motions with the bass. Tartini's reasoning cannot be conclusive, because a "musical law" apparently prevented him to develop here a rigorous method.

Figure 7: G. Tartini, scale with chord generation based on the combination tones. (Tartini, *De' Principj*, 80.)

---

45 Tartini, *De' Principj*, 79–80. The last example is not contained in the *Trattato di musica*.

4 Conclusions

It is indisputable that Tartini had a quite creative conception of scientific method. At the same time, he was certainly aware of the not easy relation between theory and practice. At the end of his demonstration of the scale, he substantiates his choice of a certain and sole rule of the octave, drawing a clear line between science and art:

> After years and centuries since the present Music has existed and been practised, one still waits to see a bass scale, in which the organic formulations agree with all composers by a certain primary law. They search for the truth where it is absent: it will never be found. [...] The very certain original law of the accompaniment of the scale, determined not by art, or by arbitrariness, but by physical-harmonic nature, is found only in this exemplar, which precisely for this reason cannot but be the first.[46]

Apart from this, the comparison with Calegari offered an opportunity of examining two different attitudes within the so-called *Scuola dei rivolti* from the 1730s onwards. On one side, Calegari and Saratelli moved to Venice in 1732 and personally embodied the ideal of the theory-led keyboard player and composer. On the other side, Tartini and Vallotti remained in Padua and are counted together with Rameau, Vallotti, or Euler among the *fisico-matematici* harmonists.[47] Can this fundamental difference be expressed in terms of practice-based or practice-oriented reasoning? Calegari's reasoning is based on past and current practice, leaving no room for a discourse within natural sciences. Tartini's use of the *third tone* goes hand in hand with the only possible accompaniment of the scale, but it is eventually limited by given premises – the historically variable laws of counterpoint. In the final analysis, a rigid Cartesianism can easily turn into an abductive argumentation scheme, as in the discussed example. Tartini's musical inference could at most furnish the best explanation for the musical practice of his time. Nevertheless, this is destined to remain a scientific hypothesis.

Bibliography

Barbieri, Patrizio. *Quarrels on Harmonic Theories in the Venetian Enlightenment.* Lucca: Libreria Musicale Italiana, 2020.

---

46 "Dopo anni, e secoli da che esiste, e si esercita la Musica attuale, si aspetta ancora a veder una scala di Basso, nelle di cui organiche formole convengano per certa primaria legge tutt'i compositori. Si cerca il vero dove non è: non si troverà mai. [...] La certissima legge originale delle formole organiche della scala, determinate non dall'arte, o dall'arbitrio, ma dalla fisico-armonica natura, si trova unicamente in questo esemplare, che appunto per tal cagione non può non esser il primo." Tartini, *De' Principj*, 79–80. English translation by the author.

47 See especially Chap. E.7 "Padre Martini and the *fisico-matematici* harmonists: Tartini, Rameau, Riccati, and Vallotti," in Barbieri, *Quarrels on Harmonic Theories*, 149–193.

Bernard, Jonathan W. "The Principle and the Elements: Rameau's 'Controversy with d'Alembert'." *Journal of Music Theory* 24, no. 1 (1980): 37–62.

Byram-Wigfield, Benjamin. "The Sacred Music of Antonio Lotti: Idiom and Influence of a Venetian Master." Doctoral dissertation, The Open University, 2016. https://doi.org/10.21954/ou.ro.0000bc4c.

Calegari, Francesco Antonio. "Ampla dimostrazione degli armoniali musicali tuoni. Trattato teorico-pratico." Manuscript Venice, 1732, copy, c.1800, A-Wn, 19103, f. 9r–126r. Music Department, Austrian National Library, Vienna.

Canale, Margherita. "Fonti per una ricostruzione della didattica di Tartini nella 'Scuola delle Nazioni'." *Muzikološki Zbornik/Musicological Annual* 28 (1992): 15–24.

Caraba, Irene Maria. "I Bassi per esercizio d'accompagnamento all'antico." *Rivista Italiana di Musicologia* 53 (1992): 57–72.

Christensen, Thomas. *Rameau and Musical Thought in the Enlightenment*. Cambridge: Cambridge University Press, 1993.

Eemeren, Frans H. van. "The Study of Argumentation." In *The SAGE handbook of rhetorical studies*, edited by Andrea A. Lunsford, Kirt H. Wilson, Rosa A. Eberly, 109–124. Thousand Oaks, CA: SAGE, 2009.

Gambino, Daniele. "Il trattato teorico-pratico di Francesco Antonio Calegari ovvero *l'Ampla dimostrazione degli armoniali musicali tuoni*." In *Barocco padano e musici francescani 2*, edited by Alberto Colzani, Andrea Luppi, Maurizio Padoan, 543–607. Padua: Centro Studi Antoniani, 2018.

Giuggioli, Matteo. "Tartini, Giuseppe." In *MGG Online*. Bärenreiter. Accessed February 12, 2022. https://www.mgg-online.com/mgg/stable/12743.

Hochstein, Wolfgang. "Vallotti, Francesco Antonio." In *MGG Online*. Bärenreiter. Accessed February 12, 2022. https://www.mgg-online.com/mgg/stable/50871.

Josephson, John R., and Susan G. Josephson. *Abductive Inference. Computation, philosophy, technology*. Cambridge: Cambridge University Press, 1994.

Koons, Robert. "Defeasible Reasoning." In *The Stanford Encyclopedia of Philosophy*. Stanford University. Accessed February 12, 2022. https://plato.stanford.edu/archives/fall2021/entries/reasoning-defeasible/.

Lumer, Christoph. "Walton's Argumentation Schemes." *OSSA Conference Archive* 110 (2016). Accessed February 12, 2022. http://scholar.uwindsor.ca/ossaarchive/OSSA11/papersandcommentaries/110.

Saratelli, Giuseppe. "Ammaestramenti Prattici dal lume de quali si apprende il vero modo di perfettamente accompagnare la parte soppra lo Stromento da tasto del Sig.r Giuseppe Saratelli Maestro della Ducal Capella di S. Marco 1732." Manuscript, Venice, 1732, copy, 18th cent., I-Vc, Giust. B. 45 n. 5. Fondo Giustiniani, Library of the Conservatory of Music "Benedetto Marcello" (Biblioteca, Conservatorio di Musica Benedetto Marcello), Venice.

Schurr, Walter William. "Francesco Antonio Calegari (d. 1742): Music Theorist and Composer." Doctoral dissertation, Catholic University of America, 1969.

Tartini, Giuseppe. *De' Principj dell'Armonia Musicale contenuta nel Diatonico genere*. Padova: Stamperia del seminario, 1767.

Tartini, Giuseppe. *Trattato di musica secondo la vera scienza dell'armonia*. Padova: Stamperia del seminario, 1754.

Valder-Knechtges, Claudia. "Giuseppe Saratelli. Ein Venezianischer Musiker des 18. Jahrhunderts." *Musikforschung* 37, no. 2 (1984): 111–114.

Vallotti, Francesco Antonio. *Della scienza teorica e pratica della moderna musica. Libro I*. Padua: Manfré, 1779.

Vallotti, Francesco Antonio. "Raggionamenti del Padre Francescantonio Calegari che servono per sostenere il di lui sistema del Tuono minore musicale armoniale nella corda, ed Ottaua di D. la sol re contro il Padre Vallotti che lo vuole fondato nella corda, ed ottava di A la mi re per le raggioni che si vedranno in risposta alle obbiezioni del sudetto Padre, senza considerare di presente gli altri validissimi fondamenti, che mirabilmente accordando in teorica, non meno che in prattica lasciano la mente libera da qualunque, benche menoma confusione con grande sensibilissimo vantaggio di chiunque si accinge alla pratica." Manuscript, Padua, 1731, autograph, 24th November 1731, I-Pca, A.VI.537, 15 fol. Music Archive, Pontifical Antoniana Library (Archivio Musicale, Pontificia Biblioteca Antoniana), Padua.

Walton, Douglas N. "Abductive, presumptive and plausible arguments." *Informal Logic* 21, no. 2 (2001): 141–169. https://doi.org/10.22329/il.v21i2.2241.

Wessely, Othmar. "Johann Joseph Fux und Francesco Antonio Vallotti. Vortrag gehalten vor der Jahreshauptversammlung der Johann-Joseph-Fux-Gesellschaft am 17. März 1966." *Jahresgabe 1966 der Johann-Joseph-Fux-Gesellschaft* (1967): 3–18.

Zanon, Giancarlo. "Il P. M.° Francescantonio Vallotti del giudizio dei contemporanei e dei posteri." Introduction to *Trattato della moderna musica* edited by Francesco Antonio Valotti, xv–xxx. Padova: Il Messaggero di S. Antonio/Basilica del Santo, 1950.

Jerneja Umer Kljun

University of Ljubljana

Understanding Tartini and His Thought: Overcoming Translation Difficulties in the Correspondence between Tartini and Martini

Abstract: The trilingual edition of letters and documents is a fundamental resource for further research into Tartini's life and character, as well as his theoretical and philosophical thought. Drawing insight from her experience in translating the collection of Tartini's letters into Slovene, the author discusses the translation difficulties in the correspondence between Tartini and Martini. Based on a linguistic analysis of these letters, the following problematic areas have been identified: the syntactic, lexical and phraseological characteristics of the eighteenth-century Italian language, the possible comprehension problems arising from a semantic shift or lack of context, as well as Tartini's inconsistent use of musical and mathematical terminology.

The specificity of eighteenth-century Italian and the complexity of the source material call for a collaborative effort between experts in the field of linguistics, translation studies, musicology and mathematics (and others) in order to produce a translation that is accessible to the modern-day target audience.

Keywords: music theory translation, historical text, context in translation, translation strategies, collaborative translation

1 Introduction

The 2020 edition of letters and documents[1] is an exceptionally valuable source for biographical research, shedding light on Tartini's complex musical, theoretical and philosophical thought, his various interests and his character. Although the compilation of letters and documents belongs to the non-fiction literature, the texts span across genres and styles due to their subject matter. The personal exchanges that reveal several aspects of Tartini's life and personality as well as the wider social and historical context at times read almost like a historical epistolary novel; other times they are purely informational and factual. The letters to his pupils and patrons feature specific instructions on violin technique and performance, providing

---

1 Giorgia Malagò, ed., *Giuseppe Tartini: Lettere e Documenti/Pisma in dokumenti/Letters and Documents*, 2 vols, trans. Jerneja Umer Kljun and Roberto Baldo (Trieste: Edizioni Università di Trieste, 2020).

insight into Tartini's pedagogy and compositional style. Tartini's exchanges with the most prominent scholars of his time, such as Leonhard Euler and especially Giovanni Battista Martini, venture into purely scientific prose, while the letters received from count Francesco Algarotti offer brief excursions into literature and poetry. This range of topics and styles along with the linguistic characteristics of the source text and other difficulties (presented below) make for a challenging read.

The purpose of this chapter is to discuss some of the translation problems identified within the source text, share an insight into the role and tasks of a translator and to emphasize the importance of a collaborative approach when dealing with source materials of this scope and nature. Taking into consideration the collection as a whole, I first present the specificities of the eighteenth-century Italian language, providing examples from Tartini and addressing the possible translation difficulties brought forth by archaic vocabulary and semantic shift. I then move on to the comprehension problems arising from a significant lack of context. Based on the definition and a specific categorization of context by scholars in the field of translation studies, I explain the terms used in the discussion, emphasizing the importance of a contextual analysis of the source material and proposing a collaborative approach as a possible means of overcoming difficulties stemming from the use of field-specific terminology and lack of context. The fifth section of the chapter brings a brief review of the relevant Slovene resources.

Finally, the focus shifts to the Tartini-Martini correspondence, which presents specific challenges regarding Tartini's use of mathematical terminology. In the discussion of a few particular terms, I compare the Slovene translation with the English edition of the letters, taking into account the models and guidelines laid out in the relevant scientific publications on the translation of ancient authors and early music theory.

2 The Language of the Settecento and Tartini's Writing Style

Many translation difficulties stem from the stylistic, syntactic, lexical and phraseological characteristics of the eighteenth-century Italian language. At the time, Italian was perceived as the language of emotion, poetry and musicality, as opposed to French, which was regarded as the language of clarity and scientific reasoning.[2] The spoken languages were prevalently dialects, while the written Italian language, which was based on the Florentine dialect, was, to some extent, still characterized by complex periods and syntactic inversions, influenced by Latin and the literary style of the Trecento. It was also veined with dialectal words and idiomatic expressions, and there were many examples of oscillating use of different word forms and spellings – for example, Tartini writes *tuono* and not *tono* (tone); he uses both *demostrazione* and *dimostratione* (demonstration), the plural form *principij*

---

2 Claudio Marazzini, *Breve storia della lingua italiana* (Bologna: Mulino, 2004), 155.

and *principi* (principles); as well as the dialectal adjective *cremese* instead of *cremisi* or *chermisi* (crimson). Some variants are easily recognizable, while others are not, and a translator must be aware of the possible orthographic variations that are characteristic of the period, in order to translate them appropriately. It is also crucial to seek out appropriate linguistic resources, such as the historical monolingual dictionaries Vocabolario degli Accademici della Crusca,[3] TLIO,[4] Tommaseo-Bellini[5] and Boerio[6] that are conveniently available online.

In the Settecento, according to Migliorini: "[…] the language of science had not yet reached the conciseness it achieved later on, neither it was so detached from the literary language not to allow for some elegance of expression."[7] This elegance of expression as well as the syntactic complexity of the scientific language can be illustrated by Tartini's introduction to his theories in his letter to Paolo Balbi from 1741:

> Condotto a mano dalla mia fortunata semplicità di pensare, aiutato infinitamente dalla scienza armonica, in cui sinora niun uomo grande si è degnato internarsi, sebben in essa solamente vi è la chiave della natura, ho scoperto molti fenomeni e fisiche demostrazioni, dalle quali illuminato, e dalla musica portato nella natura fisica universale, ho veduto chiaramente la soluzione di tutte quelle difficoltà, che sinora sono insolubili appresso li matematici; e sono tutte le incomensurabili riddotte mensurabili a misura com*m*une, siano le diagonali, sia la quadratura del circolo; la legge de' gravi, forze, resistenza etc. La natura del continuo, la natura de' centri, e in una parola sola la misura dell'uno come uno: cosa che pare contraddittoria, ma ch'è vera ver*issi*ma perché si tratta di demostrazioni, e di prove fisiche.[8]

---

3 Vocabolario degli Accademici della Crusca. Available at http://www.lessicografia.it DOI: 10.23833/BD/LESSICOGRAFIA
4 Tesoro della lingua Italiana delle Origini (Florence: Istituto del Consiglio Nazionale di Ricerche, 1997). Available at http://tlio.ovi.cnr.it/TLIO/
5 Nicolò Tommaseo and Bernardo Bellini, *Dizionario della lingua italiana* (Torino: Unione tipografico-editrice, 1861). Available at http://www.tommaseobellini.it/#/
6 Giuseppe Boerio, *Dizionario del dialetto veneziano* (Venice: Reale tipografia di Giovanni Cecchini Edit., 1867). Available at http://www.linguaveneta.net/dizionario-del-dialetto-veneziano-di-giuseppe-boerio/
7 Bruno Migliorini, *Storia della lingua italiana* (Milano: Bompiani, 2007), 458. Quotation translated by Jerneja Umer Kljun.
8 Malagò, *Tartini: Lettere*, 1:150. English translation in Malagò, *Tartini: Lettere*, 2:289: "Led on by my fortunate simplicity of thought, infinitely helped by the harmonic science, into which no great man has until now considered immersing himself, although in it alone the key of nature is to be found, I have discovered many phenomena and much physical proof; enlightened by these and led from music into universal physical nature, I have clearly seen the solution to all those difficulties that have hitherto been unsolvable for mathematicians; and these are all the immeasurables made measurable by means of a common measure, be it the diagonals, be it the squaring of the circle, the law of falling bodies, forces, resistance, etc. The nature of the continuous, the nature of centres, and in a word the measure of one

Tartini's writing is marked by long, complex periods with several subordinate and embedded clauses. Due to their complex syntactic structure, paired with an unconventional use of punctuation (from a present day perspective), indirect or vague quotes, references to the ancient Greek philosophers, the Scripture, ancient mathematicians and music theorists,[9] as well as metaphors, hyperboles and elements of Latin and the Venetian dialect, Tartini's texts often feel like a stream of consciousness that requires careful reading.

Furthermore, when dealing with a historical text, it is possible to encounter problems deriving from a semantic shift, which implies that over time words take on additional meanings. Taking another example from the Tartini-Martini correspondence, the conjunction *però* that has an adversative or concessive value nowadays (however, but, yet, nevertheless) sometimes still maintains its archaic meaning of *per questo* (therefore, for that reason) in the source text: "Il numero di queste vibrazioni dentro lo spazio d'un tempo determinato, è forza che anch'esso sia determinato, e però possa esprimersi con un numero noto."[10] Such semantic nuances can prove quite difficult to detect, yet they affect the interpretation and understanding of a period.

Not only is deciphering Tartini's thoughts difficult due to the all of the abovementioned linguistic characteristics, the author himself declared he purposely wrote in an obscure fashion, when he had some other objective, related to the metaphysical aspects of the third tone.[11] And even before that, when Tartini became frustrated with his inconclusive theoretical discussions with Giovanni Battista Martini and Paolo Balbi after a year of correspondence regarding his treatise, he stated that the treatise must be unintelligibly obscure or a work of a fanatic or that it simply does not reach the objective it aspires to.[12] In fact, other prominent scholars of his time perceived Tartini's *Trattato di musica secondo la vera scienza dell'armonia* (Treatise on Music according to the True Science of Harmony, 1754) to be completely incomprehensible. Among Tartini's harshest critics, Horvat

---

as one: something that seems contradictory but which is absolutely true, as we are dealing with demonstrations and physical proof."

9 See Sukljan's chapter in this volume. Nejc Sukljan, "Tartini and the Ancients: Traces of Ancient Music Theory in Tartini-Martin Correspondence," in *In Search of Perfect Harmony: Tartini's Music and Music Theory in Local and European Contexts*, ed. Nejc Sukljan (Berlin: Peter Lang, 2022), 141–167.

10 Malagò, *Tartini: Lettere*, 1:125. English translation in Malagò, *Tartini: Lettere*, 2: 266: "The number of these vibrations within a determined space of time is necessarily itself determined and can therefore be expressed with a known number."

11 Malagò, *Tartini: Lettere*, 1:313: "Anzi nel mio trattato di musica avendo io voluto ad arte esser oscuro dove ho avuto qualche altro fine, in codesti due libercoli voglio e so di esser chiaro […]"

12 Malagò, *Tartini: Lettere*, 1:206: "[…] deduco, che o il trattato è un fanatismo o il trattato è talmente oscuro, che non si può intendere, o il trattato non conclude la verità, che si propone."

mentions Jean le Rond d'Alembert, Jean Adam le Serre and Antonio Eximeno y Pujades.[13]

3 Missing Information and Extra-Textual References

Another set of translation difficulties arise from missing information. Malagò notes that the examination of Tartini sources revealed "a significant loss of materials, above all in the letters replying to those sent by Tartini, from his numerous correspondents".[14] Most of the time, we are, therefore, reading one side of the exchange and cannot always be sure of the extratextual references made in the letter. These range from family disputes, litigations, debts and the nephews' military appointments to historical and political events, social structure, European courts and monarchs (emphasis added):

> Se noi tutti d'accordo, io per il primo, voi, il prete (*ch'è stato uno scandalo pubblico*) viveremo in grazia di Dio, e si raccomandaremo a lui di cuore, vedrete fratello caro, che tutto si mutarà [...][15]
>
> Da persona religiosa ho fatto passar parola a sua eccellenza signor Lorenzo Grimani sopra *le vertenze presenti*, facendogli insinuare il pregiuditio, che riceve la parte contraria dalla protettione della eccellentissima Casa per ottenimento della delegatione etc.[16]
>
> giacché *li passi chiusi* mi hanno impedito di venir costì, come avevo destinato, è tempo di seguir per lettera al mio impegno.[17]
>
> [...] ella non può immaginarsi abbastanza la consolazione da me provata nel sentire dalle altri relazioni, e dalla di lei lettera il felice incontro che costì hanno avuto e la sua persona, e le sue composizioni, appresso *sua altezza reale elettrice, ed appresso cotesta corte*.[18]

---

13 Boris Horvat, "Tartini, matematik ali diletant," in *Giuseppe Tartini in njegov čas*, ed. Metoda Kokole (Ljubljana: Založba ZRC, 1997), 31–38.
14 Malagò, *Tartini: Lettere*, 1:72.
15 Malagò, *Tartini: Lettere*, 1:112. English translation in Malagò, *Tartini: Lettere*, 2:252: "If all of us – in agreement, myself first of all, you, the priest (who has been a public scandal) – live in God's grace, and heartily trust in Him, you shall see, dear brother, that everything will change [...]"
16 Malagò, *Tartini: Lettere*, 1:169. English translation in Malagò, *Tartini: Lettere*, 2:308: "Through a man of religion I have had the news about the present disputes passed on to His Excellency Signor Lorenzo Grimani, suggesting to him the bias that the opposing party receives from the protection of the most excellent household for obtaining the assignment; etc."
17 Malagò, *Tartini: Lettere*, 1:135. English translation in Malagò, *Tartini: Lettere*, 2:276: "Since the closure of the passes has prevented me from coming there, as I had decided to do, it is time to fulfil my obligation by letter."
18 Malagò, *Tartini: Lettere*, 1:307. English translation in Malagò, *Tartini: Lettere*, 2:444: "You cannot quite imagine the consolation I felt on hearing from the other

The problem is even more pronounced in the theoretical letters discussed in Section 6 of this chapter, in which the correspondents refer to figures and demonstrations that are not included in the source text. Martini's letter from 4 April 1752, in which he lists some objections to Tartini's propositions, even includes direct quotations and page references from the manuscript Tartini sent to Bologna (emphasis added):

> *Pag. 4. Ma come che &.* Si dice che il due può esser termine della progressione aritmetica 1, 2, 3, la quale esige la differenza costante, che in questa serie è l'unità. [...] *Pag. 4 [/] 5.* La seconda cosa che demostrativamente si deduce resta alquanto confusa.[19]

When reading and especially translating these texts, we have to acknowledge and address such a significant lack of context. In order to expand on the possible strategies to overcome these problems, we must first understand how context affects translation.

4 Context and Collaborative Approaches in Translation

It is widely agreed among translators and scholars in the field of translation studies that context is essential to the translation process. It is, however, an elusive notion and its definitions vary according to the traditions that approach the study of context. While Baker[20] and House[21] provide a comprehensive examination of these theoretical approaches, the matter far exceeds the scope and purpose of this chapter. Suffice it to say, that context, understood here as the circumstances and settings that form a wider frame of a text, unequivocally affect the meaning of a word or phrase and inform the translator's interpretation. To illustrate with a simple example, the Italian word *suono* can be translated as *sound* in English and *zvok* in Slovene. However, the word takes on another meaning in the phrase *terzo suono*: in the context of Tartini's discovery of the acoustic phenomenon, it can only be translated as *third tone* and *tretji ton* (see Section 6 for more examples).

Melby and Foster,[22] who treat "context as a set of resources that need to be available to translators", present a more practical approach, breaking down context

---

reports, and from your letter, the positive reaction that both your person and your compositions have had there, with Her Royal Electoral Highness and at the court."
19 Malagò, *Tartini: Lettere*, 1:208. English translation in Malagò, *Tartini: Lettere*, 2: 348: "Page 4. But how is it that &. It is said that two can be the term of the arithmetical progression 1, 2, 3, which requires the constant difference, which in this series is the unit. [...] Page 4. 5. The second thing demonstratively inferred remains quite confused."
20 Mona Baker, "Contextualization in translator- and interpreter-mediated events," *Journal of Pragmatics* 38, no. 1 (2006): 321–337. doi:10.1016/j.pragma.2005.04.010.
21 Jennifer House, "Text and context in translation," *Journal of Pragmatics* 38, no. 1 (2006): 338–358. doi:10.1016/j.pragma.2005.06.021
22 Alan K. Melby and Christopher Foster, "Context in translation: Definition, access and teamwork." *The International Journal for Translation & Interpreting Research* 2, no. 2 (2010): 1–15.

into five components that are "primarily intended to provide support for the *production* of (target) texts".[23] Starting from a general understanding of context as the interrelated conditions in which something exists and occurs, the authors define five aspects of context that are most significant in the translation process: co-text, chron-text, rel-text, bi-text and non-text. In the Melby-Foster classification, *co-text* is defined as the text surrounding (preceding and following) a word or a phrase within the same document. *Chron-text* implies there is a history of revisions to the source text that are relevant to the translation; *rel-text* refers to all related documents and other resources that facilitate understanding; and *bi-text* refers specifically to the bilingual resources, such as corpora and translation memories, that are formed after the alignment of the source text with the target text. The fifth aspect, *non-text*, goes beyond the text itself, referring to the real-world setting of a document or the paralinguistic information. For the purposes of practical translation, according to Melby and Foster, *non-text* can be regarded as

> those *aspects of context that are not accessed through written texts* during a translation project but that are nonetheless relevant to the work of a translator. They might include *technical knowledge about the subject matter* of the source text, *general knowledge about the cultures to which the source and target texts are addressed*, and a dynamic mental model of the *interaction between the author of the source text and particular readers of the source text* or *between the translator and the reader of the translation*.[24] (Emphasis added.)

Non-text also includes *intent*[25] – a translator must consider the purpose and the intended audiences of the source text as well as the purpose and the intended audiences of the target text. The categories that are most relevant for this discussion and the source text at hand are certainly *co-text*, *rel-text* and *non-text*. In the case of highly complex source texts, such as Tartini's letters, in which, sometimes, *co-text* does not suffice for a clear understanding of the source, the translator is required to do in-depth research into *rel-text* and *non-text*. It is crucial to consult relevant resources, such as historical monolingual dictionaries (mentioned in Section 2 above) and scholarly sources (see Section 5 below), but it is also equally important to establish a dialogue with experts in the various related fields to promote collaboration, all the while keeping in mind the purpose of the target text and the intended reader. Just as a word, a phrase or a text, for that matter, cannot be considered without its context, the process of translation itself cannot be carried out in isolation.

Drawing from Nord's[26] review of functionalist approaches to translation, O'Brian emphasizes the *collaborative nature* of the entire translation process: "Collaboration

---

23 Melby and Foster, "Context in translation," 3.
24 Melby and Foster, "Context in translation," 5–8.
25 See note 22 above.
26 Christiane Nord, *Translating as a Purposeful Activity – Functionalist Approaches Explained* (London: Routledge, 1997).

is evident in all types of translation scenarios and across the whole process of translation [...]" and can occur between translators and any other agent involved (author, editor, publisher, reviewer or others).[27] In a narrow meaning, a collaborative approach or collaborative translation refers to a situation, in which two or more translators work together to produce a target text, be it for commercial reasons, for a social cause or to fill a gap in the publication of popular genres.[28] Whatever the setting, O'Brian concludes that collaboration clearly brings benefits to a translation project, since "[b]eing able to consult with the source text author, or to exchange ideas and debate with a fellow translator will most likely lead to higher quality translation."[29]

To add to O'Brian's conclusion and shift back to the translation problems identified in Tartini's letters, a collaboration between a translator and scholars or other experts will not only facilitate the understanding and use of field-related lexis but could also help with the contextualization of extra-textual references by piecing together information that is necessary for the understanding of the source text.

5 Translating Tartini into Slovene: An Overview

In accordance with the Melby and Foster[30] categorization of context, previously published translations of texts by the same author as well as scholarly articles on the author and their work represent a valuable resource regarded as *rel-text*. However, the search for such publications on Tartini in Slovene renders a relatively short list of highly fragmented sources. Before the trilingual edition of the 189 letters and documents in Malagò,[31] only two of Tartini's letters were translated into Slovene, i.e. a letter to his brother Domenico from 1726 and another to his brother Pietro from 1747, chosen by Hoyer[32] to emphasize Tartini's strong bond with the town of Piran. Moreover, in 2021 the Maritime Museum "Sergej Mašera" in Piran commissioned a second translation of Tartini's letter to Maddalena Lombardini (see Žitko).[33] Tartini's theoretical works, *Trattato di musica, De' principj dell'armonia musicale contenuta nel diatonico genere* (On the Principles of Musical Harmony

---

27 Sharon O'Brian, "Collaborative translation," in *Handbook of Translation Studies*, ed. Yves Gambier, Luc van Doorslaer (Amsterdam/Philadelphia: John Benjamins Publishing Company, 2011), 2:17–20.
28 O'Brian, "Collaborative translation," 18.
29 O'Brian, "Collaborative translation," 19.
30 Melby and Foster, "Context in translation," 6.
31 Malagò, *Tartini: Lettere*.
32 Sonja Ana Hoyer, "Dvoje pisem Giuseppa Tartinija," *Primorska Srečanja: Revija za družboslovje in kulturo* 17, št. 133 (1992), 281–282.
33 Duška Žitko, *Giuseppe Tartini & Maddalena Laura Lombardini: pismo/la lettera/ the letter/la lettre/der Brief*, trans. Ravel Kodrič, Slobodan Žmikić, Charles Burney, Antoine-Léonard Thomas and Johann Adam Hiller (Piran: Pomorski muzej "Sergej Mašera", 2021).

Contained in the Diatonic Genus, 1767) and *Scienza platonica fondata nel cerchio* (Platonic Science Founded in the Circle, ca. 1767–1770), are discussed in Ravnikar,[34] Šinigoj,[35] Horvat[36] and Južnič,[37] and brief excerpts of the source texts are occasionally quoted along with their translation in Ravnikar and Šinigoj. The only attempt at a translation of a complete theoretical work, i.e. Tartini's unpublished manuscript *Quadratura del circolo* (Squaring the Circle),[38] can be seen in Bensa.[39] When consulting these related resources, the context and the purpose of the target text must be considered as well. In the case of Ravnikar and Šinigoj, the translation seems almost an afterthought, as it is relegated to the footnotes, while Bensa's translation served as a starting point for the author's BSc dissertation and cannot be regarded as a professional translation nor was it intended to reach a wider readership. Despite their fragmentedness or low quality, however, these translations of Tartini's theoretical thought provided a solid enough footing for the translation of the musical and mathematical propositions discussed in the Tartini–Martini correspondence.

6 The Tartini-Martini Correspondence: Translating the Musical and Mathematical Terminology

The collection of letters exchanged between Tartini and Martini is comprised of 98 documents, ranging from strictly personal messages, which attest to a deep friendship and mutual respect between the two musicians, to complex discussions on music theory.[40] The dilemmas discussed in the following paragraphs concern the theoretical correspondence, which can be divided into two periods. The early Tartini-Martini theoretical exchanges introduce "the matters of music theory connected with the 'system' that Tartini was already developing at the time"[41] and provide a basis for later exchanges regarding his particular mathematical approach. In Tartini's later correspondence with Martini (and indirectly Balbi), the

---

34 Bruno Ravnikar, "Tartini in kombinacijski toni" *Muzikološki zbornik*, no. 28 (1992): 41–46, http://www.dlib.si/?URN=URN:NBN:SI:doc-EIJX2P77
35 Boris Šinigoj, "Tartini in metafizika glasbe," in *Giuseppe Tartini in njegov čas*, ed. Metoda Kokole (Ljubljana: ZRC SAZU, Založba ZRC, 1997) 19–30.
36 Boris Horvat, "Tartini, matematik ali diletant," 31–38.
37 Stanislav Južnič, "Pirančan Tartini s kombinacijskim tonom proti D'Alembertu," *Annales Series Historia et Sociologia* 16, no. 1 (2006): 133–144.
38 "Quadratura del circolo," by Giuseppe Tartini, SI-Pit, SI PAK PI 334, box 3, ms. 232, *Collection Giuseppe Tartini*, Regional archives Koper, Piran Unit, Slovenia.
39 Vladimir Bensa, "Tartinijeva kvadratura kroga," (BSc dissertation, University of Ljubljana, 2007).
40 For an analysis of the evolution of their personal and professional relationship, see Malagò, *Tartini: Lettere*, 1:16–33.
41 Malagò, *Tartini: Lettere*, 1:82–83.

focus shifts towards the topic of the third tone and the squaring of the circle – the most interesting of things that can be debated among men.[42]

From a translator's perspective, these letters bring forth another set of difficulties, which concern Tartini's use of mathematical terminology. When explaining his propositions, Tartini relies on geometry and mathematics, even though he admits to use terms that are fashioned in his own way, both because he is unaware of their precise meaning, and because he would not find them useful even if he knew them.[43] In his letter to Martini from 4 August 1752, Tartini even points out one of the errors he made in a previous letter, in which he mistakenly referred to an ellipsis as a circular shape. He then defends himself by stating he already admitted that he had not studied geometry.[44]

The most emblematic case of Tartini's complex theoretical writing is the use of the highly polysemic words *ragione* and *proporzione* that frequently appear in his letters to Martini.

When discussing the translation of the semantically rich Latin word *ratio*, from which the Italian expression *ragione* derives, Ahačič[45] states that even when used as a term, i.e. an expression with a specific and unambivalent meaning that is independent of its context, *ratio* maintains a certain degree of elasticity that is nearly impossible to express with a single word equivalent in the Slovene translation. Through the analysis of the terminological and non-terminological use of *ratio* in Varro and Quintilian, Ahačič[46] observes that in the former case, a translator should strive to find a translation that maintains the singularity and the elasticity of the Latin word and use such an expression consistently, while in the latter case it is not wrong to translate it according to its wider context.

Since both *ragione* and *proporzione* are used in connection to interval quantity and quality in Tartini's theoretical letters, they must be regarded as terms and therefore translated consistently. Starting from the mathematical definition of the

---

42 Malagò, *Tartini: Lettere*, 1:190: "[…] la cosa più interessante di quante mai si possano trattare tra gli uomini?"
43 Malagò, *Tartini: Lettere*, 1:208: "Inoltre son a me conscio, che alle volte adopro termini formati a mio modo, sì perché non mi sono noti i termini delle scienze di quantità, che sono comuni; sì perché alle volte non servirebbero, seben mi fossero noti."
44 Malagò, *Tartini: Lettere*, 1:230: "Le averto, che nella mia ultima lettera ho fatto la figura di una elissi, chiamandola circolare. Già mi son prottestato sino dal principio, che io non ho studiato geometria, e però niente più facile per me, che il fallare ne' termini."
45 Kozma Ahačič, "Prevajanje termina *ratio* pri Varonu in Kvintiljanu," *Keria: Studia Latina et Graeca* 2, no. 2 (2000): 57–63, https://doi.org/10.4312/keria.2.2.57-63.
46 Ahačič, "Prevajanje termina *ratio*," 61.

Italian term *ragione* as the quantitative relation between two values expressing the number of times one value contains or is contained within the other and even as a constant relation between the terms of a progression or sequence, the term can only be translated as *ratio* in English and *razmerje* in Slovene. Similarly, in strictly mathematical terms, *proporzione* implies a statement of equality between two ratios, just as its English and Slovene equivalents *proportion* and *sorazmerje* do. Theoretically, there should not be any confusion regarding the use of these terms, which should provide for a consistent translation. However, it is Tartini's own terminological inconsistencies that prove to be problematic. In his early correspondence with Martini, Tartini uses the two terms, *ragione* and *proporzione*, in a synonymous manner, both referring to the comparison between two quantities, both abstract and concrete, as in the case of *la maggior proporzione* (the greater ratio), *proporzione dupla* (the duple ratio), compared to *ragion dupla* (the duple ratio) and *ragion sesquialtera* (the 3:2 ratio), seen in the excerpts (1), (2) and (3) below:

(1) La maggior proporzione, ch'è la sesquialtera, si divide nel ditono, e semiditono, e la minore ch'è la sesquiterza si ommette.[47]

(2) Per essempio: la maggiore, e la prima di tutte le proporzioni è la dupla.[48]

(3) Dimostrai il suono del secondo peso al suono del primo peso in ragion dupla radicale; il suono del terzo peso al suono del secondo in ragion sesquialtera radicale.[49]

In Tartini, *proporzione* never alludes to the equal value of two ratios, but rather to the ratio itself, and it is therefore impossible to translate it as *sorazmerje* in Slovene just to keep two distinct expressions, following Tartini's writing style, as it would be fundamentally wrong to interchange these concepts. Furthermore, the use of the loanwords *proporc* or *proporcija* (adopted through German from the Latin *prōportiō*, first registered in Slovene in the nineteenth century)[50] as a synonym for *razmerje* could be perceived as a stylistically questionable choice, inconsistent with the present-day musicological terminology.[51] In the English translation of the letters,[52] we can also observe a synonymous use of the terms *proportion* and *ratio* (e.g. "the greater proportion, which is the sesquialter"[53] and "[the] radical sesquialter ratio"[54]). Since the meanings of the two English terms overlap – the proportion

---

47 Malagò, *Tartini: Lettere*, 1:118.
48 Malagò, *Tartini: Lettere*, 1:120.
49 Malagò, *Tartini: Lettere*, 1:212.
50 Marko Snoj, *Slovenski etimološki slovar* (Ljubljana: Založba ZRC, 2016).
51 See, for example, Nejc Sukljan, "Istitutioni Harmoniche Gioseffa Zarlina in antična glasbena teorija," (Doctoral dissertation, University of Ljubljana, 2016), 229–245; Anicij Manlij Severin Boetij, *Temelji glasbe*, trans. Jurij Snoj (Ljubljana: Založba ZRC, 2013).
52 Malagò, *Tartini: Lettere*, vol. 2.
53 Malagò, *Tartini: Lettere*, 2:258.
54 Malagò, *Tartini: Lettere*, 2:350.

also meaning the relation of one part to another – such use is not necessarily wrong. However, when discussing Boethius's deliberate lexical inconsistencies in *De institutione musica* (Fundamentals of Music), Palisca observed that the author "used three different words for 'ratio', i.e. *proportio, habitudo* and *comparatio*, although it is obvious that he meant the same thing by all three".[55] According to Palisca[56] there is no particular advantage gained in equating these Latin terms with a set of three distinct English equivalents, when ratio is the only mathematically exact term.

To add another layer of complexity, the meanings of the two terms diverge in Tartini's later correspondence with Martini. From 1768 on, Tartini uses the term *ragione* indicating a ratio between two terms, while *proporzione* appears as an entirely separate concept (see "ragione, solitaria e separata da proporzione" in example (4) below), frequently as a part of the collocations *proporzione geometrica discreta* and *proporzione geometrica continua* (see excerpt (5) below):

(4) [...] sicché qualunque data ragione, solitaria e separata da proporzione, o serie, sia per sé armonica.[57]

(5) La dottrina ivi contenuta sì è in sostanza, che da una data proporzione geometrica continua si taglino parti, e si riportino nel mezzo, sicché si formi, e deduca una proporzione geometrica discreta, la quale certamente non può più conservare la ragione degli estremi geometrici, perché da questi dovendosi tagliar qualche parte per riporla nel mezzo, è forza che gli estremi della seconda proporzione geometrica discreta siano in minor ragione degli estremi della geometrica continua.[58]

Taking into consideration the *rel-text*, namely Tartini's theoretical discussions *Trattato di musica* and the unpublished manuscript *Quadratura del circolo*, it can be deduced that in these letters, *proporzione* (be it *armonica, geometrica, discreta, continua*) takes on the meaning of a ratio of three or more terms. While I previously argued there might be no real need for differentiation between *proporzione* and *ragione* when the terms are used synonymically, it is certainly sensible to mark the distinction between the two terms according to their use in Tartini's later correspondence, and possibly even address the matter in a footnote.

A second topic of discussion, related to the one above, concerns the translation of names of the ratios Tartini uses to define the intervals, e.g. *(ragione) dupla* (2:1), *sesquialtera* (3:2) and *sesquiterza* (4:3) that derive from the ancient nomenclature. With a certain degree of simplification these terms could be replaced by target language terms the present-day reader is much more familiar with, such as *octave, fifth* and *forth* in English and *oktava, kvinta* and *kvarta* in Slovene. However,

---

55 Claude Palisca, "Fidelities and Infidelities in Translating Early Music Theory," in *Music Discourse from Classical to Early Modern Times: Editing and Translating Texts*, ed. Maria Rika Maniates (Toronto: University of Toronto Press, 1997), 3.
56 See note 27 above.
57 Malagò, *Tartini: Lettere*, 1:323.
58 Malagò, *Tartini: Lettere*, 1:319.

Tartini does not allow for simplification in this matter, as his discussion focuses primarily on ratios, which he occasionally mentions alongside the names of the intervals: "Ogni una di queste tre parti è in proporzione sesquialtera, cioè di quinta [...]"[59] and "[...] da questa divisione nasce la sesquiterza, cioè la quarta [...]."[60] While the use of Latin loanword adjectives such as *duple, sesquialteral* and *sesquitertian* is not uncommon in English, it is not conventional in Slovene. When discussing the nature of Tartini's combination tone, Ravnikar[61] refers to these ratios simply as intervals, while Horvat also relies on the numerical expressions of the ratios: "V resnici se t. i. tretji ton pojavi samo takrat, ko se števec in imenovalec, ki opisujeta interval, razlikujeta za 1 (na primer kvinta – 3/2, vendar ne seksta – 5/3)."[62] On the other hand, Bensa[63] tried to avoid the issue by using the source term in the target text: "Če je zaigran interval sesquialtera, kar pomeni kvinto, je tretji ton A sozvočen nižjemu tonu v sesquialteri [...]."[64] Bensa argued the use of the source term is appropriate, since there seemed to be no consensus on the Slovene terminology. In the Slovene translation of Boethius,[65] Snoj tackled the same issue, providing the most accurate solution so far – by forming an adjective from the two terms of the ratio or fraction, e.g. *štiritretjinsko razmerje* from 4:3. The same approach was then adopted in the Slovene translation of Tartini's correspondence.

Another dilemma connected to Tartini's ambiguous use of geometrical terminology, mentioned at the beginning of this section, concerns the understanding and translation of the terms *linea, linea retta, linea circolare* and specifically *linea sonora*, used to represent the string in a mathematical demonstration. None of these terms are explicitly defined in the co-text, and the figures Tartini is alluding to are not included in the letters, e.g. "[...] infallibilmente è quadrato il circolo, e fisicamente, e dimostrativamente, senza che porti alcun obbietto alla quadratura il non potersi concretare la linea AX della figura XIII a quantità determinata da numero."[66] In absence of context, these terms could be translated, word-for-word, as *line, straight line, circular line* and *sounding line* in English and *črta, ravna črta, krožna črta* and *zveneča črta* in Slovene. However, doing so also means that the task to decipher Tartini's propositions is left to the reader. The only possibility we have for uncovering the meaning of these terms is to consult the related texts,

---

59 Malagò, *Tartini: Lettere*, 1:121.
60 See note 11 above.
61 Ravnikar, "Tartini in kombinacijski toni," 45.
62 Horvat, "Tartini, matematik ali diletant," 37. ("In fact, the so called third tone is produced only when the numerator and the denominator that define the interval differ by 1 (a fifth – 3/2, for example, but not a sixth – 5/3)." Translated by Umer Kljun.)
63 Bensa, "Tartinijeva kvadratura kroga," 32–33.
64 Bensa, "Tartinijeva kvadratura kroga," 38. "Se l'intervallo suonato è sesquialtero, ò sia pratticamente quinta, si ha il terzo suono A unisono al termine grave della sesquialtera; [...]." Orginal reproduced in Bensa, "Tartinijeva kvadratura kroga," 111.
65 Boetij, *Temelji glasbe*, 37.
66 Malagò, *Tartini: Lettere*, 1:230.

and observe the terminology as well as the multiple figures that illustrate Tartini's propositions.

In fact, during the process of translation into Slovene, a comparison between Tartini's propositions in the three sources, i.e. the letters, the *Trattato di musica* and the manuscript discussing the squaring of the circle, revealed that the treatise sent to Bologna to be examined by Martini and Balbi was actually the unpublished manuscript *Quadratura del circolo*,[67] and not the *Trattato di musica* as previously assumed.[68] Once this link has been identified, it could be determined that the lines Tartini is referring to in the letters have a definite length and two endpoints – he is, therefore, writing about line segments, and the terms can be translated accordingly.

Through semantic narrowing and the use of exact mathematical terms, the target text proves to be less cryptic. However, such an approach implies a certain degree of intervention into the source text, as it might attribute a better mathematical knowledge to the author. In such cases, the translator faces the dilemma of whether to "correct" the author and aim for a better comprehension, or to transfer the mistakes and inconsistencies "faithfully", producing an equally unintelligible and enigmatic text. Ultimately, it comes down to the overall aim of the target text. If the intention is to produce a translation that is accessible to the modern-day target audience, then immediate comprehension should take precedence. As Palisca states: "A translation will not hit its mark unless it is expressed in the language that the translator and readers share, and that includes the technical terminology in vogue in our time."[69]

7 Concluding Remarks

A text that presents so many linguistic and terminological difficulties and especially one that includes a number of ambiguous references to historical events and figures as well as connections to ancient theoretical traditions certainly calls for an annotated edition – not to defend the translator's interpretation but to provide for a wider context whenever the source text seems elusive. A critical edition and translation of these texts is arguably one of the most important means of understanding Tartini's reflections on music theory and his conceptualization of harmony, as well as a firm basis for further research among those who have little or no linguistic competence in Italian. It also gives us a chance to study some of the

---

67 See footnote 129 in Malagò, *Tartini: Lettere*, 1:24.
68 See Sukljan's chapter in this volume: Sukljan, "Tartini and the Ancients," 153–155.
69 Palisca, "Fidelities and infidelities," 4.

more prominent linguistic features of the eighteenth-century Italian in regards to their translation into present-day Slovene.

Furthermore, it is an endeavour that demands a collaborative interdisciplinary approach, involving experts in the fields of linguistics, translation studies, musicology, history, classical philology and the history of mathematics. While it is virtually impossible to translate texts of this nature without the help of experts, it should be noted that such experts often lack the necessary translation competences, including the linguistic, cultural and transfer competences needed to perform the task successfully. With this review of translation difficulties in Tartini's correspondence, I wanted to shed light on some of the aspects that guide the translator's decisions when dealing with complex source texts. They have to analyse and thoroughly understand the source text, taking into account its wider historical and linguistic context, in order to make the appropriate lexical, grammatical and stylistic choices that will convey the message and the overall tone of the source text in the target language. In doing so, they have to consult experts, especially regarding the field-specific lexis and the contextualization of the source material. This chapter is certainly not meant to tackle the issue in a comprehensive manner but rather to give a glimpse of the translation process and possibly open the door for further research into the translation of music theory as conceptualized by Tartini and other Italian authors of the Age of Enlightenment.

Bibliography

Ahačič, Kozma. "Prevajanje termina ratio pri Varonu in Kvintiljanu." *Keria Studia Latina et Greca* 2, no. 2 (2000): 57–63.

Baker, Mona. "Contextualization in translator- and interpreter-mediated event." *Journal of pragmatics* 38, no. 1 (2006): 321–337. doi:10.1016/j.pragma.2005.04.010

Bensa, Vladimir. "Tartinijeva kvadratura kroga." BSc dissertation, University of Ljubljana, Faculty of Mathematics and Physics, 2007.

Boerio, Giuseppe. *Dizionario del dialetto veneziano*. Venice: Reale tipografia di Giovanni Cecchini Edit, 1867.

Boetij, Anicij Manlij Severin. *Temelji glasbe*. Translated by Jurij Snoj. Ljubljana: Založba ZRC, 2013.

Horvat, Boris. "Tartini, matematik ali diletant." In *Giuseppe Tartini in njegov čas*, edited by Metoda Kokole, 31–38. Ljubljana: ZRC SAZU, Založba ZRC, 1997.

House, Jennifer. "Text and Context in Translation." *Journal of Pragmatics* 38, no. 1 (2006): 338–358. doi: 10.1016/j.pragma.2005.06.021.

Hoyer, Sonja Ana. "Dvoje pisem Giuseppa Tartinija." *Primorska srečanja: revija za družboslovje in kulturo* 17, no. 133 (1992): 281–282.

Južnič, Stanislav. "Pirančan Tartini s kombinacijskim tonom proti D'Alembertu." *Annales Series Historia et Sociologia* 16, no. 1 (2006): 133–144.

Malagò, Giorgia, ed. *Giuseppe Tartini: Lettere e documenti/Pisma in dokumenti/ Letters and Documents*. 2 vols. Translated by Jerneja Umer Kljun and Roberto Baldo. Trieste: Edizioni Università di Trieste, 2020.

Marazzini, Claudio. *Breve storia della lingua italiana*. Bologna: Mulino, 2004.

Melby, Alan K. and Christopher Foster. "Context in translation: Definition, access and teamwork." *The International Journal for Translation & Interpreting Research* 2, no. 2 (2010): 1–15.

Migliorini, Bruno. *Storia della lingua italiana*. Milano: Bompiani. 2007.

Nord, Christiane. *Translating as a Purposeful Activity: Functionalist Approaches Explained*. London: Routledge, 1997.

O'Brian, Sharon. "Collaborative translations." In *Handbook of Translation Studies*, edited by Yves Gambier, Luc van Doorslaer, vol. 2, 17–20. Amsterdam/Philadelphia: John Benjamins Publishing Company, 2011.

Palisca, Claude. "Fidelities and Infidelities in Translating Early Music Theory." In *Music Discourse from Classical to Early Modern Times: Editing and Translating Texts*, edited by Maria Rika Maniates, 1–16. Toronto: University of Toronto Press, 1997.

Petrobelli, Pierluigi. "Giuseppe Tartini." In *Grove Music Online*. Oxford Music Online. Accessed January 21, 2022. doi:https://doi-org.nukweb.nuk.uni-lj.si/10.1093/gmo/9781561592630.article.27529 .

Ravnikar, Bruno. "Tartini in metafizika glasbe." *Muzikološki zbornik*, no. 28 (1992): 41–46.

Snoj, Marko. *Slovenski etimološki slovar*. Ljubljana: Založba ZRC, 2016.

Sukljan, Nejc. "Isitutioni Harmoniche Gioseffa Zarlina in antična glasbena teorija." Doctoral dissertation, University of Ljubljana, Faculty of Arts, 2016.

Sukljan Nejc. "Tartini and the Ancients: Traces of Ancient Music Theory in Tartini-Martin Correspondence." In *In Search of Perfect Harmony: Tartini's Music and Music Theory in Local and European Contexts*, edited by Nejc Sukljan, 141–167. Berlin: Peter Lang, 2022.

Šinigoj, Boris. "Tartini in metafizika glasbe." In *Giuseppe Tartini in njegov čas*, edited by Metoda Kokole, 19–30. Ljubljana: Založba ZRC, 1997.

Tartini, Giuseppe. Quadratura del circolo. SI-Pit, SI PAK PI 334, box 3, ms. 232, *Collection Giuseppe Tartini*, Regional archives Koper, Piran Unit, Slovenia.

Žitko, Duška. *Giuseppe Tartini & Maddalena Laura Lombardini: pismo/la lettera/the letter/la lettre/der Brief*. Translated by Ravel Kodrič, Slobodan Žmikić, Charles Burney, Antoine-Léonard Thomas and Johann Adam Hiller. Piran: Pomorski muzej "Sergej Mašera", 2021.

Maestro delle Nazioni: Tartini's Influence and Reception and Dispersion of His Work

Lucija Konfic

Department for History of Croatian Music of the Croatian Academy of Sciences and Arts

Giuseppe Michele Stratico's Theoretical Thinking: Transgressing the Boundaries of Tartini's School

Abstract: Giuseppe Michele Stratico (1728–1783) was very appreciated by his teacher G. Tartini who himself stated that he "possesses the whole soul of my [Tartini's] school". That would include violin playing, composing and theoretical thinking – three areas in which Stratico was indeed adept in. But starting from the theory of his teacher, Stratico developed new theoretical ideas and a new musical system of his own. The very basis of the system included the extension of the *Sestupla* to *Ottupla*. Stratico's ideas were not acceptable to Tartini and may have been the reason for their divergence. Stratico elaborated his system in several versions of his *Trattato di musica*, but it remained unpublished. In this chapter I will present the main features of Stratico's theoretical thinking emphasizing ways in which it differs from his teacher's theory.

Keywords: Giuseppe Michele Stratico, Giuseppe Tartini, theoretical system, *Trattato di musica*, Ottupla

The work of Giuseppe Michele Stratico (Zadar, 31 July 1728 – Sanguinetto, 31 January 1783) has been recently revaluated marking him as an interesting contributor to the musical and theoretical thought of the second half of the eighteenth century. Moreover, Patrizio Barbieri in his new book *Quarrels on Harmonic Theories in the Venetian Enlightenment* states that he is one of the authors "whose direct involvement in the harmonic debate at the time has so far been overlooked or undervalued".[1]

There aren't many details about Stratico's involvement in his school, but Tartini in his letter from 7 July 1750 to the Count Francesco Algarotti (1712–1764), who at the time was in the service of Frederick II King of Prussia, writes:

> But not even this is an objection as here in Padua there is a young amateur, a student of mine (he is called Michiele Stratico and is a very civil person) who in my absence could be chosen as Instructor of the chosen youth. It is most certain that, well born

---

1 Patrizio Barbieri, *Quarrels on Harmonic Theories in the Venetian Enlightenment* (Lucca: LIM, 2020), VII.

as he is, he would not say no to such a Monarch; and it is most certain that in playing and composing he is famous, distinguished among all my students, as he possesses the whole soul of my school.[2]

Tartini's school, widely known for its violin technique teaching, was also regarded, as pointed out by Margherita Canale, as a school that educated "a complete and conscious musician"[3] in which Tartini's principle of the *terzo suono* (third tone) and his theoretical system in general had an important role. I tend to believe that the disagreements between the teacher and the student, i.e. transgressing the boundaries of his teacher's school, led Stratico from the "student who possesses the whole soul of his school" to "his declared enemy".[4] The basic premise of this chapter is therefore to show the common points of their respective systems, especially those parts where Stratico transgressed the boundaries that Tartini set in his system. Leonardo Frasson has already noticed this, pointing out: "In a certain sense, the pupil-composer Michele Stratico can be considered a follower and continuator of Tartinian theory [...] Stratico proves to have studied in-depth and well understood Tartinian thought and on the same basis he formed his personal beliefs that go beyond its limits."[5]

---

2 "Ma nemen questo è obietto, perché qui in Padova vi è un Giovane dilettante mio scolare (si chiama Michiele Straticò, et è persona civile assai) che in mia mancanza potrebbe esser scielto Maestro del Giovane destinato. È cert[issi]mo, che se ben nato tale, non direbbe di nò ad un tal Monarca; et è cert[issi]mo, che nel suonare e comporre è famoso, e distinto fra tutti li miei scolari, perchè possiede l'anima intiera della mia scuola." Guido Viverit, "Problemi di attribuzione conflittuale nella musica strumentale veneta del Settecento," (Doctoral dissertation, Università di Padova, 2015), 56. English translation in Giorgia Malagò, ed., *Giuseppe Tartini: Lettere e documenti/Pisma in dokumenti/Letters and Documents*, vol. 2, trans. Jerneja Umer Kljun and Roberto Baldo (Trieste: Edizioni Università di Trieste, 2020), 323.
3 "[...] formare un musicista completo e consapevole e non solamente ad impartire nozioni di tecnica violinistica." Margherita Canale, "Fonti per una ricostruzione della didattica di Tartini nella 'Scuola delle nazioni'," *Muzikološki zbornik*, 28 (1992): 15.
4 Barbieri, *Quarrels on Harmonic Theories*, 126.
5 "In un certo senso sequace e continuatore della teoria tartiniana può considersi l'allievo-compositore Michele Stratico [...] Lo Stratico dimostra di aver studiato a fondo e ben compreso il pensiero tartiniano e sulle stesse basi d'essersi formato convinzioni personali che ne sorpassano i limiti." Leonardo Frasson, "Bibliografia tartiniana," *Il Santo* 17, no. 1–2 (1977): 292. If not otherwise stated in a footnote, all english translations are by the author.
  Stratico's theoretical treatises were a subject of author's doctoral dissertation. Lucija Konfic, "Giuseppe Michele Stratico's Treatises on Music between Theory and Practice: Edition and Commentary," (Doctoral dissertation, Kunstuniversität für Musik und darstellende Kunst, Graz, 2016). The relationship of Tartini and Stratico as student and master was also elaborated in author's paper on the international conference *Music Migration in the Early Modern Age. Centres and Peripheries – People, Works, Styles, Paths of Dissemination and Influence* in Warsaw 2016. See Lucija Konfic,

At this point we should also mention the recent assumption of P. Barbieri who identified the previously unknown recipient of eight Tartini's letters from 1756 (from March to September)[6] as Michele Stratico. Barbieri bases his assumption on the several indications: intimacy that Tartini expresses in his letters to the recipient, the fact that he is a violinist, his considerable knowledge of music theory and the authorship of the *Octuple system*.[7] Adherence to this assumption about Stratico would give new clues about his life and work: that he translated into Latin Tartini's theoretical explanations sent to Euler; connection to a certain Mr Eliano and Padre Agostino, as well as Count Algarotti and padre Stellini.[8] Also, not only was he thoroughly acquainted with Tartini's theoretical work through Tartini's teaching and reading published works but he was also involved in the creation of his dissertation commenting and discussing problematic issues. The following connection could be in favour of this assumption: Tartini marks his interlocutor in the letter as his enemy ("[...] as between you (my sworn enemy) and I, we can pull each other's wigs (we have no hair) to our hearts' content."[9]) in a very similar way to Stratico's in his treatise *Lo spirito Tartiniano* (The Tartini's Spirit) in which the student announces to the teacher that in his critique he must observe him as an enemy ("From here on, you must consider me in the aspect of an Adversary, and I would almost say an enemy; and oh how much it pays to repeat to me such a position is ungrateful!"[10]). But, there are many yet undefined elements. Unfortunately, the place where the letter was sent is not recorded and we don't have information from this period of Stratico's life. However, definitive judgement should still be refrained from at this time until additional evidence is identified.

In his imaginary dialogue with his teacher Tartini, *Lo spirito Tartiniano*, one can find that Stratico considered that he and Tartini had the same starting point, at least, but differed in their methods of approach. He puts these words in Tartini's mouth:

"Stratico and Tartini – Student and Master. Giuseppe Michele Stratico's Music System in Comparison with Tartini's Music Theory," in *Music Migration in the Early Modern Age. Centres and Peripheries – People, Works, Styles, Paths of Dissemination and Influence*, ed. Jolanta Guzy-Pasiak and Aneta Markuszewska (Warsaw: Liber Pro Arte, 2016), 299–322.

6   For the letters in question see Malagò, *Tartini: Lettere*, 1:270–272, 274–277.
7   Barbieri, *Quarrels on Harmonic Theories*, 126–129.
8   Jacopo Stellini's letters show that he knew Michele Stratico's brother Simone well. See Letter 64 (Lettera al Sig. Co. Gianrinaldo Carli, Venezia) in Giacopo Stellini, *Opere varie di Giacopo Stellini*, vol. 6 (Padova: Stamperia Penada, 1784), 202.
9   "[...] perchè tra ella (mio dichiarato nemico) e me abbiamo a tirarsi le parrucche (non abbiam capeli) a più non posso." Malagò, *Tartini: Lettere*, 1:276; English translation in Malagò, *Tartini: Lettere*, 2:415.
10 "Voi dovete da qui innanzi considerarmi nell'aspetto di Avversario, e direi quasi d'Inimico; ed oh quanto mi convien ripeterlo a me riesce ingrato un tale aspetto!" "Lo spirito Tartiniano" by Giuseppe Michele Stratico, manuscript, Ms. It. Cl. IV, 343e (=5348), Biblioteca Marciana, Venezia, f. 173v.

Out of respect for the essential, this your summary is not lacking, it embraces it, although the exposition you make of the subjects recognizes a style and method that is different from mine. But it doesn't matter, you have my thinking and that's enough. Each has its own method of reasoning, it is difficult to convene on that.[11]

Common point to both theorists is the tendency to defend the position of music as a science – which means to supply contemporary music with a theory based on the natural (physical and mathematical) laws. This was put to question particularly in the work of Antonio Eximeno *Dell'origine e delle regole della musica colla storia del suo progresso, decadenza e rinovazione* (On the origin and rules of music with the history of its progress, decadence and renewal) published in Rome in 1774 stating that music doesn't have correlation with mathematics because all numbers and proportions related to music tones and intervals are altered related to nature, thus useless.[12] Eximeno particularly criticized Euler, Tartini and Rameau dedicating three chapters to their theories (and their rejection).

Tartini bases his theoretical system on the phenomenon of *third tone*. He considers it the true physical basis of any interval and the true fundamental bass of the melody. However, in Tartini's works we find a constant "struggle" to justify those elements that go beyond the framework of the sestuple as the framework of a consonant system. So Tartini says:

> Therefore, in the sestuple remains demonstrated the period or the fulfillment of the integral extension of the harmonic physical system; no more, no less; because respectively is integrally and intrinsically fulfilled the double ratio which in general is the universal principle of the harmonic system; and in particular and precisely it is the square root of the series deduced from the harmonic sestuple, and it is fullfilled in the harmonic sestuple. It follows, then, that by continuing the division of the diameter into 1/7, which immediately follows to 1/6, and by deducing respectively the square root, the deduced term immediately destroys the consonant system and converts it into the continuous geometric system, which as we will see in this Chapter, is the dissonant system, which means the opposite of the consonant system.[13]

---

11 "Questo vostro trasunto, per rispetto all'essenziale, non è mancante, lo abbracia, quantunque poi l'esposizione che fate delle materie riconosca uno stile, e metodo dal mio diverso; Mà non importa, v'è la mente mia, e questo basta. Ogn'uno hà suo proprio metodo nel ragionare; è difficile in ciò la convenienza." [Stratico], "Lo spirito Tartiniano," 83v.

12 See Chapter II (*Che la musica non à correlazione colla Matematica*) in Antonio Eximeno, *Dell'origine e delle regole della musica colla storia del suo progresso, decadenza e rinovazione* (Roma: Stamperia di Michel'Angelo Barbiellini, 1774), 68–75, https://books.google.hr/books?id=1u1CAAAAcAAJ&hl=hr&pg=PP7#v=onepage&q&f=false.

13 "Dunque nella sestupla resta dimostrato il periodo, o compimento della estensione integrale del sistema fisico armonico: non più, nè meno; perché a ragguaglio è consumata integralmente, e intrinsecamente la ragion dupla, che in genere è il principio universale del sistema armonico; e in specie, e precisione è radice

The definition of a consonant system within the sestuple has been questioned for the past 200 years, as Cohen very clearly presents, explaining that one of the main reasons why intervals with number seven could not be accepted among consonants is that they did not have a place in the common scale.[14] Cohen also states that "the problem of the consonance of the intervals with 7 had indeed become a crucial touchstone for every theory of consonance that was to be proposed in the future".[15] Stratico's willingness to accept crossing the border of the sestuple not only provided him with different solutions to certain problems but also opened up some new obstacles for him, especially in terms of practice and experience.

In contrast to Tartini, Stratico did not take the physical phenomenon of the *third tone* as the starting point for the construction of his theoretical system and only based it on proportions as mere mathematical categories. Nevertheless, there are similarities in thinking with respect to the natural laws on which both systems rely. One of the important elements in both authors is the importance of minimal differences such as the minimal difference of the comma 1/80:1/81. In Stratico's system this difference is sufficient to change the harmonic proportion of the major third into the arithmetic one and these two proportions give different aural effect. The minimal difference in Tartini's system is sufficient to change the third tone. To demonstrate it Tartini gave the example of the third tone of the major tone which is between 9 and 8 and the minor tone between 10 and 9 for which he concluded that one has to insist on their perfect intonation. We can illustrate these positions with following citations from Stratico's *Trattato di musica* (Treatise on music) and Tartini's *Trattato di musica secondo la vera scienza dell'armonia* (Treatise on Music according to the True Science of Harmony), respectively.

> Although the inversion of the harmonic system into the arithmetic, which is a consequence deriving from the aforementioned coma in the comparison of the two acute positions, harmonic and arithmetic, is almost imperceptible; therefore, by coupling the low positions of the octave, that demonstrably compete with each other, then

---

> quadrata della serie dedotta dalla sestupla armonica, e consumata nella, sestupla armonica. Indi ne' viene, che proseguendo la divisione del diametro in 1/7, che immediatamente succede a 1/6, e deducendo a ragguaglio la radice quadrata, il termine dedotto distrugge immediatamente il sistema consonante, e lo converte nel sistema geometrico continuo, che come si vedrà in questo Capitolo, è il sistema delle dissonanze, che vuol dire l'opposto al sistema consonante." Giuseppe Tartini, *Trattato di musica secondo la vera scienza dell'armonia* (Padova: Stamperia del Seminario, 1754), 58–59, https://books.google.hr/books?id=DMYTAAAAQAAJ&hl=hr&pg=PP5#v=onepage&q&f=false

14 Hendrik Floris Cohen, *Quantifying Music. The Science of Music at the First Stage of the Scientific Revolution, 1580–1650* (Dordrecht-Boston-Lancaster: D. Reidel, 1984).
15 Cohen, *Quantifying Music*, 230.

if the aforementioned comparison is made, your hearing will soon notice the very notable difference in the effect, which there is between one and the other position.[16]

[...] because with great difficulty the physical point of their perfect intonation is grasped, and a very small difference in quantity changes the third tone. For example, the major tone is between 9 and 8; the minor between 10 and 9. Once the two tones have been reduced to a common term, the major tone will be 90:80, and the minor 90:81. The difference is between 80 and 81. This is enough and suffices to change the third tone.[17]

The basis of Stratico's system is the harmonic and arithmetic division of the sounding string (*corda sonora*). In the first case it is divided, thus resulting in an ascending sequence of tones, and in the second it is extended and results in the same way in a descending sequence. Stratico positions himself here as an advocate of natural tuning, unlike Tartini who considered Vallotti's unequal tuning in which basic tones (white organ keys) are sought to be the best solution.[18] Thus, Stratico's system is based on the natural relationships of tones, which brings him closer to the scientific understanding of music, but away from its practical application. Moreover, Stratico's system is intended exclusively for the corpus of string instruments. This is not only because they do not have a fixed pitch of each individual tone but also because they can "change the tone", i.e. have the possibility of mobility of the tones, which is a specially developed procedure that allows modulation. For other instruments, Stratico called for different solutions on the one hand.[19] On

---

16 "Che sebbene l'inversione dell'Armco sistema, nell'Aritmco, conseguenza derivante dal coma predetto, nel confronto delle due acute posizioni, armca, ed aritmca, sia quasi insensibile, nonperciò, se a queste accoppiando le gravi posizni dell'ottava, che dimostrativamte lor si competono, facciasi poi l'accennato confronto, ne rimarca ben tosto l'udito la notabilissima differenza dell'effetto, che v'hà frà l'una, e l'altra posizione." "Trattato di musica," by Giuseppe Michele Stratico, manuscript, Ms. It. Cl. IV, 341e (=5294), Biblioteca Marciana, Venezia, f. 219r.
17 "[...] perchè a gran fatica si coglie il punto fisico della loro perfetta intonazione, e una ben piccola differenza di quantità cambia il terzo suono. Per esempio il tuono maggiore è tra 9, 8; il minore tra 10, 9. Ridotti i due tuoni a termine comune, sarà 90, 80 il tuono maggiore, 90, 81 il minore. La differenza è tra 80, 81. Questa basta, e avanza per cambiare il terzo suono." Tartini, *Trattato di musica*, 16.
18 Cf. Giuseppe Tartini, *De' principj dell'armonia musicale contenuta nel diatonico genere* (Padova: Stamperia del Seminario, 1767). https://books.google.hr/books?id=I9IfJ Bfe3s0C&printsec=frontcover&hl=hr&source=gbs_ge_summary_r&cad=0#v=onep age&q&f=false, 95.
19 For example: "[...] hence it is necessary to conclude, that new art would be needed, to reduce /in the said instruments/ to the natural perfection of the degrees of the Scale, which require the various modulation of the melodies, and new study, to exercise on the instruments in this manner and in exact form they are reduced, although they are also capable of alteration, due to an external cause of the air, or other accidents, of which their chords are susceptible, which however are inevitable." ("[...] ond'è forza conchiudere, che nuov'arte vi ci vorrebbe, per ridur /ne' Stromenti accennati/

the other, he believed that a system that functions as a scientific one can tolerate irregularities in its practical application (science – art). Since natural relations are changed in the tempered systems, this issue is one of the essential elements of the objections to the understanding of music as a science. Thus, Stratico writes:

> To which objection, let us respond briefly, sufficient for us, that Science supplies us with the paragon, with the norm by which Art can direct its operations, which then the more they become uniform with the paragon, the more exact they arise; of which we have in Music itself proof, and inexorable experience, certainly being that the ratios and proportions of which Music makes use of, presented to the ear, as far as possible, in true scientific forms, fully satisfy it; and the more they deviate from the aforesaid forms, the more they disturb it. The proposed objection, therefore, if it is considered correctly, concerns only the Art, with which it is very difficult to deal, and we would even say impossible, that of reducing the ratios and proportions in mechanical instruments to true, precise scientific forms. Nor is it peculiar to objection to Music, but it is also common to every other Science, whose axioms and precepts to the practical act want to be reduced, everyone knowing well, that mathematical precision is excluded from practice, because of the material obstacles, which are encountered there, and which are insurmountable by Art.[20]

Considering the precision of the tones and relations, Stratico particularly emphasized the importance of connecting notes (musical symbols) and numbers (mathematical symbols) to determine in the most accurate way which tone or relation

---

alla natural perfezione i gradi delle Scale, che abbisognano alla varia modulazione delle Cantilene, e nuovo studio, per farne esercizio sopra gli Stromenti in tal guisa, e forma esatta ridotti, sebbene capaci per anco di alterazione, a motivo di di [sic!] causa esteriore dell'aria, od altri accidenti, de' quali suscettibili sono le corde loro, che però inevitabili questi risultano.") "Trattato di musica," by Giuseppe Michele Stratico, manuscript, Ms. It. Cl. IV, 342 (=5347), Biblioteca Marciana, Venezia, f. 51r.

20 "Al qual obietto rispondiam brevemente, esser a noi bastante, che la Scienza ci somministri l'esemplare, colla norma di cui l'Arte diriger possa le sue operazioni, le quali poi quanto più all'esemplar s'uniforman, tanto più esatte riescono; del che abbiamo nella Musica stessa prova, ed esperienza in~egabile, certo essendo, che le ragioni, e Proporzioni, delle quali ne fà uso la Musica, presentata all'orecchio, per quanto è possibile, nelle vere scientifiche forme, pienamente lo appagano, e quanto più dalle forme predette si scostano, tanto più lo disturbano. L'obietto dunque proposto, se rettamente lo si consideri, risguarda l'Arte soltanto, a cui è difficilissimo affare, e direm anco impossibile, quello di ridurre alle vere, e precise forme scientifiche le ragioni, e proporzioni negli Strumenti meccanici. E neppur è peculiare ess' obietto alla Musica, mà egli è comune eziandio ad ogn'altra Scienza, i di cui assiomi, e precetti all'atto pratico vogliam ridursi, ben ogn'uno sapendo, che la matematica precisione dalla pratica vien'esclusa, a motivo degli ostacoli materiali, che vi s'incontrano, e che dall'Arte insuperabili sono." "Trattato di musica," by Giuseppe Michele Stratico, manuscript, Ms. It. Cl. IV, 341a (=5294), Biblioteca Marciana, Venezia, f. 11r.

was considered. An impulse to mark musical tones as precisely as possible was by no means new, but a probable impetus for the development of Stratico's system of signs can be found in Tartini's treatise. Tartini, as well as Vallotti, introduced a new sign explaining the seventh tone of the harmonic sequence of the marine trumpet. Tartini introduced the new sign ♭, explaining also that the tone ♭ B (180) is lower than ♭B (175) in relation to the minor halftone (*semituono minore*) 36:35.[21] Tartini also warned about the mentioned inaccuracy due to the lack of an appropriate sign.[22] Stratico, as he wanted to answer to Tartini's invitation, introduces new signs immediately at the beginning of his treatise, considering that the seventh and ninth tones of the harmonic and arithmetic series are not precisely marked by the note value alone.

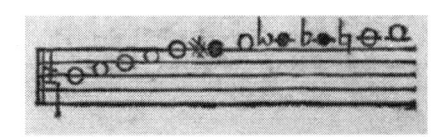

Example 1: Tartini's sign for the term 1/7. (Tartini, *Trattato di musica*, 126.)

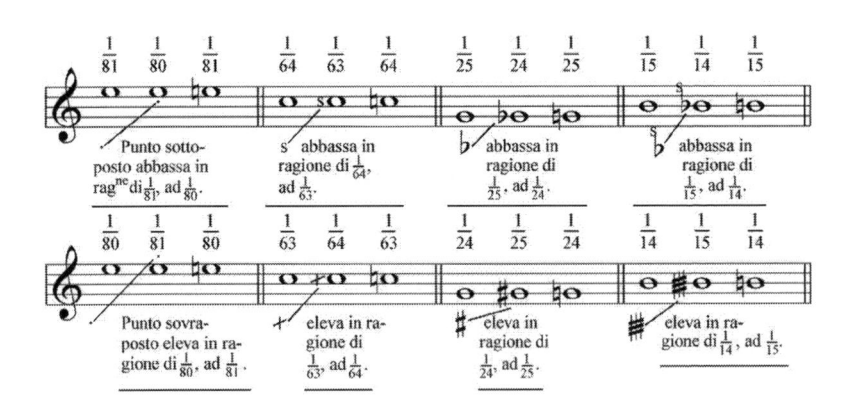

Example 2: Stratico's signs for precise notation of tone values. ([Stratico], "Trattato di musica," 341e, f. 193r.)

---

21 Tartini, *Trattato di musica*, 126.
22 "[...] molto più, perchè un tal difetto non procede intrinsicamente dal numero organico, quale per propria forza è sempre una pratica dimostrazione; ma procede dalla mancanza di un segno musicale, che in quello, e in altri casi dovrebbe aggiungersi di nuovo per dimostrare la individual differenza di que' termini, i quali sebben segnati con la stessa lettera musicale, non ostante sono tra loro diversi." Tartini, *Trattato di musica*, 166.

Let us return to the question of the sestuple, specifically the problem of the consonant seventh and its inclusion in the scale. From the treatise *Lo spirito Tartiniano* follows Stratico's critical attitude towards Tartini's indecision to clearly define the status of the minor seventh in his system. As we mentioned earlier, although Tartini clearly points out the limit of the consonant system in the sestuple, he repeatedly returns to the privileged treatment of the minor seventh. Considering it an interval that is extremely easy to intone on the violin,[23] the seventh had a "privileged" treatment compared to other dissonances in practice, which resulted in Tartini's indecisive attitude.[24] In the *Trattato di musica* he thus states that such a seventh is consonant,[25] while in *De' principj dell'armonia musicale contenuta nel diatonico genere* (On the Principles of Musical Harmony Contained in the Diatonic Genus) it places it between consonances and dissonances.[26] Stratico therefore compared him with the rascal from the parable of the bird under the hat.[27]
The inclusion of the seventh in the scale was for Tartini an absurdity.[28] Nevertheless, Stratico took his example as the only one that preceded him. When he stated:

That although the addition, which we made at the scale of common practice and use of the term 1/42 is not new, since this term was considered, and even it was added by some other Author*, it is however beyond doubt that the proportional form and

---

23 "[...] an interval of very easy intonation on the violin and which it is wanted by the harmonic nature." ("[...] intervallo di facilissima intonazione sopra il Violino, ed è voluto dalla natura armonica.") Tartini, *Trattato di musica*, 126.
24 See also Patrizio Barbieri, *Enharmonic Instruments and Music 1470–1900* (Latina: Il Levante, 2008), especially the chapter *The Enlightenment: attempts at acceptance of the 7th harmonic by some theorists and composers*, and subchapter *The 7th harmonic in the performance of violinists and singers*.
25 "Therefore such seventh is consonant, not dissonant." ("Dunque una tal settima è consonante, non dissonante.") Tartini, *Trattato di musica*, 128.
26 "[...] ♭Fa of the minor seventh which is such a homogeneous dissonance that it is used in practice with very particular privileges, which, if they do not determine it the real consonance, they certainly singularize it as a mediator between the consonances and the dissonances." ("[...] ♭fa di settima minore ch'è dissonanza talmente omogenea, che si usa in pratica con privilegj affatto particolari, i quali se non la determinano consonanza positiva, certamente la singolarizzano mezzana tra le consonanze, e le dissonanze.") Tartini, *De' principj*, 88–89.
27 Stratico chooses the following comparison: "[...] that rascal, who wanted to disappoint the oracle, by means of the bird, who he kept alive in his hands under the hat, proposing the question, was he alive, or dead; and the answer of the crafty priest, who secretly played the oracle, disappointed the malice of the rascal, by answering him: It will be whatever you want it to be." ("[...] quel Birbante, che voleva deludere l'Oracolo, per mezzo dell'Uccello, che vivo teneva frà le mani sotto la Cappa, proponendo la quistione, s'era vivo, o morto, e la risposta del furbo Sacerdote, che di nascoso favendo le parti dell'Oracolo, deluse la malizia del Birbante, col rispondergli, Sarà qual tu lo vuoi.") [Stratico], "Lo spirito Tartiniano," f. 185v (in the margin).
28 Tartini, *De' principj*, 59.

construction of the scale resulting from this addition has always been ignored; what form then gives it new shine and establishment, removes all doubts from it, and makes it, so to speak, immortal.[29] Mentioning "some other author" that have considered a scale with an inserted seventh, Stratico cites only Tartini.[30] Thus, transgressing the border of the sestuple that was set (for him) by his master, Stratico positioned himself as an advocate of the seventh as a consonance and a supporter of the ottuple system (*ottuplo sistema*). The first consequence of this was the introduction of the seventh in the scale which then acquires a proportional form that it lacked without the seventh and which was then one of the main Eximeno's objections to the foundation of music as a science.

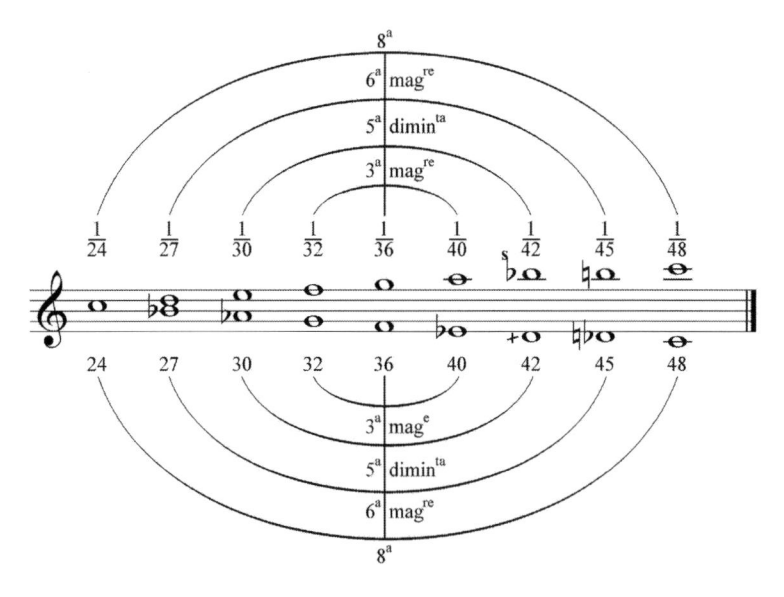

Example 3: Stratico's display of the proportional construction of the ascending and the descending scale. ([Stratico], "Trattato di musica," 341e, f. 199v.)

---

29 "Che sebbene la giunta, che facemmo alla Scala di comune pratica ed uso del termine 1/42 non sia nuova, essendochè detto termine fù considerato, ed am~esso eziandio da qualch'altro Autore*egli è però fuor di dubio, che la proporzionale forma e costruzione della Scala da tale giunta risultante, si è sempre ignorata; qual forma poi le dà nuovo lustro e stabilimento, ne allontana ogni dubbiezza, e la rende, a così dir, immortale." [Stratico], "Trattato di musica," 341e, f. 199v.
30 Stratico cited Tartini's *Trattato di musica* on the page 132. ([Stratico], "Trattato di musica," 341a, f. 11r). Tartini introduced the minor seventh into the diatonic scale to solve several problems in the relationship of the scale and the fundamental bass when descending. Maybe more obvious connection is to Tartini, *De' principj*, 91–92.

The connection that Tartini establishes between the scale and its corresponding basses on the basis of the third tone corresponds to the one made by Stratico on the basis of the proportions of the octave and the major third.

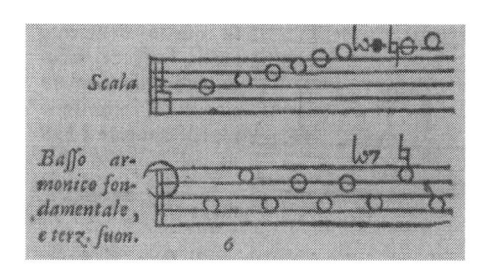

Example 4: Tartini's scale with the harmonic fundamental bass. (Tartini, *De' principj*, 62.)

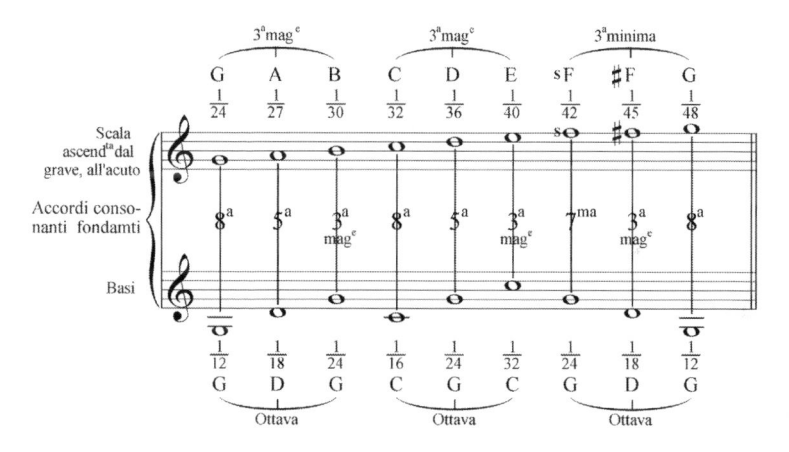

Example 5: Stratico's ascending scale with basses. ([Stratico], "Trattato di musica," 341e, f. 202v.)

Other important issues present in both authors are the problem of exclusion of the terms 1/11 and 1/13 from the scale, limitation of the harmonic series, the issue of absence of the arithmetic mean from the octaves of the fundamental tone of the harmonic series, and the question of the origin of the minor mode which will be elaborated in more detail.

Tartini sought the origin of the minor harmony in the arithmetic series facing the problem that minor harmony was not based in the same way as the major in the third tone as a physical basis, nor in his theory of the circle as a demonstrative basis.[31] Therefore, Tartini declared the arithmetic system to be of secondary importance and deficient in respect to the harmonic system which he considered to be perfect. Stratico followed Tartini's position that origin of the minor harmony is in the arithmetic series but stated that the harmonic and the arithmetic series are of equal importance but of inverse sequence. This equivalency, however, did not occur in practice, causing also Stratico to avoid discussing it in more detail. Tartini, therefore, derived the minor scale (scala di terza minore) from the major scale, while Stratico derived it as a new entity from the arithmetic series. Generally speaking, the origin of the minor mode was more problematic than the origin of the major. The harmonic series was recognized as the source of the major harmony, and some authors, like Tartini and Rameau, have found in the arithmetic series the source of the minor harmony. This, however, has often led to questioning and disagreements concerning the relationship between related tonalities (C major and f minor). Thus, for example, Vallotti, who thought that the minor scale cannot be obtained without artificiality, comments on Rameau:

> Given that the sounds would be heard precisely (given Ut, or C = 1, as Rameau suggests), the sounds, from grave to acute, would be said, as
> 5 3 1 1/3 1/5
> Ab F C G E
> and this is, for his judgement, the origin of the minor mode. But good God! what correspondence is there between the minor mode F Ab C and the major C E G?[32]

Stratico derived the minor scale from the arithmetic series in the same way as the major scale was derived from the harmonic one. We also find such an approach by Rameau,[33] but with the difference that Rameau considered the minor mode subordinate to the major, while Stratico treated them as equal (at least theoretically). Still, he encounters problems already in setting the relationship of the

---

31 Tartini, *Trattato di musica*, 66; Tartini, *De' principj*, 20–21.
32 "Atteso che si udirebbero precisamente i suoni (dato Ut, o sia C = 1, come accenna Rameau) sarebbero dissi i suoni, dal grave all'acuto, come
   5 3 1 1/3 1/5
   Ab F C G E
   ed è questa, per di lui sentenza, l'origine del modo minore. Ma buon Dio! qual corrispondenza mai del modo minore F Ab C al maggiore C E G?" Francescantonio Vallotti, *Della scienza teorica, e pratica della moderna musica*, Libro primo (Padova: Apresso Giovanni Manfrè, 1779), 10, https://books.google.hr/books?id=P7BfA AAAcAAJ&printsec=frontcover&hl=hr#v=onepage&q&f=false.
33 In a letter to Martini (29 October 1759), Rameau also informs us as following: "Moreover, I have just now discovered the origin of the minor Mode, which is nothing more than the inversion of the Major, and is derived quite naturally from the inversion of the harmonical into the arithmetical proportions." Quoted in in Erwin R. Jacobi, "Rameau and Padre Martini. New Letters and Documents," *The Musical Quarterly* 50, no. 4 (1964), 468. More on Rameau's theories in: Thomas Christensen, *Rameau and Musical Thought in the Enlightenment* (Cambridge: Cambridge University Press, 1993).

scale and bass given that the seventh member of the scale is placed lower than its bass for which reason it should be excluded from the scale. Stratico explained this by showing that the problematic tone is excluded from the consonant complex of the minor third. We can find an interestingly similar result in the presentation of the French composer and cellist Charles-Henri de Blainville's *Essay sur un troisième mode* (Essay on the third mode) from 1751 who called the new mode *troisième mode/mode mixte* (third mode/mixed mode): Mi Fa Sol La SI Ut Ut# Re Mi (30 32 36 40 45 48 50 54 60). It had eight tones and its purpose was to enrich the modulations.[34] But the more thorough comparison of this topic could be a subject of another paper, as it would be prudent to include the views of French theorists, which is a very complex subject in itself.

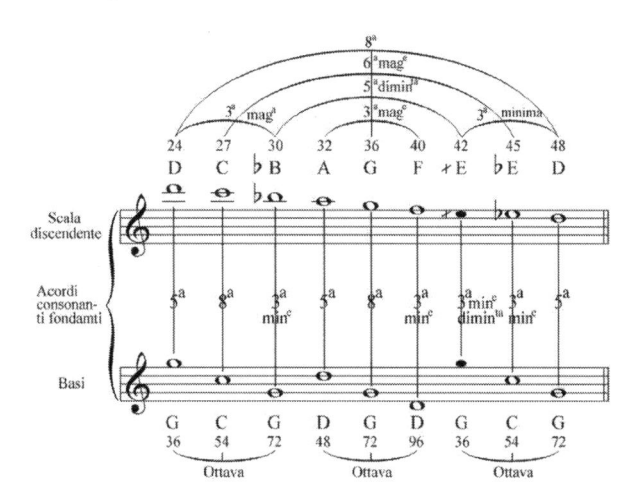

Example 6: Stratico's descending (minor) scale with basses. ([Stratico], "Trattato di musica," 341e, f. 212r.)

It should be emphasized that the scale above does not correspond to the minor scale in practice. The minor scale in practice in Stratico's system is called *mista* (mixed) since that is a scale in which particular chords with major third from the harmonic consonant complex have been replaced by the minor thirds from the arithmetic consonant complex.

In conclusion, as we have shown in this chapter, Tartini's system and some of its limitations were the starting point of Stratico's thinking in which we find the audacity to stretch and cross the boundaries of his teacher's view. It was, in

---

34 Cf. Gérard Geay, *Le Troisième mode de Blainville*, Centre de Musique Baroque de Versailles, 2005, https://www.musicologie.org/Biographies/s/m/1612270031.pdf

my opinion, the perfect and the last moment for development of such a system – moment in which experiments with sound were widely spread, challenged and debated, offering new insights on its nature, and the equal temperament was not yet fully established. Possibly encouraged by Euler's theory, looking above the *senario* led Stratico not only to criticize his teacher's weak points but also to form a new theoretical system. If we compare Stratico's and Tartini's system, we can see that Stratico's relying on proportions resulted in a clearer approach than the one offered by Tartini. It is open to discussion whether Stratico's explanations are more acceptable – either in theory or in practice. Although Stratico often invoked the practice as evidence in favour of his system, the gap between theory and practice is highly evident. Stratico's theoretical thinking is in line with the teaching of his teacher's school in terms of development as a complete musician and, encouraged by his work and influence, to engage in the defence of music as a science. Although later forgotten, being much in opposition to common practice, Stratico's theory can be considered an interesting and valuable contribution to the harmonic debates on musical theories of the eighteenth century in general.

Bibliography

Barbieri, Patrizio. *Enharmonic Instruments and Music 1470–1900.* Latina: Il Levante, 2008.

Barbieri, Patrizio. *Quarrels on Harmonic Theories in the Venetian Enlightenment.* Lucca: LIM, 2020.

Canale, Margherita. "Fonti per una ricostruzione della didattica di Tartini nella 'Scuola delle nazioni'." *Muzikološki zbornik*, 28 (1992): 15–24.

Christensen, Thomas. *Rameau and Musical Thought in the Enlightenment.* Cambridge: Cambridge University Press, 1993.

Cohen, Hendrik Floris. *Quantifying Music. The Science of Music at the First Stage of the Scientific Revolution, 1580–1650.* Dordrecht-Boston-Lancaster: D. Reidel, 1984.

Eximeno, Antonio. *Dell'origine e delle regole della musica colla storia del suo progresso, decadenza e rinovazione.* Roma: Stamperia di Michel'Angelo Barbiellini, 1774. Accessed January 24, 2022. https://books.google.hr/books?id=1u1CAAAAcAAJ&hl=hr&pg=PP7#v=onepage&q&f=false.

Frasson, Leonardo. "Bibliografia tartiniana." *Il Santo* 17, no. 1–2 (1977): 283–305.

Geay, Gérard. "Le Troisième mode de Blainville." Centre de Musique Baroque de Versailles, 2005. Accessed January 31, 2022. https://www.musicologie.org/Biographies/s/m/1612270031.pdf.

Jacobi, Erwin R. "Rameau and Padre Martini. New Letters and Documents." *The Musical Quarterly* 50, no. 4 (1964): 452–475

Konfic, Lucija. "Giuseppe Michele Stratico's Treatises on Music between Theory and Practice: Edition and Commentary." Doctoral dissertation, Kunstuniversität für Musik und darstellende Kunst Graz, 2016.

Konfic, Lucija. "Stratico and Tartini – Student and Master. Giuseppe Michele Stratico's Music System in Comparison with Tartini's Music Theory." In *Music Migration in the Early Modern Age. Centres and Peripheries – People, Works, Styles, Paths of Dissemination and Influence*, edited by Jolanta Guzy-Pasiak and Aneta Markuszewska, 299–322. Warsaw: Liber Pro Arte, 2016.

Malagò, Giorgia, ed. *Giuseppe Tartini: Lettere e documenti/Pisma in dokumenti/ Letters and Documents*. 2 vols. Translated by Jerneja Umer Kljun and Roberto Baldo. Trieste: Edizioni Università di Trieste, 2020.

Stellini, Giacopo. *Opere varie di Giacopo Stellini*. Vol. 6. Padova: Stamperia Penada, 1784.

[Stratico, Giuseppe Michele]. Manuscript treatise "Trattato di musica". Ms. It. Cl. IV, 341a (=5294), f. 1–22. Biblioteca Marciana, Venezia.

[Stratico, Giuseppe Michele]. Manuscript treatise "Trattato di musica". Ms. It. Cl. IV, 341e (=5294), f. 191–220. Biblioteca Marciana, Venezia.

[Stratico, Giuseppe Michele]. Manuscript treatise "Trattato di musica". Ms. It. Cl. IV, 342 (=5347). Biblioteca Marciana, Venezia.

[Stratico, Giuseppe Michele]. Manuscript treatise "Lo spirito Tartiniano". Ms. It. Cl. IV, 343e (=5348), f. 171–191. Biblioteca Marciana, Venezia.

Tartini, Giuseppe. *De' principi dell'armonia musicale contenuta nel diatonico genere*. Padova: Nella Stamperia del Seminario, 1767. Accessed January 31, 2022. https://books.google.hr/books?id=I9IfJBfe3s0C&printsec=frontcover&hl= hr&source=gbs_ge_summary_r&cad=0#v=onepage&q&f=false.

Tartini, Giuseppe. *Trattato di musica secondo la vera scienza dell'armonia*. Padova: Stamperia del Seminario, 1754. Accessed January 24, 2022. https:// books.google.hr/books?id=DMYTAAAAQAAJ&hl=hr&pg=PP5#v=onep age&q&f=false.

Vallotti, Francescantonio. *Della scienza teorica, e pratica della moderna musica*, Libro primo. Padova: Apresso Giovanni Manfrè, 1779. Accessed January 31, 2022. https://books.google.hr/books?id=P7BfAAAAcAAJ&printsec=frontco ver&hl=hr#v=onepage&q&f=false

Viverit, Guido. "Problemi di attribuzione conflittuale nella musica strumentale veneta del Settecento." Doctoral dissertation, Università di Padova, 2015.

Ana Lombardía

Universidad de Salamanca, Spain

The Reception of Tartini's Violin Sonatas in Madrid (*ca.* 1750–*ca.* 1800)[1]

Abstract: Spain has been virtually neglected in Tartini scholarship so far. However, a number of hitherto little-known musical and documentary sources show that his accompanied violin sonatas were known, praised, and imitated in Madrid during the second half of the eighteenth century. Amateur musicians collected this music, and professional musicians performed it in different chamber music venues in the city, as well as composing sonatas that bear clear formal similarities with those of Tartini. The following violinists played a leading role in this process: Domingo Rodil and Bonifazio Zlotek, members of Madrid's Royal Chapel; Mauro d'Alay and Christiano Reynaldi, chamber musicians of the widowed queen Elizabeth Farnese, Reynaldi being a probable student of Tartini; and Jakob Leydeck, a German disciple of the Istrian Maestro. Also, a process of canonization of Tartini's works is detected in several essays written in Madrid around the turn of the nineteenth century.

Keywords: Giuseppe Tartini, Spain, violin sonata, music dissemination, Christiano Reynaldi, Mauro d'Alay, Jakob Leydeck.

To date, Spain has been virtually neglected in scholarship about Giuseppe Tartini and his so-called School of Nations.[2] However, Tartini's works circulated in Madrid during his lifetime and the subsequent decades, as various musical and documentary sources show. Most of these sources are related to the same genre: the accompanied violin sonata. This was the most fashionable violin-music genre in the Spanish capital at that time. It was the favourite vehicle for virtuoso violinists

---

1 This publication is part of the R&D project *La música como interpretación en España: historia y recepción (1730–1930)* (PID2019-105718GB-I00), funded by MCIN/AEI/10.13039/501100011033. I am grateful to my project colleagues for their feedback on a preliminary version of this research. All translations are by the author, unless otherwise stated.
2 As exceptions, very brief mentions to Spanish musical and documentary sources related to Tartini appear in Miguel Á. Marín, "A la sombra de Corelli: componer para el violín," in *La música en el siglo XVIII*, ed. José M. Leza (Madrid: Fondo de Cultura Económica, 2014), 299; and José C. Gosálvez, "Fuentes originales de Giuseppe Tartini en la Biblioteca del RCSMM," *Música: Revista del Real Conservatorio Superior de Música de Madrid*, nos. 14–15 (2007–2008): 243–244.

to show off their technical and compositional prowess, serving as a letter of presentation to attract patrons or to secure a job. Between 1740 and 1776, a minimum of 165 accompanied violin sonatas were composed in Madrid and nearby cities, but only 62 of them have been located in musical sources so far. These are modest figures in comparison to other European cities but undoubtedly reflect the genre's popularity.[3]

Roughly half of the composers of the extant sonatas were Spanish, such as Francisco Manalt (Barcelona, ca. 1710–Madrid, 1759) and José Herrando (Valencia, ca. 1720–Madrid, 1763). The other half were mainly Italian virtuosos, such as Mauro d'Alay (Parma, ca. 1690?–Parma, 1757), Francesco Montali (Naples,?–Toledo, 1782), and Christiano Reynaldi (Cracow, 1719–Madrid, 1767), the son of a Milanese violinist. Regarding formal organization and movement types, most of these mid-century sonatas resemble the ones by Tartini and Locatelli, reflecting three standardized characteristics: (1) three-movement cycles of two main types, *slow, main fast, and light fast* or else *main fast, slow, and light fast*, (2) the use of binary forms in each movement, including rounded binary forms (antecedents of sonata forms), especially in the *main fast* movements, which were the centrepiece of the composition, and (3) a wide variety of motives and ornaments, focusing the listener's attention on the violin melody, while the bass plays an almost secondary role.[4] In contrast, only a handful of the sonatas composed in Madrid have four or five movements, like Corelli's opus 5, which was, however, a very popular didactic work in eighteenth-century Spain.[5]

It is not clear if the formal similarity with Tartini's sonatas merely responds to the general trends of the mid-eighteenth-century-accompanied violin sonata, or if it is a consequence of somewhat deep knowledge of his output. Several questions arise: when did Tartini's sonatas reach Madrid? To what extent were the city's

---

3   Ana Lombardía, "Violin Music in Mid-18th-Century Madrid: Contexts, Genres, Style," (Doctoral dissertation, Universidad de La Rioja, 2015), 735–742, https://dialnet.uniri oja.es/descarga/tesis/46783
4   Christiano Reynaldi, *Sonate di violino e basso opus 1 (1761)*/Francesco Montali, *Sonatas a violín solo y bajo (1759)*, ed. Ana Lombardía (Madrid: ICCMU, 2019), study in i–liv. The general features of the Madrid sonatas match the model that Heartz calls "galant violin sonata". Some collections that reflect these patterns are Locatelli's opuses 2 and 6, and Tartini's opus 1. See Daniel Heartz, *Music in European Capitals: The Galant Style, 1720–1780* (New York: Norton, 2003), 208–230. This model matches what Brainard considers Tartini's second period of sonata composition, roughly from 1735 to 1750 (excluding his opus 1, closer to Corelli's formal model). See Paul Brainard, *Le sonate per violino di Giuseppe Tartini. Catalogo tematico* (Padova: Carisch, 1975).
5   Miguel Á. Marín, "La recepción de Corelli en Madrid (ca. 1680–ca. 1810)," in *Arcangelo Corelli Fra Mito E Realtà Storica*, ed. Gregory Barnett (Firenze: Olschki, 2007), 573–637; Ana Lombardía, "Corelli as a Model? Composing Violin Sonatas in Mid-18th-Century Madrid," in *Miscellanea Ruspoli III*, ed. Giorgio Monari (Lucca: Libreria Musicale Italiana, 2016), 17–69.

violinists-composers and amateur performers familiar with this repertoire? Did they know Tartini's theoretical works? Did any disciples of Tartini work in the Spanish capital? What was the reaction of local critics to his works? This chapter explores these questions for the first time. It is divided into two sections. The first one focuses on a number of musical sources containing sonatas by Tartini that were produced and/or used in Madrid during his lifetime (1692–1770) or shortly afterwards, up until 1800. Both extant and non-extant sources are discussed, taking into account the information provided by inventories related to private music libraries. The physical features of the extant sources are described, and their possible models and dissemination channels are discussed. Moreover, attention is paid to the possible performance spaces and practices related to this music in Madrid. The second section focuses on documentary sources that mention Tartini specifically, focusing on the second half of the eighteenth century. Sources include commercial advertisements, short essays that were published in Madrid's local press, and the earliest known *History of Spanish Music* (*Historia de la música española*), by José Teixidor.[6] The latter states that some students of Tartini's School of Nations worked in Madrid, which seems likely considering the high proportion of Italian musicians that were active in the Spanish capital. This hypothesis is explored, paying attention to other complementary sources, such as the Maestro's own letters. Together, these various pieces of evidence provide an overall picture of the process of reception, assimilation, and dissemination of Tartini's violin sonatas in eighteenth-century Madrid. As will be shown, this process was earlier and more intense than it had been thought to date.

1 Musical Sources Containing Sonatas by Tartini

There is evidence that some of Tartini's accompanied violin sonatas reached Madrid before 1800. A series of music inventories attest to the presence of this music in private libraries belonging to members of the social elite, such as the Duke of Alba and the Duchess of Osuna. Furthermore, four extant manuscript copies of Tartini sonatas that were presumably produced and used in eighteenth-century Madrid clearly show that this repertoire circulated in the city.

The earliest historical evidence in this respect is the inventory and appraisal of the music belonging to the 12th Duke of Alba, Fernando de Silva Álvarez de Toledo (Vienna, 1714 – Madrid, 1776). The document was completed after his death but attests to the music library that he had in his Madrid residence since 1750.[7] The

---

6   José Teixidor, *Historia de la música española – Sobre el verdadero origen de la música*, ed. Begoña Lolo (Lleida: Institut d'Estudis Ilerdencs, 1996). Manuscript datable ca. 1804.
7   George Truett-Hollis, "An Eighteenth-Century Library of Chamber Music: The Inventory and Appraisal of the Music and Musical Instruments Belonging to the Twelfth Duke of Alba (d. 1776)," in *Festschrift in Honor of Theodore Front on His 90th Birthday*, ed. Darwin F. Scott (Lucca: Lim Antiqua, 2002), 29–64.

Duke of Alba was one of the most powerful noblemen in the court of King Ferdinand VI. In the late 1740s, he was Ambassador of Spain to France, and in 1750 he was appointed High Steward and State Secretary, so he returned to Madrid.[8] He was an amateur violinist and violist, as well as an eager collector of chamber music. The inventory and appraisal of his collection of musical instruments and scores mention over 1,000 chamber works. This includes 4 or 5 books of sonatas by Tartini, amounting to 46 allegedly different violin sonatas.[9] They were "duplicated", that is, a second copy was made, most likely for an accompanist.

This music library was dispersed after the duke's death. However, some of the scores remained in the family's Madrid palace (the Palacio de Liria) until their destruction in 1936, during the Spanish Civil War. A few years earlier, in 1927, musicologist José Subirá had published a detailed study describing all the musical sources preserved in the palace.[10] It mentions several printed editions of violin sonatas that must have belonged to the 12th Duke, for they were sold in Paris in the 1740s, precisely when he was living there. This includes, for example, a copy of Locatelli's opus 8 sold by Le Clerc.[11] No copies of Tartini's music were found in the Palacio de Liria, but it is very likely that the sonatas owned by Fernando de Silva were some of the printed collections published in Paris in the 1740s, such as Tartini's solo sonatas opuses 4 (1747), 5 (ca. 1747), 6 (ca. 1748), and 7 (1748), and the trio sonatas opus 8 (1749).[12]

Other inventories related to the music libraries extant in late eighteenth-century Madrid mention large quantities of chamber music, including non-identified works by Tartini. For example, the IX Duke of Osuna and his wife, the Countess-Duchess of Benavente-Osuna, owned an unspecified sonata by Tartini. Both the duke and the duchess were very relevant music patrons in Madrid, employing outstanding musicians in their orchestra, such as Luigi Boccherini. The inventory of their music

---

8   Brief biography in José L. Gómez-Urdáñez, *Fernando VI* (Madrid: Arlanza, 2001), 286.
9   Inventory and Appraisal of the Music and Musical Instruments Belonging to the Twelfth Duke of Alba, Juan Bala and Manuel Carrera, 1777: "A set of sonatas in books duplicated by Tartini./ Another book of sonatas duplicated by Tartini. /Two books of different sonatas duplicated by Tartini." (Inventory, Sonatas, f. 3r). "Forty-six [sonatas] by Tartini in five books." (Appraisal, Sonatas, f. 10r). English Transcription in Truett-Hollis, "An Eighteenth-Century Library of Chamber Music," 41.
10 José Subirá, *La música en la Casa de Alba: Estudios históricos y biográficos* (Madrid: Tipografía Sucesores de Rivadeneyra, 1927). This study shows that some of the duke's chamber musicians were the above-mentioned violinists José Herrando and Francesco Montali, who dedicated violin sonatas to him.
11 Subirá, *La música en la Casa de Alba*, 109–122 and 210–213. The edition is Pietro A. Locatelli, *X Sonate. VI a violino solo è basso, è IV a tré*, op. 8 (Amsterdam, Locatelli, 1744/ Paris, Le Clerc, ca. 1747).
12 Details in Pierluigi Petrobelli, "Tartini, Giuseppe," in Grove Music Online, Oxford Music Online, accessed January 3, 2021, https://doi.org/10.1093/gmo/9781561592630. article.27529

library mentions numerous instrumental works, including over 150 compositions by Haydn, over 100 by Boccherini, over 40 by Gaetano Brunetti (violin teacher and chamber musician of Prince Charles of Spain, later to become Charles IV), and a varied selection of music by local and international composers, including a "sonata" by Tartini.[13] This work, most likely manuscript, could have reached the Osunas library through some of the musicians they employed, such as Bonifazio Zlotek, owner of one of the extant Madrilenian copies of sonatas by the Maestro.

All four extant musical sources containing works by Tartini and presumably produced in eighteenth-century Madrid are manuscripts and contain accompanied violin sonatas (see Tables 1 and 2). These four Tartini sources are virtually unknown outside Spain, for they do not appear in RISM, in the thematic catalogue by Brainard, or in the more recent catalogue by Viverit and Olivari. They are the manuscript anthology titled *26 Sonatas de varios autores* (26 Sonatas by various composers) preserved in a private collection, and three spare manuscripts preserved in Madrid's Higher Conservatory (Real Conservatorio Superior de Música).

---

13 Music library belonging to Pedro de Alcántara Téllez de Girón y Pacheco (1755–1807) and María Josefa Alonso Pimentel y Téllez-Girón (1752–1834). Music inventory dated 1824, described in Ortega, Judith, "El mecenazgo musical de la Casa de Osuna durante la segunda mitad del siglo XVIII: El entorno musical de Luigi Boccherini en Madrid," *Revista de musicología* 27, no. 2 (2004): 643–698.

Table 1: Tartini sonatas in extant musical sources from eighteenth-century Madrid. Production and physical details.

Source	Diplomatic title	Paper type	Copy details	Owners	Origin and use
E-LPA siemens, pp. 12–17	*26 Sonatas de varios autores*	SP watermark 124 pp. (62 ff.), 296 x 212 mm 10 staffs/page	Copyist A unfigured bass	[Madrid bookshop] 6th Count of Fernán Núñez L. Siemens (1980s)	Copied Madrid *ca.* 1760–1770 Sold in a local bookshop
E-Mc, M/656	*Sonata/ à Violino solo è Cembalo o Violoncello/ del Sig.r Giuseppe Tartini/ E/ IV.*	SP watermark (f. 3) 4 ff., 297 x 220 mm 10 staffs/page margins 23 mm	Copyist B correct Italian orthography figured bass	"Rodil" = D. Rodil "Polaco" = B. Zlotek "F. Witz"	Copied Madrid *ca.* 1760–1780? Used Madrid *ca.* 1763–1787
E-Mc, M/657	*Sonata de Violino/ è Basso/ del Sig.re Giuseppe Tartini*	Unclear watermark (f. 3) 4 ff., 290 x 220 mm 10 staffs/page margins 26 mm	Copyist C correct Italian orthography musical incipit in bottom-left corner cross on top unfigured bass	"R." = Rodil? "Polaco" = "de Bonifacio Zlotek"	Copied Madrid *ca.* 1760–1780? Used Madrid *ca.* 1763–1787
E-Mc, M/658	*Sonata à solo/ Violino é Basso de el/ Signor/ GiuseppeTartini di Padoa*	GB watermark (f. 1) 4 ff., 296 x 220 mm 10 staffs/page margins 26 mm	Copyist D mixed orthography (Spanish-Italian) cross on top unfigured bass	"Polaco" = "Zlotek"	Copied Madrid *ca.* 1760–1780 Used Madrid *ca.* 1763–1787

Key: *E-LPAsiemens = Lothar Siemens' private collection, Las Palmas de Gran Canaria; E-Mc = Real Conservatorio Superior de Música de Madrid (Madrid's Higher Conservatory).*

Table 2: Tartini sonatas in extant musical sources from eighteenth-century Madrid. Contents.

Source	Brainard cat. No.*	Viverit cat. No.*	Composition date	First edition	Copy date	Key	Movements in the source	Movement types**
E-LPA siemens, pp. 12–17	B10	GT 2.Bb10	[1730–1747]	Paris, engraved by Le Hue, sold by Boivin et al., 1747: op. 4 no. 3.	ca. 1760–1770	Bb	i. Allegro ii. Grave Andante iii. Presto iv. Andante	MF S LF MinV
E-Mc, M/656	e7	GT 2.e07	[1720–1743]	Amsterdam, Le Cène, 1743: op. 2 no. 4.	ca. 1760–1780	e	i. Grave ii. Allegro iii. Presto	S MF LF
E-Mc, M/657	Es1	GT 2.Eb01	[1730–1750]	Paris, Le Clerc, ca. 1765: op. 9 no 1.	ca. 1760–1780	Eb	i. Andante largo ii. Alle[gro] iii. Alle[gro] ma non tanto	S MF LF
E-Mc, M/658	A14	GT 2.A14	ca. 1731	Amsterdam, Le Cène, 1734: op. 1 no. 1.	ca. 1760–1780	A	i. Adagio ii. Fuga iii. Allegro	S MF (fugato) LF

Key: *cat. no. = catalogue number / **Movement types: S = slow; MF = main fast; LF = light fast; MinV = minuet with variations/ E-LPAsiemens = Lothar Siemens' private collection, Las Palmas de Gran Canaria; E-Mc = Real Conservatorio Superior de Música de Madrid (Madrid's Higher Conservatory).

1.1 The *26 Sonatas* Anthology

The anthology *26 Sonatas de varios autores* belonged to the 6th Count of Fernán Núñez, Carlos José Gutiérrez de los Ríos y Rohan-Chabot (Cartagena, 1742 – Madrid, 1795). In the 1980s the manuscript was rediscovered by the musicologist Lothar Siemens, who purchased it for his private collection and presented it in an article.[14] The anthology is undated, but its content and physical characteristics point to the 1760s or early 1770s. It contains accompanied violin sonatas by eight different composers. Four of them worked in Madrid between the 1730s and 1780s: Mathias Boshoff, Mauro d'Alay, José Herrando, and Juan de Ledesma.[15] The other four composers were active in Italy: Giuseppe Tartini, Stefano Candeloro Arena, Giovanni Battista Costa, and Carlo Zuccari. The manuscript also contains an oboe sonata by Luis Misón,[16] and an anonymous virtuosic *Capricho* (capriccio) for solo violin.[17]

At the beginning of the volume, there is a contents page with prices, which indicates the commercial nature of the manuscript.[18] It specifies the price of each work, although it omits the sonata by Misón and the anonymous capriccio, and the total cost of the volume is considerably higher than the sum of the prices listed. Siemens believed that it was a sample available to the clients of a Madrid bookshop.[19] However, the fact that the final price was so high appears to indicate that the cost of the parchment binding was added. Moreover, there is evidence that different music copies made previously were gathered together before the volume was bound. For example, Alay's *Sonata 1* is the only piece in the whole manuscript that has page numbers, beginning with number 1, while it starts at the 32nd page of the anthology. All of the music in the volume was copied on the same type of

---

14 Siemens, Lothar, "Los violinistas compositores en la corte española durante el período central del siglo XVIII," *Revista de musicología* XI, no. 3 (1988): 657–766. Siemens passed away in 2017, and the manuscript remained in possession of his heirs. This collection is not in RISM.

15 Modern editions in José Herrando, *Tres sonatas para violín y bajo solo, y una más para flauta travesera o violín*, ed. Lothar Siemens (Madrid: Sedem, 1987); Juan de Ledesma, *Cinco sonatas para violín y bajo solo*, ed. Lothar Siemens (Madrid: Sedem, 1989).

16 Siemens, Lothar, "Una sonata para oboe y bajo atribuible a Luis Misón (s. XVIII)," *Revista de musicología* 15, no. 2 (1992): 761–774. This sonata appears to be written for oboe, taking into account its register and the absence of multiple stops, characteristic of idiomatic violin notation.

17 Critical edition with commentary in Anonymous, *Dos fandangos para violín y acompañamiento (ca. 1755) /Capricho para violín solo (ca. 1760–1770)*, ed. Ana Lombardía (Madrid: ICCMU, 2021).

18 *26 Sonatas de varios autores*, music manuscript, Madrid, ca. 1760–1770, page 1: "Lista de las sonatas contenidas en este libro, su valor y autores" ("List of the sonatas contained in this book, their prices and composers"). Siemens' family private collection, Las Palmas de Gran Canaria, no shelfmark.

19 Siemens, "Los violinistas compositores en la corte española," 657–661.

paper, in landscape quarto format, and featuring the watermark SP, which is very common in music manuscripts copied in Madrid between 1722 and 1773.[20] Also, all of the music is copied by the same hand, undoubtedly that of a professional copyist, considering its clarity and the virtual lack of corrections. For all of these reasons, it is more than probable that this manuscript was a commercial copy made in a Madrid bookshop for a particular client. This could have been the Count of Fernán-Núñez himself, who could have purchased the volume in Madrid before leaving for Lisbon in 1778 as Charles III's Ambassador.

Regarding prices, most sonatas in this volume cost six *reales de vellón*, except for the ones by Tartini and Ledesma, sold for 8 *reales* each. Judging from the advertisements of instrumental-music copies published in the Madrid press during the eighteenth century,[21] four complementary reasons can be hypothesized for the high prices. Firstly, it could be due to the length of each work: Tartini's sonata is six pages long (pp. 12–17), whereas most of the sonatas in the volume are four pages long. Yet this is not the case with all the sonatas by Ledesma, which also cost eight *reales* each (only the sonata in pp. 117–122 is six pages long). In addition, two sonatas by Boshoff and one by Herrando are also six pages long but cost only six *reales* (pp. 6–11 and 101–106, respectively). The second reason for a high price could be the technical difficulty of the works, which is directly related to the time needed for the copy. This makes sense in the case of this particular Tartini sonata, which instrumental writing is relatively complex (see Figure 1). Thirdly, novelty could have determined the prices; possibly,

---

20 The SP paper was used in the guitar manuscripts *Cifras selectas de guitarra* (1722), *Pasacalles y Obras de guitarra* (1732) and *Códice Saldívar* (1732), described in Santiago de Murcia, *Cifras selectas de guitarra*, ed. Alejandro Vera (Middleton-Wisconsin: A-R Editions, 2010), xv–xvi. This paper type was also used in copies of *villancicos* from the 1740s, described in Francisco Corselli, *Fiesta de Navidad en la Capilla Real Felipe V: Villancicos de Francisco Corselli, 1743*, ed. Álvaro Torrente (Madrid: Alpuerto, 2002), 43–48. This watermark appears in other copies of violin music, such as the manuscript *Divertimenti a due violini per il Duque de Fernandina*, containing violin duets by Antonio Montoro and dated 1773; shelfmark M287.A2 M81, Music Section, Library of Congress, Washington. Until recently, the SP paper had been considered Genoese, but there is evidence that it could be French. See the study of Spanish and Portuguese sources in Serguei N. Prozhoguin, "Indizi documentali e organologici sui passaggi di proprietà prima del 1835 dei 17 volumi di composizioni di Domenico Scarlatti della Biblioteca Nazionale Marciana di Venezia [BNM]," BNM, January 2019, https://marciana.venezia.sbn.it/immagini-possessori/398-barbara
21 The main two newspapers that advertised the selling of music in eighteenth-century Madrid were *Diario de Madrid* and *Gazeta de Madrid*. Transcriptions of music advertisements, respectively, in Yolanda Acker, *Música y danza en el Diario de Madrid. Noticias, avisos y artículos (1758–1808)* (Madrid: Centro de Documentación de Música y Danza, 2007); Ignacio Sustaeta, "La música en las fuentes hemerográficas del XVIII español: Referencias musicales en la Gaceta de Madrid, y artículos de música en los Papeles Periódicos Madrileños," (Doctoral dissertation, Universidad Complutense de Madrid, 1993).

the violin sonatas by Tartini and Ledesma were the newest ones available in the shop. A fourth reason could be the fame of each composer. By 1770, Ledesma was well known as viola player of Madrid's Royal Chapel, and shortly later Tartini was praised in different Madrilenian texts (as shown in Section 2). The Tartini sonata included in this manuscript is a copy of the *Sonata* in B flat major, Brainard B10, published in Paris as *Sonata* op. 4 no. 3 (1747).[22] It is not clear whether this Madrilenian copy could be based in the Paris printed collection; for example, the distribution of bars and staves is different (compare Figures 1 and 2). Furthermore, the bass part is unfigured, unlike the Paris edition. This is probably due to local performance practice: in Madrid, the melodic accompaniment was a very usual option for the performance of accompanied violin sonatas, a particularly common combination being that of violin and cello. This is shown by the lack of figured bass in most of the extant musical sources, and, most tellingly, by some work titles that are explicit in this respect, such as Francesco Montali's *Seis sonatte a violino e violoncello* (Toledo, 1754), dedicated to the Duke of Alba.[23] It is worth noting that a similar type of melodic accompaniment was used by Tartini himself in several two-movement sonatas from the 1750s; and he even used a specific term to name this type of bass, "bassetto".[24]

Figure 1: Giuseppe Tartini, *Sonata* Brainard B10 = "Sonata â solo del Sig.[no]r Tartini", first movement, *Allegro*, bars 1–21. Manuscript anthology *26 Sonatas de varios autores* (Madrid, ca. 1760–1770), Lothar Siemens' private collection (Las Palmas de Gran Canaria), p. 12, detail.

---

22 Giuseppe Tartini, *Sonates à violon seul avec la basse continue, oeuvre IVe* (Paris, engraved by Le Huë, sold by Boivin *et al.*, 1747).
23 On the accompaniment of violin sonatas, see Ana Lombardía, preface to Christiano Reynaldi, *Sonate di violino e basso opus 1 (1761)*/ Francesco Montali, *Sonatas a violín solo y bajo (1759)*, xliii–xliv.
24 Tartini's two-movement sonatas were initially considered for unaccompanied violin in Paul Brainard, "Tartini and the Sonata for Unaccompanied Violin," *Journal of the American Musicological Society* 16 (1961): 383–395. However, Gregorio Carraro has shown that they were most likely written for violin and melodic bass. He also argues that, in Padua, the term "bassetto" could refer to small, high-pitch violoncellos,

Figure 2: Giuseppe Tartini's *Sonata* Brainard B10, first movement, *Allegro*, bars 1–19. *Sonata* op. 4 no. 3, in *Sonates à violon seul avec la basse continue*, oeuvre IVe (Paris, engraved by Le Hue, sold by Boivin et al., 1747), p. 10, detail. Performers' Facsimiles, New York, undated.

Interestingly, the last sonata in the Paris edition, in C minor (*Sonata* op. 4 no. 6, Brainard c5), was presented at the time as a work by Tartini but, more recently, has been attributed to Mauro d'Alay (Parma, *ca.* 1690? – Parma, 1757).[25] In the 1720s, this virtuoso violinist was active in London, where he published this accompanied violin sonata within a six-work collection.[26] Later on, between 1739 and 1747, Alay was one of the most highly esteemed musicians of Madrid's royal court, benefitting from the direct protection of Queen Elizabeth Farnese.[27] No less than 10 unpublished sonatas by Alay appear in the *26 Sonatas* anthology, as mentioned above. Given that no concordances have been found, it seems likely that they were composed in Madrid. These sonatas feature some similarities with Tartini's op. 4: each work contains four movements, the violin writing is both virtuosic and idiomatic, and some movements are based on dance schemata that went out of fashion after 1750, such as the gigue.[28] An example is Alay's manuscript *Sonata 6*, containing

---

as some of the ones owned by Antonio Vandini (1690–1770), Tartini's colleague in Padua. See Carraro, Gregorio, "Problemi di interpretazione e prassi esecutiva nelle sonate dell'autografo I-Pca 1888–1 di Giuseppe Tartini," (Doctoral dissertation, Università di Padova, 2013), 79–87, http://paduaresearch.cab.unipd.it/5944

25 Petrobelli, "Tartini, Giuseppe".

26 Mauro d'Alay, *Cantate a voce sola e Suonate a violino solo col basso Dedicate all'ecc. za di Carlo Lenos, duca di Richmond and Lenox [...]* (London, 1728). RISM A554.

27 Ana Lombardía, "Isabel de Farnesio (1692–1766), impulsora de la música para violín italiana en Madrid," in *Las mujeres y las artes: mecenas, artistas, emprendedoras, coleccionistas*, ed. Beatriz Blasco et al., (Madrid: Abada, 2021), 269–293. Both Alay and Farnese came from Parma. This was also the city of origin of Francesco Corselli, master of Madrid's Royal Chapel from 1738 until he died in 1778.

28 The latest Tartini Thematic Catalogue lists 16 different gigues included in sonatas prior to 1750. See, Guido Viverit, Alba Luksich, Simone Olivari, eds., *Catalogo tematico online delle composizioni di Giuseppe Tartini* (tARTini-Turismo culturale

the following movements: *Adagio, Allegro, Grave*, and *Giga Allegro* (see Figure 3). There is no evidence that Alay was a student of Tartini,[29] but he probably knew some of his sonatas, and could have taken them as a compositional model.

Figure 3: Mauro d'Alay, *Sonata 6* (Madrid, ca. 1739–1747), fourth movement (*Giga Allegro*), bars 1–11. Manuscript anthology *26 Sonatas de varios autores* (Madrid, ca. 1760–1770), p. 56, detail. Lothar Siemens' private collection (Las Palmas de Gran Canaria).

1.2 The Conservatory Sonatas

Three other eighteenth-century manuscript copies of Tartini sonatas survive in Madrid's Higher Conservatory, in Manuscripts 656, 657, and 658.[30] The institution was founded in 1830, but its library contains some earlier musical sources coming from the Royal Palace collections, as is the case with these Tartini copies.[31] These sources were presented very briefly in an article, but they have not yet been discussed in depth regarding the identification of the works, the origin and date of the copies, and their possible performance contexts.[32]

---

all'insegna di Giuseppe Tartini, 2019–2020), http://catalog.discovertartini.eu/dcm/gt/navigation.xq.

29 The search for "Alay/ Alai/ Allay/ Allai" in Tartini's letters provides no results. See Giorgia Malagò, ed., *Giuseppe Tartini: Lettere e documenti/Pisma in dokumenti/Letters and Documents*, 2 vols, trans. Jerneja Umer Kljun and Roberto Baldo (Trieste: Edizioni Università di Trieste, 2020).

30 RISM shelfmarks E-Mc, M/656; E-Mc, M/657; and E-Mc, M/658.

31 A part of the royal collections was donated to Madrid's Conservatory in the 1870s by Amadeo of Savoy, then King of Spain. See Ortega, Judith, "La música en la corte de Carlos III y Carlos IV (1759–1808): De la Real Capilla a la Real Cámara," vol. 1 (Doctoral dissertation, Universidad Complutense de Madrid, 2010), 250, https://eprints.ucm.es/11739/.

32 A duplication of these sources with a brief commentary was published in Gosálvez, "Fuentes originales de Giuseppe Tartini". The author identifies one owner (Zlotek),

In the late-eighteenth century, these three manuscripts were used by two different violinists of Madrid's Royal Chapel, namely Domingo Rodil and Bonifazio Zlotek. Domingo Rodil (Figueres, Girona,? – Madrid, 1805) worked as a violinist of the institution from 1763 to 1796, when he went blind. Previously, he had been a chamber musician of the Spanish Ambassador to Poland for two years (1760–1762). In 1770 Rodil was appointed a chamber musician of Prince Charles.[33] As for Bonifazio Zlotek (Warsaw,? – Madrid, 1787), he was nicknamed "Polaco" ("Polish") due to his origin. He auditioned for Madrid's Royal Chapel in 1767 but did not become a member until 1771. He remained in the institution until he died in 1787, save for a leave period in 1772, when he travelled to Warsaw. Zlotek also took part in the musical gatherings held at Prince Charles' Royal Chamber in the 1770s.[34] Beyond the royal court, he was a chamber musician of the above-mentioned Duke and Duchess of Osuna.[35]

Rodil and Zlotek had a professional relationship as active musicians of both the Royal Chapel and the Prince's Royal Chamber. Considering Rodil's connections with Poland, it seems likely that they also had a somewhat close personal relationship (it is even possible that Rodil spoke some Polish). In any case, there is no doubt that both violinists used these copies of Tartini's sonatas in close dates and similar performance contexts. Their surnames, initials, or nicknames appear in different parts of the manuscripts. For instance, on the title page of Manuscript 656 Rodil's name was crossed out in the right-upper corner, and "Polaco" was added afterwards (see Figure 4). There is also a signature in the right-bottom corner, possibly by a later owner; it reads "F. Witz", followed by a drawing of a sacred heart. As for the indication "E. IV", it could be a class-mark from an eighteenth-century library.

Based on the owners' activity period in Madrid, these copies could have been used between 1763, when Rodil became a member of the Royal Chapel, and 1787, when Zlotek passed away. Both violinists likely used them in the musical gatherings held at Prince Charles' Royal Chamber during the 1770s and 1780s. The royal heir (who became King Charles IV in 1788) was an eager music collector and amateur violinist. He owned a wide variety of chamber works for strings, including the most modern repertoire. A central figure in the selection of the musical repertoire for his Royal Chamber was the Italian Gaetano Brunetti, his violin teacher since

---

suggests an Italian origin for these sources and proposes the approximate dates *ca.* 1760 or *ca.* 1770, but provides no explanation. Additional information on these sources, including the identification of another owner (Rodil), appears in Ortega, "La música en la corte de Carlos III y Carlos IV," 1:250.
33 Short biography in Ortega, "La música en la corte de Carlos III y Carlos IV," 2:90–92.
34 Short biography in Ortega, "La música en la corte de Carlos III y Carlos IV," 2:117–118.
35 Ortega, "El mecenazgo musical de la Casa de Osuna"; Juan P. Fernández-Cortés, *La música en las Casas de Osuna y Benavente (1733–1882): un estudio sobre el mecenazgo musical de la alta nobleza española* (Madrid: SEdeM, 2007), 172–175.

1770, and officially appointed "director of music" of the Royal Chamber in 1796, although he had been playing that role earlier.[36]

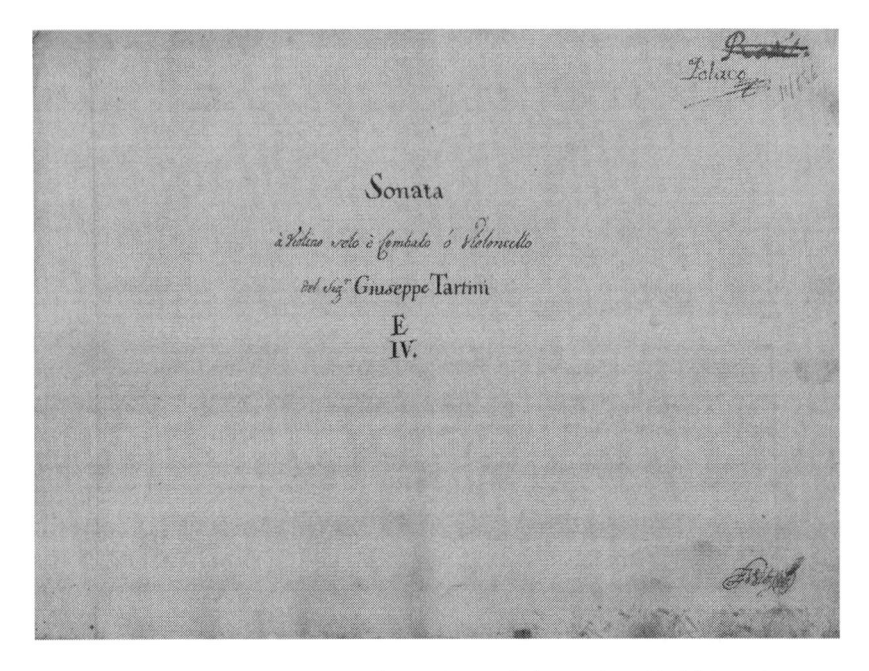

Figure 4: E-Mc, M/656: *Sonata a violino solo e cembalo o violoncello del Sigr. Giuseppe Tartini*. E. IV = G. Tartini, Sonata Brainard e7, title page.

---

36 On Gaetano Brunetti and his role in the Royal Chamber, see Germán Labrador, *Gaetano Brunetti (1744–1798). Catálogo crítico, temático y cronológico* (Madrid: Asociación Española de Documentación Musical, 2005); Ortega, "La música en la corte de Carlos III y Carlos IV," 1:165; Lluís Bertran, " 'Eligiendo las piezas': los tríos de Gaetano Brunetti en diálogo con la música instrumental europea (1760–1800)," in *Instrumental Music in Late-18th-Century Spain*, ed. Miguel Á. Marín and Màrius Bernadó (Kassel: Reichenberger, 2014), 383–424.

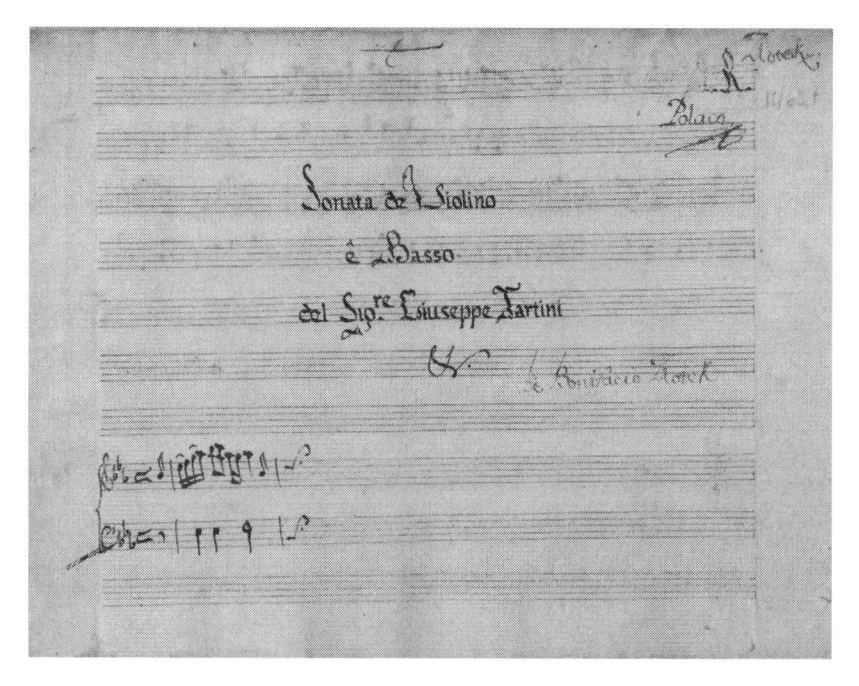

Figure 5: E-Mc, M/657: *Sonata de violino e basso del Sigre. Giuseppe Tartini* = G. Tartini, *Sonata* Brainard Es1, title page.

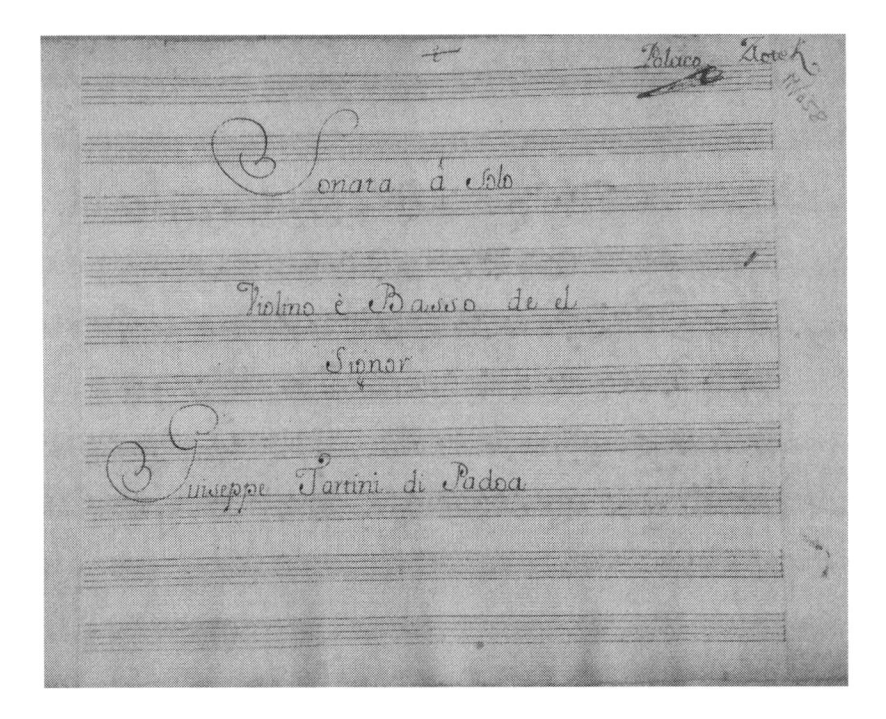

Figure 6: E-Mc, M/658: *Sonata a solo violino e basso de el signor Giuseppe Tartini di Padoa* = G. Tartini, *Sonata* Brainard A14, title page.

As for the origin of these copies, both their physical features and contents point at a Madrilenian origin, especially in the case of Manuscripts 657 and 658. All three manuscripts were copied in the same paper format: landscape octavo measuring around 290 mm wide and 220 mm high, featuring 10 musical staffs per page, and including lateral margins of over 20 mm on both sides (see Table 1). This format was common in sonata copies made in Madrid in the 1760s and 1770s, such as the anthology *26 Sonatas de varios autores*, featuring the same SP watermark as Manuscript 656 (Figure 4). Other examples of the same paper size include eight of the extant manuscripts containing works expressly composed by Francesco Corselli for the Royal Chapel's auditions between 1760 and 1776.[37] Another feature that is

---

37 Those sources contain violin sonatas by Francesco Corselli (nos. 1, 2, 3, 5, 6, and 7) and the individual parts of the *Concertino a cuatro* by the same composer (a sort of string quartet). Detailed description of the musical sources in Ortega, "La música en la corte de Carlos III y Carlos IV," 1:279–342.

typical of the royal court's sources is the presence of a small cross in the centre of the title page, as in Manuscript 657 (Figure 5) and Manuscript 658 (Figure 6).[38]

Figure 7: E-Mc, M/656: *Sonata a violino solo e cembalo o violoncello del Sigr. Giuseppe Tartini. E. IV* = G. Tartini, *Sonata* Brainard e7, f. 2v, detail.

Figure 8: E-Mc, M/657: *Sonata de violino e basso del Sigre. Giuseppe Tartini* = G. Tartini, *Sonata* Brainard Es1, f. 1v, detail.

Figure 9: E-Mc, M/658: *Sonata a solo violino e basso de el signor Giuseppe Tartini di Padoa* = G. Tartini, *Sonata* Brainard A14, f. 1v, detail.

---

38 A similar cross appears on the title page of Gaetano Brunetti's *String quintet op. 10 no. 4*, L 258, copied in 1797. Source in Sezione musicale della Biblioteca Palatina, Parma, Borb. 882, belonging to the music collection of Maria Luisa of Bourbon, Queen of Etruria, and her husband Ludovico of Parma. See Lluís Bertran, Ana Lombardía and Judith Ortega, "La colección de manuscritos españoles de los Reyes de Etruria en la Biblioteca Palatina de Parma (1794–1824): Un estudio de fuentes," *Revista de musicología* 38, no. 1 (2015): 168.

Regarding copyists, they are all different in the three Conservatory manuscripts, as the comparison of the G clefs and the capital-A letters shows (Figures 7, 8, and 9). The same hand appears on the title page and the inside of each source. They have not been identified as any of the copyists active in the royal court during the eighteenth century. However, the hand of Copyist C (that of Manuscript 657) also appears in three sources containing string quartets by Haydn, presumably copied in late eighteenth-century Madrid, although they are preserved in Barcelona.[39] As for Copyist D (that of Manuscript 658), it was most likely a Spaniard, judging from an orthographical detail: the title page reads "de el Signor Tartini" instead of "del" or "di il", in Italian.

Both Manuscript 657 and Manuscript 658 feature an unfigured bass. This is a usual trait of the Madrilenian copies of violin sonatas, related to performance practice (see above). Furthermore, the movement titles of both sources were modified, seemingly due to local copying and performance practices. Manuscript 657 contains Tartini's *Sonata* op. 9 no. 1. In other sources, it features the movements *Adagio*, *Allegro*, and *Allegro assai*,[40] but in the Madrid source, the tempo markings are *Andante largo*, *Allegro*, and *Allegro ma non tanto*. This suggests a slower and less virtuosic performance practice of the last movement than in other places. More tellingly, Manuscript 658 contains Tartini's *Sonata* op. 1 no. 1. In other sources, it features the movements *Grave*, *Allegro*, and *Presto*, the second one characterized by Corellian-fashion fugato writing.[41] In the Madrid source, the movements are titled *Adagio*, *Fuga*, and *Allegro*. Local composers used the *Fuga* marking for this kind of movement, as shown by the sources containing the violin sonatas by the above-mentioned Spaniards Manalt and Herrando.[42] Also, in the mid-century local sonatas *Grave* and *Presto* were rarely used tempo markings, while *Adagio* and *Allegro* were much more usual.

Only Manuscript 656 could have an Italian origin, considering that the orthography of all Italian words is correct and that the bass is figured, which is relatively unusual in the Madrid copies. However, there are no watermarks featuring three moons, like in the Venetian paper used in Padova, so it is unlikely that the Madrid

---

39 Santa Maria del Pi Church Archive, Barcelona (RISM sigla E-Bp), shelfmarks M 1548, M 1551, and M 2085. These sources belonged to the music amateur Sebastià Muntaner i Cabot (1740–1811), a surgeon that resided in Mallorca. He owned several manuscripts of chamber music that were presumably produced in Madrid, considering the chronology of their advertisements in the local press. When and why these sources were sent to Barcelona is ignored. I am grateful to Lluís Bertran for this information.
40 Details on other sources in Viverit et al., *Catalogo tematico online*, GT 2.Eb01.
41 Details on other sources in Viverit et al., *Catalogo tematico online*, GT 2.A14.
42 Francisco Manalt, *Obra harmonica en seis sonatas de violín y bajo solo* (Madrid, Guinea, 1757); José Herrando, *Sonatine per violino di cinque corde*, manuscript, 1754, source in International museum and library of music in Bologna (RISM sigla I-Bc), EE 188.

sources are directly related to Tartini's school, as suggested by previous studies.[43] Moreover, the presence of the SP watermark and the paper format match other Spanish copies, so the possibility of a Spanish origin should not be ruled out.

It is also worth noting that all three Conservatory sources contain three-movement accompanied violin sonatas featuring the same sequence of movement types, namely *slow, main fast, and light fast* (see Table 2). This was precisely the most usual movement cycle in the sonatas composed in mid-eighteenth-century Madrid (as mentioned above). In contrast, the sonata of the other source features a four-movement cycle; also used by Alay, but rare in the local output after 1750.

As has been shown, Tartini's violin sonatas were copied and performed in Madrid up until 50 years after their first editions in Amsterdam and Paris. This apparent delay does not necessarily indicate that the repertoire available in the Spanish capital was obsolete. On the contrary, the local press attests to the rapid arrival of novelties from abroad, especially from 1770 onwards.[44] In reality, both earlier and more modern works coexisted in the local market. For example, Corelli's *Sonatas* op. 5 had a Madrid edition as late as 1772, in contrast with the updated style of the local output in this same genre. The reason is that Corelli was considered a didactic model for violin technique, not a compositional model.[45] On the contrary, the long-lasting interest in Tartini's sonatas could be interpreted as a sign that his sonatas were canonized as a compositional model in late eighteenth-century Spain. The documentary sources discussed in the next section point precisely to this direction.

2 Documentary Sources on Tartini's Reception

The local press confirms that by 1790 Tartini was well known and admired in Madrid. He is mentioned in several commercial advertisements and short essays published in two local newspapers, *Diario de Madrid* and *Gazeta de Madrid*. In 1790, an anonymous critic stated: "I have heard saying that the adagios by Tartini, the andantes by San-Martino, and the allegros by Locatelli are very appropriate for overtures."[46] Six years later, another anonymous writer ironically commented that Tartini's harmony treatise was one of the many "rare animals" that Spanish allegedly learned people ignored: "[...] I know very well that the *Pleasures* by Galileo, the *Rules* by P. Kirker [A. Kircher], the *Harmony Treatise* by Tartini, the *Algebra* by

---

43 Gosálvez, "Fuentes originales de Giuseppe Tartini", 243–246. I am grateful to Guido Viverit for the information on the Padovan sources.
44 Miguel Á. Marín, "El mercado de la música," in *La música en el siglo XVIII*, ed. José M. Leza (Madrid: Fondo de Cultura Económica, 2014), 439–461.
45 See note 5 above.
46 "[..] Los adagios de Tartini, los andantes de San-Martino, y los alegres de Locatelli, he oído decir que son a propósito para las oberturas." Anonymous, "Fin del discurso sobre la música," *Diario de Madrid*, February 10, 1790, 161–163. Transcription in Acker, *Música y danza en el Diario de Madrid*, 103–105.

Euler, the Physics by Rameau, the *Elements* by d'Lambert [D'Alembert], the dictionary by the Genevan man [J.-J. Rousseau], and even the harmony of the hammers by Pythagoras are some of the many rare animals unknown to learned Spanish people [...]."[47] The author compares Tartini with famous scientists (Pythagoras, Galileo, Euler), music theorists (Kircher, Rameau), encyclopedists (D'Alembert), and philosophers (Rousseau). This was a way to recommend studying Tartini's theoretical works, probably *Trattato di musica secondo la vera scienza dell'armonia* (Treatise on Music Accoding to the True Science of Harmony, 1754).[48]

As regards compositions by Tartini, in 1797 *L'arte dell'arco* was for sale in two different Madrid bookshops. Campins advertised it for violin: "Campins' bookshop [...] an Andante with 50 variations for violin, composed by Mr. Tartini, aimed at the good use of the bow, for 16 r[eale]s."[49] In contrast, Alonso advertised a flute version: "Alonso Bookshop [...] an Andante with 50 variations for flute, with or without a bass, by Mr. Tartini; its price 16 r[eale]s."[50] Most likely, the edition for sale in both shops was Luigi Marescalchi's, which was published shortly earlier and contains precisely 50 variations.[51] Moreover, in the late 1760s Marescalchi had been *impresario* of the Italian opera company at the Spanish royal court, and in the 1770s reprinted some Madrilenian music editions in Venice, which were also for sale at Castillo's bookshop in Madrid.[52] Therefore, Marescalchi likely kept in touch with the Madrid music retailers during the 1780s and 1790s.

Notably, the earliest known *History of Spanish Music* (*ca*. 1804), by José Teixidor (*ca*. 1752 – *ca*. 1811), mentioned Tartini's school as a symbol of excellence in violin

---

47 "[...] Yo bien conozco que los placeres de Galileo, las reglas del P. Kirker [A. Kircher], el tratado de armonía de Tartini, la algebraica de Euler, la Física de Rameau, los Elementos de d'Lambert [D'Alembert], el Diccionario del Ginebrino [J.J. Rousseau?], y aun la armonía de los martillos de Pitágoras son otros tantos animales desconocidos de nuestros profesores españoles [...]". Anonymous, *Diario de Madrid*, November 9, 1796, 1275–1277. Transcription in Acker, *Música y danza en el Diario de Madrid*, 231–233.

48 Giuseppe Tartini, *Trattato di musica secondo la vera scienza dell'armonia* (Padova: Stamperia del Seminario, 1754).

49 "Librería Campins [...] un andante con 50 variaciones para violín, compuesto por el Sr. Tartini, dirigido al buen uso del arco, á 16 rs." *Gazeta de Madrid*, July 18, 1797, 644. Transcription in Sustaeta, "La música en las fuentes hemerográficas," 3:274.

50 "Librería Alonso [...] un andante con 50 variaciones para flauta con baxo ó sin él, por el Sr. Tartini: su precio 16 rs.". *Gazeta de Madrid*, June 6, 1797, 480. Transcription in Sustaeta, "La música en las fuentes hemerográficas," 3:273.

51 Giuseppe Tartini, *L' Arte dell'arco o siano cinquanta variazioni per violino, e sempre collo stesso basso, composte dal Sig.r Giuseppe Tartini sopra alla più bella gavotta del Corelli Opera V* (Naples, Marescalchi, *ca*. 1780–1789).

52 Rudolf Rasch, "Four Madrilenian First Editions of Works by Luigi Boccherini?" in *Instrumental Music in Late 18th-Century Spain*, ed. Miguel Á. Marín and Màrius Bernadó (Kassel: Reichenberger, 2014), 259–298.

playing. More specifically, Teixidor stated that Tartini had taught one of the most outstanding violinist-composers in mid-eighteenth-century Madrid:

> At the same time as Zarzini [recte Tartini] astonished France, and Germany[,] his new violin school redirected his most outstanding pupil Cristiano Rinaldi to Spain, who although of such great merit, that some believe he outdid his teacher, nonetheless he found Mr José Manalt in Spain, who although not superior to him in all the aspects that constitute an excellent master of this instrument, at least he disputed supremacy every day of his life.[53]

Teixidor only worked as an organist in Madrid from 1774 onwards, after the death of Christiano Reynaldi (also Rinaldi or Reinaldi), José Herrando, and Francisco Manalt. The author mistakenly combines the name and surname of the last two musicians. In all likelihood, he was familiar with the works the three violinists-composers had published in the 1750s and 1760s, and this led him to imagine a certain rivalry.

As for the possibility that Reynaldi studied with Tartini, there is evidence that it could be true. Tartini's own letters mention one of his students serving the Ambassador of Spain, and this could have been Reynaldi. More specifically, in January 1739 Tartini wrote: "In conformity with the promise made in another letter of mine, I give notice to your reverence of the fact that the pageboy of His Excellency the Ambassador of Spain has returned here to take violin lessons from me, so I am presently and shall be until July with six students."[54] This student spent six months with Tartini in Padova. Most likely, he was a chamber musician of the Ambassador of Spain to the Holy See, based in Palazzo Spagna in Rome.

Between 1735 and 1747 the Ambassador was Troiano (or Troyano) Acquaviva (Atri, 1696 – Rome, 1747), who pursued an ecclesiastical and political career. In 1732 he was appointed Cardinal priest of Saints Quirico and Giulita, but in 1733 he asked to change his title to Saint Cecilia. Also, after his death in 1747 he was buried in Saint Cecilia Chapel in Trastevere.[55] This reflects his great interest in music. In fact, Acquaviva

---

53 "En los mismos tiempos que el Zarzini [recte Tartini] asombraba la Francia, y Alemania[,] su nueva escuela de violín remitió a España su más sobresaliente discípulo Cristiano Rinaldi, el cual aunque de un mérito tan grande, que algunos opinan que sobrepujaba a su maestro, con todo halló en España [a] Dn José Manalt que cuando no le fue superior en todas las circunstancias que constituyen en un excelente profesor del tal instrumento por lo menos le disputó por todos los días de su vida la primacía." Teixidor, *Historia de la música española*, 113.
54 "[...] conforme alla promessa fatta in altra mia, do avviso a *vostra riverenza*, come il paggio di *sua eccellenza* ambasciator di Spagna è ritornato qui a prender da me lezione per il violino, onde son presentemente, e sarò sino a luglio con sei Scolari." Malagò, *Tartini: Lettere*, 1:134. English translation in Malagò, *Tartini: Lettere*, 2:274–275.
55 Fausto Nicolini, "Acquaviva d'Aragona, Troiano," in Dizionario Biografico degli Italiani, accessed January 3, 2021, https://www.treccani.it/enciclopedia/troiano-acquaviva-d-aragona_(Dizionario-Biografico)/

sponsored regular social gatherings (*tertulias*) in Palazzo Spagna, protagonized by conversation and music. He also organized cantatas for the birthdays of Charles of Bourbon, King of Naples (later to become Charles III of Spain), and his wife. The ambassador was responsible for the miscellaneous shows that accompanied their wedding in 1738, including music, dance, and different forms of visual arts. Unfortunately, the scarcity of documentary sources does not allow to identify the musicians that served Acquaviva.[56]

Christiano Reynaldi (Cracow, 1719 – Madrid, 1767) was the son of Milanese violinist Giuseppe Reynaldi, presumably his first music teacher.[57] When Tartini wrote the above-quoted letter in 1739, Christiano was 19 or 20 years old, old enough to work for the Ambassador in Rome and to travel to Padua for a six-month study period. Five years later his professional activity is documented precisely in Rome: Pier Leone Ghezzi sketched a portrait of him during a musical gathering (*accademia*) held at the artist's home, writing an explanation underneath: "Mr. Cristiano Rinaldi, excellent violinist; he is in the service of a Spanish captain who is in the armada of the King of Spain, [and] who has returned from Velletri. He plays the violin wonderfully and pleased me by coming to play at my academy [in Rome] when all of those present were amazed, and this was on 18 December 1744."[58] The Battle of Velletri (August 1744), part of the War of the Austrian Succession, was won by the troupes of Charles of Bourbon. Presumably, one of his captains had Reynaldi as a chamber musician in Rome at that time. Acquaviva, still Ambassador by then, could have acted precisely as the connection between the musician and the military members of the Spanish Bourbonic circle in Italy.

---

56 On Acquaviva's patronage of different forms of art, see Pilar Díez del Corral, "Un palacio en fiesta: Troyano Acquaviva y la celebración por los esponsales de Carlos de Borbón y María Amalia de Sajonia en el palacio de España en Roma," *Revista de historia moderna: Anales de la Universidad de Alicante* 33 (2015): 147–162; Díez del Corral, Pilar, "Il dilettevole trattenimento: el teatro del Cardenal Troyano Acquaviva en el Palacio de España en Roma," *Music in Art: International Journal for Music Iconography* 42 (2017): 59–69.

57 Biographical information about Christiano Reynaldi in Spain appears in Siemens, Lothar, "El violoncelista y compositor polaco Cristiano Reynaldi (Cracovia, 1719 – Madrid, 1767): nuevos datos para su biografía," *Revista de musicología* 13, no. 1 (1990): 221–226; Ortega, "La música en la corte de Carlos III y Carlos IV," 2:79.

58 "Il signor Cristiano Rinaldi bravissimo sonator di violino; il medesimo sta al servitio d'un capitano spagniolo che sta nell'armata del re di Spagnia, che è ritornato da Velletri. Il medesimo sona il violino a meraviglia bene, che mi ha favorito di venire a sonare alla mia accademia, che tutti i circostanti ne restorno ammirati, e questo fu il dì 18 dicembre 1744." Portrait of "Cristiano Rinaldi", Pier Leone Ghezzi, 1744, f. 80, Lat. 3119, *Fondo Ottoboni*, Biblioteca Apostolica Vaticana. Duplication of the portrait and longer discussion of it in Ana Lombardía, preface to Reynaldi, *Sonate di violino e basso opus 1 (1761)*/ Montali, *Sonatas a violín solo y bajo (1759)*, ix–xi and xxxiii– xxxv.

Therefore, it seems likely that Reynaldi was actually the student that Tartini mentioned in 1739.

In any case, from 1750 until he died in 1767, Reynaldi worked in Madrid and nearby cities as a chamber musician of the widowed queen Elisabetta Farnese, the mother of Charles of Bourbon. He was officially appointed cellist of Farnese's chamber, but was also known as a virtuoso violinist. His *Sonate di violino e basso,* op. 1 (Madrid, J. F. Martínez Abad, 1761), sponsored by the widowed queen, was the second collection of this musical genre ever printed in Spain. It is representative of the compositional trends that were in fashion in Madrid. The predominant movement cycle is *slow, main fast,* and *light fast,* like in the Tartini sonatas preserved in Madrid's Conservatory.[59] The instrumental writing is not overly complex in the first sonatas, probably aimed at amateur musicians (potential buyers) who could glance through the work in the Madrid bookshops. However, it increases towards the end of the collection, reaching flashy passages in *Sonata 6,* especially in the third movement, which functions as a brilliant ending to the collection, exploiting very idiomatic keys for the violin (G major and D major). It features a multi-sectional structure that alternates between lyrical *adagios* and virtuosic *allegros* (Figure 10). It is an atypical form in the sonatas composed in Madrid within the same time frame. The use of this pattern can be considered conservative, for it can be detected in much earlier works, like Locatelli's *Sonata* op. 2 no. 11 (1732).

In the last third of the eighteenth century, another student of Tartini spent several years in Spain. He was a German violinist whose name adopts various forms in different Italian and Spanish documents, such as "Giacomo Leydeck", "Giacomo Gaisdeck", "Santiago Leydeck", and "Santiago Laideque". Considering his German origin, his baptism name was most likely Jakob Leydeck. Various Padovan sources mention this musician. In 1770, "Giacomo Leydeck" was one of the witnesses of the opening of Tartini's testament.[60] This suggests a close relationship between the student and the teacher. Between 1793 and 1795, different mentions appear in the Chapter Acts of Basilica di Santo Antonio di Padova.[61] In 1793 "Giacomo Gaisdeck" or "Giacomo Giusdeck tedesco" (from Germany) applied for a position in the Basilica's musical chapel, arguing that he had been a student of Tartini and that he had carried out an international career. A Statement ("Memoriale") dated 2 April 1793 is particularly revealing about Spain:

---

59 Critical edition with commentary in Reynaldi, *Sonate di violino e basso opus 1 (1761).*
60 Claudio Bellinati, "Contributo alla biografia padovana di Giuseppe Tartini con nuovi documenti," in *Tartini. Il tempo e le opere,* ed. Andrea Bombi and Maria N. Massaro (Bologna: Il Mulino, 1994), 23–35. I am grateful to Guido Viverit for the bibliography about Leydeck.
61 Chapter Acts of Basilica di S. Antonio di Padova. Transcriptions in Lucia Boscolo and Maddalena Pietribiasi, eds., *La cappella musicale antoniana di Padova nel secolo XVIII* (Padova: Centro Studi Antoniani, 1997), 367–371 (Giacomo Gaisdeck) and 398–399 (Giacomo Leidek).

Figure 10: Christiano Reynaldi, *Sonata 6*/iii, *Adagio–Allegro–Adagio–Allegro*, bars 1–20. Critical edition by Ana Lombardía, Madrid, ICCMU, 2019.

Statement of Giacomo Giusdeck: Giacomo Gaisdek to the Magistratura del Camerlengo and Auditors to the Council of Ten. The German Gaisdeck asks the Magistratura to be admitted to service in the Cappella musicale del Santo. A disciple of Tartini for many years, *he served at the Royal Court of Spain for three years, then at the Royal Chapel of St. James of Galicia for 13 years as a concert musician, with the obligation to play the first violin part and to play eight concerts a year.* The prospect of settling down in the city where he received the teaching of such a famous Maestro, the fame he has acquired and the natural desire to provide himself with a permanent means of subsistence lead him to ask to be admitted to the Chapel as a concert musician, even in the second position and without prejudice to the first full professor, with the salary that the Presidency will consider most appropriate.[62]

In a later application for the same purpose, dated 26 December 1795, the musician specifies that he had been a student of Tartini for five years.[63] Considering that he took part in the opening of the Maestro's testament in 1770, he could have studied in Padova approximately from 1765 to 1770.

In 1774 "Santiago Leydeck" applied to take part in the auditions of Madrid's Royal Chapel.[64] He was not admitted to participate,[65] but, according to his own Statement, he spent three years in the Spanish capital. It is plausible that he stayed there in the early 1770s, probably serving different patrons and playing some of Tartini's music or his own (not located), allegedly in a similar style. It is even possible that Leydeck introduced specific copies of Tartini's sonatas into Spain, precisely at the time that Zlotek and Rodil were using the Madrid Conservatory copies.

By 1775 "Santiago Laideque" was a member of the musical chapel at Santiago de Compostela Cathedral and played "conciertos" in solemn services ("funciones

---

62 "Memoriale di Giacomo Giusdeck: Giacomo Gaisdek alla Magistratura del Camerlengo e Revisori alla cassa del Consiglio dei Dieci. Il tedesco Gaisdeck chiede alla Magistratura di essere ammesso al servizio nella Cappella musicale del Santo. Discepolo di Tartini per molti anni, servì alla Corte reale di Spagna per tre anni, poi alla Cappella Reale di S. Giacomo di Galizia per 13 anni come concertista, con l'obbligo di svolgere il ruolo di 1° violino e di suonare 8 concerti all'anno. La prospettiva di stabilirsi nella città in cui ha ricevuto gli insegnamenti di un così celebre Maestro, la fama acquisita e il naturale desiderio di procurarsi una sussistenza permanente lo spingono a chiedere di essere ammesso in Cappella come concertista, anche al 2° posto e senza pregiudizio del 1° professore ordinario, con lo stipendio che la Presidenza riterrà più opportuno," 2 April 1793. Transcription in Boscolo and Pietribiasi, *La cappella musicale antoniana*, 368. Italics by the author.
63 "Supplica del Sig.r Giac.[om]o Leidek," 26 December 1795. Transcription in Boscolo and Pietribiasi, *La cappella musicale antoniana*, 398.
64 Ortega, "La música en la corte de Carlos III y Carlos IV," 1:92.
65 Ortega, "La música en la corte de Carlos III y Carlos IV," 2:148–149.

solemnes") that year.[66] According to the 1793 Statement, he worked in that cathedral for 13 years, up until 1788. Leydeck might have left Spain shortly afterwards, because by 1793 he was back in Padova, applying for a post in "the city where he received the teaching of such a famous Maestro".

3 Conclusions

In sum, the evidence just discussed shows that Tartini's accompanied violin sonatas reached Madrid in his lifetime and remained in fashion for several decades. Only four sonatas have been located in eighteenth-century local copies, but documentary sources reveal that many other Tartini sonatas reached the city before 1800. They could have arrived in Madrid directly from Italy, origin of about half of the professional violinists active in the city. Most likely, they also arrived through France, considering the connections between the Paris editions and the Spanish manuscript copies and inventories.

In addition, the canonization of Tartini's music, theoretical works, and violin school is detected in the Spanish capital around the turn of the nineteenth century. Commercial advertisements and essays published in the local press praise his works, although knowledge of them was not overly deep. For instance, his harmony treatise was mentioned as a book that Spanish musicians should study but did not know enough, and one of the works for sale is of doubtful attribution, namely Marescalchi's edition of *L'arte dell'arco*.

Notably, up until 40 years after their first printed editions Tartini's violin sonatas were one of the main formal models for local composers. Several violinists-composers that were most likely familiar with Tartini's works settled down in the Spanish capital. This is the case with d'Alay in the 1740s, Reynaldi in the 1750s, and Leydeck in the 1770s. The latter was no doubt a student of Tartini in Padova, and hitherto unknown evidence has shown that Reynaldi could have also studied with him in 1739. It seems no coincidence that Reynaldi's violin sonatas, like Alay's, bear formal similarities with Tartini's, especially regarding movement types and their combinations. In the future, it would be useful to undertake a close comparison of the violin vocabulary used in the sonatas by Tartini and the Madrid-based

---

66 Chapter Acts of Santiago de Compostela Cathedral (Libro de Actas Capitulares), Archivo Capitular de Santiago de Compostela, vol. 58, fol. 164: "28-9-1775. En este cabildo se acordó que el maestro de capilla, sin embargo de lo que está resuelto, disponga en las funciones solemnes se toquen por Peroli [Juan José Perrault, violinista], Laideque [Santiago Leydeck, violinista] y Canchiani [Pascual Canchiano, oboísta], conciertos, alternando cada uno, y en los días de reliquias, aberturas o algún concierto según lo determinare el maestro." Quoted in Héctor E. Santos, "Definiciones y usos del término 'concierto' en la documentación catedralicia española entre c. 1750 y c. 1830," *Resonancias* 44 (2019): 26. The author discusses the meanings of the term *concierto* in that particular context.

composers, in search of further evidence about how the Maestro could have influenced local composition.

No doubt, by the 1770s the violinists working for the city's elite were familiar with his sonatas, as the manuscripts belonging to Rodil and Zlotek clearly show. In that decade, Leydeck could have also played some of Tartini's sonatas in the social elite's palaces. The mobility of the musicians themselves was one of the key factors in the dissemination of this music. The facts that Reynaldi, Rodil, and Zlotek had connections with Poland and that Leydeck was German show that Madrid's chamber-music scene was a cosmopolitan one that received not only influences from Italy and France, but also from further European courts. Future research may bring to light more details about the reception of Tartini's students in Spain, including, for example, the Croatian Michele Stratico, whose only known set of violin sonatas is precisely preserved in Madrid.[67]

From a broader perspective, Madrid could have been key in the dissemination of Tartini's works to Latin America. Tellingly, in 1780 the inventory of the music collection belonging to the Marquis of Jaral, in Mexico City, mentions 18 compositions by Tartini in manuscript copies, namely 12 concertos and 6 sonatas.[68] Future research may unveil the networks through which Tartini's music reached New Spain and other parts of the New World, probably via the Spanish metropolis.

Bibliography

Acker, Yolanda. *Música y danza en el Diario de Madrid. Noticias, avisos y artículos (1758–1808)*. Madrid: Centro de Documentación de Música y Danza, 2007.

Anonymous. *Dos fandangos para violín y acompañamiento (ca. 1755)/ Capricho para violín solo (ca. 1760–1770)*. Edited by Ana Lombardía. Madrid: ICCMU, 2021.

Bellinati, Claudio. "Contributo alla biografia padovana di Giuseppe Tartini con nuovi documenti." In *Tartini. Il tempo e le opere*, edited by Andrea Bombi and Maria N. Massaro, 23–35. Bologna: Il Mulino, 1994.

Bertran, Lluís. " 'Eligiendo las piezas': los tríos de Gaetano Brunetti en diálogo con la música instrumental europea (1760–1800)." In *Instrumental Music in*

---

67 Michele Stratico, *Sei sonate a violino e violoncello o clavicembalo, opera prima* (London, Welcker, ca. 1763). Source in E-Mn, M/1699. On Stratico, see the chapter by Lucija Konfic in this same volume: Lucija Konfic, "Giuseppe Michele Stratico's Theoretical Thinking: Transgressing the Boundaries of Tartini's school," in *In Search of Perfect Harmony: Tartini's Music and Music Theory in Local and European Contexts*, ed. Nejc Sukljan (Berlin: Peter Lang, 2022): 263–277.

68 Javier Marín-López, "Mecenazgo musical e identidad aristocrática en el México Ilustrado: Miguel de Berrio y Zaldívar, Conde de San Mateo de Valparaíso (1716–1779)," *Latin-American Music Review* 39, no. 1 (2018): 1–29; especially pp. 16, 21, and 22.

Late-18th-Century Spain, edited by Miguel Á. Marín and Màrius Bernadó, 383–424. Kassel: Reichenberger, 2014.

Bertran, Lluís, Ana Lombardía and Judith Ortega. "La colección de manuscritos españoles de los Reyes de Etruria en la Biblioteca Palatina de Parma (1794–1824): Un estudio de fuentes." *Revista de musicología* 38, no. 1 (2015): 107–190.

Boscolo, Lucia and Maddalena Pietribiasi, eds. *La cappella musicale antoniana di Padova nel secolo XVIII.* Padova: Centro Studi Antoniani, 1997.

Brainard, Paul. *Le sonate per violino di Giuseppe Tartini. Catalogo tematico.* Padova: Carisch, 1975.

Brainard, Paul. "Tartini and the Sonata for Unaccompanied Violin." *Journal of the American Musicological Society* 16 (1961): 383–395.

Carraro, Gregorio. "Problemi di interpretazione e prassi esecutiva nelle sonate dell'autografo I-Pca 1888-1 di Giuseppe Tartini." Doctoral dissertation, Università di Padova, 2013. http://paduaresearch.cab.unipd.it/5944/

Corselli, Francisco. *Fiesta de Navidad en la Capilla Real Felipe V: Villancicos de Francisco Corselli, 1743.* Edited by Álvaro Torrente. Madrid: Alpuerto, 2002.

Díez del Corral, Pilar. "Il dilettevole trattenimento: el teatro del Cardenal Troyano Acquaviva en el Palacio de España en Roma." *Music in Art: International Journal for Music Iconography* 42 (2017): 59–69.

Díez del Corral, Pilar. "Un palacio en fiesta: Troyano Acquaviva y la celebración por los esponsales de Carlos de Borbón y María Amalia de Sajonia en el palacio de España en Roma." *Revista de historia moderna: Anales de la Universidad de Alicante* 33 (2015): 147–162.

Fernández-Cortés, Juan P. *La música en las Casas de Osuna y Benavente (1733–1882): un estudio sobre el mecenazgo musical de la alta nobleza española.* Madrid: Sedem, 2007.

Gómez-Urdáñez, José L. *Fernando VI.* Madrid: Arlanza, 2001.

Gosálvez, José C. "Fuentes originales de Giuseppe Tartini en la Biblioteca del RCSMM." *Música: Revista del Real Conservatorio Superior de Música de Madrid* 14–15 (2008): 243–256.

Heartz, Daniel. *Music in European Capitals: The Galant Style, 1720–1780.* New York: Norton, 2003.

Herrando, José. *Tres sonatas para violín y bajo solo, y una más para flauta travesera o violín.* Edited by Lothar Siemens. Madrid: Sedem, 1987.

Konfic, Lucija. "Giuseppe Michele Stratico's Theoretical Thinking; Transgressing the Boundaries of Tartini's school." In *In Search of Perfect Harmony: Tartini's Music and Music Theory in Local and European Contexts*, edited by Nejc Sukljan, 263–277. Berlin: Peter Lang, 2022.

Labrador, Germán. *Gaetano Brunetti (1744–1798). Catálogo crítico, temático y cronológico.* Madrid: Asociación Española de Documentación Musical, 2005.

Ledesma, Juan de. *Cinco sonatas para violín y bajo solo*. Edited by Lothar Siemens. Madrid: Sedem, 1989.

Lombardía, Ana. "Corelli as a Model? Composing Violin Sonatas in Mid-18th-Century Madrid." In *Miscellanea Ruspoli III*, edited by Giorgio Monari, 17–69. Lucca: Libreria Musicale Italiana, 2016.

Lombardía, Ana. "Isabel de Farnesio (1692–1766), impulsora de la música para violín italiana en Madrid." In *Las mujeres y las artes: mecenas, artistas, emprendedoras, coleccionistas*, edited by Beatriz Blasco et al., 269–293. Madrid: Abada, 2021.

Lombardía, Ana. "Violin Music in Mid-18th-Century Madrid: Contexts, Genres, Style." Doctoral dissertation, Universidad de La Rioja, 2015. https://dialnet.uniri oja.es/descarga/tesis/46783

Malagò, Giorgia, ed. *Giuseppe Tartini: Lettere e documenti/Pisma in dokumenti/Letters and Documents*. 2 vols. Translated by Jerneja Umer Kljun and Roberto Baldo. Trieste: Edizioni Università di Trieste, 2020.

Marín, Miguel Á. "A la sombra de Corelli: componer para el violín." In *La música en el siglo XVIII*, edited by José M. Leza, 299. Madrid: Fondo de Cultura Económica, 2014.

Marín, Miguel Á. "El mercado de la música." In *La música en el siglo XVIII*, edited by José M. Leza, 439–461. Madrid: Fondo de Cultura Económica, 2014.

Marín, Miguel Á. "La recepción de Corelli en Madrid (ca. 1680–ca. 1810)." In *Arcangelo Corelli Fra Mito E Realtà Storica*, edited by Gregory Barnett, 573–637. Firenze: Olschki, 2007.

Marín-López, Javier. "Mecenazgo musical e identidad aristocrática en el México Ilustrado: Miguel de Berrio y Zaldívar, Conde de San Mateo de Valparaíso (1716–1779)." *Latin-American Music Review* 39, no. 1 (2018): 1–29.

Murcia, Santiago de. *Cifras selectas de guitarra*. Edited by Alejandro Vera. Middleton-Wisconsin: A-R Editions, 2010.

Ortega, Judith. "El mecenazgo musical de la Casa de Osuna durante la segunda mitad del siglo XVIII: El entorno musical de Luigi Boccherini en Madrid." *Revista de musicología* 27, no. 2 (2004): 643–698.

Ortega, Judith. "La música en la corte de Carlos III y Carlos IV (1759–1808): De la Real Capilla a la Real Cámara." Doctoral dissertation, Universidad Complutense de Madrid, 2010). https://eprints.ucm.es/11739/

Prozhoguin, Serguei N. "Indizi documentali e organologici sui passaggi di proprietà prima del 1835 dei 17 volumi di composizioni di Domenico Scarlatti della Biblioteca Nazionale Marciana di Venezia (BNM)." BNM, January, 2019. https://marciana.venezia.sbn.it/immagini-possessori/398-barbara

Rasch, Rudolf. "Four Madrilenian First Editions of Works by Luigi Boccherini?" In *Instrumental Music in Late 18th-Century Spain*, edited by Miguel Á. Marín and Màrius Bernadó, 259–298. Kassel: Reichenberger, 2014.

Reynaldi, Christiano. *Sonate di violino e basso opus 1 (1761)*/Montali, Francesco. *Sonatas a violín solo y bajo (1759)*. Edited by Ana Lombardía. Madrid: ICCMU, 2019.

Santos, Héctor E. "Definiciones y usos del término 'concierto' en la documentación catedralicia española entre c. 1750 y c. 1830." *Resonancias* 44 (2019): 13–35.

Siemens, Lothar. "El violoncelista y compositor polaco Cristiano Reynaldi (Cracovia, 1719 – Madrid, 1767): Nuevos datos para su biografía." *Revista de musicología* 13, no. 1 (1990), 221–226.

Siemens, Lothar. "Los violinistas compositores en la corte española durante el período central del siglo XVIII." *Revista de musicología* 11, no. 3 (1988): 657–766.

Siemens, Lothar. "Una sonata para oboe y bajo atribuible a Luis Misón (s. XVIII)." *Revista de musicología* 15, no. 2 (1992): 761–774.

Subirá, José. *La música en la Casa de Alba: Estudios históricos y biográficos*. Madrid: Tipografía Sucesores de Rivadeneyra, 1927.

Sustaeta, Ignacio. "La música en las fuentes hemerográficas del XVIII español: Referencias musicales en la Gaceta de Madrid, y artículos de música en los Papeles Periódicos Madrileños." Doctoral dissertation, Universidad Complutense de Madrid, 1993. Not online.

Teixidor, José. *Historia de la música española – Sobre el verdadero origen de la música*. Edited by Begoña Lolo. Lleida: Institut d'Estudis Ilerdencs, 1996.

Truett-Hollis, George. "An Eighteenth-Century Library of Chamber Music: The Inventory and Appraisal of the Music and Musical Instruments Belonging to the Twelfth Duke of Alba (d. 1776)." In *Festschrift in Honor of Theodore Front on His 90th Birthday*, edited by Darwin F. Scott, 29–64. Lucca: Lim Antiqua, 2002.

Viverit, Guido, Luksich, Alba, and Olivari, Simone, eds. *Catalogo tematico online delle composizioni di Giuseppe Tartini*. tARTini-Turismo culturale all'insegna di Giuseppe Tartini, 2019–2020. http://catalog.discovertartini.eu/dcm/gt/navigation.xq.

Daniel E. Freeman

University of Minnesota

The Stylistic Legacy of Giuseppe Tartini's Violin Concertos as Revealed in the Violin Concertos of Josef Mysliveček and Wolfgang Mozart

Abstract: The Czech composer Josef Mysliveček never attempted to write a concerto for any solo instrument until he began to cultivate close ties with the musical life of Padua in 1768 at the age of 31. Within 4 years, he produced 10 violin concertos that may be regarded as some of the finest produced anywhere in Europe since the heyday of Giuseppe Tartini. A number of stylistic traits mark Mysliveček as a follower of Tartini, and he likely transmitted some of them into the first violin concerto of W. A. Mozart.

Keywords: Leopold Mozart, Wolfgang Amadeus Mozart, Josef Mysliveček, Padua, Giuseppe Tartini, Vienna, violin concertos

With his adventurous nature and outgoing personality, the Czech composer Josef Mysliveček came into contact with an amazing assortment of musical figures during his long residence in Italy between 1763 and 1781. The most famous, of course, were Wolfgang and Leopold Mozart, with whom he established a close personal relationship during all three of their trips to Italy during the early 1770s.[1] Other connections are much less well known, and some were never even suspected until recently, including those that must have existed with Giuseppe Tartini as a result of Mysliveček's visits to the city of Padua. There is no question that Mysliveček found inspiration in Tartini's legacy as a composer of violin concertos, and there is also good reason to believe that he passed on creative energies to the young Mozart.

1 Josef Mysliveček and Musical Life in Padua, 1768–1774

Josef Mysliveček, one of the musicians most frequently mentioned in the Mozart family correspondence, described himself to Leopold as a "wanderer"

---

1 Connections between Josef Mysliveček and the Mozart family are thoroughly documented in Daniel E. Freeman, *Josef Mysliveček, "Il Boemo"* (Sterling Heights: Harmonie Park Press, 2009), 52–86, 225–255.

("viaggiatore").[2] He was highly unusual among the leading composers of his day for his constant movements and refusal to seek any type of permanent musical employment or permanent base of operations. In his early years in Italy, he spent most of his time in Venice and Florence for the purpose of musical study, opportunities for temporary employment, and opportunities for performances of his music.[3] In later years, he mainly travelled from city to city to supervise opera productions after the success of his *Bellerofonte* (Bellerophon) in Naples in 1767 established him as one of Italy's leading composers of serious opera almost instantaneously. He often returned to Naples but also spent time in Milan, Venice, Florence, and other cities. For six years, between 1768 and 1774, one of the cities he visited most often was Padua, perhaps originally as an extension of his activities in Venice.[4]

Mysliveček's connections with Padua are first confirmed in the summer of 1768, when one of his cantatas was performed at the Accademia dei Ricovrati.[5] He soon began to cultivate connections with the Marchese Giuseppe Ximenes of Aragon (1718–1784), a Florentine who had resided in Padua since 1762 and who began an informal academy that promoted the talents of native composers, such as Giuseppe and Antonio Calegari, and notable foreigners, such as Josef Mysliveček and Johann Gottlieb Naumann.[6] Also present in Padua during this period was the composer Giovanni Battista Ferrandini, a pensioner and agent of the Elector Maximilian III Joseph of Bavaria. Ferrandini identified composers who could be commissioned to compose operas for the carnival season at Munich, among them Tommaso Traetta, Antonio Sacchini, and Pietro Pompeo Sales.[7] Mysliveček himself was chosen for the carnival season of 1776 but was unable to travel north from Florence due to

---

2   Leopold reported Mysliveček's description of himself in a letter written from Salzburg to his son in Augsburg on 15 October 1777. Mysliveček wrote to the Mozarts strictly in Italian; the use of the word "viaggiatore" is found in a partial transcription of a lost letter written to Leopold sometime in October 1777 from Munich, where Mysliveček was convalescing from an operation in which his nose was burned off. Leopold's letter is transcribed in Wilhelm A. Bauer and Otto Erich Deutsch, eds., *Mozart: Briefe und Aufzeichnungen*, vol. 2 (Kassel: Bärenreiter, 1962), 60.
3   See Freeman, *Josef Mysliveček*, 29–47, for information on the composer's earlier activities in Italy between 1763 and 1767.
4   These connections are documented thoroughly in Freeman, *Josef Mysliveček*, 49–68.
5   This is the *Cantata per Sua Eccellenza Marino Cavalli* performed on 30 August 1768 (Cavalli was the leader of the Accademia Delian). The performance is mentioned in Elisa Grossato, "Le accademie musicali a Padova (1766–1790)," in *Mozart, Padova, e la Betulia liberata: Committenza, interpretazione e fortuna delle azioni sacre metastasiane nel '700*, ed. Paolo Pinamonti (Florence: Olschki, 1991), 203. No score or libretto survives.
6   These activities are documented in Paolo Cattelan, "'L'Accademia' nei dintorni del Santo (1768–1785)," in *Storia della musica al Santo di Padova*, ed. Sergio Durante and Pierluigi Petrobelli (Vicenza: Neri Pozza, 1990), 234–237.
7   See Paolo Cattelan, "Giovanni Ferandini, musicista 'padovano'," in *Mozart, Padova, e la Betulia liberata: Committenza, interpretazione e fortuna delle azioni sacre metastasiane nel '700*, ed. Paolo Pinamonti (Florence: Olschki, 1991), 217–244.

illness. He did provide music for the opera *Ezio* (Aetius) at the court of Munich in 1777 and the oratorio *Isacco, figura del redentore* (Isaac, Presager of the Redeemer) for the following Lent.[8] Mysliveček wrote a number of large-scale compositions for Padua, including the opera *Atide* (Atys), first performed in June 1774.[9] He also began his career as a composer of oratorios in Padua. In all, four of his eight oratorios were first performed in Padua during the late 1760s and early 1770s: *Tobia* (Tobias, 1769), *I pellegrini al sepolcro* (The Pilgrims at the Sepulchre, 1770), *Betulia liberata* (The Liberation of Bethulia, 1771), and the mysterious *Giuseppe riconosciuto* (Joseph Revealed, perhaps in the early 1770s). There is little doubt that Mozart knew the setting of *Betulia liberata* at one time (no score survives to the present day, however).

But it is Mysliveček's activity as a composer of violin concertos that is of the greatest interest for this essay. Mysliveček was the author of nine violin concertos that survive in complete form, plus one additional concerto that only survives in fragmentary form.[10] One of these violin concertos is the original version of what is generally known as Mysliveček's cello concerto, a work that has been more widely performed and recorded worldwide than any of his violin concertos.[11] He was also

---

8 These episodes are discussed in Freeman, *Josef Mysliveček*, 67–73.
9 See Freeman, *Josef Mysliveček*, 321–379, for a listing of Mysliveček's vocal works. The opera *Atide* is referred to in a letter of Wolfgang Mozart written to his father from Munich on 11 October 1777, when Mozart visited Mysliveček in the Ducal Hospital in Munich, where he sought treatment for a disease believed to be syphilis. Mozart mentioned that Mysliveček had been sick for years, and "when his illness was at its worst, he composed an opera for Padua" ("wie seine Krankheit am stärckstn war, machte er eine opera nach Padua"). This letter is discussed in Freeman, *Josef Mysliveček*, 75–79. The complete letter is transcribed in Bauer and Deutsch, *Mozart: Briefe und Aufzeichnungen*, vol. 2, 43–46.
10 An enumeration of all of Mysliveček's concertos (including complete source information) is found in Freeman, *Josef Mysliveček*, 297–301. Most of them are also listed in Angela Evans and Robert Dearling, *Josef Mysliveček (1737–1781): A Thematic Catalogue of his Instrumental and Orchestral Works* (Munich: Katzbichler, 1999), 114–126.
11 The cello concerto is listed in Evans and Dearling, *Josef Mysliveček*, 123, and Freeman *Josef Mysliveček*, 299–300. Evans and Dearling had no knowledge of the violin concerto that is undoubtedly the original version of the cello concerto, cited in Freeman, *Josef Mysliveček*, 298. There is a very good possibility that the cello version was prepared for the benefit of the renowned cellist Antonio Vandini, a close associate of Tartini who was still living in Padua at the time of Mysliveček's period of intense activity. The suitability of the cello concerto for Vandini's manner of playing is hinted at in a remark about his playing that appears in Charles Burney, *The Present State of Music in France and Italy* (London: Becket, 1773), 142. Burney noted that "the Italians say [he] plays and expresses *a parlare*, that is, in such a manner as to make his instrument speak". The melodies of the slow movement of the cello do indeed "speak" in a way that would be compatible with this description. I am grateful to Marc Vanscheeuwijck for bringing Burney's remark to my attention.

the author of two keyboard concertos and a flute concerto that has found tireless advocacy in recent years from the flautist Ana de la Vega.[12]

The quality of the violin concertos is high, indisputably some of the best violin concertos written between the great works of Vivaldi, Locatelli, and Tartini in the decades before 1750 and the appearance of Mozart's four great violin concertos of 1775. Three of Mysliveček's violin concertos were likely written in the late 1760s or just about the year 1770,[13] whereas the remaining six are preserved in a manuscript in Vienna that was likely left over from a trip that Mysliveček made to that city in 1772.[14] Presumably, the latter were used as vehicles for his own activities as a virtuoso violinist. Some or all of them might date from a slightly earlier time, but their lack of any movements in rondo form is a likely indication that they were not written in the second half of the 1770s, even if their preservation in a manuscript in Vienna has nothing to do with Mysliveček's visit in 1772.[15] Mozart's report of his acquaintance with at least one Mysliveček violin concerto in a letter from Vienna in September 1773 would tend to corroborate the suspicion that the six concertos still preserved in Vienna were brought to the city in 1772 and that one of them was the concerto that Mozart reported seeing.[16]

---

12 The sources of these concertos are detailed in Evans and Dearling, *Josef Mysliveček*, 124–126, and Freeman, *Josef Mysliveček*, 300. The keyboard concertos have recently found an advocate in the pianist Clare Hammond that is analogous to the advocacy of Ana de la Vega for the flute concerto.
13 For the *Concerto* in D major listed as *Violin Concerto 1* in Freeman, *Josef Mysliveček*, 297, a *terminus ante quem* is set up by its appearance in the 1769 catalogue of works offered for sale by the Breitkopf music publishing house in Leipzig. See Barry S. Brook, ed., *The Breitkopf Thematic Catalogue: The Six Parts and Sixteen Supplements, 1762–1787* (New York: Dover, 1966). The *Concerto* in C major listed as *Violin Concerto 2* in Freeman, *Josef Mysliveček*, 298 (the original version of what is usually heard today as the cello concerto), appears in the Breitkopf catalogue of 1770. The *Concerto* in C major listed as *Violin Concerto 3* in Freeman, *Josef Mysliveček*, 298, is dated conjecturally ca. 1768–1770 based on its stylistic compatibility with *Violin Concertos 1* and *2*.
14 The concertos in question are listed as *Violin Concertos 4–9* in Freeman, *Josef Mysliveček*, 298 (in the keys of E major, A major, F major, B-flat major, D major, and G major, respectively). They are preserved in manuscript IX 16992 (Q 16467) of the library of the Gesellschaft der Musikfreunde in Vienna. Mysliveček's presence in Vienna in September 1772 is confirmed in Charles Burney, *The Present State of Music in Germany, the Netherlands, and United Provinces*, vol. 1 (London: Becket, 1773), 364–365. Burney reported nothing more about Mysliveček than he had just returned from Italy, where he had made a great name for himself as a composer of operas and instrumental music.
15 Among the Mysliveček concertos, it is only the *Keyboard Concerto 1* in B-flat major from the late 1770s that contains a movement labeled a rondo.
16 The letter in question, dated 8 September 1773, was prepared mainly by Leopold Mozart, but includes a postscript written by Wolfgang to his mother that states he was writing on top of the bass part of a Mysliveček violin concerto. Since no musical

It is a striking coincidence that all of the Mysliveček violin concertos were apparently written just in the few years between 1768 and 1774 when he maintained close connections with the city of Padua. The importance of this coincidence becomes all the more notable when one considers how long it took for Mysliveček to begin his cultivation of the genre of violin concerto. It is known that he had been playing violin since his upbringing in Prague[17] and taught violin playing in Italy long before his close association with the city of Padua began in 1768,[18] yet he never wrote any concertos for violin until the late 1760s, when he was in his early 30s, as far as can be determined. The obvious explanation for this sudden interest in violin concertos is contact, either direct or indirect, with Giuseppe Tartini, the great violinist who still lived in Padua in the late 1760s.

There is no firm confirmation of any direct personal encounters between Mysliveček and Tartini, but it would have been very uncharacteristic of Mysliveček not to seek him out. Mysliveček possessed a charismatic personality that is vividly documented in the Mozart correspondence and other contemporary records, although he often comes off as a charming scoundrel. The young Wolfgang referred to him as an "excellent fellow", "full of fire, spirit, and life",[19] before he thoroughly betrayed the trust of the Mozart family.[20] It would not be any exaggeration to

---

incipit is recorded and the key is not specified, there is no way to match it precisely with any of the surviving violin concertos attributed to Mysliveček. The letter is transcribed in Bauer and Deutsch, *Mozart: Briefe und Aufzeichnungen*, vol. 1, 497. A facsimile of the postscript is reproduced in Freeman, *Josef Mysliveček*, 62.

17 This is confirmed in the earliest biography of Mysliveček, a short sketch prepared shortly after his death by the Prague literatus František Martin Pelcl in the collection *Abbildungen bömischer und mährischer Gelehrten und Künstler*, vol. 4 (Prague: Gerle, 1782), 189–192. Pelcl specifically indicated that as a youth, Mysliveček "played the violin with great skill" ("spielte die Violine mit grosser Geschicklichkeit").

18 During his early years of this residence in Italy in the mid-1760s, Mysliveček is known to have earned income from the Bohemian nobleman Count Vincenz von Waldstein by tutoring one of the musicians in his household in violin playing. This activity is described in Freeman, *Josef Mysliveček*, 31–34.

19 The oft-quoted phrase "full of fire, spirit, and life" ("voll Feuer, Geist, und Leben") to evoke Mysliveček's personality is found in a letter of Wolfgang Mozart to his father written from Munich on 11 October 1777, as mentioned in footnote 9. After his pithy summation of Mysliveček's personality, Mozart continued by saying that he was "a little thin, of course, but otherwise the same good and excellent fellow" ("ein wenig mager, natürlich, aber sonst der nämliche gute und aufgeweckte Mensch").

20 The specific discreditable incident that let to Mysliveček's break with the Mozart family was a broken promise to arrange Wolfgang an operatic commission for the 1779 season at the Teatro San Carlo in Naples. Mysliveček claimed that he had enough influence with the management of the San Carlo that the commission could be counted on absolutely. The first hint that such a commission would be forthcoming is found in a letter of Leopold to Wolfgang dated 1 October 1777 (transcribed in Bauer and Deutsch, *Mozart: Briefe und Aufzeichnungen*, vol. 2, 25–26). By the spring of 1778, it was clear that he actually had no ability to arrange such a

describe his personality as "magnetic" for the Mozart family. Even the elusive Maria Anna Mozart, Wolfgang's mother, fell under his spell immediately on first meeting.[21] Mysliveček constantly sought out new professional acquaintances and fresh sources of music patronage. Of many prominent musical figures in Italy that he was close to, perhaps the most important one for his career was Padre Martini,[22] but he cultivated contacts with a dizzying array of musicians, theatrical personnel, and patrons, indeed far too many to list quickly. In 1780–1781, near the end of his life, when he was living in Rome in a state of destitution, constantly in pain and hideously disfigured from an operation he endured in Munich in 1777 that resulted in his nose being burned off, he was still able to secure patronage from a papal nephew, Prince Abbondio Rezzonico, and secure financial assistance from the wealthy English dilettante musician James Hugh Smith Barry.[23] On the basis of the intense musical study required to secure Mysliveček's admission to the Accademia Filarmonica of Bologna in 1771,[24] it would be reasonable to assume that he would have had intimate acquaintance with Tartini's writings on music, probably even before he began his close association with the city of Padua. For a composer, Mysliveček was highly educated. He could boast an excellent primary and secondary education, some university study, and completion of the rigorous technical training necessary for him to attain the rank of a master miller in Prague in 1761.[25]

Mutual connections with the city of Prague and the Bohemian nobility would have provided very interesting topics of conversation between the two composers.

---

commission and had simply used the hope of it as a means to manipulate Leopold Mozart into arranging musical patronage for Mysliveček from the archbishop of Salzburg (see Freeman, *Josef Mysliveček*, 73–86). Leopold was quite successful in arranging payments for Mysliveček's music from the archbishop but found himself bamboozled by Mysliveček in the end.

21 This is clear from the postscript she attached to Mozart's letter to Leopold of 11 October 1777 cited in footnote 9. In fact, she said that she "talked to him as if I have known him all my life" ("ich habe mit ihme geredet als wan ich ihme mein Lebtag gekant hette").

22 Mysliveček first met Giovanni Battista Martini in Bologna in 1770 at about the same time when he first met Wolfgang and Leopold Mozart (see Freeman, *Josef Myslivecek*, 51–53). Martini was soon instrumental in making it possible for Mysliveček to be admitted to the Accademia Filarmonica of Bologna. Their relationship endured at least until the late 1770s.

23 For these connections, see Freeman, *Josef Mysliveček*, 92–98.

24 Mysliveček applied for admission to the Accademia Filarmonica on 15 May 1771, and his application was accepted after the submission of his motet *Veni sponsa Christi*, the only conservative *alla breve* liturgical composition that he is known to have written. The particulars of his admission are discussed in Freeman, *Josef Mysliveček*, 56–57. The composer ever after proudly attached the title *accademico filarmonico* to his name at every appropriate opportunity.

25 Mysliveček's educational background is detailed in Freeman, *Josef Mysliveček*, 19–22.

Mysliveček of course grew up in Prague, whereas Tartini lived there between 1723 and 1726 in the service of Count Philipp Joseph Kinský (1700–1749), one of the most notable members of his family.[26] Another strong Bohemian connection that Tartini had cultivated earlier in his life was the émigré Bohuslav Matěj Černohorský (1684–1742), with whom he was on close terms for decades between the 1710s and 1730s.[27]

In an age when relations between composers were more collegial than they often are today, it would have been astonishing if Mysliveček had never tried to meet Tartini while visiting Padua in the late 1760s. Detailed information about Tartini's infirmities and mental state before his death in 1770 is not available. It is known that his last public performance as a musician took place in 1765.[28] As for his ability to receive visitors, the fact that Antonio Vandini lived with Tartini in his house in Padua in the late 1760s provides good reason to believe that he would have been able to welcome visitors to his home, even if Vandini would have needed to make special arrangements or exercise special precautions.[29] Vandini and Tartini had travelled to Prague together in the 1720s; thus, he also would have had much to share about experiences in the city with Mysliveček. Whether or not Mysliveček ever made Tartini's personal acquaintance, Tartini's legacy as a composer, pedagogue, and music theorist in the city of Padua would have been impossible to escape. Simply the availability of Tartini's music in Padua and the presence of a large number of his students and colleagues would have been almost as significant as direct personal contact for the purpose of absorbing stylistic influences.

2 The Violin Concertos of Giuseppe Tartini as Stylistic Models for the Violin Concertos of Josef Mysliveček

It would be a noteworthy finding simply to conclude that Mysliveček started composing violin concertos in the late 1760s due to an exposure to the musical life of Tartini's Padua. More significant still would be the ability to assert that Mysliveček's violin concertos exhibit a degree of stylistic influence from Tartini, even though most of Tartini's concerto were written decades before Mysliveček began his association with the city of Padua. Indeed, the evidence is rather strong

---

26 Documents that describe the association of Giuseppe Tartini and Antonio Vandini with Count Kinský are transcribed and discussed in Pierluigi Petrobelli, *Giuseppe Tartini: le fonti biografici* (Venice: Universal Edition, 1968), 26–27, 62, 66–67, and 149. A useful biographical sketch of Count Philipp Joseph Kinský is found in Konstant von Wurzbach, *Biographisches Lexikon des Kaiserthums Oesterreich*, vol. 11 (Vienna: Hof- und Staatsdruckerei, 1864), 300–301 (with no mention of his association with Giuseppe Tartini).
27 These connections are documented thoroughly in Petrobelli, *Giuseppe Tartini*.
28 See Petrobelli, *Giuseppe Tartini*, 13 and 76.
29 Documentation confirming Vandini's presence in Tartini's house from April 1769 is presented in Petrobelli, *Giuseppe Tartini*, 67 and 152.

that Mysliveček did adopt certain stylistic characteristics of Tartini's violin concertos in his own writing.

The first scholar to draw attention to Mysliveček's possible affinity for Tartini's violin concertos was the American Chappell White in an edition of Mysliveček concertos published in 1994.[30] His remarks seem all the more remarkable now, because they were made at a time when accurate biographical information about Mysliveček was still very scarce in any language other than Czech. White had no apparent idea that Mysliveček had any association with the city of Padua or that he easily could have come into close personal contact with Tartini and his associates. The trait that White drew attention to specifically was the use of notated repeat signs in one of the Mysliveček movements cast in ritornello form.[31] Amalgamations of binary form and ritornello form that actually include notated repeat signs were of course one of the great hallmarks of Tartini's concertos, but they were no longer common in concertos written about the year 1770.[32]

Certain characteristics of Mysliveček's slow movements also point to reliance on models from Tartini. For example, two of the three concertos believed to be the earliest of Mysliveček's concertos conform to a format very typical of Tartini: quite short and cast in binary form without ritornellos.[33] Tartini often included repeat signs to set off the binary segments. Mysliveček did not use repeat signs in his slow movements, but the binary structures nonetheless are very well articulated. These same two slow movements feature the soloist accompanied only with two violin parts, another telltale sign of Tartini's influence (see Examples 1 and 2). The accompaniment of a soloist by two violin parts was also a notable trait of many passages in Tartini's fast movements (as illustrated in Example 3). Slow movements accompanied

---

30 See *Josef Mysliveček: Three Violin Concertos*, ed. Chappell White (Madison, Wis.: A-R Editions, 1994). The three violin concertos edited are *Concertos* 1 (D major), 7 (B-flat major), and 8 (D major) of the catalogue of instrumental music by Mysliveček in Freeman, *Josef Mysliveček*, 297–299. Mysliveček's violin concertos are highly praised in Chappell White, *From Vivaldi to Viotti: A History of the Early Classical Violin Concerto* (Philadelphia: Gordon and Breach, 1992), 182–187, but without any reference made to possible influences from Tartini.
31 The movement in question is the third movement of *Concerto* 8 (D major) in the catalogue of instrumental music found in Freeman, *Josef Mysliveček*, 298. White knew it as the fifth concerto of six in the above-mentioned manuscript in the Gesellschaft der Musikfreunde in Vienna (see Footnote 14).
32 A theoretical discussion of the implications of the use of binary-form repeat signs within ritornello structures is discussed in Daniel E. Freeman, "The Earliest Italian Keyboard *Concertos*," *The Journal of Musicology* 4 (1985–1986): 121–145.
33 These would be the slow movements for *Concertos* 1 (D major) and 3 (C major) in the catalogue in Freeman, *Josef Mysliveček*, 297–298. Discussion about the style of Tartini's violin concertos with extensive bibliography can be found in White, *From Vivaldi to Viotti*, 101–110 (with further information about his followers, 111–150), and Simon McVeigh and Jehoash Hirshberg, *The Italian Solo Concerto, 1700–1760: Rhetorical Strategies and Style History* (Woodbridge: The Boydell Press, 2004), 284–299.

only by two violin parts are an astonishing stylistic trait for a northern composer working in the period ca. 1770. These same slow movements were also a natural venue for the cultivation of the intricately ornamented melodic lines so typical of Tartini's work, which Mysliveček imitates. In slow movements of this type, only a basic melody line with minimal ornamentation would be written out with the expectation that elaborate ornamentation would be added spontaneously by a performer.

Example 1: Giuseppe Tartini, *Violin Concerto* in B-flat major, D. 78, second movement, mm.1–10.

Example 2: Josef Mysliveček, *Violin Concerto* No. 1 in D major, second movement, mm. 1–11.

[Musical notation: Violin Solo, Violin I, Violin II parts]

Example 3: Giuseppe Tartini, *Violin Concerto* in B-flat major, D. 123, third movement, mm. 66–69.

A striking feature in Mysliveček's violin concertos is the effect of unexpected repetitions of motives first heard in major key that are presented a second time in the parallel minor key. This is another trait that finds precedent in the work of Tartini (see Examples 3 and 4). Nonetheless, it is not entirely certain that Tartini's example alone would be responsible for the presence of this device in Mysliveček's work. The works of others might also be responsible, or even simply the composer's whim.

[Musical notation: Violin I part]

Example 4: Josef Mysliveček, *Violin Concerto* No. 4 in E major, first movement, mm. 53–64, Solo Violin part only.

The principal key for each of the Mysliveček violin concertos is a major key, but one of them has a slow movement in minor key (*Violin Concerto 8*). This would be another rare procedure for a northern composer of Mysliveček's day, but there is ample precedent in Tartini's work to include slow movement in minor key between two fast movements in major key. Mysliveček's minor-key movements, found in the Vienna collection of concertos,[34] has an Italianate sound that is often quite archaic in character, in fact so much that Mysliveček seems to have found inspiration from Tartini's earliest concertos, or perhaps from Vivaldi's concertos, even though there are many passages in the movement that exhibit more modern

---

34 This would be the slow movement in D minor of the *Violin Concerto 8* in D major, no. 5 in the collection of six violin concertos by Mysliveček preserved in the above-mentioned manuscript IX 16992 (Q 16467) of the library of the Gesellschaft der Musikfreunde in Vienna.

musical motives. It is very difficult to think of a reason why Mysliveček would have employed gestures as archaic as those seen in Example 5 (which includes a stereotypical old-fashioned cadence with unison octaves at mm. 25–27) unless he was under the influence of a musical figure who had notable connections to the past. Obviously, Giuseppe Tartini in Padua was a musical figure of this type.

Example 5: Josef Mysliveček, *Violin Concerto* No. 8 in D major, second movement, mm. 1–32.

As regards formal structures, the Mysliveček violin concertos were conservative, perhaps also due to the legacy of Tartini.[35] For the fast movements, Mysliveček retained structures built around four ritornellos and three solo sections, a normal pattern of Tartini's generation, instead of dropping the traditional third ritornello as some younger composers chose to do. Even though Mysliveček employed an unusually systematic and modern approach to sonata form in the fast movements of his symphonies and overtures by the year 1770,[36] the use of sonata-form elements was not nearly so consistent in his concertos. In his third movements, for example, there is generally no attempt to organize the themes of the opening ritornellos along the lines of the sonata-form exposition, a procedure that was becoming more and more common among the younger composers active about the year 1770.[37]

In other ways, Mysliveček adopted more modern procedures. Instead of the string orchestra favoured by Tartini and other Italians before 1750, Mysliveček was in the habit of using an expanded orchestra typical of the 1760s for the orchestral accompaniment in his fast movements. Usually that would involve the addition of horns and oboes.[38] An ensemble of strings, horn, and oboes was in fact the basic orchestral ensemble for Italian symphonies and opera arias at the time that Mysliveček was writing his violin concertos. The accompaniments of Mysliveček's concertos in general have much the character of contemporary symphonic style, at least in the fast movements. An excellent evocation of contemporary symphonic style can be seen in the opening of his *Violin Concerto 8* (see Example 6), whereas *Violin Concerto 1* opens with another type of replacement for the "figural" thematic types that open so many of Tartini's concertos: a syncopated pattern that was common in Italian vocal music of this era (see Example 7).[39]

---

35 The formal traits of Mysliveček's violin concertos are discussed in White, *From Vivaldi to Viotti*, 182–187, and Freeman, *Josef Mysliveček*, 202–209.
36 Formal procedures in Mysliveček's symphonies and opera overtures up to ca. 1770 are described in Freeman, *Josef Mysliveček*, 185–198.
37 For a discussion of contemporary formal practices in violin concertos, see White, *From Vivaldi to Viotti*, 67–98.
38 *Concertos 2–8* all make use of accompanimental ensembles that include horns and oboes. *Concerto 3* also survives in a version with trumpet, whereas *Concerto 9* includes horns, but no oboes. *Concerto 1* is for strings only. The makeup of the instrumental ensemble for the fragmentary *Concerto 10* is unknown.
39 The use of syncopated patterns of this type in Italian music of the early classic period is described in Freeman, *Josef Mysliveček*, 109–111.

[musical notation]

Example 6: Josef Mysliveček, *Violin Concerto* No. 8 in D major, first movement, mm. 1–17, Violin I part only.

[musical notation]

Example 7: Josef Mysliveček, *Violin Concerto* No. 1 in D major, first movement, mm. 1–8.

3 The Violin Concertos of Josef Mysliveček as Stylistic Models for the Violin Concertos of Wolfgang Mozart

It is easy to make the case that Mysliveček passed on the inspiration for initiating activity as a composer of violin concertos to the young Mozart. Before the 1980s, it was believed that all five of the Mozart violin concertos were written in the year 1775, but newer research indicates that the first one, the little-known *Concerto* in B-flat major, K. 207, was actually written in 1773. In his study of Mozart's autograph scores, Alan Tyson concluded that "K. 207 is probably from April 1773".[40] Tyson claimed that the difference in date "should matter a great deal", but never supported this observation with bold new interpretations of its stylistic origins. On the broadest level, the use of ritornello form in both of its fast movements

---

40 See Alan Tyson, *Mozart: Studies of the Autograph Scores* (Cambridge: Harvard University Press, 1987), 25.

would make much more sense for a work written in 1773 than for works written in 1775. The four Mozart violin concertos written in 1775 all conclude with rondos, consistent with trends in concerto composition all over Europe of the mid-1770s. The lack of a rondo in K. 207 is more compatible with concerto writing of the early 1770s and stylistic traditions inherited from Italian composers such as Vivaldi and Tartini. It must also be pointed out that the overall mastery of compositional technique is noticeably less advanced in K. 207 than the works written when Mozart was two years older. It very much has the character of a "first" concerto when compared to the other four.

Tyson made vague attempts to suggest central European influences that might have been at work in Mozart's first violin concerto during the year 1773, but he did not recognize the importance of Italian influences left over from Mozart's last trip to Italy (from which he returned to Salzburg in March of 1773). Considering the manner in which Mysliveček's connections with the Mozart family were almost universally ignored in Mozart research of the 1980s, it is not surprising that Tyson failed to note that K. 207 would have been produced just after Mozart came into contact with Mysliveček for the third and last time in Italy. Mysliveček was the only notable musical figure that the Mozarts encountered during all three of their trips to Italy between 1770 and 1773. The last letter in the Mozart correspondence that confirms contact with Mysliveček in Italy is dated 23 January 1773.[41] In 1773, at the time when Mozart started writing concertos, Mysliveček was certainly the most talented composer of violin concertos with whom Mozart had been in regular contact during the preceding several years.

The idea of Mysliveček being a source of inspiration for Mozart's first violin concerto was not considered by any Mozart scholar before the present century, even though Marc Pincherle claimed in the 1920s that the opening of the *Concerto in D major*, K. 218 (Mozart's *Violin Concerto No. 4*), was clearly based on the opening of a *Concerto* by Mysliveček also in D major (see Examples 6 and 8).[42] Speculation that Mozart's *Concertone* in C major for two violins, K. 190 of 1774, might owe some of its stylistic traits to models in the music of Mysliveček was also proposed already in the twentieth century.[43] But in general, no attention to

---

41 See Bauer and Deutsch, *Mozart: Briefe und Auzeichnungen*, vol. 1, 477.
42 See Marc Pincherle, "Un oublié: il divino Boemo," in *Feuillets d'histoire du violon* (Paris: Leguoix, 1927), 108. There were no catalogues of Mysliveček's works in Pincherle's time. The D-major *Concerto* with which Pincherle was acquainted was *Concerto 8* (the fifth concerto of the above-mentioned Vienna manuscript of Mysliveček concertos; see footnote 14) as listed in Freeman, *Josef Mysliveček*, 298. Neither Tyson nor anyone else recognized Italianate characteristics in K. 207 until the publication of the present author's *Josef Mysliveček* in 2009. A sense of this can be gleaned readily from the summation of research into Mozart's violin concertos presented in *The Cambridge Mozart Encyclopedia*, ed. Cliff Eisen and Simon P. Keefe (Cambridge: Cambridge University Press, 2006), 108–109.
43 Robert Levin has suggested that Mozart may have used Mysliveček as a model for the preparation of his *Concertone*, K. 190, in his entry for the piece in H. C.

Mysliveček's connections to the young Mozart was paid in almost any Mozart scholarship produced in the twentieth century after World War II, except in the former Czechoslovakia. Mysliveček's importance as a friend and stylistic model for the young Mozart was never disputed; rather, the inclination was simply not to mention him.[44] As amazing as it seems, the existence of a letter of September 1773 written to Mozart's mother from Vienna that specifically confirms Mozart's possession of one of Mysliveček's violin concertos never made any impression on anyone who made a study of the Mozart violin concertos.[45]

Example 8: Wolfgang Amadeus Mozart, *Violin Concerto* No. 4 in D major, K. 218, first movement, mm. 1–12, Violin I part only.

It is possible to interpret important features of Mozart's Italianate first *Violin concerto* as imitations of Mysliveček. The opening theme, for example, conforms to a type of Italianate syncopated motive that was very common in Mysliveček's

---

Robbins Landon, ed. *The Mozart Compendium: A Guide to Mozart's Life and Music* (London: Thames and Hudson, 1990). I am grateful to Yehuda Romem for bringing this entry to my attention. Specifically, the *Concertone*, K. 190, opens with a loud-soft alternation of motives and a figure that is very common in Italian instrumental music of the time, marked by an upward or downward succession of thirty-second notes and a dotted eighth note. See Freeman, *Josef Mysliveček*, 242–243, for more about the significance of this figure.

44 The British scholar Stanley Sadie was a key musicologist who systematically suppressed all mention of Mysliveček in his writings. Thus, the biographical entry for Mozart that he prepared for the *New Grove Dictionary of Music and Musicians* (London: Macmillan, 1980), famed as the longest biographical entry in the entire dictionary, nowhere mentions his name in the main text, even though Mysliveček is one of the composers most frequently mentioned in the Mozart correspondence and the importance of his relationship with the Mozart family between 1770 and 1778 cannot be disputed. The Mozart entry in the revised *New Grove Dictionary of Music and Musicians* (London: Macmillan, 2001) also contains no mention of Mysliveček. Even more astonishing is the suppression of Mysliveček's name in Stanley Sadie, *Mozart: The Early Years, 1756–1781* (New York: W. W. Norton, 2006).

45 See footnote 16.

work, both in vocal and instrumental style, including the opening of one of his violin concertos (see Examples 7, 9, and 10).[46]

Example 9: Wolfgang Amadeus Mozart, *Violin Concerto* No. 1 in B-flat major, K. 207, first movement, mm. 1–12 (oboes, horns omitted).

Example 10: Josef Mysliveček, aria *Scherza il nocchier talora* from Act II, scene 10, of *Motezuma* (Florence, 1771), mm. 1–15, Violin I part only.

---

46 The use of motives of this type in Mysliveček's music and their prevalence in Italian music of the eighteenth century is discussed in Freeman, *Josef Mysliveček*, 109–111.

The same type of syncopated motive is also shared with the *Concerto for Bassoon*, K. 191 of 1774 (see Example 11), and the *Concerto for Oboe*, K. 314 of 1777 (see Example 12). This type of syncopation is not found prominently in any of the keyboard concertos written by Mozart in the 1770s. Clearly, it is because central European composers would not usually turn to Italian models for the composition of keyboard concertos at this time. For violin concertos, the great prestige of Italian style was still in place.

Example 11: Wolfgang Amadeus Mozart, *Bassoon Concerto* in B-flat major, K. 191, first movement, mm. 1–6, Violin I part only.

Example 12: Wolfgang Amadeus Mozart, *Oboe Concerto* in C major, K. 314, first movement, mm. 1–7, Violin I part only.

The treatment of ritornello form in Mozart's first concerto conforms remarkably well to Mysliveček's trademark procedures, which are surprisingly consistent among his fast movements. Mysliveček's basic plan, used over and over again as an amalgamation of ritornello form and sonata form, can be diagrammed as follows:

	Rit.	Solo	Rit.	Solo	Rit.	Solo	Rit.
		(=exposition)		(=development)		(=recapitulation)	
Keys:	I	I-V	V	V-vi	vi-I	I	I

Diagram 1: Typical formal plan of the fast movements of Mysliveček's violin concertos.

This type of structure represents a significant departure from the ideal of modulatory solo sections and tonally stable ritornellos as cultivated by composers such as Vivaldi, Locatelli, and Tartini. Many procedures that employ some modulatory ritornellos and tonally stable solo sections can be found in the works of composers active after ca. 1750. In Mysliveček's time, procedures varied widely throughout Europe, thus his consistency is quite notable.[47]

The most telling features that relate the *Concerto* K. 207 specifically to Mysliveček's formal models are the characteristics of the interior portion of the diagram above. For example, the second ritornello might include a modulation, but Mysliveček's second ritornellos usually do not, and the second solo might end on a variety of closely related keys to the tonic major (or even the tonic key itself), instead of consistently ending on the submediant minor. The third ritornello of this diagram might be missing entirely in the sonata form amalgamations of concertos by other composers that leaves a structure of only three ritornellos and two solos in which the second solo combines the functions of the development and recapitulation of sonata form. When a third ritornello is present, it can be very short (which Mysliveček's are not), and the tonic key may already be established at the start of it, instead of at the end with a modulatory passage to dramatize the return of the tonic key.

The third movement of K. 207 conforms to the Myslivečkian model very closely,[48] whereas the first movement exhibits a few minor variations.[49] The third movement frequently sounds like an imitation of Mysliveček, and one cannot help note the prominence of accompaniment of the soloist only by the first and second violins of the orchestra, seemingly in imitation of the Italian tradition of accompaniment by two violins so common in the music of Tartini. This texture is also found in the first movement but is not nearly as prominent.

Significant influence from Mysliveček on Mozart's violin concertos did not endure, however. It might be possible to identify a few isolated cases of motivic borrowings from Mysliveček in Mozart's later violin concertos (e.g. the one noticed by Marc Pincherle in K. 218), and perhaps a certain feel for timing and pacing

---

47 See Freeman, *Josef Mysliveček*, 202–209, for a fuller discussion of Mysliveček's remarkably consistent formal procedures among his violin concertos and how they compare with the broader formal norms in concerto style of his day.
48 The most important musical events to make note of in the third movement thus would be the firm cadences in the dominant key at the end of the second ritornello (at mm. 163 and 171); the modulation to the submediant minor in the second solo (beginning at m. 176); the cadence in the solo part at the end of the second solo (at m. 201); the modulation to the tonic key in the third ritornello (beginning at m. 210); the conclusion of the third ritornello in the tonic key at m. 224; and the stability of the tonic key throughout the third solo.
49 In the first movement, there is a full cadence in the dominant key to signal the end of the second ritornello at m. 73, but it is extended in a way that introduces the tonal instability of the second solo (which begins at m. 75). The second solo modulates firmly to the submediant minor by m. 92 and concludes with a firm cadence in that key for the solo part at m. 99. The third ritornello returns quickly to the tonic key (ending at m. 107), and the third solo preserves tonal stability in the tonic key throughout.

of virtuosic figuration and soloistic entrances, but otherwise Mozart's abilities completely transcended Mysliveček's. The extraordinary rondo finales of Mozart's concertos of 1775 represent the most significant advance over Mysliveček's creations, but there are many other aspects of individuality and innovation to be marvelled at in the concertos of 1775. This reflects a common pattern in Mozart's musical relationship with Mysliveček. His older friend was capable of providing important models to get started in certain genres, but Mozart's genius soon surpassed the inspiration of his older friend. The same phenomenon is noticeable with operatic arias, symphonies, and opera overtures.[50]

4 Conclusion

It can be asserted with some confidence that Giuseppe Tartini, just before his death, was the source of a creative impulse that led to the composition of masterpieces in the genre of violin concerto by at least two major composers who were cultivating the genre for the first time in their lives: Josef Mysliveček and Wolfgang Amadeus Mozart. In Mysliveček's case, the inspiration is likely to have originated from direct or indirect personal contacts in the city of Padua. In Mozart's case, there certainly were no personal connections, rather an inspiration to treat the genre of violin concerto that probably came to him indirectly, courtesy of Mysliveček, who had only recently begun to write violin concertos under the partial influence of Tartini. There can be no doubt that Mysliveček would have talked about Tartini to Leopold and Wolfgang Mozart during their trips to Italy, which for Leopold would have been an opportunity to amplify his earlier knowledge about Tartini. Leopold was, of course, well acquainted with Tartini's writings and musical works long before he arrived in Italy,[51] and he was closer to Mysliveček in terms of personal rapport than Wolfgang was. Whereas Wolfgang was still a child at the time of all of his trips to Italy, Leopold and Mysliveček were both mature men who much enjoyed each other's company immensely.[52] Ironically, recent research into the life and works of Josef Mysliveček reveals that Giuseppe Tartini's musical and intellectual reach was broader than ever before suspected.

---

50 Examples of similar phenomena are discussed in Freeman, *Josef Mysliveček*, 225–255.
51 Leopold Mozart's treatise *Versuch einer gründlicher Violinschule* (Augsburg: Lotter, 1756) was based partly on his acquaintance with Tartini's writings.
52 Leopold's closeness to Mysliveček is confirmed in a letter of October 1770 written to his wife from Milan that records frequent visits from Mysliveček while Leopold and Wolfgang were in Bologna earlier that year. Leopold told his wife that Mysliveček was "an honest man" ("ein Ehrenmann") and that they had become intimate friends ("wir haben vollkomme Freundschaft mit einander gemacht"). At the time of Mysliveček's visit to Wolfgang in Munich, all initial contacts were made through Leopold. See Freeman, *Josef Mysliveček*, 69–86.

Bibliography

Bauer, Wilhelm A., and Otto Erich Deutsch, eds. *Mozart: Briefe und Aufzeichnungen*. 7 vols. Kassel: Bärenreiter, 1962–1975.

Brook, Barry S., ed. *The Breitkopf Thematic Catalogue: The Six Parts and Sixteen Supplements, 1762–1787*. New York: Dover, 1966.

Burney, Charles. *The Present State of Music in France and Italy*. London: Becket, 1773.

Burney, Charles. *The Present State of Music in Germany, the Netherlands, and United Provinces*. 2 vols. London: n.p., 1773.

Durante, Sergio, and Pierluigi Petrobelli, eds. *Storia della musica al Santo di Padova*. Vicenza: Neri Pozza, 1990.

Eisen, Cliff, and Simon P. Keefe, eds. *The Cambridge Mozart Encyclopedia*. Cambridge: Cambridge University Press, 2006.

Evans, Angela, and Robert Dearling. *Josef Mysliveček (1737–1781): A Thematic Catalogue of his Instrumental and Orchestral Works*. Munich: Katzbichler, 1999.

Freeman, Daniel E. "The Earliest Italian Keyboard Concertos." *The Journal of Musicology* 4 (1985–1986): 121–145.

Freeman, Daniel E. *Josef Mysliveček, "Il Boemo."* Sterling Heights: Harmonie Park Press, 2009.

Landon, H. C. Robbins, ed. *The Mozart Compendium: A Guide to Mozart's Life and Music*. London: Thames and Hudson, 1990.

McVeigh, Simon, and Jehoash Hirshberg. *The Italian Solo Concerto, 1700–1760: Rhetorical Strategies and Style History*. Woodbridge: The Boydell Press, 2004.

Mozart, Leopold. *Versuch einer gründlicher Violinschule*. Augsburg: Lotter, 1756.

Pelcl, František Martin. "Joseph Misliweczek: ein Tonkünstler." In *Abbildungen böhmischer und mährischer Gelehrten und Künstler: Vierter Theil*, edited by František Martin Pelcl, et al., 189–192. Prague: Gerle, 1782.

Petrobelli, Pierluigi. *Giuseppe Tartini: le fonti biografici*. Venice: Universal Edition, 1968.

Pinamonti, Paolo, ed. *Mozart, Padova, e la Betulia liberata: committenza, interpretazione e fortuna delle azioni sacre metastasiane del '700*. Florence: Olschki, 1991.

Pincherle, Marc. *Feuillets d'histoire du violin*. Paris: Leguoix, 1927.

Sadie, Stanley. *Mozart: The Early Years, 1756–1781*. New York: W.W. Norton, 2006.

Sadie, Stanley. "Mozart, Wolfgang Amadeus." In *The New Grove Dictionary of Music and Musicians*, edited by Stanley Sadie, vol. 12: 680–752. London: Macmillan, 1980.

Sadie, Stanley, et al. "Mozart, Wolfgang Amadeus." In *The New Grove Dictionary of Music and Musicians*, edited by Stanley Sadie and John Tyrell, vol. 17: 276–347. London: Macmillan, 2001.

Tyson, Alan. *Mozart: Studies of the Autograph Scores*. Cambridge: Harvard University Press, 1987.

White, Chappell. *From Vivaldi to Viotti: A History of the Early Classical Violin Concerto*. Philadelphia: Gordon and Breach, 1992.

White, Chappell, ed. *Josef Mysliveček: Three Violin Concertos*. Madison, WI: A-R Editions, 1994.

Wurzbach, Konstant von. *Biographisches Lexikon des Kaiserthums Oesterreich*. 60 vols. Vienna: Hof- und Staatsdruckerei, 1862–1891.

Index

A
Accardo, Salvatore 14
Acker, Yolanda 287, 297, 298
Acquaviva, Troiano (Troyano) 299, 300
Agostino [?] 265
Agricola, Johann Friedrich 176, 177
Ahačič, Kozma 254
Alberti, Vincenzo Camillo 204
Albinoni, Tomaso 78, 79, 82, 84, 88, 96
Alcántara Téllez de Girón y Pacheco, Pedro de 283
Algarotti, Francesco 6, 10, 14, 18, 66, 125, 126, 135, 155, 173, 203–209, 211, 213, 215, 217, 219, 221, 246, 263, 265
Allanbrook, Wye J. 135
Alonso Pimentel y Téllez-Girón, María Josefa 283
Amadeo I, King of Spain 290, 300
Anatol'evič, Aleksej 184
Angelucci, Eugenia 187
Anthony of Pauda (Antonio di Padova) 9, 16, 28, 46, 83, 96, 104, 152, 231, 232, 301
Aponensis, Petrus [see d'Abano, Pietro]
Arato, Franco 204
Aristotle 170–172, 229
Augustine (Augustinus), Aurelius 170, 174
Augustus III, King of Poland 204

B
Babitz, Sol 47
Bach, Carl Philipp Emanuel 175, 177, 179
Bach, Johann Christoph 173
Bach, Johann Sebastian 15, 28, 125, 173, 185
Baird, Julianne 176
Baker, Mona 250
Bala, Juan 282
Balbi, Paolo Battista 18, 144, 151–154, 159, 161, 207, 247, 248, 253, 258
Baldo, Roberto 15, 66, 143, 172, 204, 243, 264, 290
Barbera, Charles André 145, 171
Barbieri, Patrizio 19, 59, 64, 153, 158, 172, 208, 226, 230, 231, 233, 234, 242, 255, 263–265, 271
Barker, Andrew 145, 171
Barnett, Gregory 280
Bartel, Dietrich 30–33, 35, 37, 41, 42, 44, 47
Barsotti, Ambrogio Maria 107, 108
Bauer, Wilhelm A. 310, 311, 313, 322
Baxandall, Michael 209
Bayreuther, Rainer 177
Beck, Eleonora M. 172
Beethoven, Ludwig van 34, 40
Beghin, Tom 30
Bellinati, Claudio 301
Bellini, Bernardo 247
Bensa, Vladimir 158, 253, 257
Berdes, Jane L. 177
Berenstadt, Gaetano 131
Berkel, Klaas van 170
Bernadó, Màrius 292, 298
Bernard, Jonathan W. 233
Bernardi, Giovanni Carlo 125–127, 130
Bernardi, Francesco (Senesino) 125
Bernhard, Christoph 33, 42
Bertran, Lluís 292, 295, 296
Bini, Claudio 64
Bini, Pasquale 17
Bisi, Sofia Teresa 80, 81, 104

Index

Blainville, Charles-Henri 275
Blanchi, Giuseppe 117
Blasco, Beatriz 289
Blažeković, Zdravko 186
Boccherini, Luigi 282, 283, 298
Boerio, Giuseppe 247
Boethius, Anicius Manlius Severinus 165, 174, 255–257
Boetij, Anicij Manlij Severin [see Boethius, Anicius Manlius Severinus]
Bombi, Andrea 28, 59, 102, 104, 125, 176, 177, 187, 208, 212, 301
Bonanni, Filippo 61
Bononcini, Giovanni 82, 92, 93
Borchmeyer, Dieter 190
Borin, Alessandro 209, 220
Borsetto, Luciana 190
Boscolo, Lucia 301, 303
Boshoff, Mathias 286, 287
Boyden, David Dodge 176
Bower, Calvin 174
Braccioli, Grazio 93
Brainard, Paul 21, 28, 30, 31, 110, 111, 181, 185, 280, 283, 285, 288, 289, 292–295
Brewster, David 206
Brook, Barry S. 312
Brotherton, Sue 207
Bruhns, Nicolaus 173
Brunetti, Gaetano 283, 291, 292, 295
Bryski, Blaise David 185
Buelow, George J. 29
Bucciarelli, Melania 125
Burden, Michael 174
Burmeister, Joachim 29
Burney, Charles 16, 27, 77, 95, 177, 252, 311, 312
Busch-Salmen, Gabriele 188
Butler, Harold Edward 133
Buxtehude, Dieterich 173
Byram-Wigfield, Benjamin 231

C

Caccini, Giulio 15
Calcinotto, Carlo 141, 142
Calegari, Francesco Antonio 10, 223, 225, 230–244, 310
Cameron, Jasmin M. 209
Camilleri, Mathieu 14
Canale Degrassi, Margherita 5, 7, 9, 13, 55, 72, 83, 157, 176, 185, 212, 230, 264
Candeloro Arena, Stefano 286
Capece, Carlo Sigismondo 131
Caraba, Irene Maria 231
Carli, Gian Rinaldo (Gianrinaldo) 154, 207, 265
Carral, Sandra 59
Carraro, Gregorio 183, 184, 188, 288, 289
Carrera, Manuel 282
Carugo Adriano 172
Carter, Elisabeth 205
Carter, Stewart 173
Cartier, Jean-Baptiste 17, 188
Casarin, Chiara 5, 7, 9, 101, 103, 105
Casini, Paolo 207
Castro, Francisco José de 79
Cattelan, Paolo 310
Cavalli, Marino 310
Cavallini, Ivano 189
Cazzato, Alessandro 185
Charles III, King of Spain 287, 300
Charles IV, King of Spain 283, 291
Charles VI, Holy Roman Emperor 82
Chatziioannou, Vasileios 59
Christensen, Thomas 183, 225, 233, 274
Cicero, Marcus Tullius 133, 135
Clement XIII, pope 118
Cléton, Antonio 21
Cohen, Hendrik Floris 267
Colclough, David 48
Coltro, Dino 115
Colzani, Alberto 173, 231
Comber, John 77

Index 333

Condillac, Étienne Bonnot de 225
Conti, Antonio 207
Cooper, John Madison 170
Corelli, Arcangelo 141, 279, 280, 297, 298
Corselli, Francisco (Francesco) 287, 289, 294
Cossu, Matteo 21
Costa, Giovanni Battista 286

Č
Černohorský, Bohuslav Matěj 315

D
d'Abano, Pietro (Petrus) 171, 172
d'Alay, Mauro 279, 280, 286, 289, 290, 297, 304
d'Alembert, Jean le Rond 34, 35, 37, 39, 233, 249, 253, 298
Da Col, Paolo 9
Dall'Arche, Augusta 185
Dalla Vecchia, Jolanda 73, 104
Darwin, Charles 128, 281
De Brosses, Charles 93
De Fiores, Stefano 108
De Geronimo, Francesco 118
De Rif, Bianca Maria 190
Dearling, Robert 311, 312
DeFord, Ruth I. 184
Del Fra, Luca 143, 208
Denis, Pietro 176, 179
Deppert, Heinrich 173
Deutsch, Otto Erich 310, 311, 313, 322
Di Liscia, Daniel A. 170
Díez del Corral, Pilar 300
Dirksen, Pieter 179
Dobbs Mackenzie, Barbara 186
Don, Gary W. 189
Dooley, Brendan Maurice 207
Doorslaer, Luc van 252
Dounias, Minos 21, 105, 212
Dressler, Hilmar 190
Dunning, Albert 83

Durante, Sergio 5, 7, 9, 13, 15, 19, 21, 28, 78, 125, 126, 131, 132, 172, 185, 310

E
Eberly, Rosa A. 229
Eemeren, Frans Hendrik van 229
Eichhorn, Andreas 190
Eisen, Cliff 322
Eliano, [?] 265
Elmer, Minnie A. 183
Engelhardt, Dietrich von 19
Euler, Leonhard 9, 59, 64, 172, 206, 208, 211, 225, 233, 242, 246, 265, 266, 276, 298
Evans, Angela 311, 312
Eximeno y Pujades, Antonio 249, 266, 272

F
Fabbri, Paolo 189
Facco, Giacomo 79, 82, 86, 95, 96
Fanzago, Francesco 15, 16, 170, 179
Farina, Edoardo 21
Farnese, Elizabeth 279, 289, 301
Felici, Candida 124, 125, 185
Fend, Michael 186
Ferdinand VI, King of Spain 282
Fernán Núñez, count of [see Gutiérrez, Carlos José]
Fernández-Cortés, Juan P. 291
Ferrandini, Giovanni Battista 310
Ferreri, Pietro Maria 107, 118, 119, 120
Ferretti, Luca 124–126
Ferrone, Vincenzo 207
Feyerabend, Paul 170
Fitch, Fabrice 188
Flor, Christian 173
Flynn, Lawrence 135
Fontana, Giacinto (il Farfallino) 126
Foster, Christopher 250, 251, 252
Frasson, Leonardo 102, 264

Frederick II, King of Prussia 14, 15, 18, 184, 188, 204, 205, 208, 263
Freeman, Daniel E. 6, 7, 10, 309–314, 316, 320, 322–324, 326, 327
Freese, John Henry 171
Frederick the Great [see Frederick II., King of Prussia]
Frederick Henry Louis, Prince of Prussia 205
French, Roger Kenneth 170
Friedlein, Gottfried 174
Frigo, Gian Franco 19
Fubini, Enrico 16
Fuller, David 40, 41
Fux, Johann Joseph 93, 232

G
Gabrielli, Angelo 116
Gaffurio (Gaffurius), Franchino (Franchinus) 186
Galileo, Galilei 19, 226, 297, 298
Gallagher, Sean 28, 125, 185
Galliard, John Ernest (Johann Ernst) 134, 185
Gallo, Alberto 171
Gambier, Yves 252
Gambino, Daniele 231
Gasparini, Francesco 125, 126, 130, 131
Gatti, Enrico 13
Geay, Gérard 275
Gentili, Giorgio 79, 82, 83, 96
Ghezzi, Pier Leone 300
Ghilardi, Giovanni Tommaso 106, 117, 118
Girdlestone, Cuthbert 170
Giuggioli, Matteo 232
Gjerdingen, Robert O. 212
Gnocchi, Pietro 79
Goethe, Johann Wolfgang von 169, 189, 190
Godwin, Joscelyn 174
Gómez-Urdáñez, José L. 282

Gonzaga, Luigi 107
Gosálvez, José C. 279, 290, 297
Gossett, Philip 183
Gozza, Paolo 179
Grant, Edward 170
Grasso Caprioli, Leonella 176
Grendler, Marcella 172
Griggio, Claudio 21
Grimani, Lorenzo 249
Grimani, Pietro 18
Grossato, Elisa 310
Guanti, Giovanni 172, 174
Guarnieri, Roberta 17
Guglielmo, Federico 13
Guglielmo, Giovanni 13, 81
Gutknecht, Dieter 175
Gutiérrez de los Ríos y Rohan-Chabot, Carlos José 284, 286, 287
Guzy-Pasiak, Jolanta 265

H
Haböck, Franz 130
Hammond, Clare 312
Handschin, Jacques 170
Harmon, Roger 188
Harris, Adam 134
Harriss, Ernest C. 179
Haydn, Franz Joseph 40, 283, 296
Händel (Handel), Georg Friederich (George Frideric) 78
Heartz, Daniel 280
Hefling, Stephen E. 182
Heit, Helmut 170
Heller, Wendy 131
Hellmuth Margulis, Elizabeth 128
Hendrickson, George Lincoln 133
Heriot, Angus 130
Herlinger, Jan 171
Hermes Trismegistos 20
Herrando, José 280, 282, 286, 287, 296, 299
Hett, Walter Stanley 171
Heydorm, Petrus 173

Index

Hicks, Andrew James 171
Hill, John Walter 78
Hiller, Johann Adam 177, 252
Hiltner, Beate 178
Hirshberg, Jehoash 89, 212, 215, 316
Hochradner, Thomas 187
Hochstein, Wolfgang 232
Hoenen, Maarten J.F.M. 172
Hoffmann, Adolf 189
Hoffmann, Ernst Theodor Amadeus 17
Hoffmann-Axthelm, Dagmar 188
Honegger, Marc 179
Horn, Christoph 170
Horvat, Boris 248, 249, 253, 257
House, Jennifer 250
Hoven, Lena van der 188
Hoyer, Sonja Ana 252
Hoyt, Peter A. 29
Hubbell, Harry Mortimer 133
Hunter, Henry 206
Huron, David 128

I
Irvine, Thomas 187
Istel, Edgar 190

J
Jacobi, Erwin Reuben 170, 176, 178, 274
Jacobs, Jonathan A. 171
Jacobsson, Martin 174
Jaunslaviete, Baiba 5, 7, 9, 27
Jerold, Beverly 35, 180
Johansen, Karsten Friis 170
Johansen, Thomas Kjeller 170
Johnson, Fredric Bolan 124, 127, 129, 161, 174, 175, 183, 211, 219
Josephson, John R. 229
Josephson, Susan G. 229
Jung, Hans Rudolf 187
Juslin, Patrik N. 128
Južnič, Stanislav 253

K
Kaden, Christian 188
Kahl, Willi 180
Kalisch, Volker 188
Keefe, Simon P. 322
Kelly, Thomas Forrest 28, 125, 185
Kessler, Eckhard 170
Keym, Stefan 172
Kiel, Jacobijn 188
Kinský, Philipp Joseph 315
Kircher, Athanasius 297, 298
Kleßmann, Eckart 189
Knocker, Editha 175, 187
Kodrič, Ravel 252
Kokole, Metoda 172, 249, 253
Konfic, Lucija 6, 7, 10, 263, 264, 305
Koons, Robert 229
Kremer, Joachim 177
Kreyszig, Walter Kurt 6, 7, 10, 169, 180, 182, 184, 186, 188

L
Labrador, Germán 292
Lalande, Joseph Jérôme de 17, 46
Lami, Guglielmo 64
Landon, Howard Chandler Robbins 323
Lang, Franciscus (Franz) 134
Lange, Anny von 190
Lange, Carsten 182
Lasocki, David 179
Laufhütte, Hartmut 173
Lazari, Carlo 13
Le Cène, Michel-Charles 84
Lebègue, Nicolas 173
Ledesma, Juan de 286, 287, 288
Leemans, Pieter de 171, 172
Leisinger, Ulrich 175
Lernia, Francesco di 185
Lèsure, François 80
Levin, Robert 322
Leydeck (Laideque, Gaisdeck, Giusdeck), Jakob (Giacomo, Santiago) 279, 301, 303, 304, 305

Leza, José M. 279
Liebe, Anneliese 190
Lindley, Mark 145
Lini, Girolamo Michiel 82
Lippmann, Friedrich 187
Locatelli, Pietro Antonio 40, 77, 79, 80, 82–86, 89, 95, 97, 188, 280, 282, 297, 301, 312, 325
Lohri, Angela 59, 64, 66, 172
Lolo, Begoña 281
Lombardía, Ana 6, 7, 10, 279, 280, 286, 288, 289, 295, 300, 302
Lombardini Sirmen, Maddalena Laura 177, 252
Lotter, Dorothea 170
Lotti, Antonio 230, 231
Lubovsky, Bella Brover 6, 7, 10, 203, 205, 209, 212
Ludovico (Louis) I of Parma, King of Etruria 295
Luh, Jürgen 188
Luis, Annabelle 14
Luksich, Alba 16, 102, 289
Lully, Jean-Baptiste 173
Lumer, Christoph 229
Lunsford, Andrea A. 229
Luppi, Andrea 173, 231

M
Maffei, Scipione 207
Mancini, Giambattista 130, 134, 135
Maddox, Alan 9, 133, 134
Malagò, Giorgia 15, 18, 20, 66, 143, 144, 148–156, 159–161, 163, 172–174, 177, 203, 204, 206, 207, 211, 245, 247–250, 252–258, 264, 265, 290, 299
Mambella, Guido 186
Manalt, Francisco 280, 296, 299
Manalt, José [see Manalt, Francisco]
Maniates, Maria Rika 256
Marazzini, Claudio 246
Marcello, Alessandro 78, 79, 82

Marcello, Benedetto 40, 79, 82, 84, 92, 93, 101, 237
Marchetto da Padova [see Marchetto of Padua]
Marchetto of Padua 171, 172
Marco, Guy A. 186
Marcon, Andrea 14
Marescalchi, Luigi 298, 304
Maria Luisa of Bourbon, queen of Etruria 295
Marín, Miguel Á. 279, 280, 292, 297, 298
Marín-López, Javier 305
Marino, Carlo Antonio 79
Markuszewska, Aneta 265
Marpurg, Friedrich Wilhelm 173, 176
Martini, Giovanni Battista 6, 10, 18, 141, 143, 144, 148, 150, 151, 153, 154, 156, 158, 159, 160, 161, 163, 231, 242, 245, 246, 248, 250, 253–256, 258, 274, 314
Massaro, Maria Nevilla 28, 59, 102, 104, 125, 176, 177, 187, 208, 212, 301
Mathiesen, Thomas J. 171, 186
Mattheson, Johann 29, 37, 42, 44, 52, 179
Maunder, Richard 83
Maximilian III Joseph, elector of Bavaria 310
May, James M. 133
McVeigh, Simon 89, 212, 215, 316
Meine, Sabine 189
Melby, Alan K. 250–252
Meneghini, Giulio 70, 71
Meštrić, Vesna 59
Metastasio, Pietro 27, 28, 34, 35, 39, 125, 189
Methuen, Charlotte 170
Metzger, Heinz-Klaus 190
Meyer, Christian 179
McGlathery, James M. 190
Michel, Wilfried 184
Michelessi, Domenico 204
Michelsen, William C. 209

Migliorini, Bruno 247
Miller, Clement A. 186, 314
Miller, Fred D. 171
Mion, Marta 59
Mirka, Danuta 30
Misón, Luis 286
Mitchell, William J. 175
Mocenigo, Alvise 78
Mocenigo, Pisana 78
Monari, Giorgio 280
Montali, Francesco 280, 282, 288, 300
Montoro, Antonio 287
Morabito, Fulvia 188
Morgenstern, Anjak 176
Mortimer, Elizabeth 176
Mozart, Leopold 169, 175–178, 185–189, 309, 310, 312–314, 327
Mozart, Maria Anna 314
Mozart, Wolfgang Amadeus 6, 10, 28, 37, 125, 185, 309–314, 321–327
Mountford, James Frederick 170
Muntaner i Cabot, Sebastià 296
Murcia, Santiago de 287
Murr, Christoph Gottlieb von 17
Mysliveček, Josef 6, 10, 309–327

N
Naddaf, Gerard 170
Nardini, Pietro 17, 40
Neubacher, Jürgen 188
Neubauer, John 190
Naumann, Johann Gottlieb 310
Newton, Isaac 205, 207–209, 226
Nicolini, Fausto 299
Nikolić, Sonja 59
Noblitt, Thomas L. 176
Nord, Christiane 251
Northwood, Heidi Marguerite 170

O
O'Brian, Sharon 251, 252
Oberheim, Eric 170
Ogletree, Mary P. 35, 39
Olivari, Simone 16, 102, 283, 289

Olivieri, Luigi 172
Ortega, Judith 283, 290–292, 294, 295, 300, 303
Ottenberg, Hans-Günter 175

P
Pachelbel, Johann 173
Pachierotti, Gasparo 130
Padoan, Maurizio 173, 231
Paganini, Nicolò 7, 89, 169
Pagin, André Noel 17
Palestrina, Giovanni Pierluigi da 230, 231, 236
Palisca, Claude Victor 174, 179, 186, 256, 258
Pariati, Pietro 93
Paulovich, David Di Paoli 102, 115, 116
Pavanello, Agnese 21, 188
Pečman, Rudolf 179
Peirce, Charles Sanders 229
Pelcl, František MArtin 313
Peteh, Igor 59
Petersen, Birger 233
Petrobelli, Pierluigi 16, 17, 28–31, 66, 71, 78, 116, 133, 153, 172, 173, 178, 187, 189, 204, 206, 282, 289, 310, 315
Pfeffer, Jay Alan 190
Pietribiasi, Maddalena 28, 301, 303
Pinamonti, Paolo 310
Pincherle, Marc 322, 326
Pisendel, Georg 81
Planchart, Alejandro Enrique 211
Plantier, David 13, 14
Plato 20, 141, 155, 161–165, 170, 174, 190
Poleni, Giovanni 207
Polzonetti, Pierpaolo 22, 28, 46, 96, 116, 117, 121, 124, 125, 175, 189, 206
Poole, Marian 133
Praetorius, Michael 61
Prévost, Paul 179
Printz, Wolfgang Caspar 32, 33
Prozhoguin, Serguei N. 287

Ptolemy (Ptolemaeus), Claudius 145, 147, 240
Pythagoras 145, 298

Q
Quandt, Reinhold 190
Quantz, Johann Joachim 40, 88, 92, 129, 175–177, 179, 180, 182–188
Quintilianus, Aristides 186, 187
Quintilianus, Marcus Fabius 133

R
Rackham, Harris 171
Radicchi, Patrizia 174
Radole, Giuseppe 144
Rameau, Jean-Philippe 19, 173, 183, 225–227, 233, 234, 239, 242, 266, 274, 298
Randel, Don Michael 40
Rasch, Rudolf 176, 183, 298
Rastija, Vesna 59
Ravnikar, Bruno 253, 257
Reardon, Colleen 126
Rees, Owen 30
Reilly, Edward R. 129, 175
Reincken, Johann Adam 173
Reipsch, Brit 182
Reipsch, Ralph-Jürgen 189
Renner, Ralph Clifford 171
Revoltella, Pietro 102, 105, 111
Reynaldi, Giuseppe 300
Reynaldi (Rinaldi, Reinaldi), Christiano (Cristiano) 279, 280, 288, 299–302, 304, 305
Rezzonico, Abbondio 118, 314
Rhyner-Delon, Achilles 16
Riccati, Giordano 59, 143, 208, 225, 226, 231, 234, 241, 242
Riccati, Jacopo Francesco 207
Riccieri, Giovanni Antonio 231
Riehn, Rainer 190
Riemann, Hugo 209
Riva, Lodovico 125, 207
Rizzetti, Giovanni 207

Rodil, Domingo 279, 284, 291, 303, 305
Romem, Yehuda 323
Rouquié, Marie 14
Rosenmeier, Henrik 170
Rousseau, Jean-Jacques 189, 208, 298
Rota, Vincenzo 141
Roth, Dietrich 189
Rozanov, Ivan Vasil'evič 184
Ruffatti, Alessio 28
Ruggieri, Vanessa Elisabetta 80, 81
Rulla, Alvaro 118

S
Sacchini, Antonio 310
Sadie, Stanley 173, 323
Sales, Pietro Pompeo 310
Santos, Héctor E. 304
Saratelli, Giuseppe 231, 237, 242
Sartori, Claudio 126, 127, 131
Sauerlander, Annemarie M. 190
Scaccia, Angelo Maria 78
Scarlatti, Alessandro 45, 92, 93, 131
Scarlatti, Domenico 31, 287
Schayegh, Leila 14
Scheibe, Johann Adolph 40, 128
Scheibert, Beverly 179
Schläder, Jürgen 190
Schnitzler, Günter 190
Schramm, Gottfried 190
Schurr, Walter Wiliam 233
Schütz, Heinrich 42
Schwarzbauer, Michaela 187
Scimone, Claudio 21
Scott, Darwin F. 281
Seedorf, Thomas 176
Seidel, Wilhelm 184
Selvatici, Michele 126, 130, 132, 135
Serre, Jean Adam le 208, 227, 249
Shorey, Paul 170
Siemens, Lothar 284–286, 288, 290, 300
Silva Álvarez de Toledo, Fernando de 281, 282

Index

Siraisi, Nancy 171
Siranossian, Chouchane 14
Sloboda, John A. 128
Smith Barry, James Hugh 314
Snoj, Jurij 255, 257
Snoj, Marko 255
Soarez, Cypriano (Cipriano) 135
Solomon, Jon 171
Speck, Christian 184
Staehelin, Martin 17, 29, 172
Stampiglia, Silvio 93
Stellini, Jacopo (Giacopo) 265
Stillingfleet, Benjamin 208
Stoppino, Eleonora 131
Stratico, Giuseppe Michele 6, 10, 17, 234, 263–276, 305
Stratico, Simone 265
Strohm, Reinhard 130
Subirá, José 282
Sukljan, Nejc 6, 7, 9, 10, 59, 141, 145, 157, 169, 186, 248, 255, 258, 305
Susenbrotus, Joannes 41
Sustaeta, Ignacio 287, 298
Suzzi, Giuseppe 207

Š
Šinigoj, Boris 253
Šiškovič, Črtomir 66

T
Taglietti, Giulio 79, 82, 83
Taglietti, Luigi 79
Talbot, Michael 88, 209
Tamburini, Giovanni Battista 126
Tartini, Domenico 252
Tartini, Giuseppe 5–7, 9, 10, 13–22, 25, 27–51, 55–59, 63, 64, 66, 67, 69–73, 77–97, 101–107, 109–118, 120, 121, 123–136, 139, 141–144, 148–165, 169, 170, 172–190, 203–209, 211–212, 214, 215, 218, 219, 223–235, 239–242, 245–259, 261, 263–268, 270–276, 279–301, 303–305, 309, 311–320, 322, 325–327

Tartini, Pietro 252
Taschetti, Gabriele 9, 17
Tasso, Torquato 28, 125, 189
Tebaldini, Giovanni 101, 102, 118
Teixidor, José 281, 298, 299
Telemann, Georg Philipp 182, 189
Tesi, Vittoria 130
Teske, Hermien 184
Tessarini, Carlo 79, 82, 84–86, 89, 95, 96
Thieme, Ulrich 179
Thomas, Antoine-Léonard 252
Thompson, George W. 212
Todeschini Cavalla, Anna 174
Tommaseo, Nicolò 247
Toniolo, Ermanno M. 108
Torrance, John 170
Torrente, Álvaro 287
Tosi, Pier (Peter) Francesco (Franz) 134, 176, 177, 185
Tosi, Pierfrancesco [see Tosi, Pier Francesco]
Toso, Piero 14
Traetta, Tommaso 310
Treitler, Leo 135
Trento, Decio Agostino 18
Truett-Hollis, George 281, 282
Tyson, Alan 321, 322

U
Ughi, Uto 14
Umer Kljun, Jerneja 6, 8, 10, 15, 66, 143, 172, 204, 245, 247, 257, 260, 264, 290
Urbani, Silvia 145
Utz, Christian 205

V
Valder-Knechtges, Claudia 231
Valentini, Giuseppe 78
Valotti, Francesco Antonio (Francescantonio) 231
Vanderjagt, Arie Johan 170
Vandini, Antonio 289, 311, 315

Vanscheeuwijck, Marc 311
Varro, Marcus Terentius 254
Varwig, Bettina 128
Vecchi, Giuseppe 171
Vega, Ana de la 312
Venier, Lunardo 21
Vera, Alejandro 287
Veracini, Francesco Maria 78, 79, 82, 84, 89, 95–97
Vidic, Roberta 6, 8, 10, 223, 233
Vitali, Danilo 176
Vivaldi, Antonio 34, 40, 59, 77–82, 84–86, 89, 92–97, 130, 209, 212, 214, 218, 312, 316, 318, 320, 322, 325
Viverit, Guido 16, 102, 105, 176, 264, 283, 285, 289, 296, 297, 301

W
Waldstein, Vincenz von 313
Waldura, Markus 173
Wallace, Susan Murphree 188
Walker, Daniel Pickering 153, 158
Walther, Johann Gottfried 29–31
Walton, Douglas N. 229
Waterfield, Robin 162
Wessely, Othmar 232
White, Chappell 316, 320
Whitmore, Philip J. 89, 184
Wilberding, James 170
Wilk, Piotr 5, 8, 9, 28, 34, 77, 82, 125

Wilson, Blake 29
Wilson, Kirt H. 229
Winnington-Ingram, Reginald Pepys 186
Wisse, Jakob 133
Wittman, Michael 171
Witvogel, Gerhard Fredrik 21, 78, 80
Witz, F. 284, 291
Woodward, Beverly 177
Wurzbach, Konstant von 315

X
Ximenes of Aragon, Giuseppe 310

Z
Zachow, Friedrich Wilhelm 173
Zanon, Giancarlo 231, 232
Zanoncelli, Luisa Maria 186
Zarlino, Gioseffo 141, 144, 145–150, 157, 165, 185, 186, 209, 230
Zattarin, Alessandro 28, 125, 189
Zeno, Apostolo 126, 131
Ziani, Marc'Antonio 82
Zlotek, Bonifazio 279, 283, 284, 290, 291, 303, 305
Zuber, Barbara 190
Zuccari, Carlo 286

Ž
Žitko, Duška 252
Žmikić, Slobodan 252

Printed in Great Britain
by Amazon

f5c99884-c70d-4322-9e20-ef53c3738629R01